D1479285

ROWAN UNIVERSITY
CAMPBELL LIBRARY

# EVOLUTIONARY
# PSYCHOLOGY
# AND
# VIOLENCE

# EVOLUTIONARY PSYCHOLOGY AND VIOLENCE

## A Primer for Policymakers and Public Policy Advocates

*Edited by*
*Richard W. Bloom and Nancy Dess*

*Foreword by Joseph Graves, Jr.*

Psychological Dimensions to War and Peace
*Harvey Langholtz, Series Editor*

Westport, Connecticut
London

**Library of Congress Cataloging-in-Publication Data**

Evolutionary psychology and violence : a primer for policymakers and public policy advocates / edited by Richard W. Bloom and Nancy Dess; foreword by Joseph Graves, Jr.
     p. cm.—(Psychological dimensions to war and peace, ISSN 1540–5265)
  Includes bibliographical references and index.
  ISBN 0–275–97467–7 (alk. paper)
    1. Violence—Psychological aspects.   2. Social conflict—Psychological aspects.   3. Genetic psychology.   4. Violence—Government policy.   5. Social conflict—Government policy.   I. Bloom, Richard W., 1944–   II. Dess, Nancy Kimberly.   III. Series.

  HM1116 .E96 2003
  303.6—dc21     2002072821

British Library Cataloguing in Publication Data is available.

Library of Congress Catalog Card Number: 2002072821
ISBN: 0–275–97467–7
ISSN: 1540–5265

First published in 2003

Praeger Publishers, 88 Post Road West, Westport, CT 06881
An imprint of Greenwood Publishing Group, Inc.
www.praeger.com

Printed in the United States of America

The paper used in this book complies with the Permanent Paper Standard issued by the National Information Standards Organization (Z39.48–1984).

10  9  8  7  6  5  4  3  2  1

# Contents

# Foreword

Charles Darwin changed our view of the human animal forever when he published *The Origin of Species* in 1859 and *The Descent of Man* in 1871. In these works Darwin demonstrated that natural selection had played a decisive role in the origin of new species. An inescapable conclusion of this work was that the human species had been shaped morphologically and behaviorally by the same basic mechanism. Yet 90 years later one could still read psychology textbooks that made no mention of Darwin or evolutionary theory when discussing topics such as human aggression, violence, prejudice, or why people are attracted to each other.

The reason for this was simple. Many scholars and the public did not want to hear what Darwinism had to say about topics so central to human experience. After hearing that humans were descended from apelike ancestors a contemporary of Darwin's, Lady Ashley, was reported to have said, "Let's hope it's not true; but if it is true, let's hope that it does not become widely known." Thus, evolutionary theory met opposition from religious fundamentalists from the very beginning. Religious fundamentalist opposition was crucial in slowing down the reception of evolutionary reasoning in the United States. Even as we begin the new millennium, the teaching of evolutionary biology in the public schools is still under assault by creationists under the guise of "intelligent design theory."

However, not all opposition to evolutionary biology came from unreasonable quarters. Part of the rejection of relevance of evolutionary theory to human social affairs can be laid at the feet of evolutionists themselves. For example, many prominent biologists supported reactionary social policies and utilized evolutionary theory to justify that support. The world also had the opportunity to see the implementation of some of the proscriptions of Social Darwinism and eugenics in the form of Nazi race theory. The association of evolutionary biology with the pseudoscience claims of these ideologies was also significant in retarding the progress of the discipiline. Thus, there was a virtual absence of evolutionary ideas in psychology and sociology throughout the 1960s.

In 1975, Harvard biologist E.O. Wilson published his monumental treatise titled *Sociobiology: The New Synthesis*. This book was a synthesis of broad specialties in biology, united with Hamilton's inclusive fitness theory, theories of paternal investment, and sexual selection. Its purpose was to explain the evolution of society. He utilized a wide variety of species to make his points, and most of the controversy the book generated came from the last chapter, in which he discussed the implication of these ideas for humans. Wilson made extraordinary claims at the end of *Sociology*, in particular that the new synthesis would ultimately explain culture, religion, ethics, and other important human activities. Unfortunately, he made those claims with a very weak evidentiary base and flawed adaptationist reasoning. At this time, many, including myself, threw the baby out with the bathwater.

I now realize that Wilson's core claims must be true. Asserting the truth of this, however, is not the same as demonstrating it. This is why evolutionary psychology is such a crucial discipline for our time. In fact, I do not believe that we will be able to make meaningful progress in explaining our societies until we reassess the evolutionary history of our species, and ask how that impacts our behavior. Evolutionary psychology is already shattering some long-held misconceptions. Margaret Mead once claimed to have found idyllic societies in the South Seas where free love reigned, sex roles were reversed, and sexual jealousy was absent. Yet subsequent studies have now shown that the reports were simply false. Male sexual jealousy seems to be universal in all cultures surveyed thus far. This result is explained well by evolutionary theory in opposition to naïve views of man living in harmony with nature and each other. Indeed, the discipline is also calling into question its own naïve adaptationism. For example, it was once argued that racism should be a consequence of inclusive fitness theory. Thus, xenophobic behavior was supposed to result from the process of kin recognition, and obviously people with different physical features couldn't be your close kin. However, a recent experiment has demonstrated that social conceptions of race can be easily erased.[1] A correct analysis of evolutionary theory suggests that humans learned to recognize kinship in small geographic areas. In such circumstance no variation that could remotely considered to be racial would have been seen. This experiment showed that socialized views of race could be altered in college students by exposure to an alternative social world. By altering clues to coalitional affiliation using colored jerseys, less than four minutes of exposure eliminated the socialized views of race. The researchers were not able to produce the same response with gender. Again evolutionary psychology predicts why this should be true. Our ability to distinguish sexual identity should not have been influenced by geographic distance, and hence should be more fundamental.

The present volume extends the power of evolutionary psychology to the question of violence. It examines questions such as how we might utilize knowledge of our evolutionary history to prevent it and to make public policy surrounding it. The authors are distinguished researchers in the field, and they examine such topics as rape, mate homicide, the impact of differential environmental toxins on behavior, fear of death, intercultural conflict, and global conflict resolution. I do not believe that anyone who is seriously concerned with these issues will be able to ignore the perspective of evolutionary psychology or this volume. We should never again read a textbook in psychology, or engage in a public discussion of violence, that is not informed by evolutionary reasoning.

*Joseph Graves, Jr.*
*Professor of Evolutionary Biology*
*Arizona State University–West*

**NOTE**

1. Kurzban, Robert, Tooby, John, & Cosmides, Leda. (2001, December). Can race be erased? Coalitional computation and social categorization. *PNAS, 98,* 26, 15387–15392.

# Preface

How did this book come about? Answering this question is like answering any question exemplifying human searches for and constructions of meaning. We might refer to the beginnings of human self-consciousness and a sense of the possibilities of mastery over the self, others, and the environment. Or, the beginnings of government and intellectual history. Out of these and other beginnings, we could sincerely assert that this book is but a grain of sand in a continuous flow of mental striving to understand the world and change it. This approach might be termed a phylogenetic one that would pay homage to all those who came before with the urge to answer how anything came or comes about.

Or instead, we might each refer to their respective lives in an ontogenetic approach. With preferred psychological and social constructs and theories, each might ascribe significance to salient episodes stemming from family life, schooling, neighborhoods, personal relationships, and even political, economic, and cultural events. The most likely suspect in a book about violence for the age cohort inhabited by both editors might include the entire twentieth-century history of human atrocity unparalleled in its global scope and magnitude. More salient historical events actually lived through might include the militarization and proxy conflicts of the Cold War, the assassination of John F. Kennedy, the Vietnam War and related social upheaval in the United States, the mass murder as public policy in the Khmer Rouge's Cambodia, the rise after the Cold War in further genocide in Rwanda and ethnic conflict and cleansing in the Balkans, and the ongoing war against terrorism with global reach. Through it all would be the seemingly intractable regional conflicts in Ireland and the Mideast and global human rights violations and terrorism.

Items of personal history for us might include emotional support or lack thereof from a parent, the intellectual vitalization from am academic mentor, or the moment one's lifework crystallized in some epiphany or through a more measured process. They might also cite strong negative emotions—even revulsion—at daily examples of human violence such as murder, assault, rape, and physical and sexual abuse. To a lesser extent, they also might cite strong positive emotions toward some examples of human violence. One example might include self-sacrifice to protect others manifested by some military, law enforcement, and fire department personnel—as well as some family neighbors, neighbors, and unknown Samaritans. Even more humbly, we might admit that how this book came about is at least partly unknowable given the likely influence by phenomena that are unconscious, unrecognized, and misconstrued.

However, as far as our perceptions, cognitions, and other intrapsychic products may have some relationship with events leading to the writing of this book in a manner eliciting some acceptable degree of the reader's resonance, empathy, or consensus, the facts seem to be as follows.

The venue was the 2000 Annual Convention of the American Psychological Association (APA). The Convention can seem to the uninitiated as a formless morass of presentations, panel discussions, awards ceremonies, and even statistically deviant social encounters imbued with impressive degrees of pretentiousness, narcissism, bombast, self-righteousness, compulsiveness and impulsivity, and intellectual faddishness—along with sheer brilliance, creativity, and a sincere desire to contribute to human welfare. To the initiated there usually is more form than formlessness, recognition of the same positive and negative aspects of Convention activity, and recognition of the APA's best attempts to further psychological knowledge in science, practice, education, and the public interest.

The editors and some of the contributors to this book first met as collaborators on a panel dealing with the topic of evolutionary psychology and its possible value in understanding, preventing, attenuating, and otherwise managing human violence. Sincerely attempting to put aside matters of self-interest—even as such attempts are quite difficult to validate—the participants found that the one-hour-and-fifty-minute panel activity was both exciting and unfulfilling.

As to the former, the topic of evolutionary psychology and violence exemplified all four aspects of APA's organizational mission, as matters of science, practice, education, and the public interest were addressed and interrelated. Second, provocative questions arising between and among panel participants reinforced the interdisciplinary nature required by analyses of violence and how evolutionary psychology as a group of theoretical models was compatible with integrating interdisciplinary constructs and data and with identifying further such opportunities. Third, the potential contribution of evolutionary psychology to public policy—to actually affect discourse about how to change the world and to actually change it—was first crystallized as a significant focus by the participants. Fourth, the identification of common misunderstandings concerning evolutionary psychology impelled a strong sense of the need to replace falsehoods with truths—even in an academic world still significantly influenced by residual postmodernist advocacies of a world of relativism. In turn, the unfulfilling aspect of the panel activity was that so much appeared to be worthy of exploration and delineation, but so little time was available in the very fast-moving panel moment.

So out of the APA venue arose the motivation for this book—a book that would facilitate understanding of evolutionary psychology, apply this psychology to understanding forms of human violence, and provide public policy recommendations for public policy advocates confronting life and death matters necessarily related to violence. This motivation proved extremely resistant to the huge number of competing professional and personal demands confronting academics. Perhaps it was the editors' recognition that the social world in which human violence occurs is characterized by a huge number of competing concerns for all of humanity that provided the guidon demanding both the book's ambitious range—with chapters on themes ranging from basic brain and behavioral processes to global politics—and its completion.

Beyond the common and well-deserved thanks of authors almost everywhere to mentors, publishers, administrative support personnel, and loved ones, we most of all wish to give thanks to the entire human world—all of us who have lived, are living, and will live. It is all of us who have the potential for violence—to act violently, suffer violent consequences, and, hopefully, experience and engage in whatever features of violence may be positive. It is all of us who also have the potential to make and keep the peace. We believe that evolutionary psychology may be a significant vehicle for understanding and affecting violence. Whether correct or not, we assert our membership in a world of violence through studying it and attempting to change it; and whether correct or not, through this assertion we are affirming human life.

1

# The Evolution of Scientific Psychology and Public Policy
## On Violence and Its Antidotes

*Richard W. Bloom*

This chapter is intended to help readers of this textbook appreciate the basic issues concerning psychology, public policy, and the quest to influence human violence. By doing so, the chapter should facilitate readers' immersion with the chapters that follow.

## PSYCHOLOGY AND PUBLIC POLICY: BASIC TERMINOLOGY AND CONCEPTS

The term *psychology* seems to be used most often in three different ways. It can refer to a body of knowledge about how people think, feel, are motivated, and behave. Psychology also can refer to the process of developing this knowledge. Still again psychology can refer to the attempt at applying this knowledge to achieve various goals. Psychologists are people who are aware of or who engage in some combination of these psychologies. As such, we are all psychologists. Psychology seems to be a significant feature of humanity—not just of those who claim or are awarded professional degrees or membership in guilds that are formally labeled *psychological* by yet other people who formally invest statutory or other social authority in such degrees and guilds (Chiu et al., 1997; Derksen, 1997).

*Public policy* also seems to be used in different ways. It can refer to a body of knowledge describing how formally constituted governments, de facto governments, and other political entities—such as nonstate actors—operate. Public policy also can refer to the process of systematically and intentionally attempting to influence formally constituted and de facto governments and other political entities. Yet again, public policy can refer to the process of systematically and intentionally attempting to influence people through formally constituted and de facto governments and other political entities. Moreover, public policy can refer to the goals that governments and other political entities should or should not pursue. Thus, people, on the one hand, and various governments and other political entities, on the other hand, may engage in a hugely rich and complicated dance of reciprocal influence—in so-called representative democracies, totalitarian dictatorships, utopian communities, and dystopian terrorist cells. The complexity becomes only greater when we realize that the same individual may concurrently or in succession hold multiple social roles as representative of governments or other political entities and as someone to be acted on by the very same governments or other political entities.

Psychology and public policy most often intersect when knowledge about how people think, feel, are motivated, and behave is applied to understanding: how governments and other political entities operate; how to influence governments and other political entities and the people affected by them; and how to influence the political goals sought by governments, other political entities, and people affected by governments, political entities, and the very goals that are sought. Yet knowledge from the public policy realm also can be applied to understanding: how people think, feel, are motivated, and behave; how psychological knowledge is developed; and how psychological knowledge is applied. One might even conclude by noting that all psychologies are inevitably affected by and expressions of public policy, whereas the variants of public policy are inevitably expressions of psychology. That there are two formal knowledge areas labeled as psychology and public policy is a matter for yet a third knowledge area—the sociology of knowledge—and will not be pursued in this chapter (cf. Hogan, 1976; O'Donohue et al., 1998). Instead this chapter focuses only on how psychology is applied to a matter of public policy concern—namely, human violence—as if psychology and public policy are discrete areas of knowledge and practice that only partially intersect.

Knowledge of how people think, feel, are motivated, and behave is most often purported to be applied to public policy through *empiricism* (cf. Parsons, 1995). Empiricism refers to a route to knowledge based on posing a hypothesis and then collecting data that may or may not support that hypothesis. Psychologists claim that their hypotheses and data can render public policy more understandable, more efficient, more effective, and even more ethical and moral. Whether this claim is itself no more than a hypothesis that may or may not be supported by data, one should note that the psychologists making the claim are not even *just* using empiricism.

It turns out that there are many other routes to knowledge that are knowingly or unknowingly employed by psychologists in constructing and identifying hypotheses, in deciding what kinds of data will a priori or a posteriori support or not support hypotheses, in choosing statistical and other analytic techniques to interpret data, and even in choosing the empirical approach. Psychologists also employ *reason* and *logic*. These two routes to knowledge entail constructing and identifying associations between sequences of information that fulfill one of three different requirements. One is coming up with such associations that are similar to what a majority of people would come up with in the same situation. Another is what some substantial minority of people with some assumed privileged knowledge in psychology and/or public policy would come up with. Yet another is what very few if any people would come up with but that elicits psychological acceptance from at least enough people to ward off consensual ridicule.

Psychologists also employ the routes to knowledge of *faith* and *authority*. Faith generates beliefs about what is right and what is wrong based on deep-seated aspects of a worldview that may even seem unsupported through the tenets of empiricism. Authority furnishes the surplus value of citing research and research authorities that support and even engender faith in a belief but that do not necessarily conform to an interpretation of the preponderance of empirical data carried out by other psychologists who do not share one's world-view (cf. this textbook's chapters by Fishbein & Dess concerning authority and Solomon et al. concerning worldviews).

So, empiricism is almost always the unique weapon that psychologists bring to battles involving influencing public policy, even if said empiricism is often enough a stalking horse for other routes to knowledge and other policy-relevant beliefs. One might note that psychology's attempts to influence public policy through influencing governments and other political entities focus particularly on the latter's attempts to affect those people represented by, controlled by, or otherwise coming to the attention of said entities. In this regard, psychology—as engaged in by all individuals, not merely those claiming or attributed the formal label of the psychologist—has addressed three main facets of public policy. First, it has addressed what general and specific goals that public policy should address—that is, the *function* of public policy. Second, it has addressed how public policy should be developed, implemented, and evaluated—that is, the *process* of public policy. Third, it has addressed how to affect people as desired by a government—that is, the *content* of public policy. Although these public policy facets are discretely identified for purposes of exposition, in actuality there are a welter of concurrent facets that interact spontaneously and in a cross-lagged manner so that, for example, future evaluation can affect the prior choice of goals, content may be but an afterthought, and unconscious processes affecting policy may defy conscious attempts at logical policy analysis. In fact, the very social fact of formally labeled, scientific psychologists is itself a public policy. All in all, one might wish to at least suspend the belief that such psychologists might contribute to public policy from the vantage point of any privileged Received Word of science.

## PSYCHOLOGY, PUBLIC POLICY, AND VIOLENCE: THE HISTORICAL PICTURE

Be that as it may, has psychology been successful in influencing public policy? As an example, let's just focus on the psychology carried out by individuals

formally labeled as psychologists and cognate, applied social, cultural, and behavioral scientists—for example, sociologists, anthropologists, social workers,
psychiatrists, professional educators, and so on. And of these psychologists, the
focus should be on just those who assert a scientific praxis and embrace a logical
positivist cast to epistemology, metaphysics, and ethics—that is, an empiricism
perspective—and of these psychologists, just those who through their work
have attempted to affect the incidence, prevalence, and quality of human violence through influencing public policy. Within this last group, the results seem
to be very significant—but often not in a direction that supports the notion
that psychology can help supply even a partial antidote for human violence.
Instead, the history of pertinent psychological research suggests that psychology can significantly aid and abet violence more than it can prevent or minimize
it.

First, let's look at aiding and abetting violence through psychology. Psychologists have affected military selection, training, and management policies
so that personnel can kill more efficiently (Zeidner et al., 1997). Psychologists
have affected military health policies so that people who kill but are wounded
or injured can more quickly return to violence and kill again (Abraham et al.,
1998). Psychologists have affected education and social policies so that violence
perpetrated by and toward racial and ethnic minorities can more easily be perceived to stem from intrinsic deficiencies of these minorities (Brubaker & Laitin, 1998), thereby impeding efforts to modify other more salient contributors
to said violence. Psychologists have affected economic policies through industrial, organizational, and systemic consulting so that the *poor* and *deprived*—
so often correlated and conflated with racial and ethnic minorities—continue
to disproportionately experience violence as perpetrators and victims and to
more easily perceive and be perceived as deserving their fate (Pinn & Chunko,
1997). Psychologists have even intentionally constructed political ideologies
and systems to overtly and violently repress and oppress national majorities
in the service of a minority (Lapping, 1987). And psychologists have affected
civilian health and legal policies so that most people who are at risk to suffer
violence to the mind and soul are fated to largely depend on secondary and
tertiary intervention, while primary and putative causes of this violence are
given short-shrift (Almqvist & Brandell-Forsberg, 1998; King et al., 1998). This
last group of psychologists includes competent and well-meaning practitioners
who seek to minimize and treat the civilian casualties of political violence and
of crime—the latter making up the vast majority of the perpetrators and victims of violence today—and to help identify and apprehend the perpetrators
before they kill again (Gacono et al., 2000).

On the other hand, psychologists appear to have been singularly—in the
context of its self-professed expertise—and significantly ineffective in attempts
to prevent and minimize violence—for example, murder, war, assault and bat-
tery, and the violent aspects of rape and sexual abuse (Barish, 2001; Boast,

1999; Koss, 2000). In fact, some psychological attempts to prevent and minimize violence—for example, the violent parameters of sexual predation—seem to aid and abet it (Walcott, 2000; Wood et al., 2000).

Some readers of scientific psychological research might cite empirically validated applications that attenuate competition and foster cooperation—for example, Aronson, 1990—as part of an argument countering psychology's inadequacy in countering violence. However, one should note that competition and cooperation can both induce and be imbued with violence. Of course, some readers might also point to the previously described epistemological vulnerabilities in empirical and experimental research as caveats for asserting that psychological research shows any robust effect on the phenomenological world.

Is this the end of the story? Need we conclude at this point that violence is some prepotent, inevitable, or intractable psychological proclivity—leaving for the rest of this chapter the possibility that psychological research just cannot address violence or any other human activity? Hardly. It may well be that characteristics of psychology, of public policy, and of the relationship between the two in a larger sociohistorical context may have as much if not more to do with scientific psychological findings on violence than the presence or absence of some objective relationship between putative causal variables and violence-related consequences. What follows are some of the more likely characteristics.

## THE CONTEXT OF PSYCHOLOGY, PUBLIC POLICY, AND VIOLENCE: DOES HISTORY NEED TO REPEAT ITSELF?

### Psychological Macrotheories

Most scientific approaches to psychology are wittingly or unwittingly founded on variants and combinations of four macrotheories of social behavior: behaviorism, cognitive theory, psychoanalysis, and humanistic psychology (cf. Prilleltensky, 1994). There may be a number of interdependent reasons for this that relate to problems in the philosophy and sociology of psychology and in the developmental psychology of social cognition. And, perhaps, if these problems were better resolved, scientific psychology might be less likely to support the hypothesis that violence seems to be a prepotent human tendency resistant to the prevention and minimization of its experience and expression.

In any case, the four macrotheories, when addressing violence and other social behaviors, deemphasize social, cultural, historical, economic, political, and various other situational variables and emphasize individual differences— the latter comprising inferred traits, self- and other-described intrapsychic content and processes, and variously observed and recorded discrete behaviors (Rothschild et al., 1997). A number of these individual differences—including those related to typologies of how familial, work, and school experiences are perceived by individuals being studied by psychologists—often are construed by psychologists as more static as opposed to dynamic and, therefore, rather intractable to intervention. In fact, psychologists may actually embrace the public policies of professional identification that mitigate against psychologists attempting to preempt what will become static contributors to violence among future generations of people or within the future of the current generations regardless of how some community psychologists might aver to the contrary (cf. Watts et al., 1999).)

It turns out that individual differences often provide a meager causal increment to the prediction of violence—save for extreme examples of neurobiological dysfunction (cf. Filley et al., 2001). Thus, groundings within the four macrotheories by psychologists are problematic.

Some psychologists might object that behaviorism with its focus on linking stimuli, behavior, and consequences to the exclusion of variables "within" the individual might not be vulnerable to allegations of ignoring the social and other situational variables for individual differences. However, pure behaviorism largely focuses on external variables that are not social and situational but merely extraneous to an individual's context and that at times are comically abstract in their definitional circularity.

Some psychologists might object that cognitive theory—especially its cognitive-behavioral and social learning combinations—is not fairly described as emphasizing the language of traditional individual differences. However, the cognitions identified as suspect in being associated with violence actually are founded on individual differences of phenomenologically generated external occurrences and consequences that are usually sanitized from the social and political strivings of everyday life.

Some psychologists might object to psychoanalysis being identified as emphasizing individual differences because said theory describes social constellations that affect the dynamics of metapsychological variables—namely, the structural, ontogenetic, and so on. However, it is the intra-individual metapsychology that is deemed most responsible for healthy and unhealthy behavior.

It would seem most difficult for psychologists influenced by humanistic theory to object to the individual differences brush. After all, the putative, benign core of human psychology that is posited by humanistic theory has also been the foundation on which evaluation devices measuring variations from the benign has been constructed.

I should also note that individual differences variables of psychologists contribute to scientific psychologists' track record on violence. Theoretical and experimental propensities are often reflections of psychologists' character, their own conflicts, cognitive complexity, creativity, intelligence, formative experiences, and the all-pervading zeitgeist encompassing paradigms of professional propriety—all of which may have little to do with appropriateness for the subject at hand (cf. Lasswell, 1930).

So there seems to be a bias for embracing a stance on what should influence—especially decrease—violence among many psychologists that obviates against significant influence of violence.

## Social Ideology

Psychologists construct and are variously influenced by theories of the social world that often are compartmentalized off from psychological macrotheories. For example, many psychologists belittle social values as irrelevant or even injurious to the creation and application of knowledge (Mays & Manaster, 1999). They are still in the grasp of a putative and pristine objectivity that is putatively value-free and of an empirical and interpretive stance that is alleged to have no effect on that which is observed and interpreted.

As another example, some psychologists may not only champion and cherish values as informing science but also allow these values—for example, the wish for peace or a world of nonviolence—to help nurture illusory correlations of data supporting the desired conclusions. Many of these psychologists behaviorally perseverate by insisting on advocating for the same worn and unsubstantiated "violence killers"—that is, prescriptions and proscriptions concerning violence reduction, which do nothing of the kind.

In addition, most psychologists are constrained and blinded by reified hypothetical constructs so that the "as if" of the social world assumes an undeserved ontological validity (Barclay, 1997). Although the "as if" existential and behavioral stances can often bring power to the powerless when confronting a politically repressive and violent government, these stances too easily remain in the service of the status quo in the social world of the psychologist.

As another example, many psychologists are more affected by the quest for social prestige, money, and the pleasure of the unexamined life than they care to let on—even if the route is through the examined life. In fact, many aspects of the unexamined life quite baldly and insidiously transubstantiate the examined life into something that should not be hallowed even by lovers of knowledge.

These and other social ideological aspects mitigate against developing causal linkages and change technologies effecting reductions in human violence. The aversion to social values as antithetical to knowledge development mirrors that of the psychological macrotheories. The embracing of pacific social values impedes nonpacific psychological conclusions. And the "as if" and rewards stances of many psychologists can, respectively, yield metaphorical resonances and physical and psychological positive reinforcements that are at odds with valid knowledge development.

## Social Identity

Many psychologists—even as socially sanctioned experts on human psychology—still share the penchant for constructing a self-identity largely based on a social identity formed from social comparison processes and other variants of social cognition. This identity overtly and covertly has an influence on choice of research topics, hypotheses, methodologies, presentation strategies of results, and data interpretative strategies. And much of this seems to preclude an intellectually honest look at the adaptive and nonadaptive aspects of human violence.

For example, the American Psychological Association's (APA) proprietary research data base, PsycINFO, contains large numbers of studies on preventing or minimizing violence, few on maximizing or exacerbating violence (Bloom, 2001a). This is the case even if psychological research suggests a facility with violence resilience and exacerbation rather than reduction and prevention.

APA also contains a professional division entitled the Society for the Study of Peace, Conflict and Violence: Peace Psychology dedicated to preventing and minimizing violence. There are no APA divisions dedicated to furthering the prospects of "natural born killers."

"Of course not!" the reader might retort. "Who would ever engage in such an enterprise?" But that is exactly the point. The "who" who would and do are categorically demonized, marginalized, and pathologized—if only by a guidon of banality and the commonplace. The same is often the case for those who engage in violence—save for some perpetrators of government-sanctioned violence controlled by the same political nexus that shapes the psychology of psychologists.

## Phenomena of Control, Coercion, and Subjugation

There is tragedy for those who sincerely would like to live in a world without violence or with less violence. Most psychologists are knowingly or unknowingly protagonists in a story with the theme of attempting to attenuate violence—this story being largely constructed by those who savor and live by violence and who see only one possible ending. In fact, better the story never ends and the hope for preventing or attenuating violence persists (cf. Tetlock & Goldgeier, 2000). Here the construct of *false consciousness* comes into play.

By false consciousness, I am denoting the awareness of an individual or group that is contradicted by so-called objective relationships in the social environment. For example, one can make the case that the belief systems of socially sanctioned change agents suggest to these agents that they are, indeed, change agents, when actually their social roles focus on impeding change or inducing change that is meaningless or trivial. If various types of violence undergird the political power of political authorities, false consciousness works to the ultimate benefit of such authorities and could facilitate violence enhancement findings except in cases wherein said findings would endanger the political power of those who have it (cf. Boehm's chapter in this textbook).

## Political Power

Psychologists often are operating at the sufferance of those for whom violence undergirds political power. Relative to these power zealots, most psychologists strike an impotent stance precluding combinations of ability and will to carry out the action research—necessitating restructuring and even blows against various empires, which could make a difference. Legitimate violence reduction efforts might only be tolerated in carefully constrained areas wherein political power is unthreatened or enhanced.

## THE GENERIC EVOLUTIONARY PSYCHOLOGY PERSPECTIVE

### Introduction

What is needed, it would seem, is a concerted attempt at preventing or minimizing violence by psychologists that can be freer from the ideological, social, cultural, and psychological detritus described earlier. This attempt might also embrace a broader perspective of recommending when attempts at aiding and abetting, preventing, minimizing, or doing nothing concerning violence should occur. Is this a likely possibility?

This textbook focuses on such an attempt through a close reading of the texts prepared by eminent researchers—scientific psychologists—who favor variants of an evolutionary psychology perspective to help inform public policy. Can these researchers create valid descriptive and inferential knowledge and apply it to the goal of creating an antidote for violence or various stances on, perhaps, when and how violence should be prevented, reduced, maintained, or even increased?

As to the former—given that an antidote is a remedy for counteracting the effects of poison or disease or is something that prevents or counteracts injurious effects—these researchers risk embarking on a doomed voyage because the alien Other to be slain may be an adaptive doppelganger. However—given that affecting violence in any direction may necessarily involve an evolution of the relationship between scientific psychology and public policy—an evolutionary psychology perspective may at least possess some face validity imparting hope for success. What follows is a description of the nature of explanation of a generic evolutionary psychology perspective (GEPP) as it pertains to any social behavior including that of violence (cf. Badcock, 2000; Caporael, 2000; Cartwright, 2000; Edwards, 1999; Heyes & Hebert, 2000; Katz, 2000; Kenrick, 2001; King et al., 1998; Kirkpatrick, 1999; Mealey, 2000; Pierce & White, 1999; Revonsuo, 2000; Sober & Wilson, 1998).

### The Nature of GEPP Explanation

In explaining the various parameters of a social behavior—for example, presence, absence, strength, and frequency—GEPP assumes an environment in which social behavior occurs. The environment is not a homogenous entity, but multifaceted and characterized by continuous change as to its salience and complexity. Within this environment, various behaviors occur that differ in terms of the probability with which they help effect various goals. At other times behavior appears to be nongoal related. Sometimes, those behaviors which are more likely to effect goals within an environment are more likely to occur or more likely to reside within a person's behavioral repertoire poised and ready to help effect a goal. Other times, behaviors are likely to occur or likely to reside within a behavioral repertoire only because their very expression or possibility of being expressed is necessary for the expression or possibility of expression of other behaviors that do, indeed, help effect goals. Still other times, behaviors are likely to occur or reside within a behavioral repertoire only because of a person's physical properties and constraints, developmental constraints, and yet other constraints in interaction with various aspects of an environment. The idea that the expression of all behavior or the existence of all behavioral capabilities must ultimately reside in some purpose is neither necessary nor sufficient for an evolutionary perspective.

Things can become even more complicated because yet other behaviors are likely to occur or reside within a behavioral repertoire; these behaviors once were associated with effecting a goal but are no longer, were associated with effecting a goal but now are associated with effecting another goal, were associated only with a person's physical properties and then fluctuated among associations with effecting goals and associations with other behaviors associated with effecting goals, and so on.

Along with these complexities, GEPP also posits that the behaviors that help increase the probability of physical survival, sexual mating, sexual procreation, parenting, and the welfare of kin are of singular import in human psychology. The consequences of these behaviors will include a higher probability of the transmission of the genetic substrates of individuals manifesting said behaviors into the next human generation and yet the next and the next. In essence, a certain kind of past behavioral success will color the nature of future human psychology. These behaviors are in that sense labeled as adaptive.

The question then becomes how does behavior change or remain the same within an individual, among individuals of a specific historical moment, and across generations of people. GEPP yields four main routes of behavior maintenance and change. These routes are interdependent and reciprocally interactive. In other words, one can most profitably speak about why behaviors occur, can occur, can be maintained, or changed only by considering all four in a concurrent fashion.

The first is a *biological* route. Ultimately, there are genetic substrates of behavior through molecular development. This does not mean that there is genetic material corresponding to every social behavior—for example, a gene for producing successful hip-hop videos containing gratuitous violence or an interactive pattern of genetic functioning through time that induces the development of laser weapons as part of a ballistic missile defense system. It does mean that one's genetic makeup as expressed through various physical structures, systems, and processes has behavioral impact that varies depending on the behavior in question and the other three routes. This includes, for example, behaviors effecting goals associated with physical need states. Also, the biological is not an immutable pathway but ever changing on many levels of molecular, structural, and developmental analysis.

The second route is psychological. Here psychological denotes ever-changing conscious, preconscious, unconscious, and nonconscious mental activity of thought, emotion, and motivation. People can be aware of their goals. They can plan to achieve them. They can have thoughts and feelings about the nature of their goals, the degree of desirability, their expectations of success, and their judgments of success or failure. And they can plan on maintaining a steady behavioral course because goal achievement seems to be on track, or they can behaviorally change accordingly—based on thoughts, emotions, and motives. Just as one's behavioral fate is not solely biological, neither is it psychological. One may wish to fly unaided by an aircraft or rocket as a means to achieve a goal. But biology may stand in the way.

The third route is *cultural.* Here cultural denotes the sum total of ways of living developed by people through time and the social transmission of these ways within and across generations. Mechanisms for this transmission include formal pedagogy and the vicarious conditioning and persuasion of everyday social life. Culture provides a collective conscious and unconscious of what behaviors have worked and not worked in effecting various goals. There are actually many, ever-changing cultures impacting on behavior as perceived and misperceived, as constructed and deconstructed, and as chosen or unchosen (but introjected) by people. Moreover, there may be psychological constraints bearing on to what cultural products people attend and physical constraints on what cultural products can be emulated.

The fourth pathway is *environmental.* Goals, behaviors to effect goals, behaviors and behavioral probabilities regardless of goal relevance relate to an arena of environments. As environments change, so may the above. So also may the other pathways of behavioral change and maintenance, which, in turn, can effect maintenance and change of environments.

An added assumption of GEPP is that some aspects of all four pathways that bear on the successful effecting of goals have a greater probability of remaining throughout generations of human functioning. Some aspects of the pathways that do not, are less likely to.

## What GEPP Is Not

This brief elaboration on the nature of explanation of GEPP hopefully contests two vital points bearing on evolutionary psychology's utility for public policy on human violence and any other issue. First, a number of misconceptions about evolutionary psychology impede its consideration as a source of inspiration for public policy (cf. Buss, 1999). The four most important for public policy follow.

GEPP does *not* require social behavior to be genetically determined. Although one part of the biological pathway of behavioral change and maintenance includes genetics, genetic inheritance, and biological development, social behaviors depend on an interaction of four different pathways. For policymakers who harbor an ideology of free will or fear the political backlash of espousing a gene-controlled world, there is plenty of conceptual flexibility with GEPP. Also, GEPP should be associated with *no* particular stance on civil and criminal adjudication as to the responsibility of a defendant, suspect, accused, convicted, or the legally liable (cf. chapters by Mealey, Buss, and Kinner in this textbook).

GEPP does *not* insist that behavior cannot be changed. Many aspects of all four pathways of behavioral change and maintenance can be influenced or can change even without human intention. Policymakers do not have to be confronted a priori with undesired behaviors that are fated only to be tolerated, managed, discounted, or even ignored, but never affected in terms of amplitude, frequency, or their very presence. Change or maintenance does not have to be totally at the mercy of the Fates, but, instead, can be at least somewhat dependent on innovation and insight. However, it may turn out that violence or some other social behavior is functionally intractable to change strategies.

GEPP does *not* require that all behavior be assumed to be the best possible for human functioning at any point in time. Instead, some behavior may be "on the way out" in that it no longer helps effect a goal, still "on the way in" for helping effect a goal, or "on the way out or in" for many other reasons, including no reason at all. Given the ever-changing nature of all four pathways, one is hard pressed to claim that any behavior targeted by a public policy is already optimally designed or, for that matter, can be.

And finally, GEPP does *not* require that one conceives of people to be consciously or otherwise motivated to spread their genes wide and far. Whether one would approve of such a quest as a foundation for hedonism or utilitarianism, or disapprove of the quest as a foundation for celibacy or for a life based on some ethereal plane, the quest is not mandated by GEPP. On the other hand, one should note that such a conscious motivation, for example, could be considered an intrapsychic behavior that might at some historical time be considered adaptive.

All four of the above misconceptions contribute to construing that GEPP is not an appropriate vehicle for public policy. The essence of the misconceptions is that people are prisoners of an insidious time lag. To wit: Behaviors that "made sense" long, long ago—usually assumed to be at least as far back as when the human state-of-affairs was characterized as a hunter-gatherer era—may no longer "make sense" in terms of effecting current goals or merely in behaving. This may especially be the case for behaviors that effect goals bearing on physical survival, sexual mating, procreation, parenting, and the welfare of kin. Alas—per genetic determinism—we must wait for our genetic makeup to "catch up" with the new functional status of behaviors that are now more indicative of futility than utility. The good news is that this take on GEPP is incorrect.

## THE CONTEXT OF GEPP AND PUBLIC POLICY: IMPLICATIONS FOR RESEARCH ON VIOLENCE

A second vital point bearing on GEPP's utility for public policy on human violence and any other social behavior is a consideration of how it addresses the many failings of other theoretical perspectives addressed earlier in this chapter. This consideration is on the whole positive.

GEPP addresses social and situational variables, as well as individual differences that are biopsychosocial in nature. GEPP addresses values as pertinent to behavior change and maintenance—both via psychological and cultural pathways and their interaction with the biological and environmental. It also does not take an a priori stance on the desirability of any specific human behavior. Although the scientific literature of GEPP does contain "as if" jargon—for example, adaptation, spandrels, exaptation—that can be reified to the confusion of policymakers and scientists alike, the jargon is not necessary for exposition and application.

On the other hand, some scientists expositing and applying GEPP in a public policy context are seeking social prestige and material gain (Anonymous, 2001; Bloom, 2001b). They also are operating at the sufferance of those for whom violence undergirds political power, playacting (as described in the section on Phenomena of Control, Coercion, and Subjugation) in a script written by violence's keepers, and subject to the vagaries of character, conflicts, cognitive complexity, creativity, intelligence, formative experiences, and zeitgeist.

There are other aspects of GEPP that might render it problematic in matters of public policy. There is the philosophy of science issue of necessarily affecting that which is purported to be studied through study, so that what is being studied is not what is intended to be studied. Psychologists who employ GEPP to study behavior change and maintenance must do so with the realization or suppression of the realization that GEPP is itself a concatenation of behaviors that have been, are, and will be changing and maintained. Subject and object are concurrently identical but conceptually different. Ultimately, the self cannot study the self, because the aspect of self needed to study the self renders the study of self as less than or different than the self that one wishes to study. This reflexivity of GEPP—and other psychological macrotheories—does not allow the psychologist to assure the public policymaker of a clean bill of health for the tools of policy study.

There is also the related issue that GEPP might be—via GEPP analysis—a concatenation of behaviors that might help effect goals, express other behaviors that effect goals, or be expressed only by virtue of physical properties and constraints, developmental constraints, and yet other constraints in interaction with various aspects of an environment. How all of this plays out in terms of the search for behavior change and maintenance at the service of the public policymaker may largely remain unknown save in terms of a lay phenomenological sense.

In addition, GEPP presents a significant challenge for the public relations and overall public and political discourse of public policy. This challenge involves the facet of GEPP that can attribute the rise and fall of behavior and the label of behavioral success to successful physical survival, sexual mating, sexual procreation, parenting, and the welfare of kin—ultimately to how much of one's genetic material one spreads within and across human generations. To many public policymakers this, perhaps rightly, smacks of de facto, implicit, or a bald-faced encouragement of overpopulation and the overuse of finite resources to handle human need, immoral behavior, a breakdown of social propriety, and sin. Standard-bearers of GEPP for public policy who attempt to explain the assumptions of their theoretical tool should be ready to assert whether such encouragement is, indeed, accurate and, if not, how to explain why it's not.

A last challenge concerns GEPP challenging two closely held and related ideologies. First, it may threaten beliefs about how people *are* that serve the function of masking, repressing, or substituting for how they are and convey instead how they *should be* (cf. Solomon at al.'s chapter in this textbook). Second, it may threaten belief systems that people maintain for their own personal self-subjugation, as well as those reinforced by hegemonic political and sociocultural authorities. If these latter two contentions are accurate, theorists of evolutionary psychology—whether championing terror management (McGregor et al., 1998), reproductive success (Buss & Shackelford, 1997), or other constructs yet to be developed—may find it quite difficult to be reproductively successful in spawning disciples, acolytes, and publications and to manage terror associated with professional death. In the quest for an antidote to violence, evolutionary psychology may only approach ever closer to its own demise.

## GEPP, TERRORISM, ANTITERRORISM, AND COUNTERTERRORISM

Having considered the nature of GEPP explanation and the pros and cons of its suitability for informing public policy, this chapter now identifies implications of these issues by exploring GEPP in relationship to public policy on terrorism, antiterrorism, and counterterrorism.

### Terrorism, Prescription, and Proscription D

Definitions of terrorism continue to proliferate. Terrorism may denote the employment of violence or the threat of violence against noncombatants to achieve political objectives from a formally constituted government. Of crucial import is the psychological effect on government representatives and those they represent from the violence and threat of violence. However, a comprehensive analysis of combat and combat support—for example, personnel, intelligence, operations, logistics, policy and strategy, and communications—suggests that there are no noncombatants. Even the very young, the very old, and classes—such as women—who may be forbidden from or unlikely participants in direct combat can provide important combat and combat support functions. Much as military conflict can be conceived as politics by other means, the same may apply to terrorism. Given that politics may be defined as the sphere of goal-directed behavior wherein there are more needs than resources, terrorism becomes just another label for violence or its threat to satisfy need.

As opposed to generating obfuscatory aphorisms such as "one man's terrorist is another man's freedom fighter"—obfuscatory in that one can engage in violence for freedom or any other goal, while one can seek freedom with or without violence—GEPP provides a biopsychosocial context within which terrorism can be appropriately analyzed. Whether terrorism should be prescribed or proscribed in all or particular cases will depend on ethical elaborations on means and ends and on equalities, equities, and absolute values concerning access to means and ends among people. Positing instincts of aggression as eternally adaptive or unadaptive is unnecessary.

More interestingly, some of the nonadaptive aspects of consciousness can here be delineated. Specifically, the psychological consequences on observers and survivors of violence that facilitate terrorist political success depend on vicarious conditioning, resonance, empathy, phenomenological confrontations with mortality, and so on. Nonadaptiveness is the concern assuming terrorist demands ultimately lead to less and less success with survival and reproduction on the part of the population under terrorist siege. Of course, terrorism may lead to adaptive behaviors on the part of the population under siege that also satisfy terrorist needs. And, so too, the very notion of adaptation applied to terrorism may be missing the mark. In other words, the presence of terrorism from the earliest recorded histories may have more to do with nonsurvival and nonreproductive types of success and failure.

## Antiterrorism and Counterterrorism

Antiterrorism denotes the pursuit of preventing terrorism from occurring, whereas counterterrorism denotes the pursuit of resolving a terrorist act as satisfactorily as possible. One might well be pessimist in confronting both these pursuits in that the sophisticated terrorist entity is almost always at a decided advantage as to the who, what, where, when, how, and why of a terrorist act or campaign. In fact, the time and other resources allocated to antiterrorism and counterterrorism may also prove to the terrorist's advantage in that the expended resources could otherwise have been used for the health, education, and economic viability of the population under terrorist siege.

GEPP does suggest that terrorism does not have to be "set" at a particular level of intensity and frequency. Instead, terrorism may be modifiable.

### Forensic Psychology and Terrorism

The value and utility of forensic psychology in criminal justice settings involving allegations of terrorism seems to be settled. Moreover, public policies are being developed based on this hypothesized high value and utility (cf. Bloom et al., 2000; Casey & Rottman, 2000; Finkel et al., 2001; Schouten, 2001; Thomas-Peter & Warren, 1998). Still, GEPP might generate support or detract from this perspective.

A sine qua non of the criminal justice systems of representative democracies is an attempt at exemplifying a rule of law. One characteristic of this rule of law is a set of transgressions—each linked with a penalty, range of penalties, or other consequence to be implemented upon conviction for each transgression. Especially when an individual is convicted of a transgression that can lead to more than one possible penalty or more than one transgression—some of which lead to different penalties; forensic psychologists—(usually psychiatrists and clinical psychologists) can be called on to develop information that may affect the penalty or penalties issued forth by a court. The question is whether forensic psychologists have anything useful to contribute and, if so, whether the utility stems from any special area of expert knowledge.

For example, a psychiatrist testified for the defense in the case of Khalfan Khamis Mohamed, who already had been convicted for his role in the 1998 terrorist bombing of the United States Embassy in Tanzania (Weiser, 2001). The psychiatrist contributed information about the convicted terrorist that the defense lawyers believed would help mitigate against a death penalty. The psychiatrist asserted that Mohamed was unquestioning in obeying orders from complicit colleagues at one time but now believed that taking the lives of innocent victims was not justified under any circumstances. The psychiatrist also asserted that Mohamed's contributions to terrorism were only taken under a commitment to attenuate the suffering of Muslims around the world. As well, the psychiatrist asserted that Mohamed now expressed tearful remorse for his actions, was uneducated, lost his father at an early age, was easily led by others, and felt pained at being a minor player in the hierarchy of the terrorist plot.

What is one to do with such information based on the premises that a priori and ex post facto intent, motives, phenomenology, behavioral tendencies, and events are judged relevant in issuing a penalty by political authorities effecting the criminal justice system? It is difficult to identify the special area of expert knowledge that gives a unique status to the forensic psychologist in this case. One difficulty is that psychiatrists and clinical psychologists by definition and tradition are steeped in the art and science of psychopathology. However, psychopathology does not seem to be a mitigating issue in published accounts of the psychiatrist's testimony. Another difficulty is that the information pre-sented could be imparted by many kinds of professions and, indeed, by many kinds of people—not just the forensic psychologist. Third, forensic psycholo-gists often are no more knowledgeable of scientific research on such informa-tion than the "great unwashed"—the lay psychologists—whom are not considered forensic experts.

Thus, in the case at hand, the court was not informed that stated remorse can very effectively be an impression management strategy that, in turn, elicits expectations that a future negative act will not be committed and elicits feelings of forgiveness in others (Gold & Weiner, 2000). The same applies with findings that stated remorse has been found to affect the very nature of an assigned sentence (Pipes & Alessi, 1999); to activate belief systems concerning health, philosophy, religion, and politics that lead to forgiveness (Scobie & Scobie, 1998); to elicit forgiveness depending on what cognitions have previously been activated among potential forgivers (Takaku et al., 2001); and to be difficult to discriminate between sincere and feigned versions (Blackman & Stubbs, 2001).

One could make a strong argument that—in this case—a forensic psychol-ogist had no special expertise. One might also assert that the forensic psy-chologist could have been effectively countered with a social psychologist or other behavioral scientist familiar with the scientific literature on remorse, apology, and forgiveness. Finally, one might conclude that through letting psy-chological testimony focus only on the presence or absence of mitigating cir-cumstances as opposed to the social psychology of these circumstances in the context of a legal hearing, justice may not be served regardless of the penalty issued to the convicted terrorist.

GEPP might induce authorities and participants in terrorist cases to recognize that some common criteria that are deemed to warrant consideration in the penalty phase may have little to do with the social welfare and even help lead to further acts of terrorism by the convicted and by other potential terrorists.

## Conceptions of Competency Related to Ideological Fanatics

As explicated in the MacArthur Treatment Competency Study, there may be at least four different competency capacities (Winnick, 1996). These are the abilities to (1) appreciate a choice, (2) understand relevant information, (3) manipulate information rationally, and (4) appreciate the nature of the situa-tion and its likely consequences.

Yet at least one type of ideological fanatic, the religious, may posit absolutely no choice, for example, all acts are willed by God. The fanatic may not seem to understand information relevant to legal authorities, because the only rele-vant information is sacred, not secular. Other information is to be ignored or discounted. The fanatic may seem not to manipulate information rationally because the consequences of so-called facts, and the facts themselves, may lead to an act viewed as irrational by legal authorities, illogical by a so-called "jury of peers," as delusional by psychological authorities, but as none of the above by the fanatic. And the fanatic may appreciate a legal trial, the situation, as another test of religious legitimacy and commitment, rather than a conflict concerning legal consequences.

Are all fanatics—religious, nationalist, ethnic, and racial—uniquely incompetent in the judicial setting? If so, are trials within the United States ineluctably violating civil and, even, human rights? Psycholegal research on competency for the fanatic needs to be developed to inform legal adjudication. This research would facilitate developing reliable and valid assessment of impression management and other deceptive strategies and tactics. This development would be for conscious and unconscious phenomena and would be sensitive to cross-cultural issues.

The legal competence of alleged terrorists is a significant concern as the Central Intelligence Agency and Federal Bureau of Investigation are apparently being given greater authorization for police operations against alleged terrorists outside the United States, thereby increasing the potential pool of defendants for whom traditional approaches to competency may not apply. As it is, even certain racial subgroups of U.S. citizens, for example, African American males, are more likely to be diagnosed and misdiagnosed as schizophrenic, which is itself correlated with determinations of incompetence. Also, terrorist—even genocidal—events in Rwanda, Burundi, Zaire, Bosnia and Herzegovina, Serbia, and Croatia have increased momentum to effect an international criminal court to prosecute alleged perpetrators of such actions worldwide.

Thus, the legal competence of alleged terrorists and perpetrators of crimes against humanity should be a growing research concern for political psychologists. What GEPP can provide is the heuristic impetus to consider forensic psychological constructs as requiring not only social and cultural parsing but ontogenetic and phylogenetic parsing as well. The concrete consequences of this impetus would be the jettisoning of objective and standardized assessment techniques for ipsative and idiographic ones.

## Deception by a Defendant during a Psychological Assessment and the Probability of Conviction or of a Formal Attribution of Liability

GEPP would suggest that policy deliberations concerning the value and utility of psychological assessments should not focus on whether there is deception. There also should not be a focus on a defendant's necessary guilt and liability, if deception is detected. Instead, the focus should be on the omnipresence of the defendant's deception—some intentional, some conscious, some not, some directed against the self, some directed elsewhere. In fact, the same should apply to the psychologist or other assessor appointed by the court or legal representatives, as well as to all participants in the legal adjudication.

Deception—through a combination of interactive biological, psychological, cultural, and environmental phenomena—currently seems to be a characteristic of humanity.

Public policy on deception and forensic assessment should specify that the assessor speculate on how deception is affecting defendant responses and those of the assessor and other participants in legal adjudication. It is unlikely, however, that this policy direction would be accepted by many political authorities because of the direction's implicit and explicit challenges to political legitimacy and the nature of the rule of law on which it is founded (at least within representative democracies.) Here, GEPP might do no more than clearly illustrate huge disparities between legal dictates about human behavior and human behavior.

## CONCLUSION

As with any other tool of self-professed wisdom or Received Truth, the consequences of GEPP might include revolutionary change, reactionary movement against change, no change, or even—dare I write it—evolutionary change in public policy as applied to human behavior, including the locus of human violence. Change itself might even border on the violence beyond the slings and arrows of calumny so often employed by academics and public intellectuals. Such consequences would mirror recurring phenomena among contestants of religious—as opposed to scientific—belief and ideology as has been depicted in various historical interludes of formally constructed apostasies embracing most, if not all, the world's major religions.

In fact, application of GEPP to public policy concerning violence might even result in the very marginalization, discrediting, or discounting of GEPP itself. In this case, the highly valued, adaptive GEPP continuum from physical survival through procreation to the welfare of kin might, indeed, be threatened for GEPP purveyors and their acolytes.

Yet as the reader embarks on an intellectual adventure with the proponents of GEPP as applied to interdependent public policy issues bearing on violence and a gamut of human atrocities, is there any core consideration that might help with navigation? Given that GEPP is posited as a tool for enquiry on human understanding of human psychology, one might turn to David Hume's *Enquiry Concerning Human Understanding* (1902). In this classic text, Hume offers what has come to be known as Hume's Fork. In essence, he advocates a dichotomy exemplified by two questions. First, does the theory approach the abstract reasoning of mathematics or geometry? Second, does it contain factual statements that can be supported by empirical test? If neither, he concludes: "Commit it to the flames; for it can contain nothing but sophistry and illusion." (pp. 25–26)

The reader will find that GEPP meets the demands of the second question and, perhaps, those of the first. Is this good news? Well, I write this last paragraph on New Year's Eve 2001, after a year wherein thousands have been consigned to the flames and horrible deaths at the hands of righteous certitude. In the light of these flames, GEPP may well inform policymakers that violence is not always an evil malignancy or a human anomaly—and through this informing contribute to a reduction in violence. Thus, would it not be understandable—even irresistible—to spare GEPP from the flames as well?

## REFERENCES

Abraham, R.B., Blumenfeld, A., Stein, M., & Shapira, S.C. (1998). Advanced trauma life support versus combat trauma life support courses: A comparison of cognitive knowledge decline. *Military Medicine, 163,* 747–749.

Almqvist, K., & Brandell-Forsberg, M. (1997). Refugee children in Sweden: Post-traumatic stress disorder in Iranian preschool children exposed to organized violence. *Child Abuse & Neglect, 21,* 351–366.

Anonymous. (2001). Privileged communication.

Aronson, E. (1990). Applying social psychology to desegregation and energy conservation. *Personality & Social Psychology Bulletin, 16,* 118–132.

Badcock, C. (2000). *Evolutionary psychology: A critical introduction.* Oxford, United Kingdom: Polity Press.

Barclay, M.W. (1997). The metaphoric foundation of literal language: Towards a theory of the reification and meaning of psychological constructs. *Theory and Psychology, 7,* 355–372.

Barish, R.C. (2001). Legislation and regulations addressing workplace violence in the United States and British Columbia. *American Journal of Preventive Medicine, 20,* 149–154.

Blackman, M.C., & Stubbs, E. (2001). Apologies: Genuine admissions of blameworthiness or scripted, sympathetic responses? *Psychological Reports, 88,* 45—50.

Bloom, J.D., Williams, M.H., & Bigelow, D.A. (2000). The forensic psychiatric system in the United States. *International Journal of Law & Psychiatry, 23,* 605–613.

Bloom, R. (2001a). Personal observation.

Bloom, R. (2001b). Personal observation.

Boast, N. (1999). Homicide and failure of community care. *British Journal of Psychiatry, 175,* 585.

Brubaker, R., & Laitin, D.D. (1998). Ethnic and nationalist violence. *Annual Review of Sociology, 24,* 423–452.

Buss, D.M. (1999). *Evolutionary psychology: The new science of the mind.* Boston: Allyn & Bacon.

Buss, D.M., & Shackelford, T.K. (1997). Human aggression in evolutionary psychological perspective. *Clinical Psychology Review, 17,* 605–619.

Caporael, L.R. (2000). Evolutionary psychology: Toward a unifying theory and a hybrid science. *Annual Review of Psychology, 52,* 607–628.

Cartwright, J. (2000). Evolution and human behavior: Darwinian perspectives on human nature. Cambridge, MA: MIT Press.

Casey, P., & Rottman, D.B. (2000). Therapeutic jurisprudence in the courts. *Behavioral Sciences & the Law, 18,* 445–457.

Chiu, C., Hong, Y., & Dweck, C.S. (1997). Lay dispositionism and implicit theories of personality. *Journal of Personality & Social Psychology, 73,* 19–30.

Derksen, M. (1997). Are we not experimenting then? The rhetorical demarcation of psychology and common sense. *Theory & Psychology, 7,* 435–456.

Edwards, D.C. (1999). *Motivation and emotion: Evolutionary, physiological, cognitive, and social influences.* Thousand Oaks, CA: Sage Publications, Inc.

Finkel, N.J., Fulero, S.M., Haugaard, J.J., Levine, M., & Small, M.A. (2001). Everyday life and legal values: A concept paper. *Law & Human Behavior, 225,* 109–123.

Gacono, C.B., Meloy, J.R., & Bridges, M.R. (2000). A Rorschach comparison of psychopaths, sexual homicide perpetrators, and nonviolent pedophiles: Where angels fear to tread. *Journal of Clinical Psychology, 56,* 757–777.

Gold, G.J., & Weiner, B. (2000). Remorse, confession, group identity, and expectancies about repeating a transgression. *Basic and Applied Social Psychology, 22,* 291–300.

Heyes, C., & Huber, L. (Eds.). (2000). *The evolution of cognition.* Cambridge, MA: MIT Press.

Hogan, R. (1976). "On the conflicts between biological and social evolution and between psychology and moral tradition." Comment. *American Psychologist, 31,* 363–366.

Hume, D. (1902). *An Enquiry Concerning Human Understanding,* Page 25–26, Section IV, Part I, Paragraphs 20–21, 2nd ed., (Ed. L.A. Selby-Bigge). (Oxford: Oxford University Press.

Katz, L. (Ed.). (2000). *Evolutionary origins of morality: Cross-disciplinary perspectives.* Thorverton, England: Imprint Academic.

Kenrick, D.T. (2001). Evolutionary psychology, cognitive science and dynamical systems: Building an integrative paradigm. *Current Directions in Psychological Science, 10,* 13–17.

King, L.A., King, D.W., Fairbank, J.A., Keane, T.M., & Adams, G.A. (1998). Resilience-recovery factors in post-traumatic stress disorder among female and male Vietnam veterans: Hardiness, postwar social support, and additional stressful life events. *Journal of Personality & Social Psychology, 74,* 420–434.

Kirkpatrick, L.A. (1999). Toward an evolutionary psychology of religion and personality. *Journal of Personality, 67,* 921–952.

Koss, M.P. (2000). Blame, shame, and community: Justice responses to violence against women. *American Psychologist, 55,* 1332–1343.

Lapping, B. (1987). *Apartheid, a history.* New York: Braziller.

Lasswell, H. (1930). *Psychopathology and politics.* Chicago: University of Chicago Press.

Mays, M., & Manaster, G.J. (1999). Research: Facts, values, theory, practice, and unexamined assumptions. *Journal of Individual Psychology, 55,* 248–255.

McGregor, H.A., Lieberman, J.D., Greenberg, J., Solomon, S., Arndt, J., Simon, L., & Pyszczynski, T. (1998). Terror management and aggression: Evidence that mortality salience motivates aggression against worldview-threatening others. *Journal of Personality & Social Psychology, 74,* 590–605.

Mealey, L. (2000). *Sex differences: Development and evolutionary strategies.* San Diego, CA: Academic Press, Inc.

O'Donohue, W.T., Callaghan, G.M., & Ruckstuhl, L.E. (1998). Epistemological barriers to radical behaviorism. *Behavior Analyst, 21,* 307–320.

Parsons, W. (1995). *Public policy: An introduction to the theory and practice of policy analysis* (pp. 1–84). Cheltenham, United Kingdom: Edward Elgar.

Pierce, B.D., & White, R. (1999). The evolution of social structure: Why biology matters. *Academy of Management Review, 24,* 843–853.

Pinn, V.W., & Chunko, M.T. (1997). The diverse faces of violence: Minority women and domestic abuse. *Academic Medicine, 72,* S65–S71.

Pipes, R.B., & Alessi, M. (1999). Remorse and a previously punished offense in assignment of punishment and estimated likelihood of a repeated offense. *Psychological Reports, 85,* 246—248.

Prilleltensky, I. (1994). *The morals and politics of psychology* (pp. 45–97). New York: SUNY Press.

Revonsuo, A. (2000). The reinterpretation of dreams: An evolutionary hypothesis of the function of dreaming. *Behavioral & Brain Sciences, 23,* 877–901; 904–1018; 1083–1121.

Rothschild, B., Dimson, C., Storaasli, R., & Clapp, L. (1997). Personality profiles of veterans entering treatment for domestic violence. *Journal of Family Violence, 12,* 259–27.

Scobie, E.D., & Scobie, G.E.W. (1998). Damaging events: The perceived need for forgiveness. *Journal for the Theory of Social Behaviour, 28,* 373–401.

Sober, E., & Wilson, D.S. (1998). *Unto others: The evolution and psychology of unselfish behavior.* Cambridge, MA: Harvard University Press.

Takaku, S., Weiner, B., & Ohbuchi, K.I. (2001). A cross-cultural examination of the effects of apology and perspective taking on forgiveness. *Journal of Language and Social Psychology, 20,* 144–166.

Tetlock, P.E., & Goldgeier, J.M. (2000). Human nature and world politics: Cognition, identity, and influence. *International Journal of Psychology, 35,* 87–96.

Thomas-Peter, B.A., & Warren, S. (1998). Legal responsibilities of forensic psychologists. *Expert Evidence, 6,* 79–106.

Walcott, D.M. (2000). Sexually violent predator commitment successfully challenged on basis of conditions of confinement and treatment. *Journal of the American Academy of Psychiatry & the Law, 28,* 244–245.

Watts, R.J., Griffith, D.M., & Abdul-Adil, J. (1999). Sociopolitical development as an antidote for oppression—theory and action. *American Journal of Community Psychology, 27,* 255–271

Weiser, B. (June 28, 2001). Defense psychiatrist tells jury of Embassy bomber's remorse. *New York Times* [On-line]. Available: http://www.nytimes.com.

Winnick, B.J. (1996). Foreword: A summary of the MacArthur Treatment Competence Study and an introduction to the special theme. *Psychology, Public Policy, & Law, 2,* 3–17

Wood, R.M., Grossman, L.S., & Fichtner, C.G. (2000). Psychological assessment, treatment, and outcome with sex offenders. *Behavioral Sciences & the Law, 18,* 23–41.

Zeidner, J., Johnson, C.D., & Scholarios, D. (1997). Evaluating military selection and classification systems in the multiple job context. *Military Psychology, 9,* 169–186.

# 2

# The Social Implications of Evolutionary Psychology
## Linking Brain Biochemistry, Toxins, and Violent Crime[1]

*Roger D. Masters*

Although recent neuroscientific research has revolutionized our understanding of brain function, studies in this field usually focus on the individual central nervous system (CNS). This emphasis has been necessary given the immense complexity of cytoarchitecture, neurochemistry, and function. Now, however, it is time to link our growing knowledge of brain function and evolutionary psychology to public policy. Such a linkage, with a particular focus on the links between neurotoxins and violent crime, shows the growing importance of evolutionary psychology, which—unlike earlier psychological theories—provides a solid framework for understanding new findings in neuroscience, toxicology, and behavior.

## EVOLUTIONARY PSYCHOLOGY AND VIOLENCE

Evolutionary psychology teaches that human behavior needs to be understood in the perspective of hominid evolution and behavioral biology. In addition to describing the repertoire of primate social behaviors as well as the likely developments associated with the appearance of hominids over the last 100,000 years, evolutionary psychology is open to insights from genetics, neuroscience, and ecology. As experience teaches us only too well, individuals differ in behavioral propensities for reasons that include genetic predispositions, personal experiences, and environmental contingencies.

Unlike classical behaviorism, for example, evolutionary psychologists recognize a species-typical repertoire of behavior that includes threat and aggression, as well as communication, bonding, sexuality, and other behaviors such as those linked with hunting and gathering. This approach, which integrates nature and nurture, facilitates analysis of the characteristic brain structures and neurotransmitter functions associated with distinct behavioral patterns in diverse situations. From this perspective, although it is important to understand the individual and environmental conditions that elicit particular behaviors, it is equally important to consider inhibitory processes. Even more important, by integrating ecological factors in behavioral analysis, evolutionary psychology makes it possible to reconsider how economic activities and public policies can modify the environment in ways that have unintended effects on individual behavior.

One promising area for such analyses concerns the harmful effects of toxins on brain chemistry and behavior (Gottschalk et al., 1991). Lead, for example, lowers intelligence and learning ability, as Ben Franklin learned from British printers.[2] More recently, neurotoxicologists have shown an association between lead uptake and poor impulse control, learning disabilities, and violence (Bellinger et al., 1994; Bryce-Smith, 1983; Cook et al., 1995; Cory-Slechta, 1995; Kahnet al., 1995; Minder et al., 1994; Needleman, 1989, 1999; Needleman & Gatsonis, 1991; Tuthill, 1996). In many instances, exposure to lead and other toxins is due to human activities and can be exacerbated by governmental policies (Wollan, 1968). As a result, could differences in rates of violent behavior be traced to brain dysfunction that is made worse by ill-advised legal or bureaucratic decisions?[3]

From the perspective of evolutionary psychology, aggressive impulses and violent behaviors are part of the human behavioral repertoire. Among hominids, as in the social behavior of other primates, in addition to violent actions directed at potential predators, such behaviors sometimes occur between conspecifics. Although threat displays often occur within a band (especially in the context of behaviors that establish and maintain social dominance), within group bonding usually inhibits violent outcomes from aggressive interactions. In contrast, between group competition seems more likely to lead to a violent attack. On the one hand, aggressors may seek to deprive members of another band of access to crucial resources; on the other, individuals—and especially high-status males—sometimes respond to between-group threat with what has been classified as kin-based altruism. In short, from the perspective of evolutionary psychology, violent behavior is an element in the human repertoire that is normally inhibited within bonded groups but more likely to occur when directed to external threats to families or communities.

In a civilized society, the acts classified as "violent crime" represent a different form of aggressive behavior. Social norms and laws establish expectations that include those acts of within-group violence that are customarily inhibited by individuals experiencing aggressive impulses toward others. Consider two examples in terms of evolutionary psychology. First, I see a masked man approaching my house with a drawn revolver at 8:00 P.M., take out my own gun, and shoot him as I open the door. This violent behavior could well be judged as an act of self-defense rather than a crime. Second, I see a salesman selling trinkets approaching my house at 2:00 P.M. on a sunny afternoon, take out my gun and shoot him as I open the door. In this case, I would probably be accused and convicted of murder. The first case is acceptable violent behavior if it can be judged under norms founded on the impulses of individual survival and defense of one's family. The second is violent crime if judged under norms that include civility to strangers and inhibition of aggressive impulses where no threat is involved.

From this perspective, when analyzing violent crime, evolutionary psychology can both clarify motives and—more important—explain the failure to inhibit aggressive impulses that contradict the law. And in addition to genetic predisposition and brain structure, recent research shows that the effects of toxins on neurotransmitter function are often a factor that can undermine normal inhibition of aggression (Masters, Hone, & Doshi, 1998). In the development of evolutionary psychology, this level of analysis may be especially important because it often reveals causal patterns that other psychological and sociological theories can neither predict nor explain.

## BRAIN CHEMISTRY, ENVIRONMENTAL TOXINS, AND VIOLENT CRIME

Although the link between brain chemistry and violent crime may seem implausible, evidence that reduced exposure to toxins can lower the frequency of crime and other costly behaviors is provided by the Congressional ban on the sale of leaded gasoline (Kitman, 2000).[4] In this case, the harmful effects of lead pollution from gasoline were apparently strongest during an infant's early neurological development. Although the correlation between each year's sales of leaded gasoline (as a measure of average exposure to fumes from tetraethyl lead) and that year's crime rate is virtually nil, the correlation rises sharply as the time lag between leaded gas sales and violent crime rates is extended; with a lag of 17 years, the correlation is over 0.90 (Table 2.1). Because children 17 years or younger rarely engage in violent crime, the very high correlation between lead gas sales and violent crime rates 18 to 26 years later points to fetal or neonatal exposure to lead as a significant but not generally noted factor in violent crime. As a result, these data suggest that the drop in U.S. homicide rates since 1991 was facilitated by the Congressional ban on leaded gasoline (Masters, 2001).

Exploration of such questions is important because behavioral dysfunctions associated with neurotoxicity are often attributed to the individual's choice, education, or other personal defects. This tendency is noticeable even when the problem has been traced to a defect that is clearly beyond voluntary control. Several years ago, for instance, I presented a seminar on "Neuroscience and Learning" at the Harvard Graduate School of Education. At that time, three participants asserted that hyperactivity and other learning disabilities do not exist as CNS deficits but are merely "moral" failings of unruly children.

The consequence of the gap between neuroscientific findings and our educational system is often costly. In classes at Dartmouth College, it has not been

**Table 2.1**
**Correlations between Gasoline Sales and U.S. Violent Crime Rates Lagged
by Increasing Time Intervals (1976–1997) (Source: FBI, Supplementary
Homicide Reports, 1976–1997)**

| Year Lag | Correlation | n | | Year Lag | Correlation | n | |
|---|---|---|---|---|---|---|---|
| 0 | -0.906 | 26 | | 25 | 0.910 | 24 | |
| 1 | -0.897 | 27 | | 26 | 0.900 | 23 | |
| 2 | -0.88 | 28 | | 27 | 0.885 | 22 | |
| 3 | -0.85 | 29 | | 28 | 0.882 | 21 | |
| 4 | -0.79 | 30 | | 29 | 0.878 | 20 | |
| 5 | -0.74 | 30 | | 30 | 0.874 | 19 | |
| 6 | -0.675 | 30 | | 31 | 0.859 | 18 | |
| 7 | -0.610 | 30 | | 32 | 0.856 | 17 | |
| 8 | -0.542 | 30 | | 33 | 0.868 | 16 | |
| 9 | -0.465 | 30 | | 34 | 0.878 | 15 | |
| 10 | -0.369 | 30 | | *Average 25-34:* | | | 0.879 |
| 11 | -0.247 | 30 | | 35 | 0.891 | 14 | |
| 12 | -0.111 | 30 | | 36 | 0.880 | 13 | |
| 13 | 0.050 | 30 | | 37 | 0.819 | 12 | |
| *Average 0-13:* | | | -0.57 | 38 | 0.728 | 11 | |
| 14 | 0.236 | 30 | | 39 | 0.642 | 10 | |
| 15 | 0.431 | 30 | | 40 | 0.439 | 9 | |
| 16 | 0.618 | 30 | | *Average 37-40:* | | | 0.702 |
| 17 | 0.778 | 30 | | | | | |
| *Average 14-17:* | | 0.516 | | | | | |
| 18 | 0.902 | 30 | | | | | |
| 19 | 0.961 | 30 | | | | | |
| 20 | 0.979 | 29 | | | | | |
| 21 | 0.964 | 28 | | | | | |
| 22 | 0.956 | 27 | | | | | |
| 23 | 0.939 | 26 | | | | | |
| 24 | 0.919 | 25 | | | | | |
| *Average 18-24:* | | 0.95 | | | | | |

unusual to discover about one student out of every ten with a previously undiagnosed learning disability. Indeed, when *Science* published an analysis of brain function among dyslexics in three countries (Paulesu et al., 2001), the positron emission tomography (PET) scans showing the brain loci not active among dyslexic children seem to have been—for some educators—the first concrete evidence that this condition has a basis in brain function.

Even where hyperactivity and learning disabilities are viewed as needing treatment, the neurological factors that might underlie each child's problem

are often ignored. To be sure, a specific learning disability or behavioral problem may be traced to various factors. Among CNS characteristics that have
been linked to attention deficit hyperactivity disorder (ADHD) are damage to
a specific brain structure (the nucleus accumbens; Cardinal et al., 2001) as well
as deficits in dopaminergic or serotonergic activity (Bellinger et al., 1994; Needleman & Gatsonis, 1991). Where neurotransmitter dysfunction is implicated,
lead toxicity is often one of the factors involved (Brockel & Cory-Slechta,
1998).

Because hyperactivity due to a loss of impulse control can also be observed
in violent behavior, the role of neurotoxins in ADHD deserves special attention.
Although excessive cellular uptake of lead can be treated by chelation, teachers
and physicians often give hyperactive children medications such as Ritalin
without screening for known risk factors. In the United States alone, it has
been estimated that as many as 11 million children are receiving Ritalin or
other drugs that improve behavior by activating inhibitory circuits in the brain
(such as dopaminergic pathways in the basal ganglia). For ADHD children,
such medications provide a "quick fix" that masks underlying problems and
creates a danger of long-term drug abuse from a "medication" that has effects
parallel to those of cocaine (Walker, 1998). Indeed, journalistic reports that
Ritalin has become a popular recreational drug underscore the need to adopt a
more scientific approach to the analysis and treatment of learning disabilities
or behavioral problems with an identified neurological basis. Obviously, such
uses of Ritalin can mask the problem and could actually increase the risks of
violent behavior in later years.

Dealing with such issues is unlikely to be successful unless neuroscientific
research is linked with the social dimensions of environment, individual behavior, and public policy. To illustrate the potential of such an approach, I
present evidence of the neurotoxic effects of two largely untested chemicals
that are currently added to the drinking water consumed by 140 million Americans. These compounds—hydrofluosilicic acid ($H_2SiF_6$) and sodium silicofluoride ($Na_2SiF_6$)—are more generally called "silicofluorides" (SiFs).[5] Despite their
widespread use, SiFs have never been properly tested for safety; as an EPA
official put it, his agency has no evidence on "the health and behavioral effects"
of silicofluorides.[6]

Because the public policy decisions responsible for this situation are not
relevant for present purposes (Rymer, 2000), this chapter focuses on a series
of questions that are essential in attempts to link neuroscience and evolutionary
psychology to violent behavior. First, what characteristics of the suspected
chemicals make the inquiry plausible and indeed necessary? (Part I: "Why
Silicofluorides May Be Harmful to Humans"). Second, based on known effects
of these chemicals, what mechanism could trigger neurotoxic harm to humans?
(Part II: "Biochemical Effects of Silicofluoride: Mechanisms of Neurotoxicity").
These two steps culminate in the description of biochemical mechanisms that

are predicted to have specific biological and behavioral consequences, including increased risks of violence. Finally, given the research hypothesis developed to this point, is there empirical evidence consistent with the predicted effects? (Part III: "Testing the Hypothesis: Enhanced Lead Uptake and Behavioral Dysfunctions Due to SiF"). As this outline suggests, in addition to building on research linking evolutionary psychology to neuroscience, analysis of this sort will also require knowledge of such disparate fields as chemistry, toxicology, and public policy.

## WHY SILICOFLUORIDES MAY BE HARMFUL TO HUMANS

In the mid 1940s, the injection of sodium fluoride (NaF) in public water supplies was initiated in the United States as an experiment to ascertain whether rates of tooth decay would be reduced by fluoridated drinking water. In 1950, midway through a projected 10–12 year experiment, the U.S. Public Health Service allowed the substitution of SiFs for NaF. Although tests had been conducted on NaF but not on SiFs, the implications of this shift have been generally ignored by both supporters and critics of public "fluoridation" of water supplies.[7]

Whereas NaF hydrolizes on injection into water, completely dissociating fluoride ion from sodium, no empirical evidence of dissociation rates of SiFs at 1 ppm was available when they were judged acceptable—in 1950. At that time, the use of SiF was justified on the basis of a *theoretical* argument by P.J. McClure (of the Public Health Service) that the dissociation of SiFs would be "virtually complete."[8] Twenty-five years later, German laboratory studies by Westendorf revealed major differences between SiF and NaF. Under conditions comparable to those of a water treatment plant, SiFs are incompletely dissociated, and their residues have significant experimental effects on vital enzymes, including acetyl-cholinesterase (AChE) and serum cholinesterases (or pseudocholinesterases), including butyryl-cholinesterase (BChE) (Knappwost & Westendorf, 1974; Westendorf, 1975).[9]

Despite recent assertions of two EPA scientists (Urbansky & Schock, 2000),[10] this difference between NaF and SiF is consistent with other experimental findings. SiF anion $[SiF_6]^{2-}$ remains intact at pH 7 at room temperature. It must be exposed to boiling water at pH 9 in order to effect total fluoride release so that no residues of partially dissociated SiF remain in solution. Moreover, because the dissociation process is reversible, reassociation of SiF from its components is possible (e.g., when SiF treated water is used in cooking). Hence the assumed identity of NaF and SiF, which persists in many discussions of public health and dentistry (American Public Health Association, 2001; U.S. Department of Health and Human Services, 2000),[11] and was reinforced in the Centers for Disease Control's recent publication of a study group's "Recommendations" on fluoridation,[12] can no longer be sustained without disconfirming existing research on these compounds.

When Westendorf set out to study SiF dissociation under more realistic conditions than had been tried previously, he used a refined technique. Measuring fluoride ions released from SiF at physiological conditions (pH 7.4, 37 °C) in Ringer's solution at 1–5 ppm of total fluoride, Westendorf could only detect 67% of that fluoride with the fluoride ion specific electrode. He proposed that the remaining fluoride was still bound in a partially dissociated residue of SiF in the form of $[SiF_2(OH)_4]^{2-}$. Whether that particular species was the only SiF dissociation residue, Westendorf's finding was evidence for the survival of some partially undissociated SiF residue.

Translated into water plant parameters, Westendorf's findings would mean that dilution of SiFs to the 1 to 2 ppm level used in water fluoridation at the pH and temperatures customarily obtaining in the water plant would induce each $[SiF_6]^{2-}$ ion to release only four fluorides to be replaced by hydroxyls. The concentration of resulting SiF dissociation residue $[SiF_2(OH)_2]^{2-}$ would be in the order of 1–5 ppm by weight. Incidentally, the same quantitative release of fluoride from $SiF_4$ would correspond with leaving behind the nonionic species $SiF_2(OH)_2$ at about the same concentration.

Thus, contrary to the total release of fluoride from SiF at water plant conditions (which has been assumed by supporters of fluoridation as a public policy),[13] Westendorf found only two-thirds fluoride release by actual experiment. Hence, at a pH close to common water plant practice, Westendorf's experiments show that SiFs are incompletely dissociated when injected in a public water supply and that the resulting residual complexes can have significant biochemical effects.

These characteristics of SiFs indicate that, in the absence of extensive testing of their safety, a harmful chemical may currently be distributed in the public water supplies of many communities. The scale of the potential problem is sufficient to justify concern, because over 90% of water fluoridation in the United States uses SiFs. With over 140 million Americans exposed to them (Centers for Disease Control, 1992), it is prudent to examine whether SiF residues or other harmful consequences of SiF injection in public water supplies (including the potential for reconstituting SiF in cooking or digestion) have neurotoxic effects that could modify behavior.

## BIOCHEMICAL EFFECTS OF SILICOFLUORIDES AND MECHANISMS OF NEUROTOXICITY[14]

### Enzymatic Inhibition

That SiF and NaF have different enzymatic effects was shown long before Westendorf completed his laboratory studies in 1975. In 1933, when reporting on his doctoral research, F.J. McClure (1933) reported that fluoride (in the form of NaF) can act as an enzyme inhibitor.

Experimental evidence has established the fact that there is also a specific influence of fluorides on certain enzymatic changes associated particularly with carbohydrates and fats. Thus, the results of a systematic study conducted by Kastle and Loevenhart on the effect of antiseptics on the reactions of pancreatic and liver extracts revealed an effect of most substances and also a particularly remarkable destructive action of NaF on the reaction of lipase. . . . Dilutions of NaF as low as 1:15,000,000 [0.07 ppm] may inhibit the action of lipase on ethyl acetate as much as 50 per cent. . . . Leake et al have obtained evidence that NaF inhibits the action of this enzyme *in vivo.*"[15]

Two years later (in 1935), Kick et al. found the excretion pathways of fluoride differ depending on whether test animals have ingested NaF or SiF (Kick et al., 1935).

Little additional work on the biological effects of these chemicals was conducted until Westendorf found that SiF inhibits AChE without a concentration threshold, whereas NaF inhibition of AChE starts at about 5 ppm of fluoride ion. Moreover, at equal fluoride levels beyond the NaF threshold level, SiF is about two to four times more powerful an inhibitor of AchE than is NaF. The kinetics indicated that NaF inhibition was only competitive (i.e., worked by blocking the enzyme active site), whereas SiF inhibition was both competitive and noncompetitive. Competitive inhibition is explained by the presence of hydrofluoric acid (HF), formed from free fluoride ion, which could find and occupy the active site in the enzyme molecule. That would occur whether inhibition was due to NaF or SiF, because both release free fluoride under physiological conditions at 1 ppm of fluoride. However, whereas NaF releases all of its fluoride ions by simple dilution/ionization, SiFs release fluoride ions in a complicated sequence of dissociation steps that depend on concentration and pH.

The chemical structures of likely SiF residues—$[SiF_2(OH)_4]^{2-}$ or $SiF_2(OH)_2$— would make each one a logical precursor for the creation of mono-silicic acid in the bloodstream. Mono-silicic acid is not a commonplace form of hydrated silica in blood and, according to the following hypothesis, has the potential for serious damage to health and behavior in a number of ways.

## Residual Complexes Due to Incomplete Dissociation

A partially dissociated monomeric SiF species either survives into the stomach or is reformed there at gastric pH. It then passes into the bloodstream where it hydrolyzes to mono-silicic acid and/or forms low molecular weight silicic acid oligomers. These readily bind via their silanol hydroxyls to any polypeptide backbone with a reactable amine or hydroxyl. That alone would interfere with normal polypeptide structure and function. However, subsequent reaction of as-yet unreacted pendant silanols with one another would also create siloxane bonds or more linkages to the polypeptide backbone in such a way as to disrupt the natural chain folding of proteins.

A recent report (Coradin & Livage, 2001) amplifies this hypothesis and adds significantly to its credibility:

The polymerization of silicic acid in aqueous solutions at different pH was followed by the colorimetric molybdosilicate method. The role of four amino acids (serine, lysine, proline and aspartic acid) and the corresponding homopeptides was studied. All four amino acids behave the same way and favor the condensation of silicic acid. Peptides exhibit a stronger catalytic effect than amino acids but they appear to behave in very different ways depending on the nature of side-groups and pH. Polylysine and polyproline for instance lead to the precipitation of solid phases containing both silica and peptides. The role of these biomolecules on the polymerization of silicic acid is discussed in terms of electrostatic interactions, hydrogen bonds and solubility.

This report supports the proposition that silicic acid reaction with blood proteins could well be the root cause for SiF's powerful inhibition of AChE and "pseudo-cholinesterases" (PChEs), which are also known as "serum cholinesterases" and include butyryl-cholinesterase (BChE).

## Effects of Cholinesterase Inhibition

The implications for human health of this SiF-induced biomechanism are numerous and in some instances can be extremely serious. One of the most important of these effects concerns the interference with cholinesterases. Although acetylcholinesterase (AChE) is known due to its regulatory role for acetylcholine, a neurotransmitter with multiple functions throughout the body, even today the role of butyryl-cholinesterase (BChE) and its relationship to AChE are not entirely understood. According to Allderdice et al. (1991):

Human tissues have two distinct cholinesterase activities: acetylcholinesterase and butyrylcholinesterase. Acetylcholinesterase functions in the transmission of nerve impulses, whereas the physiological function of butyrylcholinesterase remains unknown.

At least one function believed to be served by BChE is to protect AChE by scavenging toxins:

Butyrylcholinesterase must be differentiated from acetylcholinesterase, which cannot hydrolyse succinylcholine. The physiological action of butyryl-cholinesterase remains unknown, although it can hydrolyse many drugs. (Lejus et al., 1998)

It is not inconceivable that the role of BChE as a protector of AChE goes beyond the capacity to hydrolyze drugs to a sacrificial role in absorbing heavy metals. In any case, powerful inhibition of BChE by SiF would indirectly modify an indirect impact on the proper function of AChE. Moreover, their interaction has been associated with brain dysfunction:

Evidence about nonclassic functions of acetyl- (AChE) and butyryl-cholinesterase (BChE) during embryonic development of vertebrate brains is compared with evidence of their expression in Alzheimer disease (AD). Before axons extend in the early neural tube, BChE expression shortly precedes the expression of AChE. BChE is associated with neuronal and glial cell proliferation, and it may also regulate AChE. AChE is suggested to guide and stabilize growing axons. Pathologically, cholinesterase expression in AD shows some resemblance to that in the embryo. (Layer, 1995)

Regarding AChE inhibition, Westendorf found that fluoride released by NaF acted only in the competitive mode, but SiF had a much more powerful effect and acted in two modes. The first mode was competitive, as expected, due to the 67% of the SiF fluoride released as free fluoride. In addition, however, the nondissociated fluoride-bearing SiF residue enhanced net inhibition significantly in the noncompetitive mode. Westendorf suggested that the species $[SiF_2(OH)_4]^{2-}$ mentioned earlier somehow distorted the morphology of the AChE molecule, but he did not offer an explanation for how that occurred. Without referring to Westendorf's work at all, a hint of an explanation for this effect appeared in the English language literature a few years later (Margolis, 1976, as cited in Iler, 1979).

The "Margolis mechanism" discussed by Iler (1979) suggests how low molecular weight poly-silicic acid oligomers formed in the bloodstream could disrupt polypeptide chain morphology:

The effect of silica was described by Margolis as due to the adsorption and denaturation of a globular protein, the Hageman factor. The proposed mechanism was that on sufficiently large particles or on flat surfaces of silica, the protein molecule was stretched out of shape by adsorption forces as it formed a monolayer on the surface. When the silica particles were very small, the molecular segments of the protein could become attached to different particles without segment stretching. . . . When protein is adsorbed on a larger silica particle or a coherent aggregate of smaller particles, the chain stretched and certain internal hydrogen bonds which hold the protein molecule in a specific configuration are broken. On small single particles no such stretching occurs.

Any of the partially dissociated SiF species just described—for example, $[SiF_2(OH)_4]^{2-}$, SiF4, or $SiF_2(OH)_2$ derived from $SiF_4$—would be candidates for producing low molecular weight polysilicic acid oligomers in the bloodstream, after crossing over from the stomach at pH around 2. Most enzymes are globular proteins, so many enzymes besides AChE would be likely to experience at least noncompetitive inhibition by the "Margolis mechanism."

## Ferry Molecules and Enhanced Heavy Metal Uptake

A wide array of nonenzyme polypeptides whose chain folding determines their function would also be subject to this morphological disruption. As a result, adverse effects of the partially dissociated SiF residue are not limited to adsorption by globular proteins or on flat surfaces. Given covalent bonding with any protein hydroxyl and amino sites by silicon-bound fluorine as described earlier, many other specific polypeptide morphology effects besides enzyme inhibition would also be susceptible to disruption.

Other mechanisms that enhance lead uptake or modify neurotransmitter function might also exist. For instance, if undissociated or reassociated SiF reaches the brain, its function as an AchE and BChE inhibitor could reinforce the effects of other cholinesterase inhibitors (such as organo-phosphate pesticide residues). Because Abou-Donia's experimental work shows that AChE inhibition has cumulative effects, this suggests that even relatively small residues might enhance the effect of other toxins in this class (Abou-Donia, Goldstein, Dechovskaia, et al., 2001; Abou-Donia, Goldstein, Jones, et al., 2001).

It is especially noteworthy that Westendorf's SiF experimental data on incomplete dissociation are consistent with a biochemical mechanism that could enhance gut/blood lead transport and hence increase uptake of lead from environmental exposures. The compound Westendorf postulated as the partially hydrolyzed ionic species $[SiF_2(OH)_4]^{2-}$ closely resembles the $SiF_2(OH)_2$ molecule that we have proposed as a "ferry molecule" capable of chelating a heavy metal ion via the hydroxyls, with the enhanced ability to permeate lipophilic membranes due to the two residual fluorines. In addition, the two fluorines still bound to silicon at the 67% dissociation of SiF found by Westendorf could be due to survival of a half hydrolyzed $SiF_4$ molecule, as well as to a two-thirds hydrolyzed $[SiF_6]^{2-}$.

If the strong noncompetitive enzyme inhibition by SiF found by Westendorf was the result of disruption of protein chain folding by low molecular weight polysilicic acid oligomers, a partly hydrolyzed $SiF_4$ molecule would be as likely to have that effect as the $[SiF_2(OH)_4]^{2-}$ anion. Defective protein morphology could result by the adsorption process suggested by Margolis (1976, as cited in Iler, 1979) or by covalent bonding between active silicon-fluorine bonds in partially dissociated SiFs with blood proteins.

The result could be the formation of molecules that can "ferry" a toxin such as lead to the brain or other organs, thus short-circuiting such natural detoxification enzymes as glutathione or metallothionines. Prior to Westendorf's research in Germany, although there was evidence that SiF had potentially harmful effects not found for NaF, there is little indication that American researchers were aware of this possibility.[16] The shift from NaF to SiFs as fluoridation agents was endorsed in 1950, at which time no one could have known of Westendorf's findings (first partly revealed in 1974, when *Naturwissenschaft* carried a brief account of the findings more fully reported in Westendorf's thesis in 1975; Knappwost & Westendorf, 1974). The situation today differs due to the radical advances in neuroscience combined with the availability of extensive empirical evidence (including the English translation of Westendorf's thesis).

Under these circumstances, it is now reasonable to test the hypothesis that children living in communities with SiF treated water are more likely to absorb lead from their environment and to exhibit behaviors that have been linked to lead neurotoxicity or cholinesterase inhibition. Because the Centers for Disease Control monitors the chemicals used in water fluoridation, if geographic data are sufficiently precise these data can be used to test these hypotheses. Four types of data were available for statistical analysis: (1) the chemicals used for water fluoridation in each community; (2) children's blood lead levels from either state health surveys or the National Health and Nutrition Evaluation Survey (NHANES III), (3) socioeconomic and ecological data from the U.S. Census, and (4) rates of violent crime as reported by the Federal Bureau of Investigation (FBI). We began, therefore, by examining whether SiF usage is associated with an enhanced uptake of lead from such environmental sources as old housing with lead paint or high-lead levels in public water supplies (obviously, the absence of significant effects at this level would falsify the hypothesis). Then, having confirmed that blood lead uptake reflects something akin to the proposed "ferry molecules" or residual complexes due to SiF water treatment, we test whether the use of silicofluorides is associated with increased rates of behavioral dysfunctions linked to blood lead, focusing on violent crime and substance abuse by criminals.

## TESTING THE HYPOTHESIS: ENHANCED LEAD UPTAKE AND BEHAVIORAL DYSFUNCTIONS DUE TO SiF

To assess predictions of social phenomena based on neuroscientific and toxicological findings at the individual level, it is necessary to examine aggregate data with care. Geographically diverse samples of individuals need to be studied using multivariate statistical techniques to control for the effects of potentially confounding variables. More than one sample should be studied, and samples should be large enough to insure that tests of statistical significance are meaningful. For any one sample, moreover, it is useful to analyze the data in more than one way, using different statistical techniques (such as multiple regression, logistic regression, and analysis of variance) and examining subsamples to explore the incidence of observed effects among individuals of different race, age, or sex. Finally, but of particular importance, it is important to examine aggregate data *both* for a biological effect known to influence behavior (e.g., levels of blood lead as a test of uptake of a dangerous neurotoxin) *and* for behaviors that might have been made more likely by the toxin (e.g., substance abuse and violent crime).

Multiple analyses are therefore necessary to test the hypothesis that SiF-treated water exposes individuals to residues that enhance lead uptake (such as the "ferry molecules" described above) and thereby increase rates of behavioral dysfunction. As an illustration of the methodological problems facing any such endeavor, at least four distinct empirical issues need to be addressed:

- Population samples should provide evidence of biological differences between those exposed and not exposed to the presumed source of neurotoxicity. In the present case, *do children living in communities with SiF-treated water have, controlling for other variables, higher blood lead levels?*

- These effects should include evidence consistent with the presumed mechanism. In the present case, *does exposure to SiF increase the risks of high blood lead from such known environmental sources of lead as old housing and lead levels over 15 ppb in public water supplies?*

- The effects should occur among different types of individuals—and, insofar as there is variation by population subgroups, the differences should correspond with previously known variations. In the present case, *how does SiF exposure affect blood lead levels among children of different races and ages—and, in particular, how do these effects relate to the generally higher blood lead levels usually found among blacks in the United States?*

- Behaviors previously linked to the toxins in question should be more frequent in times and places where the environmental problem of interest is present. In the present case, *are rates of crime and substance abuse higher in communities using SiF than in comparable localities whose water is not treated with these chemicals?*

The first three questions will be explored using several geographic samples for which we have data on children's blood lead levels (usually based on samples of venous blood lead as well as capillary blood lead). First, for the state of Massachusetts, we have data from capillary blood lead tests of children in 213 communities (constituting virtually all localities with a population over 3,000, including all but one of the communities using SiF-treated water).[17] This sample provided data for approximately 280,000 children, and was analyzed both for all 213 towns and for venous blood lead measurements in a subset of 76,566 children from 30 communities with and 30 communities without SiF treatment (Masters & Coplan, 1999a). Second, for the state of New York, we studied a sample of venous blood tests from 151,225 children in 103 communities with populations between 15,000 and 75,000 (Masters et al., 2000). Finally, we examined blood lead data for almost 4,000 children in the National Health and Nutrition Evaluation Survey III (NHANES III) who lived in 35 counties with populations of over 500,000 (Masters et al., 1999).

Whereas the first two of these samples had data by community, permitting unambiguous evidence of whether children were exposed to SiF, the NHANES III data (only available by county) were divided into counties with less than 10% of the population exposed to SiF, between 10% and 80% exposed to SiF, and more than 80% exposed to SiF. For most purposes, the best assessments here were a contrast between counties with less than 10% SiF exposure (on aggregate, about 6% of children in this category drank SiF-treated water) and counties with over 80% exposure (on aggregate, 92% of children in this group drank SiF-treated water).

For an epidemiological study of behavioral outcomes, we can then use national FBI county-level data for rates of violent crimes. This makes it possible to compare counties for the effects of industrial lead pollution and SiF-treated water while controlling for socioeconomic and demographic factors using census data. For substance abuse, a sample of over 30,000 criminals in 24 cities studied by the National Institute of Justice (NIJ) was assessed for the association between cocaine use at time of arrest and age of first substance abuse. Although further studies are desirable, it should be evident that these datasets are sufficiently diverse to provide a reasonable test of the twin hypotheses that SiF-treated water contains residues (such as the postulated "ferry molecules") that enhance lead uptake, and that the resulting neurotoxicity is associated with costly behavioral dysfunctions.

## Higher Blood Lead Levels Where Silicofluorides Are in Use

In Massachusetts communities using SiF, children's average blood lead levels were higher and the probabilities of a level over $10\mu g/dL$ were greater:

Whereas a community's average uptake of lead by children is weakly associated with the so-called "90th percentile first draw" levels of lead in public water supplies (adjusted $r^2 = .02$), the fluoridation agents used in water treatment have a major effect on lead levels in children's blood. Average levels of lead in capillary blood were 2.78 $\mu g/dL$ in communities using fluosilicic acid and 2.66 $\mu g/dL$ in communities using sodium silicofluoride, while they were significantly lower in communities that used sodium fluoride (2.07 $\mu g/dL$) or did not fluoridate (2.02 $\mu g/dL$) (one way ANOVA, p = .0006; DF 3, 209, F 6.073). The prevalence rate of individuals whose capillary blood lead was above the maximum permissible level of $10\mu g/dL$ was also significantly higher in the communities using either of the silicofluoride compounds (fluosilicic acid = 2.9%, sodium silicofluoride = 3.0%; sodium fluoride = 1.6%; untreated = 1.9%; p < .0001; DF 3,212, F 8.408). Despite smaller samples tested, similar findings were obtained using venous blood uptake. These findings are independent of recorded 90th percentile first draw lead levels in the public water supplies.[18]

Overall, roughly four times as many SiF-treated communities as nonfluoridated or NaF-treated communities have over 3% children with blood lead over $5\mu g/dL$. Moreover, these effects are evident where environmental lead sources are below average, but they are exacerbated when lead levels in water or the percent of old houses are above average. For instance, in communities using sodium fluoride where first draw lead in pubic water exceeded 15 ppb, average blood lead levels were actually lower (1.9$\mu g/dL$) than in communities using this chemical with less lead in their water (2.11$\mu g/dL$). In contrast, in 25 communities using fluosilicic acid with over 15 ppb lead in water, children's blood lead averaged 3.27$\mu g/dL$ compared with only 2.31$\mu g/dL$ in 26 communities using fluosilicic acid where lead in 90th percent first draw water was under 15 ppb. Effects in a smaller number of communities using sodium silicofluoride were comparable, with blood lead averaging 4.38$\mu g/dL$ where first draw lead was above 15ppb ($n = 1$) compared with 2.37 where lead in water was under

15 ppb ($n$ = 6).[19] (For further analysis of the hypothesis that SiF residues enhance uptake of lead from environmental sources such as old housing or lead in public water supplies, see next section.)

The association between SiFs and higher blood lead was confirmed by comparing a subsample of 30 nonfluoridated Massachusetts communities with 30 matched communities using SiF (Table 2.2). Here, although the SiF-treated towns had 50% more lead in public water supplies, more poor, and more minorities, they also had slightly higher per capita income, higher elementary school budgets, and a larger percentage of college graduates. None of these differences fully explain why 1.94% of screened children had blood lead levels in excess of 10μg/dL where SiF was in use, whereas only 0.76% had such high blood lead in the comparable nontreated towns.

New York data are consistent with an association between the use of SiF and higher venous blood lead levels among children. Overall, the percentage of children with venous blood lead over 10μg/dL was significantly higher (DF 3, 104, $F$ = 9.13, $p$ = .0001) if water was treated with fluosilicic acid (4.52%) or sodium silicofluoride (4.20%) than if water was untreated (3.78%) or treated with sodium fluoride (3.05%). Among blacks tested, 20.6% of the 8,685 exposed to SiF had venous blood lead over 10μg/dL, whereas only 7% of the 9,556 blacks in non-SiF communities had blood lead at this level (with similar effects at different blood lead level cutting points) (Masters et al., 2000, p. 1093). Although communities using SiF had somewhat higher levels of seven risk factors associated with higher blood lead (Table 2.3), these sources of lead

**Table 2.2**
**Percent Screened with Blood Lead above 10μg/dL and Other Characteristics, Matched Sample of 30 Nonfluoridated and 30 Fluoridated Communities—Massachusetts**

|  | 30 Non-fluoridated Communities | 30 Fluoridated Communities |
|---|---|---|
| Population (1,000s) | 837.3 | 845.1 |
| Children 0-5 years | 57,031 | 56,446 |
| % children screened with >10μmg/dL | 0.76 | 1.94 |
| Lead in water (ppb) | 21 | 30 |
| 4th grade MEAP* | 5,440 | 5,455 |
| % Poor | 4.60% | 5.10% |
| % Nonwhite | 6.60% | 11.50% |
| % College degree | 23.60% | 30.50% |
| Income per capita | $116,600 | $119,600 |

*MEAP is a state standardized educational text.

Table 2.3
**Community Demographics and Risk Factors, New York Sample: Distribution of 1990 U.S. Census Variables in 105 NY State Communities of Population 15,000–75,000 by SiF Status**

|  | SiF | No SiF |
|---|---|---|
| *Demographics* | | |
| Number of Communities | 28 | 77 |
| Mean Community Size | 34,778 | 25,627 |
| Children 0-5 as % of Pop. | 8.50% | 8.00% |
| No. Children 0-5 years per Community | 2,960 | 2,046 |
| *No. Children Tested, 1994–1998* | | |
| Total Number of VBL Tests | 56,934 | 94,291 |
| Total Number Capillary Tests | 36,791 | 68,357 |
| Total of All Blood Lead Tests | 93,725 | 162,648 |
| Percent of Tests for VBL | 61% | 58% |
| *Risk Factors Associated with High Blood Lead* | | |
| Housing pre-1939 | 49.4% | 23.3% |
| % Age 0-5 in Poverty | 22.3% | 8.5% |
| % Unemployed | 3.5% | 2.5% |
| % B.A. | 7.4% | 9.3% |
| Pop Density (per Sq. Km) | 155 | 143 |
| Total Population | 973,785 | 1,973,336 |
| Per Capita Income | $14,698 | $19,415 |

uptake do not fully explain the results; on the contrary, as hypothesized, SiF enhances lead uptake from environmental sources and hence increases the odds of high blood lead even more where these factors are present (see next section).

Data from the Third National Health and Nutrition Evaluation Survey (NHANES III) were only available for the subset of about 4,000 children living in 35 counties having populations of over 500,000. Using the CDC's 1992 Fluoridation Census, the percent of each county's population receiving silicofluoride-treated water was calculated, and each county was assigned to one of three groups. As noted, the "high" group comprised counties in which a total of 92% of the population received SiF-treated water. The "low" group comprised a population only 6% of which received SiF-treated water. A relatively small group of counties with "intermediate" exposure comprised a population with about a 50% chance of receiving SiF-treated water. Controlling at the individual level for covariates usually associated with lead uptake, the association between more SiF usage and elevated blood lead was statistically significant ($p < 0.001$), with high/low risk ratios in the range of 1.5 to 2.0, depending on age and race.

## Enhanced Uptake of Lead from Environmental Sources

We have predicted that the lead uptake from environmental sources of lead is significantly higher where SiF-treated water exposes children to residues, including compounds like the suggested "ferry molecules." As a result, mere association between SiF usage and higher blood lead levels is insufficient to test the research hypothesis. Two-way or three-way analysis of variance (AN-OVA), which simultaneously considers the relative association between several predictive variables, can also indicate whether the combination of two or three of these predictors (as measured by the "interaction term" of the ANOVA) has significantly stronger effects than the sum of their independent effects. Our hypothesis predicts significant interaction terms between SiF usage and such environmental risk factors as lead in public water supplies or paint in old housing. Conventionally, when a two- or three-way ANOVA has a significant interaction term, statisticians often give weight to the results because such effects are rarely due to measurement error in one of the variables.

The data from Massachusetts (Masters & Coplan, 1999a) are clearly consistent with the research hypothesis that SiF-treated water carries residual complexes, including "ferry molecules" that enhance lead uptake from the environment:

When both fluoridating agents and 90th percentile first draw lead levels are used as predictors of lead uptake, the silicofluoride agents are only associated with substantially above average infant blood lead where lead levels in water are higher than 15ppm. This interaction between the use of silicofluorides and above average lead in water as predictors of children's lead uptake is statistically significant (p = .05; DF 3,204, F 2.62). To confirm this effect, we assessed the extent to which silicofluoride usage might increase the risk from lead paint in old housing as well as lead in the water. Towns were dichotomized according to whether they use silicofluoride agents, whether percent of houses built before 1940 was above the state median, and whether 90th percentile first draw water lead was over 15 ppb. In towns with both more old housing and high levels of lead in water, average blood lead is 3.59 µg/dL in 20 towns where silicofluorides are used, and only 2.50 µg/dL (slightly above the average of 2.23 µg/dL) in the 26 towns not using these agents.[20]

These effects show a tendency for SiF to increase the harmful effects of known risk factors of blood lead uptake that were consistently found in analyses of other samples.

To assess the overall vulnerability of those in high-risk environments in the New York sample, we assigned to each individual a value indicating whether his/her community was above or below the median for each of the seven covariate risk factors in Table 2.3. We then used these as covariates in our analysis, dividing the sample of individuals into those who live in communities with four or fewer risk factors and those who live in communities with five or more risk factors. Although exposure to five or more risk factors increases the risk of blood lead above 10µg/dL, exposure to this number of risks where SiF is used more than doubles a child's chance of having elevated blood lead. As is shown below, these effects were confirmed by computing age-adjusted logistic regressions of odds ratios for venous blood lead over 10µg/dL for children living in communities using SiF compared with those not using these chemicals (Figures 1 and 2 in Masters et al., 2000, p. 1095).

The NHANES III data are less useful for such statistical analyses due to smaller sample size and organization of data by county (which makes it difficult to assume that a high level of an environmental variable applies to each child in a given county). Such limitations reinforce the importance of assessing interaction effects in different racial and age groups of children.

## SiF Exposure and Blood Lead Levels among Children of Different Races and Ages

Prior studies have generally shown that minorities—and especially blacks— are particularly at risk for high levels of blood lead. NHANES III data, showing average blood lead levels for black, Hispanic, or white children aged 3–5 (Figure 2.1) and 5–17 (Figure 2.2) provide a useful urban sample. For each race and each age, lead levels are significantly higher for children exposed to SiF-treated water ($p < .0001$), with effects of exposure to SiF that are significantly worse for minorities than for whites, and worse for blacks than for Hispanics.

Because a similar effect had already been noted for children in our New York State sample, we sought a more precise measure of the impact of SiF-treated water on environmental factors associated with higher blood uptake for blacks as compared with whites. For white and black children living in towns above and below the median for each risk factor, we computed the odds ratio for higher blood lead among those exposed versus not exposed to SiF-treated water (1.0 equals chances that are 50–50 whether water does or does not have these chemicals). Logistic regression was used to assess these odds ratios. The results show that SiF-treated water consistently increases the odds of high blood lead, but that this effect is exacerbated where risk factors for high blood lead are above average. Moreover, as seen in other statistical tests, this enhancement of environmental risks by SiF is much greater for black children than for whites.

In the Massachusetts sample, the vulnerability of black children is also evident. When data are analyzed by community, although average blood lead levels are significantly higher where silicofluorides are in use, average blood lead was substantially higher where blacks comprise a larger proportion of the population (Figure 2.3). Consistent with established findings, higher blood lead levels are also found in communities with an above average proportion of pre-1940 housing (where lead paint is often found) and in communities with more

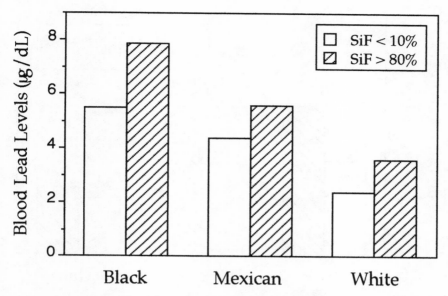

**Figure 2.1.** Average blood lead for NHANES III—Children 3–5 (Counties over 500,000). Mean blood lead is significantly associated with fluoridation status (DF 3, $F$ = 17.14, $p < .0001$) and race (DF 2, $F = 19.35$, $p < .0001$), as well as for poverty-income ratio (DF 1, $F = 66.55$, $p < .0001$). Interaction between race and fluoridation status: DF 6, $F = 3.33$, $p = .0029$.

blacks in the population. When silicofluoride use is added to the analysis, however, the higher levels of children's blood lead usually associated with communities with larger black populations is *only* found where there are *both* more older housing *and* silicofluorides in water treatment (Figure 4 in Masters et al., 2000). From this perspective, the enhanced lead uptake due to exposure to silicofluoride-treated water seems to be a critical factor explaining high blood lead among American blacks.

In the New York sample, the vulnerability of blacks is also evident from the effect of exposure to SiF on the proportion of children with various blood lead levels (Figure 2.4). Virtually all black children in the New York sample with blood lead levels of 10–15μg/dL or 15–20μg/dL lived in SiF communities. In contrast, blacks with less than 5μg/dL of blood lead were less likely to live in SiF communities. Although it has long been noted that blacks tend to be more vulnerable to lead uptake (due to characteristics such as low calcium in diet, which is perhaps associated with lactose intolerance), SiF water treatment increases this risk substantially.

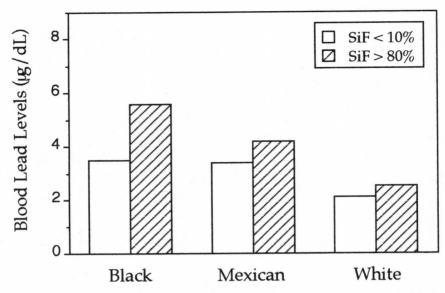

**Figure 2.2.** Average blood lead NHANES III—Children 5–17 (Counties over 500,000). Significance: fluoridation status (DF 3, $F = 57.67$, $p < .0001$), race (DF 2, $F = 28.68$, $p < .0001$), poverty-income ratio (DF 1, $F = 252.88$, $p < .0001$). Interaction between race and fluoridation status: DF 6, $F = 11.17$, $p < .0001$.

Data from the NHANES III sample also are consistent with this effect. In the counties with fewer percent living in poverty and where silicofluorides are *not* in use, there is virtually no difference between the average blood lead levels of whites (3.62µg/dL) and blacks (3.90µg/dL). For similar counties with silicofluoride use, blood lead in white children averages 4.62µg/dL, whereas it is 5.95µg/dL among blacks. Similar increases occur in the counties with above average poverty: in both environments, blacks are affected more strongly than whites by SiF-treated water. Hence a two-way ANOVA for the sample as a whole shows that SiF treatment is a significant predictor of higher blood lead ($F = 6.63$, $p = .0042$), whereas community poverty is not significant ($F < 1$).

Similar results for the increased lead from environmental risk factors in Massachusetts indicate that the harmful effects of SiF-treated water are not primarily due to toxins in the SiF delivered to water treatment plants (Masters et al., 2000). Rather, mechanisms like that of the postulated ferry molecule or other residual complexes from SiF apparently increase the uptake

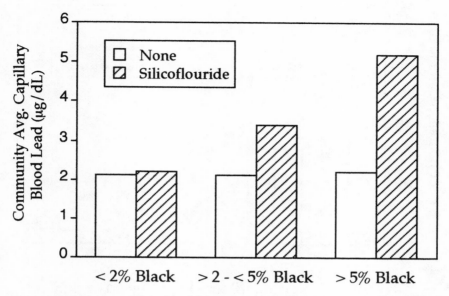

**Figure 2.3.** Average capillary blood lead in Massachusetts by community, effects of silicofluoride use and percentage of the population that is black. Significance: silicofluoride use, $p = .0001$; % black, $p = .0001$; interaction between SiF use and % black, $p = .0001$.

of lead from old housing and from lead in public water supplies. Because the policy of water fluoridation has been justified by the poor dental health of minorities, it is ironic that the principal chemicals used for this purpose seem to have especially deleterious effects on blacks and other minorities.[21]

## Increased Violent Crime and Other Behavioral Dysfunctions

Because lead is a neurotoxin that lowers dopaminergic function in the inhibitory circuits of the basal ganglia, it is not surprising that researchers have repeatedly found that higher bodily burdens of lead are linked to increased rates of violent crime (Stretesky & Lynch, 2001). Individual data to this effect imply that ecological data ought to show that communities with industrial lead pollution are associated with higher rates of violent crime. Such research reveals effects at the *social* level and illustrates how governmental decisions could improve human health and welfare by reducing the impact of environmental poisons.

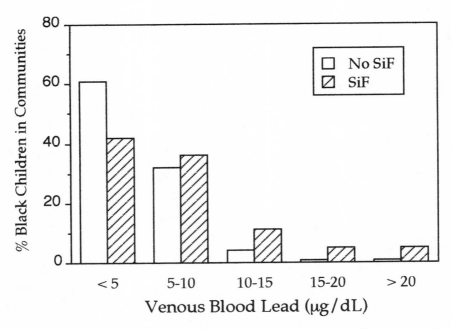

**Figure 2.4.** Venous blood lead levels in black children (Communities of 15,000–75,000), with and without SiF treatment.

Geographic variations in violent behavior had been analyzed before our research turned to SiF. Because data on individual offenders had indicated that violent behavior could be linked to the toxic effects of lead or manganese, crime rates in 1991 were compared for all U.S. counties with or without EPA-reported toxic releases of either of these heavy metals. Using aggregate data for all U.S. counties, both heavy metals significantly contribute to higher rates of violent crime, with a significant "interaction" effect showing that the combination of lead and manganese has a stronger effect than the sum of each toxin separately. With counties as the unit of analysis, multiple regression equations, including other factors associated with crime, such as poverty, unemployment, and race, indicate that lead pollution was probably an *additional* contributory factor in 1991 crime rates (Table 2.4).

It is logical to predict that if lead pollution is a factor in violent crime, and SiF increases the uptake of environmental lead, then using SiF in water treatment should be associated with higher rates of violent crime. Using a multiple regression model including both lead and manganese pollution (as measured in the EPA's Toxic Release Inventory) and percent of county receiving SiF-treated water, as well as socioeconomic and demographic factors linked to violent behavior, this prediction was tested for 1985 rates of violent crime in all U.S. counties (Table 2.5). The results show not only that SiF usage is a signifi-

**Table 2.4**
**Multiple Regression Analysis of Violent Crime Rates in the United States—1991**

| Variable | Unstandardized Coefficient | t-value | p-value |
|---|---|---|---|
| Population Density | 82.42 | 20.24 | <.0001 |
| Per capita income | -0.0007 | -2.74 | <.0001 |
| Unemployment | Not Significant | | |
| % Black Poverty | 40.06 | 2.33 | <.05 |
| % Hispanic Poverty | 62.11 | 2.79 | <.005 |
| Police per Capita | 153423 | 16.56 | <.0001 |
| Infant Death Rate | 1.813 | 2.78 | <.005 |
| % housing pre-1950 | 526.75 | -13.43 | <.0001 |
| Public water per capita | 225.34 | 4.07 | <.0001 |
| Median Grade Complete | 24.68 | 3.5 | <.005 |
| Lead TRI present | 40.8 | 4.67 | <.0001 |
| Manganese TRI | 58.71 | 6.68 | <.0001 |
| Alcohol Death Rate | 101.62 | 11.55 | <.0001 |
| #Alcohol x Lead | 21.48 | 2.54 | <.05 |
| #Alcohol x Manganese | 55.4 | 6.54 | <.0001 |
| #Lead x Manganese | 34.89 | 4.11 | <.0001 |
| #Alcohol x Lead x Manganese | 19.21 | 2.27 | <.05 |

DF 17,2783; adjusted $R$-squared $= 0.369$; $F = 97.45$; $p < .0001$
# interaction terms.

cant additional factor for higher crime rates, but that once SiF is included in the analysis, toxic releases of lead and manganese are no longer significant predictors of county-level violent crime rates. Consistent with this analysis, although crime rates are always increased by industrial releases of manganese, the national data show that this effect is aggravated where silicofluorides are used (Figure 2.5).

Because the choice of variables in a multiple regression model can sometimes influence the outcome, a slightly different set of variables was used in regression equations to predict county level rates of violent crime in both 1985 (Table 2.6) and 1991 (Table 2.7). In both cases, SiF is a significant predictor of violence. Moreover, the contrast between Tables 2.4 and 2.5 indicates that, where SiF is

**Table 2.5**
**Factors Influencing U.S. Violent Crime Rate, 1985. Results of Multiple Regression on Data from 2,880 U.S. Counties. (Variables Listed in Order of Strength of Standardized Coefficient)**[†]

| Variable | Standardized Coefficient | t-value | p-value |
|---|---|---|---|
| % Black | 0.2798 | 15.9 | 0.0001 |
| Poverty/Wealth Ratio | 0.2262 | 6.56 | 0.0001 |
| Population Density | 0.1956 | 9.38 | 0.0001 |
| % SiF | 0.115 | 6.19 | 0.0001 |
| % HS Graduate | 0.0795 | 3.46 | 0.0005 |
| Per Capita Income | 0.0457 | 1.85 | 0.0642 |
| % Houses pre 1939 | -0.1071 | 5.09 | 0.0001 |
| Population | -0.02587 | 0.82 | n.s. |
| Lead Toxic Releases | 0.0042 | 0.262 | n.s. |
| Manganese Toxic Releases | 0.0196 | 1.246 | n.s. |

[†]*Note:* When both % of population on silicofluorides and toxic release inventory (TRI) of lead and manganese are included in the analysis, silicofluoride usage is a significant predictor of violent crime whereas heavy metal pollution ceases to have a significant additional effect. This probably explains the significance of the variable "public water supply per capita" in the 1991 multiple regression in Table 2.4, which was calculated before the author knew of the issue of silicofluoride toxicity.

not used in public water supplies, industrial pollution with either lead or manganese has a much weaker impact on violent crime rates. This finding is consistent with the evidence that SiF enhances heavy metal uptake by biochemical mechanisms like those outlined earlier.

Other population-level tests of behavioral harm due to silicofluoride usage are limited by the lack of reliable measures of conditions such as hyperactivity (ADHD) that have been linked to lead toxicity. An exception, however, is an NIJ study of substance abuse by violent offenders. This study recorded the age of first use of alcohol and drugs as well as drug use at the time of arrest for a sample of over 30,000 criminals from 24 cities. Such data are especially relevant because BChE has recently been found to "accelerate cocaine metabolism in such a way as to potentially lessen the behavioral and toxic effects of cocaine" (Carmona et al., 2000).[22] As a result, BChE inhibition by SiF residues would increase the effect of cocaine, leading to the prediction that drug use would be more pronounced among violent offenders in cities that inject SiF in public water supplies.

Once again, the data are consistent with the hypothesis. In the NIJ sample, controlling for the percent of blacks in the population (which by itself is never significant), use of SiFs was significantly associated with the average age of the

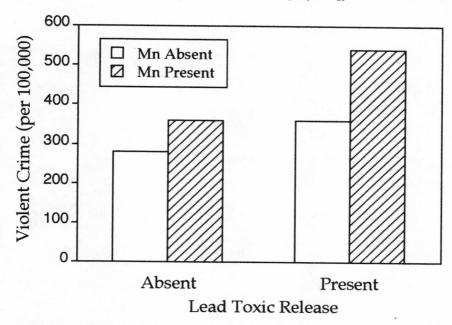

**Figure 2.5.** Violent crime rates in counties without (Absent) and with (Present) toxic releases of lead and manganese (EPA toxic release inventory, TRI). Recalculated from Masters et al. (1998).

first use of alcohol ($p = .06$), of PCP ($p = .0155$), and of crack ($p = .027$) (Masters & Coplan, 1999b). Moreover, the age of first use of alcohol, crack, or cocaine is significantly associated with rates of violent crime (in each case, $p < .0001$), and crimes rates are significantly higher in the 13 sampled cities using fluosilicic acid (2,123 per 100,000) or the 6 cities using sodium silicofluoride (1,704 per 100,000) than in the 5 cities not using SiF (1,289 per 100,000) (Masters & Coplan, 1999b).

As a check, rates of drunken behavior per capita were analyzed in our county dataset. To illustrate yet another statistical technique, step-wise regression was used: The best of a set of predictor variables was identified and the variance it accounted for was removed, then the next best predictor of the remaining variance was identified, and so on until no additional significant variables remained. In this analysis, SiF was one of seven variables that significantly predicted rates of drunken behavior whereas five variables (including the EPA's Toxic Release Inventory for lead and manganese) had no significant effect on county level rates (Table 2.8).[23]

Table 2.6
**Factors Associated with Rates of Violent Crime: Results of Multiple Regression on Data from All U.S. Counties, 1985**

| Variable | Coefficient | Std. Error | Std. Coefficient | t-value | p-value |
|---|---|---|---|---|---|
| Intercept | -0.005056 | | | | |
| ** % SiF | **0.000368** | **0.000133** | **0.045** | **2.78** | **0.0055** |
| Unemployment | 0.000076 | 0.000013 | 0.106 | 5.99 | 0.0001 |
| PC Income Blacks . . . | -9.92E-09 | 5.69E-09 | -0.029 | 1.74 | 0.0816 |
| PC Income | 9.53E-08 | 1.91E-08 | 0.115 | 4.99 | 0.0001 |
| Median Grade . . . | 0.000205 | 0.000069 | 0.082 | 2.97 | 0.003 |
| Median Year . . . | 0.000003 | 0.000004 | 0.0123 | 0.72 | 0.4722 |
| % Black | 0.00005 | 0.000003 | 0.313 | 17.56 | 0.0001 |
| % Graduate . . . | -0.000022 | 0.000007 | -0.096 | 2.96 | 0.0031 |
| % Rural | -0.000027 | 0.000001 | -0.350 | 18.73 | 0.0001 |

| Confidence Intervals Variable | 95% Lower | 95% Upper | 90% Lower | 90% Upper | Partial F |
|---|---|---|---|---|---|
| ** % SiF | **0.000108** | **0.000628** | **0.00015** | **0.000587** | **7.72** |
| Unemployment . . . | 0.000051 | 0.000101 | 0.000055 | 0.000097 | 35.86 |
| PC Income Blacks | -2.11E-08 | 1.25E-09 | -1.93E-08 | -5.50E-10 | 3.04 |
| PC Income | 5.78E-08 | 1.33E-07 | 6.39E-08 | 1.27E-07 | 24.89 |
| Median Grade . . . | 0.00007 | 0.00034 | 0.000091 | 0.000318 | 8.83 |
| Median Year | -0.000005 | 0.000011 | -0.000004 | 0.00001 | 0.52 |
| % Black | 0.000044 | 0.000056 | 0.000045 | 0.000055 | 308.54 |
| % Graduate . . . | -0.000036 | -0.000007 | -0.000034 | -0.00001 | 8.79 |
| % Rural | -0.00003 | -0.000024 | -0.000029 | -0.000024 | 350.75 |

Table 2.7
**Factors Associated with Rates of Violent Crime: Results of Multiple Regression on Data from All U.S. Counties, 1991**

| Variable | Coefficient | Std. Error | Std. Coefficient | t-value | p-value |
|---|---|---|---|---|---|
| Intercept | -0.026874 | | | | |
| ** %SiF | **0.000922** | **0.00019** | **0.076136** | **4.84725** | **0.0001** |
| Unemployment | 0.000064 | 0.000017 | 0.062928 | 3.692 | 0.0002 |
| PC Income Blacks . . . | -3.96E-09 | 8.09E-09 | -0.007926 | 0.489639 | 0.6244 |
| PC Income | 1.28E-07 | 2.63E-08 | 0.108872 | 4.869223 | 0.0001 |
| Median Grade . . . | 0.000504 | 0.000095 | 0.140963 | 5.304905 | 0.0001 |
| Median Year . . . | 0.000014 | 0.000006 | 0.039495 | 2.411564 | 0.0159 |
| % Black | 0.00008 | 0.000004 | 0.351002 | 20.358866 | 0.0001 |
| % Graduate . . . | -0.000058 | 0.00001 | -0.178521 | 5.719072 | 0.0001 |
| % Rural | -0.000041 | 0.000002 | -0.376415 | 20.749842 | 0.0001 |

| Confidence Intervals Variable | 95% Lower | 95% Upper | 90% Lower | 90% Upper | Partial |
|---|---|---|---|---|---|
| ** %SiF | **0.000549** | **0.001295** | **0.000609** | **0.001235** | **23.50** |
| Unemployment | 0.00003 | 0.000098 | 0.000035 | -0.000038 | 13.64 |
| PC Income Blacks . . . | -1.98E-08 | 1.19E-08 | -1.73E-08 | 9.36E-09 | 0.24 |
| PC Income | 7.65E-08 | 1.80E-07 | 8.48E-08 | 1.71E-07 | 23.71 |
| Median Grade . . . | 0.000317 | 0.00069 | 0.000347 | 0.00066 | 28.14 |
| Median Year . . . | 0.000003 | 0.000026 | 0.000004 | 0.000024 | 5.82 |
| % Black | 0.000072 | 0.000088 | 0.000074 | 0.000087 | 414.48 |
| % Graduate . . . | -0.000078 | -0.000038 | -0.000075 | -0.000041 | 32.71 |
| % Rural | -0.000045 | -0.000037 | -0.000044 | -0.000038 | 430.56 |

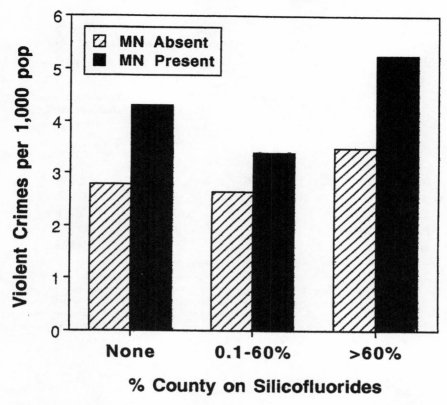

**Figure 2.6.** Manganese and silicofluorides as factors in violent crime (1991). Significance: SiF usage, $F = 27.60$, $p = .0001$; manganese pollution, $F = 79.00$, $p = .0001$; interaction between SiF and Mn: $F = 3.74$, $p = .0239$. For the 369 U.S. counties where over 60% received water treated with SiFs and there is no Toxic Release Inventory record for manganese (MN Absent), the violent crime rate in 1991 (3.53 per 1000) was intermediate between rates in the 109 counties with manganese TRI (MN Present) and no SiFs (4.40) or the 217 counties with between 0.1 and 60% receiving SiFs (3.49). Where both SiFs are delivered to over 60% of the population and manganese TRI is present, the crime rate was 5.34. In 1991, the national county average was 3.12 violent crimes per 1000.

In all samples studied, therefore, we found evidence that the behavioral effects of SiF residues increase rates of costly behaviors that have previously been linked to lead. As a result, the evidence suggests that a moratorium on the use of SiF in public water supplies would be a relatively low-cost policy capable of lowering rates of substance abuse and violent crime. Indeed, given indications that hyperactivity is often linked to lead toxicity, such an initiative might also reduce learning disabilities and improve educational outcomes.

**Table 2.8**
**Factors Associated with Rates of Drunkenness Per Capita, 1991: Stepwise Regression on Data from 3,139 U.S. Counties (Variables Listed in Order of Entry)**[†]

| Variable | Standard Coefficient | F to Remove | Total Adj R-square after variable entry |
|---|---|---|---|
| % HS Graduate | -0.316 | 171.334 | 0.089 |
| % Hispanic | 0.208 | 150.238 | 0.143 |
| Median Year Housing Built | 14.70% | 68.23 | 0.158 |
| % Black | -0.123 | 48.825 | 0.168 |
| % SiF | 0.054 | 10.832 | 0.171 |
| Per Capita Income | 0.051 | 4.896 | 0.173 |
| Pop Density | 0.037 | 4.355 | 0.174 |

[†]*Notes:* $F$ to remove criterion was 4. Variables not entered: population size, unemployment, social inequality [poverty/per capita income], Lead TRI, Manganese TRI. To confirm that the year chosen did not influence the result, the same stepwise regression was run for rates of drunkenness in all U.S. counties for the years from 1990 through 1995. The percent of county population receiving silicofluoride-treated water was a significant predictor for 1990, 1992, 1994, and 1995 (in each case, one of six variables) as well as in 1991 (above, one of seven variables). The strength of the standardized coefficient was similiar in all these cases. For 1993, however, percent SiF was not significant and was replaced by unemployment as one of six significant predictors. In contrast, when the same stepwise regression model was used to predict property crime rates in these years, percent SiF was *not* significant for 1990, 1991, 1992, and 1995, and had a negative coefficient for 1993 and 1994 (for each year, six or seven variables were significant). These results are consistent with the hypothesis that the behavioral effects of silicofluoride-treated water were associated with enhanced lead uptake or other neurotoxic effects that weaken impulse control.

## CONCLUSION

The foregoing analysis, like the controversy over lowering the permissible levels of arsenic in American public water supplies, suggests that conflicts between science and public policy may be of increasing importance in coming years. In such issues, the central concern has hitherto been cancer and other mortal diseases. As our analysis shows, it is now time to link neuroscience, evolutionary psychology, and toxicology to such social behavior as violence. Just as the ban on leaded gasoline seems to have lowered rates of violent crime since 1991, other initiatives may have substantial benefits by reducing the risks of dysfunctional behavior caused by toxins.

To illustrate a policy derived from this approach, I have proposed a moratorium on injecting fluosilicic acid or sodium silicofluoride in a public water supply until extensive testing proves their safety. Such testing is especially necessary for chemicals that are distributed to the general public in a manner not subject to individual choice. Moreover, because prudent policy initiatives need to consider costs as well as benefits, the use of untested chemicals cannot be justified merely on the presumed benefit to a single medical condition. It must be stressed that this proposal only concerns the use of fluosilicic acid or sodium silicofluoride in water treatment. Although there is much controversy over the costs and benefits of water fluoridation using sodium fluoride as well, our data do not indicate that NaF is a major factor in enhancing children's blood lead levels.

In comprehensive cost-benefit analyses of chemicals in our environment, behavioral harm may often be more costly or more widespread than cancer and other mortal diseases. As neuroscientists and evolutionary psychologists unravel biological factors in human social behavior, scientists and policymakers in other fields can no longer ignore the costs of learning disabilities, substance abuse, or criminal behaviors that have often proven resistant to traditional treatments or governmental policies based on sociological and economic theories of behavior. In the era of Prozac, Ritalin, and brain imaging with PET and other technologies, ignoring the revolutionary advances of neuroscientific research is neither prudent nor reasonable.

## NOTES

1. Research on silicofluoride toxicity described in this paper has been conducted in collaboration with Myron J. Coplan (Intellequity Consulting, Natick, MA), whose expertise in chemical engineering and the history of fluoridation has been invaluable. Former vice president of a multinational firm, Coplan has experience that includes direct professional work with silicofluorides, as well as numerous areas of public policy. Our collaboration reflects the extent to which research on many issues linking environmental toxicity, brain chemistry, and public policy can no longer be conducted by a solitary researcher.

2. See the letter from Benjamin Franklin to Benjamin Vaughan "on the bad Effects of Lead taken inwardly" (31 July 1786), in Lemay (1987).

3. For the example to be discussed below, see the Web site http://www.dartmouth.edu/~rmasters/ahabs.htm.

4. This article includes especially revealing information on the origins of adding tetrethyl lead to gasoline with knowledge of the toxicity of these additives—and on the continued sales of these products in the Third World.

5. See Myron J. Coplan and Roger Masters, "Should Silicofluoride Be Used to Fluoridate Municipal Water?" Submitted to Congressman Kenneth Calvert, Chair of Subcommittee on Energy and the Environment, Committee on Science, U.S. House of Representatives. April, 2000; idem, Response to EPA Staff Unsupportable Dismissal of Evidence of Adverse Silicofluoride Health Effects. Report to EPA, June 12, 2000; idem, Scientific Misconduct at EPA. Report to Hon. Kenneth Calvert, Chair of Subcommittee on Energy and the Environment, Committee on Science, U.S. House of Representatives, September 25, 2000.

6. "To answer your first question on whether we have in our possession empirical scientific data on the effects of fluosilicic acid or sodium silicofluoride on health and

behavior, our answer is no. . . . We have contacted our colleagues at NHEERL and they report that with the exception of some acute toxicity data, they were unable to find any information on the effects of silicofluorides on health and behavior." Robert C. Thurnau (Chief, Treatment Technology Evaluation Branch, Water Supply and Water Resources Division, U.S. EPA National Risk Management Research Laboratory, Cincinnati, OH) to Roger Masters, November 16, 2000.

7. For example, in 1951, a principal proponent of extending water fluoridation—Francis Bull—explicitly told a dental convention never to mention the chemicals to be used and admitted he had no evidence on toxicity. This practice has persisted. For instance, in the recent report on Oral Health in the United States—2000, Surgeon General Satcher speaks of "fluoridation" without mentioning the chemicals used. With few exceptions, critics of water fluoridation have long addressed the issue in similar terms.

8. Years later, several experiments were published that purported to confirm this prediction, but the studies used an ion specific electrode method that required conditions unlike those of a water treatment facility and the reported results rounded figures to the nearest whole number (thereby hiding evidence of incomplete dissociation).

9. An English translation of Westendorf's doctoral dissertation is available at http://www.dartmouth.edu/~rmasters/slub.htm. To access, follow instructions at the end of the "forward" to the translation by Jakob von Moltke. Although this research seems to have escaped the attention of U.S. health authorities, it provides important evidence that SiF-treated water is not "just like" NaF treated water that has not been taken into account by either critics or supporters of water fluoridation.

10. Available on the Web at http://fluoride.oralhealth.org/papers/urbansky.pdf.

11. National Institutes of Health, Transcript of Proceedings, Surgeon General's (Koop) Ad Hoc Committee on "Non-Dental Health Effects of Fluoride," Day I (April 18, 1983), Bethesda, MD: Stenotech, Inc., 1983), I, esp. 132–139 (Dr. Frank Smith's description of the experimental studies of "fluoride absorption" and "fluoride in blood" without reference to specific chemicals to which research animals were exposed).

12. Fluoride Recommendations Work Group, "Recommendations for Using Fluoride to Prevent and Control Dental Caries in the United States" (2001), available at http:www.cdc.gov/mmwr/. See also CDC Press Release "CDC releases new guidelines of fluoride use to prevent tooth decay" (2001), available at http://www.cdc.gov/od/oc/media/pressrel/4r010817.htm.

13. For a detailed critique of Crosby's methodology, including his selective use of rounding to whole numbers to hide incomplete dissociation, see Myron J. Coplan's correspondence with the APHA, available at http://www.dartmouth.edu/~rmasters/ahabs.htm.

14. For a fuller analysis of this topic, from which the following section is adapted, see Myron J. Coplan, Reply to APHA Oral Health Section Objections to Proposed APHA Resolution (July 2000).

15. It should be noted that the fluoride level in this experiment was far lower than 1 ppm.

16. By the same token, though McClure was interested in amyulase inhibition by fluorides, there is no indication that he was aware of fluoride inhibition of AchE (McClure, 1939).

17. We thank Adrian Bailey and James Sargent for making available to us these data, for which they previously showed the role of lead residues from industrial activities (Bailey et al., 1994).

18. Regarding Masters and Coplan (1999a), pp. 440–441: A footnote added to this passage indicates, "Towns using sodium fluorosilicate reported lower first draw water lead values (11.7 ppb) than unfluoridated towns (21.2 ppb) or towns using sodium fluoride (17.5 ppb); communities using fluosilicic acid had significantly higher levels of lead than in others (39.3 ppb). Although the difference between usage of fluosilicic acid and all other treatment conditions is highly significant ($p < .0001$, DF 3, 223, F 9.32), differences in lead in first draw water cannot account for the fact that levels of children's blood lead are comparable in towns using sodium silicofluoride and fluosilicic acid. In any event, there is one order of magnitude difference between lead levels reported in water supplies (in parts per billion or 10–9) and measures of lead uptake in blood (micrograms per deciliter are equivalent to parts per one hundred million or 10–8)."

19. Regarding Masters and Coplan (1999a), it should be noted that the increment in average children's blood lead from use of sodium fluoride (compared with unfluoridated water) is relatively small (0.14µg/dL) if lead levels in 90th percentile first draw water are under 15 ppb; if lead levels in water are above 15 ppb, children's blood lead levels are actually 0.28µg/dL lower where sodium fluoride is used than where water is not fluoridated. In contrast, where lead in the water is above 15 ppb, the increment compared with nonfluoridated communities is 1.09µg/dL for the 25 communities using fluosilicic acid and 2.2µg/dL in the one community using sodium silicofluoride. Put another way, if the level of lead is above 15 ppb in the public water supply, the effect of water fluoridation is roughly three or four times worse if the chemical agent is a silicofluoride rather than sodium fluoride (see Table II, p. 443). Analysis of variance shows that this effect, measured as the interaction between silicofluorides and lead levels in water over 15 ppb, is statistically significant: $p = .042$; $F = 4.18$ (Figure 1, p. 444).

20. In Masters and Coplan (1999a), after controlling for other sources of lead, silicofluoride usage remained significant, which (a footnote adds) "is all the more impressive because multiple regression reveals that percentage of housing built before 1940 is a significant predictor of which towns use silicofluorides (controlling for population density, % vacant housing, per capita income, racial composition, and other demographic variables)."

21. The January 2002 issue of *American Journal of Public Health* had two articles germane to this issue. On prejudices and discrimination in the delivery of dental health care to poor minority children, see Mofidi et al. (2002, pp. 53–58). For the serious epidemic of dental health among blacks in Harlem, where water is treated with silicofluorides, see Zabos et al. (2002, pp. 49–52).

22. The entire abstract of this study is worth citing:

Butyrylcholinesterase (BChE) is known to metabolize cocaine in humans. In the present study, three different experiments were performed to determine whether the addition of horse serum-derived BChE would accelerate the metabolism of cocaine. In the first experiment, the addition of BChE to squirrel monkey plasma in vitro reduced the half-life of cocaine by over 80%, decreased the production of the metabolic product benzoylecgonine, and increased ecgonine methyl ester formation. The effect of BChE on cocaine metabolism was reversed by a specific BChE inhibitor. In the second, in vivo, experiment, exogenously administered BChE reduced peak cocaine concentrations when given to anesthetized squirrel monkeys. Finally, incubation of cocaine with added BChE in human plasma in vitro resulted in a decrease in cocaine half-life similar to that observed with squirrel monkey plasma. The magnitude of the decrease in cocaine half-life was proportional to the amount of added BChE. Together, these results indicate that exogenously administered BChE can accelerate cocaine metabolism in such a way as to potentially lessen the behavioral and toxic effects of cocaine. Therefore, BChE may be useful as a treatment for cocaine addiction and toxicity.

23. In a stepwise regression for violent crime for 1991, percent SiF was fifth of seven variables removed (with a stronger standardized coefficient than either per capita income or population density); percent SiF also was a significant predictor in 1990, 1992, 1994, and 1995.

## REFERENCES

Abou-Donia, M.B., Goldstein, L.B., Dechovskaia, A., Bullman, S., Jones, K.H., Herrick, E.A., Abdel-Rahman, A.A., & Khan, W.A. (2001). Effects of daily dermal application of DEET and permethrin, alone and in combination, on sensorimotor performance, blood-brain barrier, and blood-testis barrier in rats. *Journal of Toxicology and Environmental Health, Part A, 62,* 523–541.

Abou-Donia, M.B., Goldstein L.B., Jones, K.H., Abdel-Rahman, A.A., Damodaran, T.V., Dechkovskaia, A.M., Bullman, S.L., Amir, B.E., & Khan, W.A. (2001). Locomotor and sensorimotor performance deficit in rats following exposure to pyridostigmine bromide, DEET, and permethrin, alone and in combination. *Toxicological Sciences, 60,* 305–314.

Allderdice, P.W., Gardner, H.A., Galutira, D., Lockridge, O., LaDu, B.N., & McAlpine, P.J. (1991). The cloned butyrylcholinesterase (BCHE) gene maps to a single chromosome site, 3q26. *Genomics, 11,* 452–454.

American Public Health Association (2001). Resolution LB-00–7: Support the framework for action on oral health in America: A report of the Surgeon General. *American Journal of Public Health, 91,* 520.

Bailey, A.J., Sargent, J.D., Goodman, D.C., Freeman, J. & Brown, M.J. (1994). Poisoned landscapes: The epidemiology of environmental lead exposure in Massachusetts children 1990–1991. *Social Science Medicine, 39,* 757–776.

Bellinger, D., Leviton, A., Allred, E., & Rabinowitz, M. (1994). Pre- and postnatal lead exposure and behavior problems in school-aged children. *Environmental Research, 66,* 12–30.

Brockel, B.A., & Cory-Slechta, D.A. (1998). Lead, attention, and impulsive behavior: Changes in a fixed-ratio waiting-for-reward paradigm. *Pharmacology Biochemistry & Behavior, 60,* 545–52.

Bryce-Smith, D. (1983). Lead induced disorder of mentation in children. *Nutrition and Health, 1,* 179–94.

Cardinal, R.N., Pennicott, D.R., Sugathapala, C.L., Robbins, T.W., & Everitt, B.J. (2001). Impulsive choice induced in rats by lesions of the nucleus accumbens core. *Science, 292,* 2499–2501.

Carmona, G.N., Jufer, R.A., Goldberg, S.R., Gorelick, D.A., Greig, N., Yu, Q.S., Cone, E.J., & Schindler, C.W. (2000). Butyrylcholinesterase accelerates cocaine metabolism: In vitro and in vivo effects in nonhuman primates and humans. *Drug Metabolism and Disposition, 28,* 367–371.

Centers for Disease Control (1992). Fluoridation Census 1992. Atlanta, GA: Department of Health and Human Services.

Cook, E.H., Stein, M.A., Krasowski, M.D., Cox, N.J., Olkon, D.M., Kieffer, J.E., & Leventhal, B.L. (1995). Association of attention deficit disorder and the dopamine transporter gene. *American Journal of Human Genetics, 56,* 993–998.

Coradin, T., & Livage J. (2001). Effect of some amino acids and peptides on silicic acid polymerization. *Colloids and Surfaces B: Biointerfaces, 21,* 329–336.

Cory-Slechta, D. (1995). Relationships between lead induced learning impairments and change in dopaminergic, cholinergic, glutamatergic neurotransmitter system functioning. *Annual Review of Pharmacology and Toxicology, 35,* 3337–3395.

Crosby, N.T. (1969). Equilibria of fluorosilicate: Solutions with special reference to the fluoridation of public water supplies. *Journal of Applied Chemistry, 19,* 100–102.

Gottschalk, L., Rebello, T., Buchsbaum, M.S., Tucker, H.G., & Hodges, H.L. (1991). Abnormalities in trace elements as indicators of aberrant behavior. *Comprehensive Psychiatry, 342,* 229–237.

Iler, R.K. (1979). *The chemistry of silica; solubility, polymerization, colloid and surface properties, and biochemistry.* New York: John Wiley & Sons.

Kahn, C.A., Kelly, P.C., & Walker, W.O. (1995). Lead screening in children with attention deficit hyperactivity disorder and developmental delay. *Clinical Pediatrics, 34,* 498–501.

Kick, C.H., Bethke, R.M., Edgington, B.H., & Wilder, O.H.M. (1935). Fluorine in animal nutrition. *Ohio Agricultural Experiment Station Bulletin, 558,* 1–77.

Kitman, J.L. (March 20, 2000). The secret history of lead (use of leaded gasoline). *The Nation, 270,* 11–44.

Knappwost, A., & Westendorf, J. (1974). On the inhibition of acetylcholinesterase by fluoride. *Naturwissenschaft, 61,* 274–275.

Layer, P.G. (1995). Nonclassical roles of cholinesterases in the embryonic brain and possible links to Alzheimer disease. *Alzheimer Disease and Associated Disorders, 9 Suppl 2,* 29–36.

Lejus, C., Blanloeil, Y., Burnat, P., & Souron, R. (1998). Cholinesterases. *Annales Francaises d'Anesthesie et de Reanimation, 17,* 1122–1135.

Lemay, J.A. (Ed.) (1987). *Benjamin Franklin: Writings (The Autobiography, Poor Richard's Almanack, Bagatelles, Pamphlets, Essays, & Letters)* (pp. 1163–1166). New York: Library of America.

Masters, R.D. (2001). Biology and politics: Linking nature and nurture. *Annual Reviews of Political Science, 4,* 345–369.

Masters, R.D., & Coplan, M.J. (1999a). Water treatment with silicofluorides and lead toxicity. *International Journal of Environmental Studies, 56,* 435–490.

Masters, R., & Coplan, M. (1999b). A dynamic, multifactorial model of alcohol, drug abuse, and crime: Linking neuroscience and behavior to toxicology. *Social Science Information, 38,* 591–624.

Masters, R.D., Coplan, M.J., Hone, B.T., & Dykes, J. (October 17–20, 1999). Heavy metal toxicity, cognitive development, and behavior. Presented at the 17th Annual Neurotoxicology Conference, Little Rock, AR.

Masters, R.D., Coplan, M.J., Hone, B.T., & Dykes, J.E. (2000). Association of silicofluoride treated water with elevated blood lead. *Neurotoxicology, 21,* 1091–1100.

Masters, R.D., Hone, B.T., & Doshi, A. (1998). Environmental pollution, neurotoxicity, and criminal violence. In J. Rose (Ed.), *Environmental toxicology: Current developments* (pp. 13–48. London: Gordon and Breach.

McClure, F.J. (1933). A review of fluorine and its physiological effects. *Physiological Reviews, 13,* 277–300.

McClure, F.J. (1939). The effect of fluorides on salivary amylase. *Public Heath Reports*, 54, 2165–2171.

Minder, B., Das-Smaal, E.A., Brand, E.F., Orlebeke, J.M., & Jacob, F. (1994). Exposure to lead and specific attentional problems in schoolchildren. *Journal of Learning Disabilities*, 27, 393–398.

Mofidi, M., Rozier, R.G., & King, R.S. (2002). Problems with access to dental care for Medicaid-insured children: What caregivers think. *American Journal of Public Health*, 92, 53–58.

Needleman, H.L. (Ed.). (1989).*Human lead exposure*. Boca Raton, FL: CRC Press.

Needleman, H.L. (1999). Environmental neurotoxins and attention deficit disorder, presentation at conference on environmental neurotoxins and developmental disability. Presented at the meetings of the New York Academy of Medicine, New York, May 24–25.

Needleman, H.L., & Gatsonis, B. (1991). Meta-analysis of 24 studies of learning disabilities due to lead poisoning. *Journal of the American Medical Association*, 265, 673–678.

Paulesu E., Démonet, J. F., Fazio, F., McCrory, E., Chanoine V., et al. (2001). Dyslexia: cultural diversity and biological unity. *Science*, 291, 2165–7.

Rymer, A. (2000). *The (political) science of fluoridating public water supplies*. Senior honors thesis, Dartmouth College, Hanover, NH.

Stretesky, P.B., & Lynch, M.J. (2001). The relation between lead exposure and homicide. *Archives of Pediatric and Adolescent Medicine*, 155, 579–582.

Tuthill, R.W. (1996). Hair lead levels related to children's classroom attention-deficit behavior. *Archives of Environmental Health*, 51, 214–220.

Urbansky, E.T., & Schock, M.R. (2000). Can fluoridation effect lead (II) in potable water? Hexafluorosilicate and fluoride equilibria in aqueous solution. *International Review of Environmental Studies*, 57, 597–637.

U.S. Department of Health and Human Services (2000). *Oral health in America: A report of the surgeon general*. Rockville, MD: U.S. Department of Health and Human Services.

Walker, S. (1998). *The hyperactivity hoax: How to stop drugging your child and find real medical help*. New York: St Martin's Press.

Westendorf, J. (1975). *Die kinetik der acetylcholinesterase hemmung und die beeinflussung der permeabilitat von erythrozytenmembranen durch fluorid und flurocomplex-jonen*. Doctoral dissertation, Universitat Hamburg Fachbereich Chemie, Hamburg.

Wollan, M. (1968). Controlling the potential hazards of government-sponsored technology. *George Washington Law Review*, 36, 1105–1120.

Zabos, G.P., Northridge, M.E., Ro, M.J., Trinh, C., Vaughan, R., Howard, J.M., Lamster, I., Bassett, M.T., & Cohall, A.T. (2002). Lack of oral health care for adults in Harlem: A hidden crisis. *American Journal of Public Health*, 92, 49–52.

# 3

# Psychopathy as an Adaptation
## *Implications for Society and Social Policy*

*Stuart Kinner*

The majority of crimes, including violent crimes, are committed by only a small proportion of offenders. In fact prevalence studies typically report that about 5% of offenders account for over 50% of violent crimes (Farringtonet al., 1986). Compared with other offenders, these "life-course persistent" offenders (Moffitt, 1993) begin their criminal careers earlier, offend more frequently and in a wider range of situations, and continue offending later in life (Loeber & Farrington, 2000; Moffitt, 1993; Moffitt & Caspi, 2001). For a subset of this group, the majority of whom are male, persistent antisocial behavior is accompanied by a callous, manipulative, superficial and often violent interpersonal style. These individuals are known as psychopaths.

Psychopaths are estimated to constitute about 1% of the North American population (Hare, 1991), but around 20% to 30% of incarcerated North American male offenders (Hare, 1991, 1993). Nevertheless, psychopaths account for over 50% of serious crimes (Hare, 1993). Furthermore, their rate of recidivism is about twice that of other offenders, and their rate of violent recidivism is about three times that of other offenders (Hare, 1993). Compared with other criminals, the crimes of psychopaths are more often instrumental (i.e., goal-oriented as opposed to emotional, reactive), and are more often committed against strangers: two-thirds of the victims of psychopaths are strangers, whereas two thirds of the victims of nonpsychopaths are known to the offender (Williamson et al., 1987).

Psychopaths often gain notoriety through their socially reprehensible behavior. An oft-cited 1992 study in the United States reports that 44% of offenders who killed a law enforcement officer on duty matched the psychopathic profile (Federal Bureau of Investigation, 1992). Charming and infamous serial killers Ted Bundy, Kenneth Bianchi, and John Wayne Gacy were almost certainly psychopaths (Clarke & Shea, 2001; Hare, 1993); however, by no means are all psychopaths gruesome serial killers. In fact, not all psychopaths are killers, or even criminals. Who, then, are the "psychopaths among us"? Hare (1998b) puts it succinctly:

These are individuals who, lacking in conscience and feelings for others, find it easy to use charm, manipulation, intimidation and violence to control others and to satisfy their own selfish needs. They . . . form a significant proportion of persistent criminals, drug dealers, spouse and child abusers, swindlers and con men, mercenaries, corrupt politicians, unethical lawyers, terrorists, cult leaders, black marketers, gang members, and radical political activists. (pp. 128–129)

Psychopaths exist in every culture, every race, almost every walk of life, and even though their presence among us is not new, our understanding of their nature and their development is far from complete. In fact it was not until around the end of the eighteenth century that a scientific description of these individuals emerged. In his *Treatise on Insanity* (1806/1962), French psychiatrist Philippe Pinel coined the term *"manie sans delire"* (insanity without delirium), arguing that it was possible to be insane (*manie*) without a corresponding "lesion of the understanding" (*delire*). Pinel and other authors of the time promulgated the notion that it was possible to behave in an irrational and often deviant manner, despite intact intellectual functioning (Millon et al., 1998).

Possibly the first author to actually use the term psychopath was German psychiatrist Emil Kraepelin, who in the fifth edition of his influential work *Psychiatry: A Textbook* (1896) referred to individuals suffering from "psychopathic states." In the seventh edition of the text, published in 1903–1904, Kraepelin adopted the term "psychopathic personalities" (Millon et al., 1998).

The concept of psychopathic personality had been refined considerably by 1941, when American psychiatrist Hervey Cleckley published his well-known text *The Mask of Sanity*, in which psychopaths were described as emotionally deficient and hiding behind "a thin veneer of normalcy"—a "mask of sanity." According to Cleckley, psychopaths are characterized by a kind of "semantic aphasia," such that the emotional significance of events is lost on them—they "know the words but not the music" (Johns & Quay, 1962). Of particular note, Cleckley highlighted the existence of "successful" psychopaths, providing examples of psychopathic businessmen, scientists, psychiatrists, and physicians (Cleckley, 1941/1988). Cleckley also provided a set of personality-based criteria (e.g., superficial charm and good intelligence, lack of remorse or shame, pathological egocentricity and incapacity for love) by which psychopaths could be identified and described.

When the American Psychiatric Association released the first edition of its *Diagnostic and Statistical Manual of Mental Disorders* (American Psychiatric Association, 1952), psychopathy was referred to as "sociopathic personality," and was defined along the lines of Cleckley's criteria. Similarly, the DSM-II (American Psychiatric Association, 1968) described what was by then called "antisocial personality" largely in terms of inferred personality features, consistent with Cleckley's clinical conceptualization of the psychopath.

In 1980, with the release of the third edition of the manual (DSM-III, American Psychiatric Association, 1980), the term *antisocial personality disorder* (ASPD) was introduced, and the diagnostic focus shifted from generally deviant and irresponsible behavior to specifically criminal and antisocial conduct, and from inferred personality traits to explicit behavioral criteria. A requirement that the individual display behavioral problems before the age of 15 was also introduced. The purported reason for this shift was to increase the reliability of diagnosis (Lilienfeld, 1994; Widiger et al., 1996), as clearly defined behavioral criteria are more easily agreed upon by clinicians than are inferred personality traits. However, this increased reliability was offset by a corresponding decrease in validity, with a much larger and more heterogeneous group of individuals receiving the ASPD label (Hare, 1996). Despite some attempt in the latest edition of the manual (DSM-IV-TR, American Psychiatric Association, 2000) to incorporate more traditional concepts of psychopathy, the emphasis on antisocial behavior remains.

Although the DSM-IV criteria remain problematic, researchers and clinicians are increasingly differentiating between ASPD (or sociopathy) and psychopathy. For example, in a recent study of 550 Australian prisoners and heroin users, Darke, Kaye, and Finlay-Jones (1998) found that 94% of those receiving a diagnosis of psychopathy ($N = 32$) also received an ASPD diagnosis, whereas only 11% of those with an ASPD diagnosis ($N = 236$) were also diagnosed as psychopaths. Typically, in North American forensic samples, 90% of psychopaths receive an ASPD diagnosis, whereas only 20% to 30% of those with an ASPD diagnosis are also psychopaths (Hare, 1991).

Psychopathy, as currently defined, is usually assessed by means of the Hare Psychopathy Checklist—Revised (PCL-R), a 20-item measure with demonstrably high reliability and validity (Hare, 1991). Consistent with Cleckley's notion of the psychopath, the PCL-R measures both the interpersonal/affective and the socially deviant behavioral aspects of psychopathy. PCL-R scores are strongly predictive of recidivism and of violence, including institutional and sexual violence, in a wide range of populations including incarcerated offenders and forensic and civil psychiatric patients (e.g., Harris, Rice, & Cormier, 1991; Hill et al., 1996; Quinsey, 1995; see also Quinsey et al., 1998; Rice & Harris, 1995; Salekin et al., 1996).

Although research and discourse with regard to psychopathy have for many years been hampered by definitional and diagnostic confusion, this confusion is gradually giving way to a consensus that psychopaths are characterized by personality traits like those described by Cleckley, and that psychopathy is most effectively measured by the PCL-R, a highly reliable and valid measure of psychopathy, derived from Cleckley's personality-based criteria.

## PROXIMATE EXPLANATIONS OF PSYCHOPATHY

Despite considerable scientific and social interest in the phenomenon, empirical exploration of the characteristics and causes of psychopathy was unusual until the middle of the twentieth century. Over the last 50 years, a variety of models of psychopathy have been proposed and subjected to empirical evaluation. Although often complementary, these various approaches have divergent policy implications. For example, some conceive of psychopathy as a congenital abnormality, whereas others consider psychopaths to be essentially "normal." Those in the former group might consider treatment an option for psychopathic offenders, whereas for the latter group, there is no "illness" to treat.

### Psychopathy as an Extreme Variant of Normal Personality

Although psychopaths are often considered to be qualitatively different from "normal people," some authors have argued that psychopathy is not a distinct personality type, but is in fact an extreme variant of normal personality, and thus that the small proportion of psychopaths in the population are complemented by a much larger number of "subclinical" psychopaths. For example, according to Eysenck (1977, 1987, 1998) psychopaths are by definition those individuals who score high on all three scales of the Eysenck Personality Questionnaire (EPQ): Psychoticism (P), Extraversion (E), and Neuroticism (N). The EPQ is not the only general personality measure that has been used to describe psychopaths: the MMPI (Blackburn, 1975), the Interpersonal Circle (Blackburn, 1988) and the Five Factor model (e.g., Dyce & O' Connor, 1998; Widiger, 1998; Widiger & Lynam, 1998) have been similarly successful in describing psychopathic individuals.

From the field of social psychology has come a somewhat different conceptualization of "subclinical" psychopathy, in the form of a growing body of research on the concept of Machiavellianism (see Christie & Geis, 1970; Fehr et al., 1992 for reviews). Based largely on the writings of sixteenth-century Italian author Niccolo Machiavelli, the concept of Machiavellianism has been captured in self-report measures known as the Mach-IV and Mach-V (Christie & Geis, 1970). "High Machs" those who score high on the measures are exploitative, calculating, and deceitful; they also view others as weak, untrustworthy, and self-serving (Fehr et al., 1992).

Based on a vast quantity of research conducted over the last 50 years, high Machs have been found to be more dominant, more hostile in their attitudes, more authoritarian, more emotionally detached, yet higher in trait anxiety than their peers. On an interpersonal level, high Machs are more manipulative and persuasive, but are themselves less easily persuaded; high Machs also behave less ethically in some situations, and are in general more "morally flexible" (Christie & Geis, 1970; Fehr et al., 1992; Geis, 1978). Furthermore, high Machs, like psychopaths, score high on the P and E dimensions of the EPQ

(Allsopp et al., 1991), on the Psychopathic Deviate (Pd) scale of the MMPI (Smith & Griffith, 1978), and on the more maladaptive subscales of the Narcissistic Personality Inventory (McHoskey, 1995). Machiavellianism also shows the same sex difference as psychopathy (Christie & Geis, 1970; Mealey, 1995).

Most important for the present purpose, however, is the direct relationship between Machiavellianism and psychopathy. Based on a sample of 343 individuals and using a subset of 10 PCL-R items, Widiger et al. (1996) found a correlation between Mach-IV scores and psychopathy of .22. Using a self-report measure of psychopathy (the PPI, Lilienfeld & Andrews, 1996) with a sample of 30 Australian prison inmates, Kinner, Mealey, and Slaughter (2001) found a correlation between Mach and psychopathy of .44. Finally, based on a sample of 100 prison inmates, Hare (1991) reported correlations between Mach-IV score and PCL-R Factors 1 and 2 of .27 and .15, respectively, suggesting a stronger relationship between Mach and the personality (vs. behavioral) component of psychopathy.

Machiavellianism and psychopathy may therefore be converging, albeit distinct, constructs (Fehr et al., 1992; McHoskey et al., 1998), with high Machs in many respects resembling the prototypical psychopathic personality type. From this perspective not all high Machs are psychopaths, but one would expect a psychopath to be a high Mach.

Although it is almost inevitable that scores on personality measures will be distributed normally in the population, this does not necessarily imply that psychopathy itself is normally distributed, or even on a continuum with normal personality. Rather, underlying normally distributed scores on personality measures, there may exist a discrete personality class or taxon: psychopaths may be qualitatively different from "normal" people, and from so-called "subclinical" psychopaths (see Gangestad & Snyder, 1985).

Evidence is gathering that a taxon does indeed underlie severe, lifelong antisocial behavior (e.g., Ayers, 2000; Harris, Rice, & Quinsey, 1994; Skilling et al., 2001). To date this evidence bears more on antisocial behavior than on psychopathic personality; nevertheless, the existence of a psychopathy taxon would explain the nonreciprocal overlap commonly found between psychopathy and other measures of antisociality.

## The Low Fear/Low Arousal/Weak BIS Hypothesis

Considerable scientific interest in the construct of psychopathy was sparked by a 1957 article suggesting that the core deficit of the psychopath was a relative absence of fear. Lykken (1957) compared incarcerated psychopaths identified according to Cleckley's criteria, with other incarcerated offenders and with "normals" taken from the community. He found that the psychopathic offenders showed poorer passive avoidance of punishment (i.e., they continued to choose an incorrect option that resulted in a painful electric shock) in a task involving negotiation of a maze. This finding of poor "passive avoidance learn-ing" has been replicated numerous times (see Lykken, 1995a for a review) and suggests that psychopaths, in effect, experience relatively little fear or anxiety in the face of punishment. According to Lykken (1982, 1995a, 1998), this rela-tive fearlessness is a heritable trait which, in combination with poor parenting, results in an unsocialized, relatively fearless adult—a psychopath. Regrettably, these temperamentally difficult children are often born to incompetent parents, who were themselves hard to socialize, and are therefore "doubly disadvan-taged."

A related proposal is that psychopathy, and antisocial behavior in general, stem from a congenitally low level of physiological arousal. According to the "General Arousal Theory of Criminality" (Eysenck & Gudjonsson, 1989), in-dividuals with an underaroused physiotype will be extraverted, impulsive, and sensation seeking, and will tend to engage in high-risk activities, including crime, in an attempt to raise their level of physiological arousal to a more optimal level. In addition, such individuals will be relatively insensitive to low levels of stimulation (including small electric shocks). This proposal is consis-tent with the low-fear hypothesis and finds additional empirical support in the literature: Criminality in general and psychopathy in particular are associated with measures of sensation seeking and impulsivity (e.g., Daderman & af Klin-teberg, 1997; Daderman, 1999; Lalumiere, Quinsey, & Craig, 1996; Zuckerman et al., 1980), and with a variety of indicators of suboptimal arousal including childhood hyperactivity (Lynam, 1996), recreational drug use (Kaye et al., 1997), sexual promiscuity, risk taking, and failure to persist on tasks (Ellis, 1987). Interestingly, like psychopathy and Machiavellianism, risk-taking and sensation-seeking behavior is much more common among males than among females (Campbell, 2001; Zuckerman, 1979).

Researchers have made some progress in explaining the psychopath's ap-parent underarousal on a physiological level. Based on Gray's (1982, 1987) model of fear processing, Newman and Wallace (1993) have argued that psy-chopaths suffer from an underactive Behavioral Inhibition System (BIS). The BIS reflects the functioning of the hippocampus and serotonergic activity, and is activated by punishment and novel stimuli (Lösel, 1998). Suffering from an underactive BIS, psychopaths are deficient in altering ongoing, goal-directed behavior, in the face of cues for punishment (Newman, 1998).

## Empathy and Theory of Mind

One of the cardinal traits of the psychopath is a lack of empathy. Although this is hardly a new concept (e.g., Cleckley, 1941/1988; McCord & McCord, 1964), the precise nature of the apparent deficit is still unclear. One possible explanation relates to the psychopath's theory of mind (ToM): the ability to represent and attribute independent mental states to self and others (Happé,

1994; Happé, Winner, & Brownell, 1998). Perhaps the psychopath lacks a ToM module, and is thus incapable of empathizing with his or her victims.

In an initial test of this hypothesis Blair et al. (1996) compared the ToM ability of 25 psychopaths and 25 incarcerated controls, using Happé's (1994) Advanced Theory of Mind (A-ToM) test. The two groups did not differ in ToM ability, and all participants performed within the normal range. Blair et al. concluded that psychopaths do not suffer from a ToM deficit.

The A-ToM test, however, is relatively easy for normal adults to pass, raising the possibility that ceiling effects could explain Blair et al.'s findings (1996). Alternatively, it may be that psychopaths are capable of representing others' mental states, but that they do not do so in the same way as nonpsychopaths. In other words, psychopaths may not lack a ToM module, but the nature of their ToM may differ from that of nonpsychopaths.

Happé and Frith (1996) compared the ToM of normally developing and conduct-disordered children. Like Blair et al. (1996), they found no ToM deficit using standard tests. However they did observe significant "real-world" social impairment suggestive of higher-level ToM module deficits. Happé and Frith suggested that conduct-disordered children may be characterized by a combination of a subtle ToM deficit and a hostile attributional bias, applying a "theory of nasty minds" (p. 395). Similarly, in a sample of 37 children aged 9 to 12, Repacholi, Slaughter, Pritchard, and Gibbs (2001) found that high Machs exhibited a negative attributional bias in judging the intent of story characters. Perhaps adult psychopaths are characterized by a similar bias: perhaps their ToM module is intact, but their perception of others' mental states is skewed.

A related possibility is that psychopaths' perceptions of others are skewed not by an attributional bias, but by the very nature of the "inputs" to their ToM module: According to Mealey (1995, 1997) the psychopath's ToM module is itself intact, but because the psychopath does not experience the social emotions (e.g., guilt, shame) the experiential inputs to this ToM module are deficient—the psychopath cannot "embody" or "simulate" these emotions. Accordingly, the psychopath conceives of others in purely instrumental terms, unencumbered by thoughts of others' emotional distress or suffering (Mealey & Kinner, in preparation; Preston & de Waal, in press). In fact Mealey and Kinner (in press) argue that "it is the failure of the psychopath's emotional simulations, and consequent forced reliance on theory, which allows the intelligent psychopath to be functionally and successfully Machiavellian while demonstrating a marked lack of empathy and apparent 'cold-heartedness.'"

Although questions remain about the ToM of psychopaths, it is clear that these individuals have difficulty attributing some types of emotions to others: In a study of British psychopaths Blair, Sellars, Strickland, Clark, Smith, and Jones (1995) found that although psychopaths and nonpsychopaths performed equally in attributing happiness, sadness, and embarrassment to others, in stories involving "guilt" psychopaths attributed relatively little emotion, or even a positive emotional state, to the character. Clearly, psychopaths do suffer from some form of deficit in the processing of attributed emotion, even though the precise nature of this deficit remains unclear.

## EVOLUTIONARY APPROACHES TO PSYCHOPATHY

For over a century, clinicians have studied and attempted to "treat" psychopathic individuals, based on the assumption that psychopathy constitutes a form of mental illness. The very term psychopathy comes from the Greek words psyche (mind) and pathos (disease). However, over the last quarter of a century the notion that psychopathy may constitute a successful life strategy—an evolutionary niche—has slowly crept into the clinical literature. Among the first to frame psychopathy as an adaptation was Theodore Millon, who in 1975 noted that "the majority of these personalities do not exhibit flagrant antisocial behaviors, finding a sanctioned niche in conventional rules" (cited in Millon et al., 1998, p. 23). Millon recognized that psychopathy is not uniformly synonymous with antisocial behavior or criminality, and suggested that psychopathic individuals might even engage in some forms of sensation-seeking, prosocial behavior.

### Individual Differences, Resources, and Reproduction

A central tenet of the evolutionary approach is that criminality is in some sense inherited. From a neo-Darwinian perspective, criminality is not only inherited, but also is maintained by natural selection. Criminologists Lee Ellis and Anthony Walsh (2000) have reviewed five evolutionary models of criminality, each based on the assumption of natural selection for criminal traits. Three of these assume that the genetic predisposition for criminality is normally distributed in the population, whereas the other two argue that all humans have an equal genetic potential for criminal behavior. Nevertheless, all recognize that criminal behavior is much more common among males than among females.

Proponents of the latter models (e.g., Belsky, 1997; Cohen & Machalek, 1988; Machalek, 1995; Vila, 1994) argue that although the potential for criminal behavior has been selected by evolutionary forces, this potential is more or less equal in everybody. In other words, for most people criminal behavior is largely the facultative result of environmental rather than genetic forces. According to Belsky (1997) criminal behavior represents one aspect of an "opportunistic" life strategy that has been developmentally canalized during a critical period early in life, as an adaptive response to an unstable and hostile environment. This "conditional adaptation" is characterized by sexual promiscuity, unstable pair bonds, low investment in parenting, and (sometimes) criminal behavior.

Cohen and Machalek (1988) and Vila (1994) present a similar model, arguing that most "expropriative" crime (i.e., crime that involves illegally obtaining others' resources) is an adaptive response to an environment in which resources are, or are expected to become, scarce. According to this model, we are all genetically predisposed to organize our lives around the acquisition of resources, whether by legitimate or illegitimate means. Both the conditional adaptation and expropriative models assert that criminality is an adaptive response to environmental contingencies, and that all humans have an equal (genetic) potential for crime.

Evidence from behavior genetics, however, indicates that in this regard, we are not "all created equal" (Rowe, 1996; Rowe & Rodgers, 1989). Rather, it appears that a polygenetic predisposition for crime is normally distributed in the population such that a small proportion of individuals have a strong genetic predisposition for crime, a small proportion have virtually no criminal tendencies, and the majority of people will be more or less "average" in this regard. Rowe (1996) argues that the tendency to engage in antisocial behavior is part of a heritable cluster of deviant traits he refers to as "d": Individuals high on "d" tend to emphasize mating effort over parenting effort, and are typically sensation seeking, aggressive males with a high sex drive.

Commensurate with their genetic propensities, these individuals tend toward more immediate methods of resource acquisition, lacking the intelligence and impulse control necessary to employ more complex, long-term strategies. Their behavior is thus adaptive for them: In the context of their genetic inheritance, they are "making the best of a bad job" (Dawkins, 1980). Furthermore, according to Rowe, criminality is a frequency dependent strategy: It will be successful if and only if it is employed by a small proportion of individuals in a population.

A complementary model of criminality, based on the notion of $r$ versus $K$ selection, has been proposed by Lee Ellis (1988). All animal species can be described on a continuum of reproductive strategies with one extreme defined by an $r$ approach to reproduction: frequent copulation, large numbers of offspring, but little parental effort; and the other end by a $K$ approach: few offspring, but with considerable parental investment in each. Humans are clearly a $K$-selected species, but among humans there is still some variation. According to the $r/K$ theory of criminality, criminal behavior is essentially a by-product of a heritable tendency to favor mating effort over parenting effort: a "behavioral accompaniment of an $r$ approach to reproduction" (Ellis & Walsh, 2000).

A third model that assumes individual differences in the genetic propensity for crime has been referred to as "cheater theory" (Ellis & Walsh, 2000). This model makes the important distinction between sociopaths (the more common antisocial individual, whose antisocial behavior is more attributable to environmental forces) and psychopaths. Cheater theory argues that even though the psychopath is qualitatively *different* from the rest of us, this difference does not constitute a *deficit*. One version of this model, which has gathered an increasing amount of empirical support, is outlined below.

## Cheater Theory

According to Mealey (1995), both psychopaths and sociopaths can be described in evolutionary terms as "cheaters." In all social species, including humans, the notion of reciprocity is fundamental to the establishment and
maintenance of mutually beneficial, adaptive relationships. Cheaters are those
who exploit this reciprocity by soliciting a cooperative response from another,
then "defecting," taking whatever resources have been made available and,
rather than reciprocating, moving on to another trusting "victim."

A cheater strategy may be either facultative (i.e., developed as an adaptive
response to environmental contingencies) or obligate (i.e., a consequence of the
individual's genetic endowment). According to Mealey (1995) the obligate
mechanism leads to psychopathy and is the result of "frequency-dependent,
genetically-based individual differences in the use of a single (antisocial) strategy" (p. 526). Mealey argues that psychopaths constitute a discrete personality
type that predisposes them to antisocial behavior: Due to inborn temperamental factors (such as those described in the first section), psychopaths are relatively unresponsive to the environmental factors necessary for normal
socialization. At the same time, their particular physiology predisposes them
to seek out arousing (and often deviant) stimuli in the environment. In other
words, psychopaths are genetically "primed" to behave antisocially, and are
genetically canalized to adopt a "cheater strategy" in their interactions with
others. Consistent with Rowe (1996), Mealey argues that psychopathy is a
frequency-dependent life strategy that is effective and in evolutionary equilibrium only when potential victims greatly outnumber their psychopathic aggressors.

The second developmental pathway described by Mealey leads to sociopathy
and stems from an "environmentally contingent, facultative cheating strategy
not as clearly tied to genotype" (p. 539). In other words, sociopaths are individuals who have not been genetically canalized to adopt a "cheater" strategy,
but who in response to environmental contingencies (e.g., scarce resources, an
unpredictable environment) nevertheless adopt an antisocial, sometimes par-
asitic lifestyle. These are the individuals described in Cohen and Machalek's
(1988), Belsky's (1997), and Vila's (1994) theories of criminality, and many will
be diagnosed with ASPD. According to this two-path model, although psychopaths will exist in low, relatively stable numbers in all societies, the prevalence
of sociopaths (or those diagnosed with ASPD) will vary considerably with environmental forces, as immediate social circumstances modify the size of the
"niche" available for cheaters.

Mealey's two-path evolutionary model of criminality maps neatly onto the
two-path developmental model proposed by Moffitt (Moffitt, 1993; Moffitt &
Caspi, 2001). The developmental model was formulated in order to explain
how antisocial behavior can exhibit bothimpressive continuity over the life

span and a massive increase in prevalence around adolescence. Moffitt distinguished between life-course persistent and adolescence-limited offenders, arguing that although the former result from an interaction of inborn neuropsychological factors and environmental influence, the latter result from environmental factors alone.

According to both the evolutionary and the developmental two-path models, there are two basic forms of antisocial person. Psychopaths are inherently asocial, emotionally flat, manipulative, and sensation seeking; for these individuals, an antisocial lifestyle is *almost* inevitable. Sociopaths, by contrast, are "normal" individuals who have responded in an adaptive way to immediate environmental factors by adopting an antisocial lifestyle, much as Ellis (1988), Rowe (1996), and others suggest. In sum, psychopaths are argued to constitute a discrete type, whereas sociopaths are not.

## Psychopathy as an Adaptive Personality Type

There is little doubt that psychopathic individuals are often destructive to those around them and to society as a whole. But are psychopaths self-destructive? That is, are psychopathic individuals better characterized as "damaged" or simply "damaging"? Although psychiatric medicine considers psychopaths to be "personality disordered" (American Psychiatric Association, 2000), from an evolutionary perspective psychopathy seems to be an adaptation rather than a disease.

A growing body of research (e.g., Anderson & Phelps, 2001; Blair & Frith, 2000; Blair et al., 1997; Blair et al., 1999; Intrator et al., 1997) has identified neurological abnormalities in psychopaths. These occur primarily in the amygdala and frontal lobe, and seem to correspond to the psychopath's unusual processing of emotional information, and to their impulsive, sensation-seeking behavior. A neurological *abnormality*, however, does not necessarily constitute an *adaptive disadvantage* (Mealey, 1997). From an evolutionary perspective, any strategy that results in average or better than average reproductive success is adaptive. Recent research suggests that psychopathy is an adaptive life strategy for males. It is a strategy characterized by coercion, deception, and short-term sexual relationships—in short, by a relatively *r* reproductive strategy (Ellis, 1988; Mealey & Kinner, in preparation; see also Mealey, this volume).

Seto, Khattar, Lalumiere, and Quinsey (1997) found that psychopathy was related to the use of deception, both sexual and nonsexual, and to the use of a short-term sexual strategy. Similarly, Lalumiere and Quinsey (1996) found that the strongest predictor of sexual coercion in heterosexual men was psychopathy—which was itself positively associated with mating effort. Finally, Seto, Lalumiere, and Quinsey (1995) also found that among a sample of 279 heterosexual males sensation seeking, a strong correlate of psychopathy, was related to various indicators of sexual promiscuity.

Further evidence that psychopathy is a successful male life strategy comes from a recent study by Lalumiere, Harris, and Rice (2001). Contrary to the view that "life-course persistent" offenders are characterized by neurological defects (Moffitt, 1993), Lalumiere et al. found no evidence of a relationship between psychopathy and either developmental perturbations or neurological defects. Psychopathy, they argue, is not a disorder but an adaptive, frequency-dependent male life strategy or, as Mealey (1997) describes it, an "ethical pathology"—a life strategy that is "functional and adaptive for one individual in an interaction . . . but which [has] dysfunctional, maladaptive consequences for one or more other participants" (p. 531).

For the cheater strategy to be successful, the cheater must avoid developing a "reputation" (Frank, 1988). Once identified, a "cheater" will be unable to effectively manipulate, deceive, and take advantage of a victim. It is therefore in their best interests to interact with a given individual for only a limited time, moving on to a new victim once their duplicity is detected (Dugatkin & Wilson, 1991). Notably, although "roving" males can increase their reproductive success by mating with then deserting or deceiving a series of partners (e.g., consider bigamy), as a reproductive strategy this behavior would be less effective for females, who must carry then nourish their child in order to pass on their genetic material. This important sex difference in the adaptiveness of "roving" is reflected in the much greater prevalence of psychopathy among males than among females.

Also consistent with the cheater model is the fact that crime rates are markedly higher in large urban communities than in rural areas (Ellis & Walsh, 2000). Although large cities are arguably made up of a number of smaller subcommunities, evidence suggests that cheaters can be successful in this context (Dugatkin & Wilson, 1991), because they can still move readily among the subcommunities, preserving anonymity and making use of their "superficial charm" (Hare, 1991). In fact Lykken (1995b) has argued that the move away from small-community or extended family living, to which we are evolutionarily adapted, has contributed to the escalating crime rate.

It is also the case that psychopaths are more likely to be found in communities with a more transient population, where their cheater reputation will be less likely to precede them. Communities with a stable population, and few strangers, are less attractive to those who aim to cheat. Similarly, psychopaths may be more common in occupations involving frequent travel, such as traveling salesperson or interstate truck driver. Occupations of this kind allow the psychopath to move between communities, locating victims who are unaware of their duplicity.

Cooke (1998a) has noted that psychopathy is more likely to be a successful life strategy in an individualistic society, such as America, than in a more collectivist society. Consistent with this view, psychopathy appears to be considerably more prevalent in North America than in Europe, at least in correctional centers, with one analysis yielding rates of 29% and 8% in North

America and Scotland, respectively (Cooke, 1997). According to both Rieber (1997) and Hare (1993), psychopathy is actually becoming increasingly adaptive in North American society, which "is moving in the direction of permitting, reinforcing, and in some instances actually valuing some of the traits listed in the Psychopathy Checklist—traits such as impulsivity, irresponsibility, lack of remorse" (Hare 1993, p. 177). One reason for the relatively low prevalence of psychopathy observed in Scotland is what Cooke (1997) terms "psychopathic drift." Consistent with the "rover" model of psychopathy (Dugatkin & Wilson, 1991), it appears that Scottish psychopaths are more likely to "drift" from place to place, often being drawn to the excitement and anonymity of populous southern England (Cooke, 1998b). The niche for a psychopathic life strategy may be larger in southern England, where the transient population and densely populated cities provide the psychopath with anonymity and an unending supply of potential victims.

## IMPLICATIONS OF AN EVOLUTIONARY APPROACH

The evolutionary model, which characterizes psychopathy as a discrete, adaptive life strategy, has significant implications for society's understanding of, and response to, the existence of psychopathic individuals. By viewing psychopathy as a frequency-dependent, adaptive "ethical pathology," policymakers can move beyond the medical model and legal rhetoric to consider new ways of responding to and minimizing the impact of these individuals.

### Assessment and Measurement

The evolutionary model argues that psychopathy is not synonymous with ASPD and that psychopaths are characterized by both a callous and manipulative interpersonal style and antisocial (although not necessarily criminal) behavior. From this perspective, the distinction between psychopathy (a discrete, adaptive life strategy) and ASPD (a pervasive pattern of antisocial behavior) is crucial (Arrigo & Shipley, 2001; Hare, 1996). In implementing policies based on the evolutionary approach, it is therefore essential that the construct of psychopathy be measured in a reliable and valid manner. As discussed in the introduction, the most reliable and valid measure of psychopathy currently available is the Psychopathy Checklist Revised (PCL-R, Hare, 1991), which measures both the interpersonal/affective and the behavioral components of psychopathy. If used by appropriately trained and qualified individuals (Hare, 1998a), PCL-R scores can be considered a reliable (if imperfect) indicator of the likelihood that a given individual is a member of the psychopathy taxon (Harris et al., 1994).

## Culpability

Haycock (2001) has observed that with the growing body of evidence that psychopaths are characterized by neurological and information-processing "deficits," a diagnosis of psychopathy may actually be advantageous: What was previously the "kiss of death" for an offender on death row might instead become the "kiss of life." At the crux of this issue is the question of whether psychopathy constitutes a *disorder* in the legal sense (i.e., an absence of *mens rea*), or simply a *difference*—an alternative life strategy.

In Queensland, Australia, the Criminal Code Act (1899) provides that

§27(1) A person is not criminally responsible for an act or omission if at the time of doing the act or making the omission the person is in such a state of mental disease or natural mental infirmity as to deprive the person of *capacity to understand* what the person is doing, or of *capacity to control* the person's actions, or of *capacity to know* that the person ought not to do the act or make the omission. (Emphasis added.)

The relevant question thus becomes: *Is the psychopath's ability to appreciate the nature of his actions, or to control those actions, impaired?*

According to some authors, the answer is yes. Fatic (1997), for example, argues that the behavior of psychopaths reflects an inability to integrate the cognitive knowledge that a behavior is proscribed and the desire to act out the behavior. In essence, Fatic argues that psychopaths do not inhibit their behavior, and therefore "can't help themselves." However, this "slippery and dangerous form of reasoning" (Restak, 1992, p. 20) is circular: Behaving in a morally reprehensible manner does not imply insanity. Psychopaths are, from an evolutionary perspective, truly *"manie sans delire"* (Pinel, 1806/1962).

Similarly, the notion that a genetic basis for psychopathy makes the psychopathic offender less culpable is flawed. Regardless of one's position on genetic determinism, the issue of a genetic basis for psychopathy is irrelevant. Psychopaths have the *cognitive* capacity to distinguish right from wrong, and should therefore be held legally responsible for their actions.

The psychopath, who has no additional handicaps, is capable of *understanding* his actions, and *knowing* right from wrong. Although impulsive, the psychopath is also capable of inhibiting behavior, and can therefore *control* his actions. In addition, with an intact Theory of Mind (Blair et al., 1996), the psychopath is able to foresee the adverse impact of his actions on victims (see Mealey & Kinner, in preparation). In short, psychopaths do not meet the criteria for diminished responsibility, at least in Queensland. Similarly, in the United States, the Model Penal Code Rule formulated by the American Law Institute (ALI) specifies that an offender cannot be exculpated on the basis of repeated criminal or antisocial conduct, and psychopathy is clearly excluded as a basis for an insanity defense (Bartol & Bartol, 1994).

Psychopathy cannot currently be used as a defense in legal proceedings, and from an evolutionary perspective, the view that psychopathy constitutes an adaptive, alternative life strategy does not reduce the offender's culpability in the eyes of the law.

## Incarceration

Two important goals of incarceration are to punish the offender and to act as a deterrent against future crime. Unfortunately, psychopathic offenders are relatively unresponsive to either punishment or the threat of punishment, and as impulsive risk-takers, are unlikely to be dissuaded by a vague threat of possible incarceration at some time in the (seemingly) distant future. Consequently, incarceration is a relatively ineffective strategy with psychopaths—a fact reflected in their considerably higher rate of recidivism, particularly violent recidivism (Hemphill et al., 1998). Perhaps if punishment could be made more immediate and more inevitable, it would be more effective (Mealey, 1995); however, it would be both difficult and costly to make significant improvements in this regard, and errors in the application of justice would be more common and more severe.

On the other hand, even though imprisonment does not deter psychopaths from offending, their incarceration does serve to protect the public. Thus, one partial solution to the problem of psychopathic offenders might be selective long-term incapacitation of individuals diagnosed as psychopaths (Gosling, 1998; Lösel, 1998). Evidence suggests that psychopathic offenders tend to "burn out" around the age of 35–40, with their rate of offending dropping to that of nonpsychopathic offenders, although their personality does not change (Hare, 1993, 1996). It may therefore be possible to reduce the offending of psychopathic individuals by maximizing the length of their custodial sentences.

In Australia and North America, sentencing and parole decisions have been and, arguably, should continue to be influenced by whether an offender is psychopathic (see Rice, 1997). With reference to such offenders, one Australian District Court judge remarked that "it bears on the court's *statutory duty* to assess the risk of physical harm to members of the community if a custodial sentence is not imposed. It is clear now that the PCL-R is a robust predictor of recidivism, particularly violent recidivism" (Pratt in Pratt & McCulloch, 1998, p. 47, emphasis added).

## Treatment

From an evolutionary perspective, it makes little sense to "treat" psychopaths, as psychopathy is not considered an illness, but rather a life strategy. Psychopaths demonstrate less effort in treatment than do nonpsychopaths, and are less likely to complete the treatment program (Hare, 1996). Not surprisingly, current treatments are ineffective with psychopathic offenders, and may even be counterproductive (Rice et al., 1992; Seto & Barbaree, 1999).

In light of the known neurological correlates of psychopathy, a number of researchers (e.g., Lösel, 1998; Panksepp et al., 1995) have suggested that pharmacotherapies might hold more promise in curbing the behavior of psychopathic individuals. However, there is at this stage little empirical support for this position, and it raises a difficult ethical question: Would pharmacological intervention constitute "treatment" or suppression of adaptive impulses? If psychopathy is an adaptive life strategy that is only pathological in the sense of harm done to others (Mealey's "ethical pathology"), then the latter may be true.

Perhaps more promising is the idea that psychopaths' impulses could be "redirected" into less socially destructive activities which would still meet their needs for sensation seeking, dominance, and (arguably) a Machiavellian sense of control (Hare, 1993; Mealey, 1995; Panksepp et al., 1995). Although this proposition has only limited empirical support so far, it may offer promise for psychopathic offenders, whose antisocial behavior is argued to be an expression of basic needs and drives.

Following from this notion is the possibility of developing a treatment strategy specifically for psychopathic offenders. Such a program has been developed in Canada (Wong & Hare, in press), but as yet has not been widely implemented. Consistent with the view that psychopathy is a life strategy rather than an illness, it has been argued that such a program would "be less concerned with attempts to develop empathy or conscience than with intensive efforts to convince them that their current attitudes and behavior are not in their own best interest . . . [and to] . . . show them how to use their strengths and abilities to satisfy their needs in ways that society can tolerate" (Hare, 1993, p. 204).

## Prevention

What, then, can be done? Psychopaths are not insane in a legal or an evolutionary sense, and are unresponsive to either incarceration or current treatments. A number of authors (e.g., Bailey, 1995; Lykken, 1995a; Mealey, 1995; Patrick, 1997) have argued that psychopathy is not synonymous with criminal or antisocial behavior, and that in fact "the hero and the psychopath may be twigs on the same genetic branch" (Lykken, 1995a, p. 118). From this point of view, prevention is a two-step process involving (a) going "upstream" to identify the "fledgling psychopath" (Lynam, 1996) and then (b) much as Hare (1993) has suggested, redirecting their impulses into less socially destructive channels.

Unfortunately, there is at this stage no accepted approach to early identification. However, children with psychopathic tendencies may be a subset of those with conduct disorder who are characterized by the same callous/unemotional traits as their adult counterparts (Frick, 1998; Frick et al., 1994). Alternatively, comorbid conduct disorder and attention deficit hyperactivity disorder (ADHD) may be an early indicator of psychopathy (Lynam, 1996,

1997, 1998). Psychopathic individuals are also likely to be among those who develop symptoms of conduct disorder relatively early in life, as their behavioral problems are an expression of inborn temperamental factors rather than adverse social influences. Agreement has yet to be reached regarding the characteristics of "fledgling psychopaths," much less the best approach to measuring these characteristics. In light of the enormous social impact of psychopathic offenders, further research in this area should be a high priority.

Although there is little agreement with regard to the early distinguishing features of psychopaths, the evolutionary model provides some clear direction for responding to these individuals. Much as Hare (1993) has suggested for adult psychopathic offenders, early interventions should be designed to redirect potentially antisocial, sensation-seeking impulses into less socially destructive activities—perhaps extreme sports or even the performing arts. If psychopathic individuals are incapable of experiencing "true empathy" (Mealey & Kinner, in press; Preston & de Waal, in press), then traditional empathy training will be unproductive at best. To be successful, any intervention will have to teach these youths that antisocial behavior is not in their *own* best interests.

Any preventive efforts at a societal level will have to be complemented by effective intervention on an individual level—within the family unit. Lykken (1995a, 1995b, 1997, 1998) has argued convincingly that although more temperamentally difficult children require more skillful parenting, the inverse is usually the case: Psychopathic children have a better than average chance of being born to psychopathic parents, who have themselves assortatively mated, producing a "double whammy effect" (Krueger et al., 1998, p. 183). These congenitally hypoaroused children do not respond well to punishment (see Section "low fear / low arousal / weak BIS hypothesis" 1.2) but can be reinforced for prosocial behavior, by sufficiently patient and persistent parents. According to Lykken (1982), "the right sort of parent will encourage the desired behavior and then ladle on the praise" (p. 27). One rather extreme solution to the problem of poor parenting would be to introduce parental licensure (Lykken, 1995a, 1998), compelling prospective parents to meet some basic criteria (e.g., financially self-sufficient, absence of drug dependency) before being permitted to have children. Less controversially, Vila (1997) suggests that as a society we should move away from reactive crime control measures (protection, avoidance, deterrence) and toward "nurturant" strategies, designed to enhance children's quality of life and to channel their development, to ensure that their needs are met in socially acceptable ways.

## Changing Society

If we cannot change psychopaths, then perhaps we can change ourselves, as a society, to reduce the negative impact that psychopathic individuals can have. One approach might be to increase society's awareness of the existence and modus operandi of psychopathic individuals, both criminal and noncriminal.

Popular books and media articles about psychopathic conmen and violent psychopathic predators abound; however, these individuals continue to manipulate and prey upon unsuspecting victims. If psychopathy is an adaptive, frequency-dependent life strategy as the evolutionary model suggests, then increased sensitivity to cheaters will be countered by an equally enhanced ability to deceive, resulting in nothing more than a "coevolutionary arms race" (Mealey, 1995, p. 525).

As previously noted, the prevalence of psychopathy in a given society is influenced by the size and stability of communities and by dominant cultural norms and attitudes. By manipulating these variables, it may be possible to reduce the size of the niche for psychopathy. On a practical level, this might entail initiatives to encourage the development of distinct, stable communities within large cities, or even the development of a stable group of "community elders," to reduce the psychopath's ability to move anonymously through the community. Strategies of this sort are, of course, long term, and will only succeed with the support of the public. In this sense, increasing public awareness of the psychopaths among us may be beneficial after all.

## SUMMARY AND CONCLUSIONS

A number of proximate models of psychopathy have emerged over the last 50 years, each providing some insight into the development and characteristics of psychopathic offenders. More recently, an ultimate, evolutionary explanation of psychopathy has been advanced to synthesize the proximate models and explain why psychopaths continue to exist in small numbers, in every society. This evolutionary model characterizes psychopathy as an adaptive, frequency-dependent life strategy—a cheater strategy. The evolutionary model does not attempt to justify the antisocial behavior of psychopaths, and in fact argues that in the eyes of the law, psychopathic offenders should be held fully accountable for their crimes.

A major contribution of the evolutionary approach has been to help us understand why psychopaths constitute a small percentage of our population, but a considerably larger minority of our prison population. Having accepted that there is a niche in human society for the psychopath, we can begin to develop strategies for identifying psychopathic individuals and channeling their impulses into more acceptable behaviors. Recognizing that psychopaths may constitute a discrete taxon, we can begin to develop specific and targeted interventions designed for implementation throughout the life span of these individuals. The institutional treatment program for violent psychopaths, developed by Wong and Hare (in press), is but one example.

The very concept of psychopathic personality has been, and continues to be, controversial in both academic and criminal justice circles. Nevertheless, the construct has both considerable clinical and predictive utility, and extensive theoretical support. A diagnosis of psychopathy should inform the decisions of judges, juries, parole boards, mental health tribunals, and clinicians alike. An evolutionary understanding of psychopathy as an adaptive, discrete, frequency-dependent life strategy should likewise inform the decisions of policymakers concerned with reducing crime, minimizing violence and maximizing the potential of at-risk youth. Antisocial behavior is neither desirable nor adaptive, but with appropriate, intensive and timely intervention, psychopathic individuals might be challenged to make their mark on the world in asocial, if not prosocial, ways.

## REFERENCES

Allsopp, J., Eysenck, H.J., & Eysenck, H.B.G. (1991). Machiavellianism as a component in psychoticism and extraversion. *Personality and Individual Differences, 12*(1), 29–41.

American Psychiatric Association. (1952). *Diagnostic and statistical manual of mental disorders* (1st ed.). Washington, DC: American Psychiatric Association.

American Psychiatric Association. (1968). *Diagnostic and statistical manual of mental disorders—Second edition* (2nd ed.). Washington, DC: American Psychiatric Association.

American Psychiatric Association. (1980). *Diagnostic and statistical manual of mental disorders—Third edition* (3rd ed.). Washington, DC: American Psychiatric Association.

American Psychiatric Association. (2000). *Diagnostic and statistical manual of mental disorders—Fourth edition text revision* (4th revised ed.). Washington, DC: American Psychiatric Association.

Anderson, A.K., & Phelps, E.A. (2001). Lesions of the human amygdala impair enhanced perception of emotionally salient events. *Nature, 411,* 305–309.

Arrigo, B.A., & Shipley, S. (2001). The confusion over psychopathy (I): Historical considerations. *International Journal of Offender Therapy and Comparative Criminology, 45*(3), 325–344.

Ayers, W.A. (2000). *Taxometric analysis of borderline and antisocial personality disorders in a drug and alcohol dependent population.* New York: Fordham University.

Bailey, K.G. (1995). The sociopath: Cheater or warrior hawk? *Behavioral and Brain Sciences, 18*(3), 542–543.

Bartol, C.R., & Bartol, A.M. (1994). *Psychology and law.* Pacific Grove, CA: Brooks/Cole.

Belsky, J. (1997). Attachment, mating, and parenting: An evolutionary interpretation. *Human Nature, 8*(4), 361–381.

Blackburn, R. (1975). An empirical classification of psychopathic personality. *British Journal of Psychiatry, 127,* 456–460.

Blackburn, R. (1988). On moral judgements and personality disorders: The myth of psychopathic personality revisited. *British Journal of Psychiatry, 153,* 505–512.

Blair, J., & Frith, U. (2000). Neurocognitive explanations of the antisocial personality disorders. *Criminal Behavior and Mental Health, 10,* S66–S81.

Blair, J., Sellars, C., Strickland, I., Clark, F., Williams, A., Smith, M., & Jones, L. (1996). Theory of mind in the psychopath. *Journal of Forensic Psychiatry, 7*(1), 15–25.

Blair, R.J.R., Jones, L., Clark, F., & Smith, M. (1997). The psychopathic individual: A lack of responsiveness to distress cues? *Psychophysiology, 34*(2), 192–198.

Blair, R.J.R., Morris, J.S., Frith, C.C., Perrett, D.I., & Dolan, R.J. (1999). Dissociable neural responses to facial expressions of sadness and anger. *Brain, 122*(5), 883–893.

Blair, R.J.R., Sellars, C., Strickland, I., Clark, F., Williams, A.O., Smith, M., & Jones, L. (1995). Emotion attributions in the psychopath. *Personality and Individual Differences, 19*(4), 431–437.

Campbell, A. (2001). Staying alive: Evolution, culture, and women's intrasexual aggression. *Behavioral and Brain Sciences, 22*, 203–214.

Christie, R., & Geis, F. L. (Eds.). (1970). *Studies in Machiavellianism.* New York: Academic Press.

Clarke, J., & Shea, A. (2001). *Touched by the devil: Inside the mind of the Australian psychopath.* Sydney, Australia: Simon & Schuster.

Cleckley, H. (1941/1988). *The mask of sanity* (5th ed.). St Louis, MO: Mosby.

Cohen, L.E., & Machalek, R. (1988). A general theory of expropriative crime: An evolutionary ecological approach. *American Journal of Sociology, 94*(3), 465–501.

Cooke, D.J. (1997). Psychopaths: Oversexed, overplayed but not over here? *Criminal Behavior and Mental Health, 7*(1), 3–11.

Cooke, D.J. (1998a). Cross-cultural aspects of psychopathy. In T. Millon, E. Simonsen, M. Birket-Smith, & R.D. David (Eds.), *Psychopathy: Antisocial, criminal, and violent behavior* (pp. 260–276). New York: Guilford.

Cooke, D.J. (1998b). Psychopathy across cultures. In D.J. Cooke, A. Forth, & R.D. Hare (Eds.), *Psychopathy: Theory, research and implications for society* (pp. 13–45). Dordrecht: Kluwer Academic Publishers.

Daderman, A., & af Klinteberg, B. (1997). *Personality dimensions characterizing severely conduct disordered male juvenile delinquents* (Reports from the Department of Psychology, University of Stockholm. No. 831). Stockholm: University of Stockholm.

Daderman, A.M. (1999). Differences between severely conduct-disordered juvenile males and normal juvenile males: The study of personality traits. *Personality and Individual Differences, 26*(5), 827–845.

Darke, S., Kaye, S., & Finlay Jones, R. (1998). Antisocial personality disorder, psychopathy and injecting heroin use. *Drug and Alcohol Dependence, 52*(1), 63–69.

Dawkins, R. (1980). Good strategy or evolutionarily stable strategy? In G.W. Barlow & J. Silverberg (Eds.), *Sociobiology: Beyond nature/nurture?* Boulder, CO: Westview.

Dugatkin, L.A., & Wilson, D.S. (1991). Rover: A strategy for exploiting cooperators in a patchy environment. *American Naturalist, 138*(3), 687–701.

Dyce, J.A., & O' Connor, B.P. (1998). Personality disorders and the five-factor model: A test of facet-level predictions. *Journal of Personality Disorders, 12*(1), 31–45.

Ellis, L. (1987). Relationships of criminality and psychopathy with eight other apparent behavioral manifestations of sub-optimal arousal. *Personality and Individual Differences, 8*(6), 905–925.

Ellis, L. (1988). Criminal behavior and r/K selection: An extension of gene-based evolutionary theory. *Personality and Individual Differences, 9*(4), 697–708.

Ellis, L., & Walsh, A. (2000). *Criminology: A global perspective.* Needham Heights, MA: Allyn & Bacon.

Eysenck, H.J. (1977). *Crime and personality* (3rd ed.). London: Routledge and Kegan Paul.

Eysenck, H.J. (1987). The definition of personality disorders and the criteria appropriate for their description. *Journal of Personality Disorders, 1*(3), 211–219.

Eysenck, H.J. (1998). Personality and crime. In T. Millon & E. Simonsen (Eds.), *Psychopathy: Antisocial, criminal, and violent behavior* (pp. 40–49). New York: Guilford.

Eysenck, H.J., & Gudjonsson, G.H. (1989). *The causes and cures of criminality.* New York: Plenum.

Farrington, D.P., Ohlin, L., & Wilson, J.Q. (1986). *Understanding and controlling crime.* New York: Springer-Verlag.

Fatic, A. (1997). Psychopathy: Cognitive aspects and criminal responsibility. *Criminologist, 21*(2), 66–75.

Federal Bureau of Investigation. (1992). *Killed in the line of duty.* Washington, DC: Department of Justice.

Fehr, B., Samson, D., & Paulhus, D.L. (1992). The construct of Machiavellianism: Twenty years later. In C.D. Spielberger & J.N. Butcher (Eds.), *Advances in personality assessment* (Vol. 9, pp. 77—116). Hillsdale, NJ: Lawrence Erlbaum.

Frank, R.H. (1988). *Passions within reason: The strategic role of the emotions.* New York: W.W. Norton.

Frick, P.J. (1998). Callous-unemotional traits and conduct problems: Applying the two-factor model of psychopathy to children. In D.J. Cooke, A.E. Forth, & R.D. Hare (Eds.), *Psychopathy: Theory, research, and implications for society.* Dordrecht, Netherlands: Kluwer.

Frick, P.J., O' Brien, B.S., Wootton, J M., & McBurnett, K. (1994). Psychopathy and conduct problems in children. *Journal of Abnormal Psychology, 103*(4), 700–707.

Gangestad, S., & Snyder, M. (1985). "To carve nature at its joints": On the existence of discrete classes in personality. *Psychological Review, 92*(3), 317–349.

Geis, F.L. (1978). Machiavellianism. In H. London & J.E. Exher (Eds.), *Dimensions of personality* (pp. 305–363). New York: Wiley Interscience Publications.

Gosling, M. (1998). How to identify a psychopath. *Victoria Police Association Journal, 64*(12), 40–41.

Gray, J.A. (1982). *The neuropsychology of anxiety: An enquiry into the functions of the septo-hippocampal system.* New York: Clarendon Press/Oxford University Press.

Gray, J.A. (1987). *The psychology of fear and stress* (2nd ed.). New York: Cambridge University Press.

Happé, F.G.E. (1994). An advanced test of theory of mind: Understanding of story characters' thoughts and feelings by able autistic, mentally handicapped, and normal children and adults. *Journal of Autism and Developmental Disorders, 24*(2), 129–154.

Happé, F.G.E., & Frith, U. (1996). Theory of mind and social impairment in children with conduct disorder. *British Journal of Developmental Psychology, 14*(4), 385–398.

Happé, F.G.E., Winner, E., & Brownell, H. (1998). The getting of wisdom: Theory of mind in old age. *Developmental Psychology, 34*(2), 358–362.

Hare, R.D. (1991). Manual for the Hare Psychopathy Checklist—Revised. Toronto: Multi-Health Systems.

Hare, R.D. (1993). *Without conscience: The disturbing world of the psychopaths among us.* New York: Guilford.

Hare, R.D. (1996). Psychopathy and antisocial personality disorder: A case of diagnostic confusion. *Psychiatric Times, 13,* 39–40.

Hare, R.D. (1998a). The Hare PCL-R: Some issues concerning its use and misuse. *Legal and Criminological Psychology, 3,* 99–119.

Hare, R.D. (1998b). Psychopathy, affect and behavior. In D.J. Cooke & A.E. Forth & R.D. Hare (Eds.), *Psychopathy: Theory, research and implications for society* (Vol. 88). Dordrecht: Kluwer Academic Publishers.

Harris, G.T., Rice, M.E., & Cormier, C.A. (1991). Psychopathy and violent recidivism. *Law and Human Behavior, 15*(6), 625–637.

Harris, G.T., Rice, M.E., & Quinsey, V.L. (1994). Psychopathy as a taxon: Evidence that psychopaths are a discrete class. *Journal of Consulting and Clinical Psychology, 62*(2), 387–397.

Haycock, D. (2001). Images of violence: What use are psychopaths' brain scans? *HMS Beagle.* Available at: http://news.bmn.com/.

Hemphill, J.F., Templeman, R., Wong, S., & Hare, R.D. (1998). Psychopathy and crime: Recidivism and criminal careers. In D.J. Cooke & A. Forth & R.D. Hare (Eds.), *Psychopathy: Theory, research and implications for society* (Vol. 88). Dordrecht: Kluwer Academic Publishers.

Hill, C.D., Rogers, R., & Bickford, M.E. (1996). Predicting aggressive and socially disruptive behavior in a maximum security forensic psychiatric hospital. *Journal of Forensic Sciences, 41*(1), 56–59.

Intrator, J., Hare, R., Stritzke, P., Brichtswein, K., Dorfman, D., Harpur, T.J., Bernstein, D., Handelsman, L., Schaefer, C., Keilp, J., Rosen, J., & Machac, J. (1997). A brain imaging (single photon emission computerized tomography) study of semantic and affective processing in psychopaths. *Biological Psychiatry, 42*(2), 96–103.

Johns, J.H., & Quay, H.C. (1962). The effect of social reward on verbal conditioning in psychopathic and neurotic military offenders. *Journal of Consulting Psychology, 26*(3), 217–220.

Kaye, S., Darke, S., Finlay-Jones, R., & Hall, W. (1997). *The relationship between antisocial personality disorder, psychopathy and injecting heroin use* (Monograph 32). Sydney: National Drug and Alcohol Research Center (NDARC).

Kinner, S., Mealey, L.J., & Slaughter, V.P. (2001). *Psychopathy, Machiavellianism, risk-taking and career preferences.* Paper presented at the Australian and New Zealand Association of Psychiatry, Psychology and Law (ANZAPPL) Annual Conference, Melbourne, Australia.

Kraepelin, E. (1896). *Psychiatrie: Ein lehrbuch* (5th ed.). Leipzig: Barth.

Krueger, R.F., Moffitt, T.E., Caspi, A., Bleske, A., & Silva, P.A. (1998). Assortative mating for antisocial behavior: Developmental and methodological implications. *Behavior Genetics, 28*(3), 173–186.

Lalumiere, M.L., Harris, G.T., & Rice, M.E. (2001). Psychopathy and developmental instability. *Evolution and Human Behavior, 22*(2), 75–92.

Lalumiere, M.L., & Quinsey, V.L. (1996). Sexual deviance, antisociality, mating effort, and the use of sexually coercive behaviors. *Personality and Individual Differences, 21*(1), 33–48.

Lalumiere, M.L., Quinsey, V.L., & Craig, W.M. (1996). Why children from the same family are so different from one another: A Darwinian note. *Human Nature, 7*(3), 281–290.

Lilienfeld, S.O. (1994). Conceptual problems in the assessment of psychopathy. *Clinical Psychology Review, 14*(1), 17–38.

Lilienfeld, S.O., & Andrews, B.P. (1996). Development and preliminary validation of a self-report measure of psychopathic personality traits in noncriminal populations. *Journal of Personality Assessment, 66*(3), 488–524.

Loeber, R., & Farrington, D.P. (2000). Young children who commit crime: Epidemiology, developmental origins, risk factors, early interventions, and policy implications. *Development and Psychopathology, 12*(4), 737–762.

Lösel, F. (1998). Treatment and management of psychopaths. In D.J. Cooke, A.E. Forth, & R.D. Hare (Eds.), *Psychopathy: Theory, research and implications for society.* Dordrecht: Kluwer Academic Publishers.

Lykken, D.T. (1957). A study of anxiety in the sociopathic personality. *Journal of Abnormal and Social Psychology, 55,* 6–10.

Lykken, D.T. (1982). Fearlessness: Its carefree charm and deadly risks. *Psychology Today* (September), pp. 20–28.

Lykken, D.T. (1995a). *The antisocial personalities.* Hillsdale, NJ: Lawrence Erlbaum.

Lykken, D.T. (1995b). Fatherless rearing leads to sociopathy. *Behavioral and Brain Sciences, 18*(3), 563–564.

Lykken, D.T. (1997). The American crime factory. *Psychological Inquiry, 8*(3), 261–270.

Lykken, D.T. (1998). The case for parental licensure. In T. Millon & E. Simonsen (Eds.), *Psychopathy: Antisocial, criminal, and violent behavior* (pp. 122–143). New York: Guilford.

Lynam, D.R. (1996). Early identification of chronic offenders: Who is the fledgling psychopath? *Psychological Bulletin, 120*(2), 209–234.

Lynam, D.R. (1997). Pursuing the psychopath: Capturing the fledgling psychopath in a nomological net. *Journal of Abnormal Psychology, 106*(3), 425–438.

Lynam, D.R. (1998). Early identification of the fledgling psychopath: Locating the psychopathic child in the current nomenclature. *Journal of Abnormal Psychology, 107*(4), 566–575.

Machalek, R. (1995). Basic dimensions and forms of social exploitation: A comparative analysis. *Advances in Human Ecology, 4,* 35–68.

McCord, W., & McCord, J. (1964). *The psychopath: An essay on the criminal mind.* New York: D. Van Nostrand.

McHoskey, J. (1995). Narcissism and Machiavellianism. *Psychological Reports, 77*(3, Pt 1), 755–759.

McHoskey, J.W., Worzel, W., & Szyarto, C. (1998). Machiavellianism and psychopathy. *Journal of Personality and Social Psychology, 74*(1), 192–210.

Mealey, L. (1995). The sociobiology of sociopathy: An integrated evolutionary model. *Behavioral and Brain Sciences, 18*(3), 523–599.

Mealey, L. (1997). Heritability, theory of mind, and the nature of normality. *Behavioral and Brain Sciences, 20*(3), 527–532.

Mealey, L.J.M., & Kinner, S.A. (in preparation). Psychopathy, Machiavellianism, and theory of mind. In W. Schiefenhovel (Ed.), *The social brain: Evolution and pathology.* New York: Wiley.

Mealey, L.J.M., & Kinner, S.A. (in press). The perception-action model of empathy and psychopathic "cold-heartedness." *Behavioral and Brain Sciences.*

Millon, T., Simonsen, E., & Birket Smith, M. (1998). Historical conceptions of psychopathy in the United States and Europe. In T. Millon & E. Simonsen (Eds.), *Psychopathy: Antisocial, criminal, and violent behavior* (pp. 3–31). New York: Guilford.

Moffitt, T.E. (1993). Adolescence-limited and life-course-persistent antisocial behavior: A developmental taxonomy. *Psychological Review, 100*(4), 674–701.

Moffitt, T.E., & Caspi, A. (2001). Childhood predictors differentiate life-course persistent and adolescence-limited antisocial pathways among males and females. *Development and Psychopathology, 13*(2), 355–375.

Newman, J.P. (1998). Psychopathic behavior: An information processing perspective. In D.J. Cooke, A.E. Forth, & R.D. Hare (Eds.), *Psychopathy: Theory, research and implications for society.* Dordrecht: Kluwer Academic Publishers.

Newman, J.P., & Wallace, J.F. (1993). Diverse pathways to deficient self-regulation: Implications for disinhibitory psychopathology in children. *Clinical Psychology Review, 13*(8), 699–720.

Panksepp, J., Knutson, B., & Bird, L. (1995). On the brain and personality substrates of psychopathy. *Behavioral and Brain Sciences, 18*(3), 568–570.

Patrick, C.J. (1997). Deconstructing psychopathy. *Psychogical Inquiry, 8*(3), 244–251.

Pinel, P. (1806/1962). *A treatise on insanity* (M.D.D. Davis, Trans.). New York: Hafner.

Pratt, E.C.E., & McCulloch, S. (1998). *Forensic reports—The right of the present to govern itself so far as it can—Some advances in forensic psychology—Relevance to social needs.* Unpublished manuscript, Brisbane.

Preston, S.D., & de Waal, F.B. (in press). Empathy: Its ultimate and proximate bases. *Behavioral and Brain Sciences.*

Quinsey, V.L. (1995). The prediction and explanation of criminal violence. *International Journal of Law and Psychiatry, 18*(2), 117–127.

Quinsey, V.L., Harris, G.T., Rice, M.E., & Cormier, C.A. (1998). *Violent offenders: Appraising and managing risk.* Washington, DC: American Psychological Association.

Repacholi, B., Slaughter, V., Pritchard, M., & Gibbs, V. (2001). *Theory of mind, Machiavellianism, and peer relationships in childhood.* Paper presented at the Macquarie Center for Cognitive Science Workshop: Mind-reading and behavior: Individual differences in theory of mind and implications for social functioning, July 2001, Sydney, Australia.

Restak, R.M. (1992). See no evil: The neurological defence would blame violence on the damaged brain. *The Sciences,* July/August, 16–21.

Rice, M.E. (1997). Violent offender research and implications for the criminal justice system. *American Psychologist, 52*(4), 414–423.

Rice, M.E., & Harris, G.T. (1995). Violent recidivism: Assessing predictive validity. *Journal of Consulting and Clinical Psychology, 63*(5), 737–748.

Rice, M.E., Harris, G.T., & Cormier, C.A. (1992). An evaluation of a maximum security therapeutic community for psychopaths and other mentally disordered offenders. *Law and Human Behavior, 16*(4), 399–412.

Rieber, R. W. (1997). *Manufacturing social distress: Psychopathy in everyday life.* New York: Plenum.

Rowe, D.C. (1996). An adaptive strategy theory of crime and delinquency. In J.D. Hawkins (Ed.), *Delinquency and crime: Current theories* (pp. pp. 268–314). New York: Cambridge University Press.

Rowe, D.C., & Rodgers, J.L. (1989). Behavioral genetics, adolescent deviance, and "d": Contributions and issues. In G.R. Adams & R. Montemayor (Eds.), *Biology of adolescent behavior and development. Advances in adolescent development: An annual book series, Vol. 1* (Vol. 1, pp. 38–67). Thousand Oaks, CA: Sage.

Salekin, R.T., Rogers, R., & Sewell, K.W. (1996). A review and meta-analysis of the Psychopathy Checklist and Psychopathy Checklist—Revised: Predictive validity of dangerousness. *Clinical Psychology: Science and Practice, 3*(3), 203–215.

Seto, M.C., & Barbaree, H.E. (1999). Psychopathy, treatment behavior, and sex offender recidivism. *Journal of Interpersonal Violence, 14*(12), 1235–1248.

Seto, M.C., Khattar, N.A., Lalumiere, M.L., & Quinsey, V.L. (1997). Deception and sexual strategy in psychopathy. *Personality and Individual Differences, 22*(3), 301–307.

Seto, M.C., Lalumiere, M.L., & Quinsey, V.L. (1995). Sensation seeking and males' sexual strategy. *Personality and Individual Differences, 19*(5), 669–675.

Skilling, T.A., Quinsey, V.L., & Craig, W.M. (2001). Evidence of a taxon underlying serious antisocial behavior in boys. *Criminal Justice and Behavior, 28*(4), 450–470.

Smith, R.J., & Griffith, J.E. (1978). Psychopathy, the Machiavellian, and anomie. *Psychological Reports, 42*(1), 258.

Vila, B. (1997). Human nature and crime control: Improving the feasibility of nurturant strategies. *Politics and the Life Sciences, 16*(1), 3–21.

Vila, B.J. (1994). A general paradigm for understanding criminal behavior: Extending evolutionary ecological theory. *Criminology: An Interdisciplinary Journal, 32*, 311–359.

Widiger, T.A. (1998). Psychopathy and normal personality. In D.J. Cooke, A.E. Forth, & R.D. Hare (Eds.), *Psychopathy: Theory, research and implications for society.* Dordrecht: Kluwer Academic Publishers.

Widiger, T.A., Cadoret, R., Hare, R., Robins, L., Rutherford, M., Zanarini, M., Alterman, A., Apple, M., Corbitt, E., Forth, A., Hart, S., Kultermann, J., Woody, G., & Frances, A. (1996). DSM-IV antisocial personality disorder field trial. *Journal of Abnormal Psychology, 105*(1), 3–16.

Widiger, T.A., & Lynam, D.R. (1998). Psychopathy and the five-factor model of personality. In T. Millon & E. Simonsen (Eds.), *Psychopathy: Antisocial, criminal, and violent behavior* (pp. 171–187). New York: Guilford.

Williamson, S., Hare, R.D., & Wong, S. (1987). Violence: Criminal psychopaths and their victims. *Canadian Journal of Behavioral Science, 19*(4), 454–462.

Wong, S., & Hare, R.D. (in press). *Program Guidelines for the Institutional Treatment of Violent Psychopaths.* Toronto, ON: Multi-Health Systems.

Zuckerman, M. (1979). *Sensation seeking: Beyond the optimal level of arousal.* Hillsdale, NJ: L. Erlbaum Associates.

Zuckerman, M., Buchsbaum, M.S., & Murphy, D.L. (1980). Sensation seeking and its biological correlates. *Psychological Bulletin, 88*(1), 187–214.

4

# Combating Rape
*Views of an Evolutionary Psychologist*

*Linda Mealey*

According to traditional etiquette, the topics "sex, politics, and religion" are taboo for polite dinner conversation because they can lead to heated and acrimonious debate, charged with emotion and fueled by personal experience. Yet it is for exactly these reasons that we should talk about them; these are topics that have deep personal meaning and are amongst the most salient of the social dynamics that impact human life.

Progressively, what were once only private discussions have been moving out of bedrooms and boardrooms into public forums, and with this open airing of opinions has come the airing of grievances and "dirty laundry." Significant among these are the high incidence of, and often callous attitudes toward, rape. Although no one knows what rape rates really are, compared with the ideal of zero, they are grotesque. Further, it is clear that social institutions have not performed as well as they might in terms of preventing rape—and in some ways they have contributed to attitudes and situational circumstances that increase the incidence of rape.

This chapter briefly summarizes recent changes in the normative understanding of post-pubertal heterosexual rape; uses an evolutionary perspective to identify the core feature shared by all such rapes; presents a more complex evolutionary approach that acknowledges the situational and motivational multiplicity of the acts that fall into this category; and applies an evolutionary lens to evaluate a variety of proposals that have been offered to address social concerns regarding rape, rape offenders, and rape victims.

## HISTORICAL PERSPECTIVES ON RAPE

In many cultures throughout history, rape was one of several ways to obtain a sexual partner—or even a wife. In the Middle Ages, "marriage by rape" was not uncommon. Indeed, it is likely that this was one of the social institutions that contributed to the fairy-tale scenario of the princess being rescued by the knight in shining armor: knights were the henchmen of the aristocracy and their job was to protect their lord's lands and his family—especially his daughters. In some non-Western cultures, marriage by abduction was even more common and was practiced well into the twentieth century. (See White, 1988, for a list of 58 cultures that, even into the 1900s, continued to use abduction as a normative means of obtaining a wife.)

Throughout history and across cultures, men have conceived of women as a kind of property to be purchased, sold, traded, or stolen (Broude & Greene, 1976). Even where rape was frowned upon, most marriages were "arranged" as a socioeconomic transaction between the parents of the potential bride and groom or between the father of the potential bride and a suitor; the most common custom involved payments (of money or other forms of property) from the groom or his family to the father of the bride. (See Borgerhoff Mulder, 1995, for contemporary examples and Gies & Gies, 1987, for historical ones.)

## MODERN PERSPECTIVES ON RAPE

It was acknowledgment of the ancient, ubiquitous, and insidious nature of this notion that women are a kind of property that led to the modern portrayal of rape as a historical outcome of the patriarchal objectification of women. With the rise of the feminist movement in the United States, researchers and activists alike began to analyze the phenomenon of rape within a context of social and political power relations. (See especially Brownmiller, 1975, and Sanday, 1981.)

Somewhere over the course of this 20-year analysis, there occurred a subtle shift from the notion of women as economic property to the notion of women as an oppressed and manipulated class. This change in perspective ushered a further change in the conceptualization of the motive for rape. Specifically, prior to feminist analysis, rapists were seen as being sexually motivated: property ownership was desirable in relation to the functionality and productivity of the property and the consequent benefits conferred by its ownership; thus, ownership of a woman was desirable in relation to her sexual function and reproductive productivity. With the shift in emphasis from women as individual items of property to women as a faceless political class came a new concept of rape as an impersonal tool of social oppression. Rape came to be seen as a political act motivated by the desire for power, rather than as an individual act motivated by the desire for a sexual partner.

In the context of the feminist social zeitgeist, the work of Nicholas Groth (1980) provided a new taxonomy of rapists' motivations. Based on prison interviews of convicted rapists, Groth produced profiles of sexual offenders who were motivated by anger, power, or sadism—but not by sex. The fact that the majority of the rapists' victims were of peak reproductive age was deemed irrelevant, as was the fact that among the largest group of offenders, the so-called "power rapists," most had targeted an individual woman and had fantasized an inappropriate but clearly sexual script (see, e.g., Baker, 1999a). During the decades of the 1980s and 1990s, both academic and public ascriptions of the motivation for rape changed from "rape is a violent form of sex" to "rape is a sexual form of violence."

Most analysts agree about how and why this shift in the attribution of motive to rape occurred—but they differ in their assessment of the usefulness and veridicality of the modern view. Sociologists tend to focus on the successes and applied value of the "rape is violence" model, whereas biologists tend to criticize its narrowness and its proponents' faulty conflation of utility and fact (see, e.g., Darke, 1990; Jones, 1999; Muehlenhard et al., 1996; and Palmer et al., 1999).

Certainly the consequences of relabeling rape as an act of violence, rather than an act of sex, were manifold. It is much easier to mobilize people to lobby against violence than to poke their nose into other people's private matters and try to legislate against particular varieties of sex (e.g., Baker, 1999a). As a result, changes in public attitudes toward rape were accompanied by progressive legal reforms such as the implementation of "rape shield" laws (precluding the introduction in court of a rape victim's sexual history to be used as character evidence against her), the removal of the legal requirement that a victim somehow "prove" that she was not complicit (a burden placed upon rape victims which stood in marked contrast to the lack of such a requirement for victims of other crimes), and the removal of the automatic exclusion of "marital rape" from legal definitions (exclusions that legitimized the concept of women as being the property of individual men). (See Koss, 2000, or Spohn, 1999, for a historical summary of these reforms.) It was also at this time that the concept of "date rape" was introduced—the idea that sexual coercion, being an expression of male-on-female power, could happen just as easily within a friendship or dating relationship as it could in a stereotypical "stranger rape."

Without intending to minimize the successes of the feminist program against rape, and with great respect and gratitude for the strength, bravery, and skills of those who promoted it, it still needs to be said that the scientific and philosophical premises that underlie it are overly simplistic (Dutton, 1994) and that with this shift in emphasis from sex to power and politics, "the baby has been thrown out with the bathwater." Rape does not have to be "not sexual" to be violent, nor does it have to be "not violent" to be sexual. Taking an evolutionary perspective on rape allows us to expand our vision beyond the merely historic and the uniquely human, to see that violent sex/sexual violence occurs in other species as well. By expanding our view of the contexts in which sexual violence occurs, we see that "rape" is not simply an act of violence motivated by anger or the desire for power, but is the label we give to the similar outcome of a large set of behavioral dynamics, each of which is motivated by a different combination of desires and circumstances.

## EVOLUTIONARY PERSPECTIVES ON RAPE

Evolutionary biologists have documented aggression in the sexual interactions of many species other than humans. Although the type of aggression observed and the situational context in which it takes place vary from species to species, in all cases the aggression is overwhelmingly exhibited by males and directed toward females, just as it is in humans. (See, e.g., Barash, 1977; Briskie & Montgomerie, 1997; Clutton-Brock & Parker, 1995; Crawford & Galdikas, 1986; Nadler, 1999; Palmer, 1988, 1989; Smuts & Smuts, 1993; Thornhill, 1980.) Although an explanation of the immediate, proximate causes of a particular form or incident of sexual aggression would require comprehensive, multilevel analysis of the species, the individuals involved, and the circumstances of the setting (an effort that has been accomplished for many species and incidents but that is beyond the scope of this report), an explanation of the overall pattern of male-on-female sexual violence is readily forthcoming.

### Cross-Species Analysis

Because production of sperm is "cheap" relative to production of eggs (Symons, 1979), we find that across the animal kingdom, relative to females of their own species, males tend to dedicate more of their reproductive energy toward mating and less toward parenting. In species with internal fertilization, evolution further primes males, but not females, to attempt to maximize the number of matings and mating partners they can achieve; for females, on the other hand, "quality" of couplings is far more important than "quantity." This difference in the reproductive strategy of the two sexes leads to a greater "demand" for sex on the part of males than there is "supply" offered by females. As a result, there develops a competition among males for what might be considered a limited resource: sexual access to females.

In his 1994 magnum opus, *Sexual Selection,* Malte Andersson summarized five well-known processes via which males compete for limited mating opportunities: scrambles, endurance rivalry, contests, female choice, and sperm competition. It wasn't until a 1996 article that he added two more strategies to the list: sexual coercion and infanticide (Andersson & Iwasa, 1996). The lateness of these additions reflects the fact that for a long time, biologists had considered male aggression toward females to be aberrant behavior—the result of the occasional failure of ritualized dominance displays to constrain outbreaks of violence following intraspecific power struggles; it took the work of pioneering feminist biologists and primatologists (e.g., Hrdy, 1979; Small, 1993; Smuts & Smuts, 1993) to demonstrate the widespread use of antifemale reproductive tactics by males of other species. Ironically, it was during the same period that the influence of feminism in politics and the humanities was leading us to see human rape as dominance, not sex, and that the influence of feminism in the biological sciences was leading us to see nonhuman sexual violence as rape, not dominance.

Why do evolutionary biologists consider nonhuman sexual violence to be rape—and all that term connotes—and not just a form of intersexual domination? Because ever since Darwin, the concept of female mate choice has been crucial for our understanding of the evolution of species.

The courtship of animals is by no means so simple and short an affair as might be thought. The females are most excited by, or prefer pairing with, the more ornamented males, or those which are the best songsters, or play the best antics; but it is obviously probable, as has actually been observed in some cases, that they would at the same time prefer the more vigorous and lively males. Thus the more vigorous females, which are the first to breed, will have the choice of many males; and though they may not always select the strongest or the best armed, they will select those that are vigorous and well armed, and in other respects the most attractive. (Darwin, 1871/1981, p. 262)

In some species, females do not have much, if any, choice among potential sex partners, or even when or whether they copulate. In some insects, for example, a female may be literally carried away by a male who copulates with her while in midair; in other cases, females are mated before they even emerge as adults. Even in vertebrates, if females are receptive only briefly and/or population density is very low, they may have no options in terms of mate choice other than to accept or not accept the only available partner. For such species, mate choice is not a relevant concept. (See, e.g., Thornhill & Alcock, 1983, on insects; Briskie & Montgomerie, 1997, on birds; and Komers & Brotherton, 1997, on mammals.)

However, in most species, females do have the opportunity to exercise choice and discretion in terms of the timing of mating and who their partner(s) will be. For these species, the concept of "rape" implies, as it does for humans, *the coercive negation of a female's opportunity to exercise choice.* As law professor Katharine Baker (2000) points out in her (excellent) review "Biology for Feminists," "It is not the degradation, violence, (or) danger that makes certain reproductive acts rape. It is the fact that women do not want to be participating in those acts" (p. 815). In other words, it is the psychology of the victim, not some arbitrary level of violence or forcefulness, that defines what is and isn't rape. Baker continues, "'[rape] is the ultimate violation of self,' (and) comparison to other primates suggests that 'nonviolent' forms of coercion may be just as devastating as violent forms of coercion" (p. 817).

Indeed it is quite clear that females of many species are sometimes forced into reproductive acts that they are unable to resist (Barash, 1977; Crawford & Galdikas, 1986; Palmer, 1989; Smuts & Smuts, 1993). Such confrontations range from sneak attacks to persistent harassment and brutal assault (Mesnick, 1997). With no intention of demeaning the human experience, it remains the case that for those who have witnessed such an event in another species, the parallels of the non-human female's experience with that of a human rape victim are all too agonizingly apparent. In fact, Nancy and Randy Thornhill (Thornhill, 1996, and Thornhill & Thornhill, 1983, 1992) have made the point that female fear of, resistance to, and psychological trauma after rape are all indicators of the evolutionary significance of female mate choice and, reciprocally, of its loss. They have also pointed out that these aspects of female psychology and behavior would not have evolved and would not now appear in such strong and predictable fashion unless coercive negation of female mate choice had been a recurring event in evolutionary history.

### The "Making the Best of a Bad Job" Model

In what circumstances do males use coercion as a sexual tactic? The evolutionary model that most closely fits the conception of rape as a negation of female mate choice might best be called the "making the best of a bad job" model (after a phrase used by Dawkins, 1980, in a general discussion of alternative life strategies). In this scenario, rape is a "last-ditch" means by which an otherwise unsuccessful male might gain sexual access to an otherwise unapproachable female (e.g., Clutton-Brock & Parker, 1995; Starks & Blackie, 2000; Thornhill, 1999; Thornhill & Thornhill, 1983, 1992). According to this model, unattractive and subdominant males—those that are the least likely to attract consensual sexual partners through female choice—are the most likely to use a coercive strategy. Finding themselves at the bottom of the social heap with no other perceivable options for sexual interaction, they risk this strategy because, for them, none of the noncoercive strategies work.

The risks of opting for coercive strategies are many. Even among nonhuman species they include physical damage and/or reprisal from the female, her mate, and/or her allies. In social species there is the added risk of further degradation of an already low social status and reputation, with consequent loss of the benefits associated with group membership. Humans additionally risk costly legal penalties and reprisals. Yet according to this model, for some males, assessment of the relative risks versus probabilities of success leads to discarding the more standard (and socially acceptable) sexual strategies in exchange for a reliance on tactics of force. In this line, Randy Thornhill (Thornhill, 1999, and Thornhill & Palmer, 2000) has postulated six specific "rape adaptations," that is, evolved, specialized heuristics that serve as calculation devices to (subconsciously) determine when and under what circumstances use of force is likely to be (statistically and evolutionarily) an effective tactic.

### The "By-product" Model

On the other hand, Thornhill's recent coauthor, Craig Palmer (Palmer, 1989, and Thornhill & Palmer, 2000) argues that postulating the evolution of specialized "rape adaptations" is not the most parsimonious explanation of sexual violence in most species. In many species—most especially mammals—other

forms of male competition for females have led to significant sexual dimorphism in body size, strength, aggressiveness, and weaponry. Palmer suggests
that in these species sexual violence is a by-product of the physical and psychological differences between males and females. Given that males are more
sexually driven than females (cf. the sex difference in "quantity" vs. "quality"
mating strategies addressed earlier), among those species in which males are
also larger, stronger, and more aggressive than females, Palmer argues that use
of physical advantage as a means to coerce sexual compliance does not require
any further special adaptations or explanations.

Mammals are a strongly dimorphic class, with primates among the most
dimorphic of orders. Among primates, our closest relatives, the great apes, are
the most dimorphic of all (Weckerly, 1998). Males of all of the great apes are
known to use this physical advantage to force females into intercourse under
expedient circumstances, just as do humans (Crawford & Galdikas, 1986; Nadler, 1999; Smuts & Smuts, 1993).

In our own species, sexual dimorphism in body size is approximately 10%
by height and 20% by weight (Alexander et al., 1979; Gaulin & Boster, 1985;
Wolfe & Gray, 1982); dimorphism in strength, especially of the arms and upper
body, is much greater (Fox et al., 1993; Laubach, 1976; Ross & Ward, 1982).
Certainly men can (and do) use their physical strength to sometimes get what
they want, and the by-product model predicts that men who tend to rely on
tactics of physical aggression as a means to an end (generally) will also be likely
to use physical aggression as a means to sexual ends (Ellis, 1991a, 1991b). A
variety of studies have documented this to be the case—for both partnered and
unpartnered men (Dean & Malamuth, 1997; DeMaris, 1997; Malamuth, 1996;
Malamuth et al., 1980; Malamuth & Malamuth, 1999; Malamuth et al., 1991).
In contrast to the common interpretation of these studies—that because physical power is the means, psychological power must be the end—the by-product
model is more parsimonious, stating that physical power is the means, but
sexual access is the end.

## The "Mate Guarding" Model

That sexual coercion might occur even in the context of long-term partnered
relationships makes sense if we retain the notion that men have traditionally
conceived of women as property (Wilson & Daly, 1992, 1996). But keep in
mind that property is *valuable* and that its value is in relation to its functionality and its productivity—so, from an evolutionary perspective, being in a
long-term relationship is not valuable (in terms of reproductive fitness) if one's
partner is infertile or sexually inaccessible. DeMaris (1997) considers that
within the marital relationship, male violence is used to "[create] a climate of
fear in which women are coerced into having sex more often than they would
otherwise assent to" (p. 361). He reported that couples experiencing male-on-
female violence have intercourse, on average, two-and-a-half times more often

per month than other couples and, after controlling for other relevant factors, he concluded that male-on-female violence is a tactic of "sexual extortion."

It is also important to keep in mind that a property's value is in relation to the benefits it confers *upon its owner:* Property that is stolen or regularly used by others comes to be of considerably less worth. From this perspective it is not surprising to see that males of sexually dimorphic primate species aggressively guard their fertile female consort(s) against the sexual advances of other would-be suitors—even against the will and to the physical detriment of the consort(s) (Mesnick, 1997; Smuts, 1995; Smuts & Smuts, 1993). The physical and sexual harassment of women by abusive husbands and lovers can, thus, be seen as a kind of proprietary mate guarding similar to that found in other species (Buss, 1988a, 1996; Flinn, 1985; Smuts, 1992/1996).

The fact that shared property is less valued than property to which one has exclusive use is also consistent with the fact that abusive men typically impose restrictions on their partners that prevent them from other social contacts. Abused partners are often forbidden to use the telephone, get a driver's license, visit with relatives, and so on (Schumacher et al., 2001), and women who attempt to circumvent these attempts at control and/or to leave their abusive partner (i.e., from their "owner's" perspective, women who share themselves with others) are more likely to be murdered by their partner than those who remain within the abuser-specified confines of the relationship (Daly & Wilson, 1996; Wilson & Daly, 1996; Wilson et al., 1997).

Further evidence that spousal abuse is an extreme form of proprietary mate guarding comes from analysis of the circumstances in which it most commonly occurs. Partner abuse is almost exclusively directed: by men toward women (Dobash et al., 1992); at women of child-bearing age (Daly & Wilson, 1996); at women with children by a previous partner (Daly et al., 1993; Daly et al., 1997); and at women whose history or behavior might be interpreted by a jealous male as an indication of sexual infidelity (Counts et al., 1992; Figueredo & McCloskey 1993). In the eyes of a partnered, abusive male, part of the marriage "contract" is an exchange of his resources (house, income, social standing) for her sexual exclusivity; he feels he must use force to enforce the contract and prevent any possibility of defection. (See Crawford & Johnston, 1999, for an evolutionary, mathematical model of sexual exchange.)

### The "Cad/dad" Model

Another evolutionary model that fits better to cases of marital than of stranger rape is what might be called the "cad/dad" model. In 1982, Patricia Draper and Henry Harpending published a now-classic article that provided an evolutionary explanation for within—and cross-cultural patterns in partnering and parenting. They noted that men and women who had grown up in a father-absent family or culture were likely to engage in sexual activity at an earlier age, and with more partners, than those who had grown up in a dual-parent household or culture. In essence, compared with those who grew up in a dual-parent household, individuals of both sexes who came from mother-only households were more likely to adopt a "quantity" strategy than a "quality" strategy. Because males can shift further toward "quantity" than can females (who, unlike males, almost always provide parental care for their children), males who took the "quantity" ("love 'em and leave 'em") strategy got nicknamed "cads," whereas males who took the "quality" ("bringing home the bacon") strategy got nicknamed "dads." (See also Biller, 1981, and Stevenson, & Black, 1988, for documentation of this pattern.)

There has been significant debate over the roles of genetic versus socioenvironmental "causes" of this transgenerational behavioral pattern—that is, over the relative extent to which "cads" and "dads" might be "born" or "made" (Belsky, 1997, 2000; Belsky et al., 1991; Chisholm, 1996; Gangestad & Simpson, 1990; Hill et al., 1994; Mealey, 1995, 2000a; Rowe, 2000; Rowe et al., 1997; Wilson & Daly, 1997). However, regardless of their position in this debate, all participants agree that the pattern reflects individual differences in allocation of reproductive effort toward maximizing mating opportunities (the "quantity" strategy) versus maximizing investment in a single partner and set of offspring (the "quality" strategy). Research also suggests that "cads," in addition to using a "love 'em and leave 'em" strategy, are more likely than "dads" to use deceptive, antisocial, and coercive tactics in their sexual (and nonsexual) interactions (Hersch & Gray-Little, 1998; Lalumiere & Quinsey, 1999; Malamuth et al., 1995; Rowe et al., 1997; Seto et al., 1997; Tooke & Camire, 1991).

### The "Macho BMOC" Model

The "cad/dad" model also provides a good fit to patterns of date rape; in this context, I prefer to call it the "macho BMOC" model. Specifically, in contrast to the frustrated, disenfranchised, socially inadequate loner who must rely on a coercive strategy to "make the best of a bad job," among date rapists, the opposite profile is more often the case: Male college students who admit to behavior that would legally qualify as rape are typically more popular and report more consensual sexual partners than their peers (Kanin, 1985; Lalumiere et al., 1996; Lalumiere & Quinsey, 1999; Malamuth et al., 1991). These "macho" Big-Men-On-Campus consider themselves (correctly) to be attractive and sexually successful, but because their self-assessment is so positive, they feel no need to offer any personal attention, concern, or commitment to their potential sexual partner(s). In the language of social exchange theory, they believe that they have already brought something extremely valuable to the bargaining table—so how could anyone possibly say "no"? As a consequence of this attitude, they sometimes don't take no for an answer. (See Kenrick et al., 1993, and Regan, 1998, for excellent integrations of social exchange theory and evolutionary theory as related to mating strategies in general. See Mosher, 1991, for an equally excellent discussion of machismo and male sexuality.)

## The "Sexy Son" Model

And then there's the indecorous suggestion that sometimes the macho BMOC is right, and his conquest's no doesn't really mean no. Muehlenhard and Hollabaugh (1988) reported that approximately 40% of a sample of U.S. college women admitted that they had, on at least one occasion, "said 'no' when they meant 'yes.'" This result was replicated in three more groups by Sprecher et al. (1994) with almost exactly the same results. Furthermore, at least four studies have found that a significant minority of date rape "victims" continue to date the perpetrator subsequent to the rape (Ellis, 1998; Koss, 1988; Murnen, Perot & Byrne, 1989; Wilson & Durrenberger, 1982). Thus, one rather counterintuitive possibility is that male coercive sexuality is actually selected through the process of female choice. This is what I refer to as the "sexy son" model of rape (Mealey, 1992, 2000b).

Consider this. From an evolutionary perspective, one viable female mating strategy is to pick as the father of one's offspring an individual whose own sons will be highly likely to be reproductively successful. Thus, if sexually coercive males father more offspring than other males, females who have sons by those males (either by force or by choice) will pass on more of their own genes through the success of their own sons (who inherit their father's coercive attributes). Furthermore, because these females will, on average, have more female descendants as well, whatever aspects of their own attributes or behaviors contribute to their mate choice *or seeming lack of mate choice* will also be passed on to future generations of females.

Evidence that this form of selection might occur in humans resides in the fact that an identifiable minority of women (women labeled "hyperfeminine" based on their scores on personality and sex roles questionnaires) are specifically attracted to "macho" and "sexually coercive" men (Maybach & Gold, 1994). Furthermore, in all four studies (cited earlier) that documented that a significant percentage of women continue to date a date rapist after the rape, it was found that a larger percentage of women continue to date the perpetrator of a *completed* rape than of an *attempted, but uncompleted* rape—as if they were testing the persistence of their partner. Despite that the majority of women are psychologically traumatized after such an experience, the contrary but not entirely anomalous behavior of a noticeable minority not only encourages and rewards coercive sexual behavior at the individual level, but also allows it to be genetically selected as one of several evolutionarily effective strategies.

## Phenocopies and the Multiplicity of Rape

In the evolutionary literature, it is acknowledged that similar phenotypes (observable traits) might result from different genotypes and genotype-environment interactions, producing what are referred to as "phenocopies" (Dobzhansky, 1962, p.112). I suggest that the phenomenon we call "rape" is actually a collection of phenocopies: a set of somewhat different behaviors that occur under somewhat different circumstances but that all have a similar outcome—that is, the coercive negation of female mate choice (Mealey, 1999). (For other arguments suggesting the "multiplicity" of rape, see also Baker, 1997; Barbaree & Marshall, 1991; Becker & Kaplan, 1991; Hall & Hirschman, 1991; Knight, 1999; Knight & Prentky, 1993; Prentky & Knight, 1991.)

If rapists are using a variety of coercive strategies under a variety of conditions, it would behoove us to explore those strategies so that we can understand the different motivations of rapists and the different circumstances that can sometimes lead to rape (Baker, 1997, 1999b; Cleveland et al., 1999; Mealey, 1999). Based on the preceding discussion, I suggest the following as a beginning:

- *"Making the best of a bad job"*—when men who are perceived to be socially undesirable resort to stealth, deceit, and force to "take whatever they can get"

- *"By-product"*—when men who, having been rewarded in the past for using aggressive tactics, do not hesitate to use similar tactics when their objective is sexual access to a woman

- *"Mate guarding"*—when men perceive their sexual partnership as exclusive and unretractable and (therefore) "defend their property" not only against all challengers, but also against any change of heart or "renegotiation" initiatives of their partner

- *"Cad/dad"*—when men in matrifocal cultures or subcultures learn to direct their sexual interests casually and opportunistically, without particular interest in the relational aspects of sexuality

- *"Macho BMOC"*—when men of desirable social status equate that status with psychological power over others, and then use that power to usurp the discretional mate choice of women

- *"Sexy son"*—when sexually aggressive tactics are reinforced (consciously or not) by female mate choice (or lack thereof)

I hasten to add that the above conditions are neither mutually exclusive nor entirely comprehensive. Other circumstances or sources of motivation to rape are also plausible, and the list should be expanded. For example:

- *"Social facilitation"*—when men who are under peer pressure to "prove" themselves vis-à-vis other men use sexual exploitation of women as one means to earn or to signal status (e.g., as in gang rape or rape during war)

This type of behavior is not motivated by sex per se; rather, sex is the means to the ends. In this regard, the social facilitation model does fit the feminist model of rape as violence. From an evolutionary perspective, such behavior has two potential "payoffs": the social benefits of increased prestige, power, and reputation, as well as the possible direct reproductive benefits. The circumstances of group rape and group-facilitated rape also entail fewer risks than other situations leading to rape, in that there is reduced probability of social reprisal. (See, e.g., Baker, 1999a, 1999b; Mosher, 1991.)

I would also add:

- *"Cycle of violence"*—when men who, as a result of early trauma (such as child abuse), are psychologically or physiologically damaged and consequently cannot develop normal social/sexual relationships

In evolutionary terms this would be an example of what is called "developmental canalization"—whereby one of many potential developmental outcomes is effected in relation to the environmental stimuli and conditions that impinge during critical periods. As with cad/dad behaviors, the transgenerational pattern of abuse could be mediated through genetic or sociocultural inheritance. (See, e.g., Dutton, 1995; Marshall et al., 1993; Money, 1986; and Sappington, 2000.)

Baker (1997) has argued that a typology of rape is necessary in order to aid judges in determining whether particular kinds of evidence are relevant to possible motive, and whether they should, therefore, be admissible in court. I would add that having such a typology will also prove useful for rape prevention. *Although the situation-sensitivity of behavioral strategies precludes identification and labeling of individual men or rapists as "types," identification of different situations that increase the various motivations to rape will surely help us to identify points at which social intervention is likely to be feasible and effective* (Cleveland et al., 1999; Hall & Barongan, 1997; Hall & Hirschman, 1991).

## POLICY IMPLICATIONS

If there are many different circumstances and (therefore) motives that lead to coercive negation of female choice, then many different intervention strategies will be required. Kennan (1998) and Baker (1997, 2000) have offered suggestions for legal reform and judicial procedure that would increase rape conviction rates, but legal reforms that simply increase conviction rates do not prevent harm. Furthermore, even if increased conviction rates were to have a deterrent effect (a topic of debate), if those convictions were only for one type of rape occurring under one constellation of circumstances, other types of rape would still continue. Some men might even switch tactics, but for, and with, the same end (Cleveland et al., 1999).

### Rape as an "Ethical Pathology"

How can an evolutionary perspective help us to determine what interventions might be effective for rape prevention? In 1997, I suggested that we use the term *ethical pathologies* to refer to behaviors that represent a potentially adaptive strategy for one individual, but which have dysfunctional, maladaptive consequences for one or more other parties (Mealey, 1997). Rape is clearly a behavior that falls in this category (Mealey, 1999).

Because, by definition, they involve interactions between two or more parties, the dynamics of ethical pathologies will have *coevolved* over time: strategies of the antagonist(s) will elicit corresponding *counterstrategies* from the victim(s) or potential victim(s). Deception, for example, will be countered by deception-detection measures, whereas theft will be countered by protective measures. (See Alexander, 1987, Axelrod, 1987, and Hirshleifer & Coll, 1988, for general discussion of "evolutionary arms races" in human morality. See Cosmides, 1989; Ekman, 1985/1992; Frank, 1988; Lewis & Saarni, 1993; and Mealey et al., 1996, more specifically on deception-detection. See Machalek & Cohen, 1991; Mealey, 1995/1997; Vila, 1997; Vila & Cohen, 1993, on crime prevention.)

In an ethical pathology, we should find that rape is countered by rape-avoidance and rape-response strategies. Indeed, if rape is actually a set of phenocopies that are differentially motivated and occur under different conditions, but that all have a similar outcome, then we should expect to find a set of rape-avoidance strategies to counter the differentially motivated rapes, but only one rape-response strategy (as would be appropriate to the one outcome: expropriation or loss of mate choice). I would argue that this is the case.

Certainly we are all familiar with the predictable and coordinated unfolding of what has come to be called the Rape Trauma Syndrome (e.g., Becker & Kaplan, 1991; Kahn, 1984; van Berlo & Ensink, 2000). First comes shock and a generalized stress response (itself an evolutionary adaptation), then anger and depression (which are, respectively, adaptive responses to cheating or betrayal and diminished capacity or status). In addition, there are rape-specific responses such as sexual disinterest/dysfunction and fear or distrust of men (e.g., Resick, 1990). As mentioned previously, Randy and Nancy Thornhill (Thornhill, 1996; Thornhill & Palmer, 2000; Thornhill & Thornhill, 1992) have made the argument that this complex psychological response to rape is an adaptation, and the fact that the Rape Trauma Syndrome is generalizable across so many different women, situations, and types of rape, suggests that it is a counter to what the evolved psyche perceives—regardless of modus operandus—to be a single outcome: expropriation of mate choice. In contrast, rape avoidance strategies, like the motivations and circumstances of rape, are multitudinous. They range from individual precautionary measures and situational risk assessment, to personalized social alliances (individual "protector" males as well as all-female social groupings), organized self-defense classes, rape crisis centers, and military, business, and campus educational workshops.

Interestingly, many recent intervention attempts have been framed in terms of the metaphor of predator and prey coevolution. Although the motivations of predators and rapists are not analogous (making overgeneralization of the terminology somewhat dangerous), the metaphor is indeed apt with regard to the coevolutionary fact that predators draw on a diversity of strategies that prey must be able to counter if they are to become "survivors" rather than "victims." Depending on circumstances, predators may rely on stealth, pursuit, overwhelming strength, and even deception. Prey must respond with reciprocal counterstrategies such as increased vigilance, escape tactics, self-defense, and finely tuned senses of discrimination.

## Rape Prevention and the "Extended Phenotype"

If rape and rape avoidance strategies have coevolved, then the first place to look for successful rape avoidance strategies is in the psychology and behavior of potential victims. In this regard, evolutionary and feminist perspectives converge: it is scientifically wise, as well as socially prudent, to listen to the voices of women.

From an evolutionary perspective, institutions (such as schools, legislatures, courts, prisons) and service providers (such as counselors, lawyers, health care providers, police) are part of the "extended phenotype" (Dawkins, 1982) that individuals, families, and societies have "evolved." They are, in essence, tools that enable us to enhance and elaborate the tactics that we use in our many (coevolutionary) social interactions. Thus, one immediately obvious implication of the coevolutionary perspective is that women need to be abundantly represented in policymaking and policy-implementing organizations. Yet, for a variety of reasons (too many and too complex to deal with here), they are not (see Mealey, 2000b). To the extent that women are not represented in decision-making bodies and among service providers, social policies and interpersonal power dynamics will reflect male perspectives more than female perspectives.

Feminists, psychologists, and evolutionary biologists all agree that men and women do perceive, frame, and interpret things differently—especially sexual behaviors, intentions, and motivations (Abbey et al., 1996; Beyers et al., 2000; Geer, 1996; Geer & Manguno-Mire, 1996; Miller & Simpson, 1991; Pryor et al., 1997). Men are more likely than women to interpret ambiguous body language (e.g., nonsexual touch, eye contact) as sexual signaling (Abbey & Melby, 1986); they are also more likely than women to interpret a friendly gesture as sexual (Kowalski, 1992) and a sexual gesture as friendly (Gutek, 1992, cited in Browne, 1997). Some men even interpret unfriendly gestures as sexual (Malamuth & Brown, 1994)! As Browne (1997) puts it, "men inhabit a more sexualized world than women do" (p. 22).

This, of course, makes sense: greater salience of sex, greater sensitivity to sexual cues, and lower threshold for sexual action are all reflections of the greater likelihood of success of the "quantity strategy" for men than for women (Mealey, 2000b). Yet the fact of such (frequently dramatic) differences between a typical male's perspective on an incident and a typical female's perspective of the same incident means that interpretation of events by police, psychiatrists, judges, legislators, and so on, will likely be biased in relation to gender and in relation to gender representativeness in the various occupations. The recent increases seen in the numbers of women police officers, psychologists, physicians, and politicians (due in large part to efforts of feminist activists) can only be helpful in this regard, and should be further encouraged.

It is also the case that, given the general consensus that men's and women's perceptions differ, some courts have started to consider testimony in light of a "reasonable woman standard" as opposed to the traditional "reasonable person standard" (e.g., Blumenthal, 1998; Browne, 1997). This approach has been helpful in that it highlights the victim's psychological experience of negated mate choice (the *outcome* of any form of sexual coercion) as opposed to the *tactic* used to achieve it—thereby circumventing the sometimes insurmountable problem of defining what tactics qualify as "coercion" or "use of force." This approach is controversial, however, in that it seems to shift the burden of proof from the accuser to the accused, and, thereby, to assume the accused is guilty until proven innocent. Furthermore, although the task of "scripting" a normative or stereotypical "reasonable woman" is important and desirable at this juncture in time, it is an unenviable task, fraught with danger, and although evolutionary biology could clearly be of help here, I fear that the discipline will be forced to shoulder the blame for the inevitable shortcomings of any such script. (See related discussion in Denno, 1999; Jones, 1999, Part V.B.; and Jones, 2000.)

## Sex Education

Drawing on a "reasonable woman" standard in the courts will help to increase conviction rates. More important, however, is educating men to understand the "reasonable" woman's perspective before a rape occurs. Feminist initiatives have already generated a plethora of education programs targeted at boys and men in all walks of life. These typically attempt to draw on human empathy by portraying the psychological devastation that follows rape. However, by stating flatly that "rape is violence, not sex," the psychology and experience of men is not considered. In the long run, although such messages may "hit home" with women listeners, the targeted audience of men often remains unreached and unmoved. It is thus no wonder that men "just don't get it."

For boys and men to "get it," that is, to come to understand a woman's perspective, differences between the male and female psyche have to be addressed: sex differences in emotion and cognition cannot be denied or swept under the rug. Our resolve to institute and uphold equal rights for men and women *neither requires nor means* that men and women are psychologically identical, and acknowledgment of real sex differences does not have to be an evil slippery slope toward a two-class society that uses pseudoscience to justify repression of women. Most people already believe that, and even understand

at some level how and why, men and women are different. We should acknowledge this correct instinct and build upon people's inherent (albeit rudimentary)
knowledge, rather than try to teach something that is not only wrong, but is
what animal psychologists would call "contraprepared"—so unrealistic that the
mind will not *ever* "get it" (Seligman, 1970).

Once men (and women) have a better understanding of sex differences, it
would not be a bad idea to further educate men in the arts of seduction from
a woman's perspective. Men and boys want to know "what women want." By
framing sex education in positive light—offering men new sexual perspectives,
knowledge, and skills rather than saddling them with restrictions, blame, and
unilateral responsibilities—I suggest that we might create incentives for lis-
tening rather than create hostility, reactance, and disbelief.

## Men as Allies

Men's sometimes hostile reactions to feminist education initiatives should
not be surprising. If we conceive of rape in terms of a coevolutionary dynamic,
then we should expect to see battle lines drawn between those who stand to
gain from it and those who stand to suffer. Because it is almost uniformly men
who stand to gain and women who stand to suffer, sexual coercion is often
perceived to be solely a "women's issue" (Studd, 1996). On the other hand,
every woman is some man's daughter and, very likely, some man's sister,
cousin, or niece; she is certainly a member of some man's community. We
might, therefore, draw upon the predilection of men to support the interests
of their kin and their communities, regardless of sex. How?

There is significant cross-cultural variance in male support of women and
male investment in "women's issues." According to Smuts (1992/1996), men
are less likely to support women—even their women kin—"when male alliances are particularly important." That is, whether a man will support his wife
or his women kin against the aggressions of other men is culturally contingent
and is mediated through perception of the relative social and political costs and
benefits of each option. (See also Low, 1992). Therefore, judicious modification
of these social and political costs might be implemented to make prowomen
actions more frequently rewarded and antiwomen actions more frequently
costly.

For example, Miller (1996) has suggested that much of male politicking is a
form of social display, and that many (especially young) men take on female-
friendly positions and social causes as a way of impressing and attracting
women. If the same behaviors that naturally earn the respect and favor of
women can be framed so as to also earn the respect of other men, many gender
gaps could be simultaneously bridged. This strategy would require putting
money where our mouth is by showering a variety of awards and attention on
profeminist men and boys, and educating youths about the successes of profeminist male role models. Universities and businesses that have instituted the

use of volunteer or paid safety escorts have, for example, established desirable prosocial roles for men, just as education campaigns have recreated the respectable, prosocial role of "designated driver" out of what before was often seen as the undesirable role of "spoiler" or "party pooper." Generally, if social status can be conferred upon men who "get it" and who support the rights of women (rather than upon those who compete for the most "notches" in their "gun"), some of men's natural competitive energies could be channeled into female-friendly rather than female-aggressive activity (Baker, 1997, 1999a).

Success of this particular counterstrategy would require not just support of profemale efforts, but also the elimination (by example and by law) of antifemale forms of male bonding exercises promulgated by the leaders of all or mostly male groups such as the military, some corporate bodies, social clubs, and fraternities. Although the "bonding" of any in-group inevitably requires the formation of an out-group, there is no reason that the out-group of a mostly-male in-group has to be females—or, for that matter, any group of people. Bonded social groups can be (and often are) formed to "battle" common "enemies" such as genetic disease, pollution, fire, and so on, and many men's groups are involved in such prosocial activities. Organizations that enroll and appeal to young men and boys must banish antifemale traditions and rituals, and substitute other forms of bonding activities.

In many ways the above social-psychological and educational strategies parallel ongoing feminist initiatives to rewrite "social scripts" about what constitutes manliness. But because men will always strive for respect from other men, suggested revisions of our "social scripts" cannot come only from women (Dutton, 1994); the good efforts and works of feminist, masculinist, and humanist men and men's groups must also be acknowledged, advertised, and supported. Men's leadership, especially of mostly male groups, can harness some of the inherent power of in-groups, peer pressure, social conformity, and modeling, and use that power for prosocial, rather than antisocial, action.

## Women as Allies

Of course, women also can draw on the help of other women to help deter or avoid sexually aggressive males. Just the presence of another person can be sufficient to dissuade a potential perpetrator from escalating a casual exchange into an assault. Implicit knowledge of this fact leads many women to travel and even date in pairs or groups, and presumably leads batterers to restrict even the female friendships of their abused partners. Expressions of the rape counterstrategy to form coalitions of mutually supportive women can be seen not only in the form of personal friendships and associations, but also in "extended phenotypes" such as rallies, women's centers, political action groups, and even laws and academic publications.

Women's coalitions have been enormously valuable and successful at both the individual and the societal level. On the other hand, in an interesting and rather personal essay, law professor Cheryl Hanna (1999) notes a possible downside of some aspects of the most recent incarnation of the women's movement. "Girl power," she says,

sells not just empowerment, but also protection by encouraging girls to be aggressive and self-assertive. [This] represents a significant shift in the way young women are being taught to relate to the world. . . . (E)arly feminists . . . would be quite pleased, I believe, to see young women today play as tough as the boys. (But) one of the dangers of the "girl power" movement is that it fails to explicitly teach young women that their sexual motivations may not be the same as their male counterparts. . . . Because of their newfound sexual freedom . . . girls may be putting themselves in situations where they are more, rather than less, vulnerable to male aggression. (p. 264)

With a good deal of insight into the complexity of coevolved sociosexual systems, she continues:

The "girl power" movement can be understood biologically as part of a female counter-strategy to reduce male violence by refusing to be sexually passive. Yet, paradoxically, rather than decrease male sexual coercion, the culture of "girl power" may simply be shifting the variables upon which females compete for males. . . . [(Our] new-found aggressiveness may not be turning men off, but turning them on. (pp. 264, 266)

Female sexual assertiveness is certainly one sign that males interpret to mean that a potential partner is interested in a short-term sexual encounter (Buss, 1988b, 1992, 1998; Wiederman & Dubois, 1998), and Hanna suggests that modern young women "may attract men without a clear understanding that the sexes may have very different long-term expectations" (p. 267). This possibility may be particularly likely and dangerous at this point in history when, as a result of increased nutrition (and perhaps, environmental estrogens), girls as young as eight and nine years old are reaching sexual, but not intellectual or emotional, maturity (Herman-Giddens et al., 1997). Hanna suggests that young women need to be educated about "the costs as well as the benefits of their mating strategies" (p. 267). Thus, women and girls, like men and boys, would profit from sex education that explains, rather than denies, sex differences in psychology and sexuality.

### Learning to Say Yes

Of course, a sexual act is not rape if it's an outcome of, rather than a negation of, female choice, and many men accused of rape (especially date rape) later claim that their victim really was "asking for it." This leads us to the question: If female sexual assertiveness has long been used to signal interest in a short-term sexual encounter, but now is used as a badge of emancipation (i.e., flaunting one's power of choice without using it), how is a man to know when a woman is "asking for it" and when she is not?

The "obvious" answer according to some, is that an explicit yes means yes and all else means no (see, e.g., Baker, 1999a). But, as discussed in the section on the "sexy son" model, many women are attracted to aggressive sexuality. In fact, "rape" fantasies consistently rate high on lists of women's techniques of self-arousal (e.g. Masters et al., 1995), and many women do "play games" by saying no when they mean yes. The result of this ambiguity in communication is that the same behavior—even by the same man in the same circumstances—might be perceived by one woman as rape, but by another as proof of his desire (and her desirability).

In these circumstances it is simplistic (and unfair) to expect men to interpret all ambiguous signals as a lack of interest. A more reasonable solution to this dilemma is to reduce signaling ambiguity by creating a tolerance of, and social scripts for, women who want to say yes. We have experienced two decades of teaching young people to "just say no," but when all one knows how to say is no, then of course communication becomes muddled.

## Prostitution

It should also be considered that one possible option to which an informed woman might say yes is prostitution (e.g., Almodovar, 1990/1991). Throughout history and across cultures, women have exchanged sex—with its risks of sexual disease, possible pregnancy, and reduced attractiveness as a long-term mate—for money, food, or gifts (Bullough & Bullough, 1996; Burley & Symanski, 1981). Unfortunately, because of the stigma attached to the profession and many of the circumstances associated with it, most prostitutes have not arrived at their profession through informed choice. Decriminalization of prostitution, with the consequent licensing, health care service, and unionization that would go with it, would reduce the physical and social costs of prostitution while increasing the education, status, options, and power of both those who choose to pursue it, as well as those who would prefer not to, but who, under current conditions, are unable to choose anything else (see, e.g., Bullough & Bullough, 1996).

Some might say that to legitimize the commercialization of a person's body—no matter what the financial payoff—is equivalent to, or at least as bad as, rape. For evolutionary psychologists, however, female choice is the key. Prostitution resultant from coercion or lack of choice would, indeed, be equivalent to rape; but prostitution arrived at through informed choice and from an array of options would be viewed as one possible outcome of the interplay of male and female strategies *in which females maintain control of their sexuality.*

Decriminalization of prostitution would provide an acceptable sexual outlet to those who are sexually disenfranchised, and thus would decrease rape rates to the extent that rape is a strategy of those trying to "make the best of a bad job" and "take what they can get." More important, empowerment of prostitutes and destigmatization of their profession would decrease the abuse and rape of prostitutes that is currently encouraged by social scripts that allow others to view them as degraded and choiceless minions rather than as legitimate business partners.

## Pornography

Like prostitution, pornography is a topic that spurs heated debate. In fact, many of the arguments are the same: Is posing for pornography inherently degrading? Could it ever result from truly free and informed choice? If/when freely chosen, does it have social costs for others? Is one of those costs increased risk of rape? If so, would that risk increase or decrease if pornography became more freely available and/or less stigmatized? (See, e.g., Koop, 1987; McCormack, 1988.)

Results of social science research have converged on the conclusion that although depictions of sexual violence can reduce inhibitions that normally restrain aggression, it is the violence component of those depictions, not the sexual component, that has an effect, and even then, only on certain individuals and only in the presence of other risk factors (e.g., Barnes, Malamuth & Check, 1984; Donnerstein & Linz, 1986; Linz, Penrod & Donnerstein, 1986; Murrin & Laws, 1990; Seto, Maric & Barbaree, 2001). In fact, the bulk of evidence suggests that availability of pornography does not encourage sexual violence (e.g., Linz, Donnerstein & Penrod, 1987; Murrin & Laws, 1990; Smith, 1987; Wilcox, 1987) and may actually decrease it (e.g., Diamond & Uchiyama, 1999; Kutchinsky, 1991; but see concerns in Zillmann, 2000).

Although it is, thus, probably unwise to allow the indiscriminant pairing of images of violence with images of sexuality, unfortunately, as with prostitution, the criminalization of a commodity or an activity that is in demand can lead to both psychological reactance and the debasing of the activity through association with organized and/or street crime. Regulation of images is, therefore, a better alternative than unilateral banning. Of course regulation is the intent of current obscenity laws, but these have proven impossible to uniformly interpret and enforce. An alternative is to encourage self-censorship through education, peer support, and the creation of new social scripts. Japan, for example, is known for its ease of availability of violent pornography and also a very low rape rate. This combination has generally been attributed to (a) the lack of taboo and compartmentalization of sex in Japan and (b) strong social sanctions against aggression (e.g., Diamond & Uchiyama, 1999; Murrin & Laws, 1990). Reformulation of sexual assault and obscenity laws needs to be part of a greater enterprise dedicated toward collectivist reframing of what constitutes legitimate use, versus abuse, of sexuality (Baker, 1999a; Hall & Barongan, 1997).

## Retribution and Restoration

So far the theme of these recommendations has been for revision of social scripts in order to minimize the kinds and numbers of social situations that might encourage various forms of coercive negation of female choice. Certainly prevention is a better goal than post-hoc retribution. But until the time that there is no rape, what does evolutionary theory have to say in terms of punishment?

In theory, to the extent that retributive punishment might serve as a deterrent, it must be swift, predictable, and consistent (e.g., Bartol & Bartol, 1994). Yet these features of punishment are not achievable in a system of justice in which protection of the innocent comes first and foremost, and every benefit of the doubt is given to the accused. Further, humans are not utterly rational automatons, and even when punishment is swift and consistent, psychological reactance sometimes stimulates offenders to act emotionally and take revenge upon their accusers, actually increasing overall levels of violence (e.g., Koss, 2000). Thus, even though we may try to make punishments for rape more costly and more salient—and, therefore, more likely to be included in a potential rapist's (conscious or unconscious) cost/benefit analysis (Thornhill & Palmer, 2000)—it is unlikely that we will be able to significantly reduce rape rates in this way.

There is, however, another feature of retribution besides its potential value in deterrence; that is, its value in helping to heal the victim. Calling once again upon the concepts of "ethical pathologies" and "extended phenotypes," we can look at the legal system not only as a meter of punishment of offenders, but also as a support system for victims.

Historically, rape victims have suffered what has come to be called the "second injury" (Kahn, 1984); that is, they have tended to suffer further victimization and degradation as they make their way through the various bureaucracies that constitute our medical and social "services," the police, and the courts. Through social activism of the 1970s, and 1980s, the feminist movement helped to change much of this (Koss, 2000; Spohn, 1999). More recently, similar initiatives have helped to implement victims' assistance programs and programs of "restorative justice" that better address the psychological needs of victims, their families, and their communities (e.g., Davis & Henley, 1990; Kelly, 1990; Maguire & Shapland, 1990; Umbreit & Jacobson, 1997).

Restorative justice and other mediation efforts draw—often explicitly—on the kinds of social interventions that traditional cultures have relied upon to resolve conflicts and "keep the peace" (Lombardi, 1997). In the small social groups that characterized most of human evolutionary history, family and community networks provided emotional and practical support for victims, forums for mediation of disputes, and "punishments" for offenders that simultaneously shamed them (providing both specific and general deterrence) while offering a chance for redemption and reintegration into the community (Gaulin & McBurney, 2001; Koss, 2000; Walsh, 2000). Promoters of modern forms of restorative justice are drawing upon a long history of victim empowerment structures designed by cultural evolution as "extended phenotypes" of victims and potential victims.

## CONCLUSION

Viewing the phenomenon of rape through an evolutionary lens allows us to:

1. Appreciate the fact that sexual coercion is widespread across species and not just a phenomenon restricted to humans and consequent to a particular social history or dynamic
2. Define rape in a way that, by drawing on biologically and psychologically meaningful concepts, can far better than current social and legal conceptions, "carve nature at its joints" and, thereby, clarify debate about what rape is (and isn't)
3. Reconsider the motivations underlying rape and acknowledge the multiplicity of circumstances that can all lead to negation of female choice
4. Use our understanding of coevolution, ethical pathologies, and extended phenotypes, to promote social changes that will reduce the motivational and situational factors that contribute to rape, and help heal individual perpetrators, victims, and communities

## REFERENCES

Abbey, A., & Melby, C. (1986). The effects of nonverbal cues on gender differences in perceptions of sexual intent. *Sex Roles, 15,* 283–298.
Abbey, A., Ross, L.T., McDuffie, D., & McAuslan, P. (1996). Alcohol, misperception, and sexual assault: How and why are they linked? In D. Buss & N. Malamuth (Eds.), *Sex, power, conflict: Evolutionary and feminist perspectives.* New York: Oxford University.
Alexander, R.D. (1987). *The biology of moral systems.* Hawthorne, NY: Aldine deGruyter.
Alexander, R.D., Hoogland, J.L., Howard, R.D., Noonan, K.M., & Sherman, P.W. (1979). Sexual dimorphisms and breeding systems in pinnipeds, ungulates, primates and humans. In N.A. Chagnon & W. Irons (Eds.), *Evolutionary biology and human social behavior: An anthropological perspective.* Belmont, CA: Wadsworth.
Almodovar, N.J. (1990/1991). Prostitution and the criminal justice system. *The Truth Seeker,* Summer 1990. Reprinted in R.T. Francouer (Ed.), *Taking sides: Clashing views on controversial issues in human sexuality,* 3rd edition (1991). Guildford, CT: Dushkin.
Andersson M. (1994). *Sexual selection.* Princeton, NJ: Princeton University.
Andersson, M., & Iwasa, Y. (1996). Sexual selection. *Trends in Ecology and Evolution 11,* 52–58.
Axelrod, R. (1986). An evolutionary approach to norms. *American Political Science Review, 80,* 1095–1111.
Baker, K. (1997). Once a rapist? Motivational evidence and relevancy in rape law. *Harvard Law Review, 110,* 563–624.
Baker, K. (1999a). Sex, rape, and shame. *Boston University Law Review, 79,* 663–716.
Baker, K. (1999b). What rape is and what it ought not to be. *Jurimetrics, 39,* 233–242.
Baker, K. (2000). Biology for feminists. *Chicago Kent Law Review, 75,* 805–835.

Barash, D.P. (1977). Sociobiology of rape in mallards (*Anas platyrhynchos*): Responses of mated males. *Science, 197,* 788–789.

Barbaree, H.E., & Marshall, W.L. (1991). The role of male sexual arousal in rape: Six models. *Journal of Clinical and Consulting Psychology, 59,* 621–630.

Barnes, G.E., Malamuth, N.M., & Check, J.V.P. (1984). Personality and sexuality. *Personality and Individual Differences, 5,* 159–172.

Bartol, C., & Bartol, A. (1994). *Psychology and law.* Pacific Grove, CA: Brooks/Cole.

Becker, J.V., & Kaplan, M.S. (1991). Rape victims: Issues, theories, and treatment. *Annual Review of Sex Research, 2,* 267–292.

Belsky, J. (1997). Attachment, mating and parenting: An evolutionary perspective. *Human Nature, 8,* 361–381.

Belsky, J. (2000). Conditional and alternative reproductive strategies: Individual differences in susceptibility to rearing experience. In J.L. Rodgers, D.C. Rowe, & W. Miller (Eds.), *Genetic influences on human fertility and sexuality.* London: Kluwer Academic Publishers.

Belsky, J., Steinberg, L., & Draper, P. (1991). Childhood experience, interpersonal development and reproductive strategy: An evolutionary theory of socialization. *Child Development, 62,* 647–670.

Beyers, J.M., Leonard, J.M., Mays, V.K., & Rosen, L.A. (2000). Gender differences in the perception of courtship abuse. *Journal of Interpersonal Violence, 15,* 451–466.

Biller, H.B. (1981). Father absence, divorce, and personality development. In M.E. Lamb (Ed.), *The role of the father in child development* (2nd ed.). New York: John Wiley & Sons.

Blumenthal, J.A. (1998). The reasonable woman standard: A meta-analytic review of gender differences in perceptions of sexual harassment. *Law and Human Behavior, 22,* 33–57.

Borgerhoff Mulder, M. (1995). Bridewealth and its correlates (with commentary and rejoinder). *Current Anthropology, 36,* 573–603.

Briskie, J.V., & Montgomerie, R. (1997). Sexual selection and the intromittent organ in birds. *Journal of Avian Biology, 28,* 73–86.

Broude, G.J., & Greene, S.J. (1976). Cross-cultural codes on twenty sexual attitudes and practices. *Ethnology, 15,* 409–429.

Browne, K.R. (1997). An evolutionary perspective on sexual harassment: Seeking roots in biology rather than ideology. *Journal of Contemporary Legal Issues, 8,* 5–77.

Brownmiller, S. (1975). *Against our will: Men, women, and rape.* New York: Simon & Schuster.

Bullough, B., & Bullough, V.L. (1996). Female prostitution: Current research and changing interpretations. *Annual Review of Sex Research, 7,* 158–180.

Burley, N., & Symanski, R. (1981). Women without: An evolutionary and cross-cultural perspective on prostitution. In R. Symanski (Ed.), *The immoral landscape: Female prostitution in Western societies.* Toronto, Canada: Butterworth & Co.

Buss, D.M. (1988a). From vigilance to violence: Tactics of mate retention in American undergraduates. *Ethology and Sociobiology, 9,* 291–317.

Buss, D.M. (1988b). The evolution of human intrasexual competition: Tactics of mate attraction. *Journal of Personality and Social Psychology, 54,* 616–628.

Buss, D.M. (1992). Mate preference mechanisms: Consequences for partner choice and intrasexual competition. In J. Barkow, L. Cosmides, & J. Tooby (Eds.), *The adapted mind.* New York: Oxford University.

Buss, D.M. (1996). Sexual conflict: Evolutionary insights into feminism and the "Battle of the Sexes." In D. Buss & N. Malamuth (Eds.), *Sex, power, conflict: Evolutionary and feminist perspectives.* New York: Oxford University.

Buss, D.M. (1998). The psychology of human mate selection: Exploring the complexity of the strategic repertoire. In C. Crawford & D.L. Krebs (Eds.), *Handbook of evolutionary psychology: Issues, ideas, and applications.* Mahwah, NJ: Lawrence Erlbaum.

Chisholm, J.S. (1996). The evolutionary ecology of attachment organization. *Human Nature, 7,* 1–37.

Cleveland, H.H., Koss, M.P., & Lyons, J. (1999). Rape tactics from the survivor's perspective. *Journal of Interpersonal Violence, 14,* 532–547.

Clutton-Brock, T.H., & Parker, G.A. (1995). Sexual coercion in animal societies. *Animal Behaviour, 49,* 1345–1365.

Cosmides, L. (1989). The logic of social exchange: Has natural selection shaped how humans reason? Studies with the Wason selection task. *Cognition, 31,* 187–276.

Counts, D.A., Brown, J.K., & Campbell, & J.C. (Eds.). (1992). *Sanction and sanctuary: Cultural perspectives on the beating of wives.* Boulder, CO: Westview.

Crawford, C., & Galdikas, B.M.F. (1986). Rape in non-human animals: An evolutionary perspective. *Canadian Psychology, 27,* 215–230.

Crawford, C.C., & Johnston, M.A. (1999). An evolutionary model of courtship and mating as social exchange: Implications for rape law reform. *Jurimetrics, 39,* 181–200.

Daly, M., Singh, L.S., & Wilson, M. (1993). Children fathered by previous partners: A risk factor for violence against women. *Canadian Journal of Public Health, 84,* 209–210.

Daly, M., & Wilson, M. (1996). Evolutionary psychology and marital conflict. In D. Buss & N. Malamuth (Eds.), *Sex, power, conflict: Evolutionary and feminist perspectives.* New York: Oxford University.

Daly, M., Wiseman, K.A., & Wilson, M. (1997). Women with children sired by previous partners incur excess risk of uxoricide. *Homicide Studies, 1,* 61–71.

Darke, J.L. (1990). Sexual aggression: Achieving power through humiliation. In W.L. Marshall, D.R. Laws, & H.E. Barbaree (Eds.), *Handbook of sexual assault: Issues, theories and treatment of the offender.* New York: Plenum Press.

Darwin, C. (1871/1981). *The descent of man and selection in relation to sex.* Princeton, NJ: Princeton University Press.

Davis, R.C., & Henley, M. (1990). Victim service programs. In A.J. Lurigio, W.G. Skogan, & R.C. Davis (Eds.), *Victims of crime: Problems, policies, and programs.* Newbury Park, CA: Sage.

Dawkins, R. (1980). Good strategy or evolutionary stable strategy? In G.W. Barlow & J. Silverberg (Eds.), *Sociobiology: Beyond nature-nurture?* Boulder, CO: Westview Press.

Dawkins, R. (1982). *The extended phenotype.* New York: W.H. Freeman.

Dean, K., & Malamuth, N. (1997). Characteristics of men who aggress sexually and of men who imagine aggressing: Risk and moderating variables. *Journal of Personality and Social Psychology, 72,* 449–455.

DeMaris, A. (1997). Elevated sexual activity in violent marriages: Hypersexuality or sexual extortion? *Journal of Sex Research, 34,* 361–373.

Denno, D.W. (1999). Evolutionary biology and rape. *Jurimetrics, 39,* 243–254.

Diamond, M., & Uchiyama, A. (1999). Pornography, rape, and sex crimes in Japan. *International Journal of Law and Psychiatry, 22*, 1–22.

Dobash, R.P., Dobash, R.E., Wilson, M., & Daly, M. (1992). The myth of sexual symmetry in marital violence. *Social Problems, 39*, 71–91.

Dobzhansky, T. (1962). *Mankind evolving.* New Haven, CT: Yale University Press.

Donnerstein, E., & Linz, D. (1986). Mass media sexual violence and male viewers. *American Behavioral Scientist, 29*, 601–618.

Draper, P., & Harpending, H. (1982). Father absence and reproductive strategy: An evolutionary perspective. *Journal of Anthropological Research, 38*, 255–273.

Dutton, D.G. (1994). Patriarchy and wife assault: The ecological fallacy. *Violence and Victims, 9*, 167–182.

Dutton, D.G. (1995). Male abusiveness in intimate relationships. *Clinical Psychology Review, 15*, 567–581.

Ekman, P. (1985/1992). *Telling lies: Clues to deceit in the marketplace, politics, and marriage.* New York: Norton.

Ellis, L. (1991a). The drive to possess and control as a motivation for sexual behavior: Applications to the study of rape. *Social Science Information, 30*, 663–675.

Ellis, L. (1991b). A synthesized (biosocial) theory of rape. *Journal of Consulting and Clinical Psychology, 59*, 631–652.

Ellis, L. (1998). Women's continuing sexual relationships with rapists following completed and blocked sexual assaults. Paper presented at the Colloquium on Biology and Sexual Aggression, Center for the Study of Law, Science and Arizona State University.

Figueredo, A.J., & McCloskey, L.A. (1993). Sex, money, and paternity: The evolutionary psychology of domestic violence. *Ethology and Sociobiology, 14*, 353–379.

Flinn, M.V. (1985). Mate guarding in a Caribbean village. *Ethology and Sociobiology, 9*, 1–28.

Fox, E.L., Bowers, R.W., & Foss, M.L. (1993). *The physiological basis for exercise and sport* (5th ed.). Madison, WI: WCB Brown & Benchmark.

Frank, R.H. (1988). *Passions within reason: The strategic role of the emotions.* New York: W.W. Norton.

Gangestad, S.W., & Simpson, J.A. (1990). Toward an evolutionary history of female sociosexual variation. *Journal of Personality, 58*, 69–95.

Gaulin, S., & Boster, J. (1985). Cross-cultural differences in sexual dimorphism: Is there any variance to be explained? *Ethology and Sociobiology, 6*, 219–225.

Gaulin, S.J., & McBurney, D. (2001). Psychology: An evolutionary approach. Englewood Cliffs, NJ: Prentice-Hall.

Geer, J.H. (1996). Gender differences in the organization of sexual information. *Archives of Sexual Behavior, 25*, 91–107.

Geer, J.H., & Manguno-Mire, G.M. (1996). Gender differences in cognitive processes in sexuality. *Annual Review of Sex Research, 7*, 90–124.

Gies, F., & Gies, J. (1987). *Marriage and the family in the Middle Ages.* New York: Harper & Row.

Groth, A.N. (1980). Rape: The sexual expression of aggression. In P.F. Brain (Ed.), *Multidisciplinary approaches to aggression research.* New York: Elsevier/North Holland.

Hall, G.C.N., & Barongan, C. (1997). Prevention of sexual agggression: Sociocultural risk and protective factors. *American Psychologist, 52*, 5–14.

Hall, G.C.N., & Hirschman, R. (1991). Toward a theory of sexual aggression: A quad-ripartite model. *Journal of Consulting and Clinical Psychology, 59,* 662–669.

Hanna, C. (1999). Sometimes sex matters: Reflections on biology, sexual aggression, and its implications for law. *Jurimetrics, 39,* 261–269.

Herman-Giddens, M.E., Slora, E.J., Wasserman, R.C., Bourdony, C.J., Bhapkar, M.V., Koch, G.G., & Hasemeier, C.M. (1997). Secondary sexual characteristics and menses in young girls seen in office practice: A study from the pediatric research in office settings network. *Pediatrics, 99,* 505–512.

Hersch, K., & Gray-Little, B. (1998). Psychopathic traits and attitudesed with self-reported sexual aggression in college men. *Journal of Interpersonal Violence, 13,* 456–471.

Hill, E.M., Young, J.P., & Nord, J.L. (1994). Childhood adversity, attachment security, and adult relationships: A preliminary study. *Ethology and Sociobiology, 15,* 323–338.

Hirshleifer, J., & Coll, J.C. (1988). What strategies can support the evolutionary emer-gence of cooperation? *Journal of Conflict Resolution, 32,* 367–398.

Hrdy, S. (1979). Infanticide among animals: A review, classification, and examination of the implications for the reproductive strategies of females. *Ethology and So-ciobiology, 1,* 13–40.

Jones, O.D. (1999). Sex, culture, and the biology of rape: Toward explanation and pre-vention. *California Law Review, 87,* 827–941.

Jones, O.D. (2000). Law and the biology of rape: Reflections on transitions. *Hastings Women's Law Journal, 11,* 151–178.

Kahn, A.S. (Ed.). (1984). Victims of crime and violence: Final report of the APA Task Force on Victims of Crime and Violence. Washington, DC: American Psycho-logical Association.

Kanin, E.J. (1985). Date rapists: Differential sexual socialization and relative deprivation. *Archives of Sexual Behavior, 14,* 219–231.

Kelly, D.P. (1990). Victim participation in the criminal justice system. In A.J. Lurigio, W.G. Skogan, & R.C. Davis (Eds.), *Victims of crime: Problems, policies, and programs.* Newbury Park, CA: Sage.

Kennan, B. (1998). Evolutionary biology and strict liability for rape. *Law and Psy-chology Review, 22,* 131–177.

Kenrick, D.T., Groth, G.E., Trost, M.R., & Sadalla, E.K. (1993). Integrating evolutionary and social exchange perspectives on relationships: Effects of gender, self-appraisal, and involvement level on mate selection criteria. *Journal of Person-ality and Social Psychology, 64,* 951–969.

Knight, R.A. (1999). Validation of a typology for rapists. *Journal of Interpersonal Vi-olence, 14,* 303–330.

Knight, R.A., & Prentky, R.A. (1993). Exploring characteristics for classifying juvenile sex offenders. In H.E. Barbaree, W.L. Marshall, & S.M. Hudson (Eds.), *The ju-venile sex offender.* New York: Guilford.

Komers, P.E., & Brotherton, P.N.M. (1997). Female space use is the best predictor of monogamy in mammals. *Proceedings of the Royal Society of London, B, 264,* 1261–1270.

Koop, C.E. (1987). Report of the surgeon general's workshop on pornography and public health. *American Psychologist, 42,* 944–945.

Koss, M.P. (1988). Hidden rape: Aggression and victimization in a national sample of students in higher education. In A. Burgess (Ed.), *Rape and sexual assault II.* New York: Garland.

Koss, M.P. (2000). Blame, shame, and community: Justice responses to violence against women. *American Psychologist, 55,* 1332–1343.

Kowalski, R.M. (1992). Nonverbal behaviors and perceptions of sexual intentions: Effects of sexual connotativeness, verbal response, and rape outcome. *Basic and Applied Social Psychology, 13,* 427–445.

Kutchinsky, B. (1991). Pornography and rape: Theory and practice? *International Journal of Law and Psychiatry, 14,* 47–64.

Lalumiere, M.L., Chalmers, L.J., Quinsey, V.L., & Seto, M.C. (1996). A test of the mate deprivation hypothesis of sexual coercion. *Ethology and Sociobiology, 17,* 299–318.

Lalumiere, M.L., & Quinsey, V.L. (1999). A Darwinian interpretation of individual differences in male propensity for sexual aggression. *Jurimetrics, 39,* 201–216.

Laubach, L.L. (1976). Comparative muscular strength of men and women: A review of the literature. *Aviation, Space, and Environmental Medicine, 47,* 534–542.

Lewis, M., & Saarni, C. (Eds.). (1993). *Lying and deception in everyday life.* New York: Guilford.

Linz, D., Donnerstein, E., & Penrod, S. (1987). The findings and recommendations of the attorney general's commission on pornography. *American Psychologist, 42,* 946–953.

Linz, D., Penrod, S., & Donnerstein, E. (1986). Issues bearing on the legal regulation of violent and sexually violent media. *Journal of Social Issues, 42,* 171–193.

Lombardi, M.J. (1997). Restorative justice: For victims, communities and offenders. Video produced and distributed by the University of Minnesota Center for Restorative Justice and Mediation.

Low, B.S. (1992). Sex, coalitions, and politics in preindustrial societies. *Politics and the Life Sciences, 11,* 63–80.

Machalek, R., & Cohen, L.E. (1991). The nature of crime: Is cheating necessary for cooperation? *Human Nature, 2,* 215–233.

Maguire, M., & Shapland, J. (1990). The "victim movement" in Europe. In A.J. Lurigio, W.G. Skogan, & R.C. Davis (Eds.), *Victims of crime: Problems, policies, and programs.* Newbury Park, CA: Sage.

Malamuth, N.M. (1996). The confluence model of sexual aggression: Feminist and evolutionary perspectives. In D. Buss & N. Malamuth (Eds.), *Sex, power, conflict: Evolutionary and feminist perspectives.* New York: Oxford University.

Malamuth, N.M., & Brown, L.M. (1994). Sexually aggressive men's perceptions of women's communications: Testing three explanations. *Journal of Personality and Social Psychology, 67,* 699–712.

Malamuth, N., Haber, S., & Feschbach, S. (1980). Testing hypotheses regarding rape: Exposure to sexual violence, sex differences, and the "normality" of rapists. *Journal of Research in Personality, 14,* 121–137.

Malamuth, N., Linz, D., Heavey, C., Barnes, G., & Acker, M. (1995). Using the confluence model of sexual aggression to predict men's conflict with women: A 10-year follow-up study. *Journal of Personality and Social Psychology, 69,* 353–369.

Malamuth, N., & Malamuth, E.Z. (1999). Integrating multiple levels of scientific analysis and the confluence model of sexual coercers. *Jurimetrics, 39*, 157–179.

Malamuth, N.M., Sockloskie, R.J., Koss, M.P., & Tanaka, J.S. (1991). Characteristics of aggressors against women: Testing a model using a national sample of college students. *Journal of Counseling and Clinical Psychology, 59*, 670–681.

Marshall, W.L., Hudson, S.M., & Hodkinson, S. (1993). The importance of attachment bonds in the development of juvenile sexual offending. In H.E. Barabee, W.L. Marshall, & S.M. Hudson (Eds.), *The juvenile sex offender.* New York: Guilford.

Masters, W.H., Johnson, V.E., & Kolodny, R.C. (1995). *Human sexuality,* 5th ed. New York: HarperCollins.

Maybach, K.L., & Gold, S.R. (1994). Hyperfeminity and attraction to macho and non-macho men. *Journal of Sex Research, 31*, 91–98.

McCormack, T. (1988). The censorship of pornography: Catharsis or learning? *American Journal of Orthopsychiatry, 58*, 492–504.

Mealey, L. (1992). Alternative adaptive models of rape. *Behavioral and Brain Sciences. 15*, 397–398.

Mealey, L. (1995). The internal working model: Cause, effect, or covariate? *ASCAP: Newsletter of the Society for Sociophysiological Integration, 8*, 5–22.

Mealey, L. (1995/1997). The sociobiology of sociopathy: An integrated evolutionary model (with commentary and rejoinder). *Behavioral and Brain Sciences, 18*, 523–599. Reprinted in S. Baron-Cohen (Ed.), *The Maladapted Mind.* London: Erlbaum/Taylor-Francis.

Mealey, L. (1997). Heritability, theory of mind and the nature of normality. *Behavioral and Brain Sciences, 20*, 527–532.

Mealey, L. (1999). The multiplicity of rape: From life history strategies to prevention strategies. *Jurimetrics, 39*, 217–226.

Mealey, L. (2000a). Commentary. In J.L. Rodgers, D.C. Rowe, & W. Miller (Eds.), *Genetic influences on human fertility and sexuality.* London: Kluwer Academic Publishers.

Mealey, L. (2000b). *Sex differences: Developmental and evolutionary strategies.* San Diego, CA: Academic Press.

Mealey, L., Daood, C., & Krage, M. (1996). Enhanced memory for faces of cheaters. *Ethology and Sociobiology, 17*, 119–128.

Mesnick, S.L. (1997). Sexual alliances: Evidence and evolutionary implications. In P.A. Gowaty (Ed.), *Feminism and evolutionary biology.* New York: Chapman & Hall.

Miller, G.F. (1996). Political peacocks. *Demos, 10*, 9–11.

Miller, S.L., & Simpson, S.S. (1991). Courtship violence and social control: Does gender matter? *Law and Society Review, 25*, 335–365.

Money, J. (1986). *Lovemaps: Clinical concepts of sexual/erotic health and pathology, paraphilia, and gender transposition in childhood, adolescence, and maturity.* New York: Irvington Press.

Mosher, D.L (1991). Macho men, machismo, and sexuality. *Annual Review of Sex Research, 2*, 199–247.

Muehlenhard, C.L., Danoff-Burg, S., & Powch, I.G. (1996). Is rape sex or violence? Conceptual issues and implications. In D. Buss & N. Malamuth (Eds.), *Sex, power, conflict: Evolutionary and feminist perspectives.* New York: Oxford University.

Muehlenhard, C.L., & Hollabaugh, L.C. (1988). Do women sometimes say no when they mean yes? The prevalence and correlates of women's token resistance to sex. *Journal of Personality and Social Psychology, 54*, 872–879.

Murnen, S.K., Perot, A., & Byrne, D. (1989). Coping with unwanted sexual activity: Normative responses, situational determinants, and individual differences. *Journal of Sex Research, 26*, 85–106.

Murrin, M.R., & Laws, D.R. (1990). The influence of pornography on sexual crimes. In W.L. Marshall, D.R. Laws, & H.E. Barbaree (Eds.), *Handbook of sexual assault: Issues, theories and treatment of the offender.* New York: Plenum Press.

Nadler, R.D. (1999). Sexual aggression in the great apes: Implications for human law. *Jurimetrics, 39*, 149–155.

Palmer, C.T. (1988). Twelve reasons why rape is not sexually motivated: A skeptical examination. *Journal of Sex Research, 25*, 512–530.

Palmer, C.T. (1989). Rape in nonhuman animal species: Definitions, evidence, and implications. *The Journal of Sex Research, 26*, 355–374.

Palmer, C.T., DiBari, D.A., & Wright, S.A. (1999). Is it sex yet? Theoretical and practical implications of the debate over rapists' motives. *Jurimetrics, 39*, 271–282.

Prentky, R.A., & Knight, R.A. (1991). Identifying critical dimensions for discriminating among rapists. *Journal of Consulting and Clinical Psychology, 59*, 643–661.

Pryor, J.B., DeSouza, E.R., Fitness, J., Hutz, C., Kumpf, M., Lubbert, K., Pesonen, O., & Erber, M.W. (1997). Gender differences in the interpretation of social-sexual behavior: A cross-cultural perspective on sexual harassment. *Journal of Cross-cultural Psychology, 28*, 509–534.

Regan, P.C. (1998). What if you can't get what you want? Willingness to compromise ideal mate selection standards as a function of sex, mate value, and relationship context. *Personality and Social Psychology Bulletin, 24*, 1294–1303.

Resick, P.A. (1990). Victims of sexual assault. In A.J. Lurigio, W.G. Skogan & R.C. Davis (Eds.), *Victims of crime: Problems, policies, and programs.* Newbury Park, CA: Sage.

Ross, W.D., & Ward, R. (1982). Human proportionality and sexual dimorphism. In R.L. Hall (Ed.), *Sexual dimorphism in Homo Sapiens: A question of size.* New York: Praeger.

Rowe, D.C. (2000). Environmental and genetic influences on pubertal development: Evolutionary life history traits? In J.L. Rodgers, D.C. Rowe, & W. Miller (Eds.), *Genetic influences on human fertility and sexuality.* London: Kluwer Academic Publishers.

Rowe, D.C., Vazsonyi, A.T., & Figueredo, A.J. (1997). Mating-effort in adolescence: A conditional or alternative strategy. *Personality and Individual Differences 23*, 105–115.

Sanday, P.R. (1981). The socio-cultural context of rape: A cross-cultural study. *Journal of Social Issues, 37*, 5–27.

Sappington, A.A. (2000). Childhood abuse as a possible locus for early intervention into problems of violence and psychopathology. *Aggression and Violent Behavior, 5*, 255–266.

Schumacher, J.A., Smith Slep, A.M., & Heyman, R.E. (2001). Risk factors for male-to-female partner psychological abuse. *Aggression and Violent Behavior, 6*, 255–268.

Seligman, M.E.P. (1970). On the generality of the laws of learning. *Psychological Review, 77*, 407–418.

Seto, M.C., Khattar, N.A., Lalumiere, M.L., & Quinsey, V.L. (1997). Deception and sexual strategy in psychopathy. *Personality and Individual Differences, 22*, 301–307.

Seto, M.C., Maric, A., & Barbaree, H.E. (2001) .The role of pornography in the etiology of sexual aggression. *Aggression and Violent Behavior, 6*, 35–53.

Small, M.F. (1993). *Female choices: Sexual behavior of female primates*. Ithaca, NY: Cornell University.

Smith, T.W. (1987). The use of public opinion data by the attorney general's commission on pornography. *Public Opinion Quarterly, 51*, 249–267.

Smuts, B. (1992/1996). Male aggression against women: An evolutionary perspective. *Human Nature, 3*, 1–44. Reprinted in D. Buss & N. Malamuth (Eds.), *Sex, power, conflict: Evolutionary and feminist perspectives*. New York: Oxford University.

Smuts, B. (1995). The evolutionary origins of patriarchy. *Human Nature, 6*, 1–32.

Smuts, B., & Smuts, R. (1993). Male aggression and sexual coercion of females in nonhuman primates and other animals. *Advances in the Study of Behavior, 22*, 1–63.

Spohn, C.C. (1999). The rape reform movement: The traditional common law and rape law reforms. *Jurimetrics, 39*, 119–130.

Sprecher, S., Hatfield, E., Cortese, A., Potapova, E., & Levitskaya, A. (1994). Token resistance to sexual intercourse: College students' dating experience in three countries. *Journal of Sex Research, 31*, 125–132.

Starks, P.T., & Blackie, C.A. (2000). The relationship between serial monogamy and rape in the United States (1960–1995). *Proceedings of the Royal Society of London, B, 267*, 1259–1263.

Stevenson, M.R., & Black, K.N. (1988). Paternal absence and sex-role development: A meta-analysis. *Child Development, 59*, 793–814.

Studd, M.V. (1996). Sexual harassment. In D. Buss & N. Malamuth (Eds.), *Sex, power, conflict: Evolutionary and feminist perspectives*. New York: Oxford University.

Symons, D. (1979). *The evolution of human sexuality*. Oxford: Oxford University Press.

Thornhill, N.W. (1996). Psychological adaptation to sexual coercion in victims and offenders. In D. Buss & N. Malamuth (Eds.), *Sex, power, conflict: Evolutionary and feminist perspectives*. New York: Oxford University Press.

Thornhill, R. (1980). Rape in Panorpa scorpionflies and a general rape hypothesis. *Animal Behaviour, 28*, 52–59.

Thornhill, R. (1999). The biology of human rape. *Jurimetrics, 39*, 137–147.

Thornhill, R., & Alcock, J. (1983). *The evolution of insect mating systems*. Cambridge, MA: Harvard University Press.

Thornhill, R., & Palmer, C. (2000). *The natural history of rape: Biological bases of sexual coercion*. Cambridge, MA: MIT Press.

Thornhill, R., & Thornhill, N.W. (1983). Human rape: An evolutionary analysis. *Ethology and Sociobiology, 4*, 137–173.

Thornhill, R., & Thornhill, N.W. (1992). The evolutionary psychology of men's coercive sexuality (with commentary and rejoinder). *Behavioral and Brain Sciences, 15*, 363–421.

Tooke, W., & Camire, L. (1991). Patterns of deception in intersexual and intrasexual mating strategies. *Ethology and Sociobiology, 12*, 345–364.

Umbreit, M., & Jacobson, S. (1997). Restorative justice: Victim empowerment through mediation and dialogue. Video produced and distributed by the University of Minnesota Center for Restorative Justice and Mediation.

van Berlo, W., & Ensink, B. (2000). Problems with sexuality after sexual assault. *Annual Review of Sex Research, 11,* 235–257.

Vila, B. (1997). Human nature and crime control: Improving the feasibility of nurturant strategies. *Politics and the Life Sciences, 16,* 3–21.

Vila, B.J., & Cohen, L.E. (1993). Crime as strategy: Testing an evolutionary ecological theory of expropriative crime. *American Journal of Sociology, 98,* 873–912.

Walsh, A. (2000). Evolutionary psychology and the origins of justice. *Justice Quarterly, 17,* 841–964.

Weckerly, F.W. (1998). Sexual-size dimorphism: Influence of mass and mating systems in the most dimorphic mammals. *Journal of Mammalogy, 79,* 33–52.

White, D.R. (1988). Rethinking polygyny: Co-wives, codes, and cultural systems (with commentary and rejoinder). *Current Anthropology, 29,* 529–572.

Wiederman, M.W., & Dubois, S.L. (1998). Evolution and sex differences in preferences for short-term mates: Results from a policy capturing study. *Evolution and Human Behavior, 19,* 153–170.

Wilcox, B.L. (1987). Pornography, social science, and politics: When research and ideology collide. *American Psychologist, 42,* 941–943.

Wilson, M., & Daly, M. (1992). The man who mistook his wife for a chattel. In J.H. Barkow, L. Cosmides, & J. Tooby (Eds.), *The adapted mind.* New York: Oxford University Press.

Wilson, M., & Daly, M. (1996). Male sexual proprietariness and violence against wives. *Current Directions in Psychological Science, 5,* 2–7.

Wilson, M., & Daly, M. (1997). Life expectancy, economic inequality, homicide, and reproductive timing in Chicago neighbourhoods. *British Medical Journal, 314,* 1271–1274.

Wilson, M., Daly, M., & Scheib, J. (1997). Femicide: An evolutionary psychological perspective. In P.A. Gowaty (Ed.), *Feminism and evolutionary biology.* New York: Chapman & Hall.

Wilson, W., & Durrenberger, R. (1982). Comparison of rape and attempted rape victims. *Psychological Reports, 50,* 198.

Wolfe, L.D., & Gray, J.P. (1982). Latitude and intersocietal variation of human sexual dimorphism of stature. *Human Ecology, 10,* 409–416.

Zillmann, D. (2000). Influence of unrestrained access to erotica on adolescents' and young adults' dispositions toward sexuality. *Journal of Adolescent Health, 275,* 41–44.

5

# Homicide

## An Evolutionary Psychological Perspective and Implications for Public Policy

*David M. Buss and Joshua D. Duntley*

Why people kill other people is a question that fascinates everyone and for good reason. Understanding causal origins concerns everyone who wishes to curtail this universally abhorrent behavior. A host of theories has been proposed to explain why nearly 20,000 individuals within the United States have their lives prematurely terminated at the hands of another human each year. From a public policy perspective, understanding the causal origins of killing may be useful in guiding efforts to decrease its prevalence. Scientifically incorrect and incomplete theories of the causal origins of homicide, however, can result in wasted policy efforts and potentially preventable loss of life.

Existing theories of homicide include those that invoke social learning, media influences, specifics of culture, ills of upbringing, brain damage, and genetic abnormalities. In our view, all these theories have some merit, each accounting for a piece of the homicide variance pie. Rates of homicide, for example, vary tremendously across cultures. Canadians, for example, kill at a higher rate than do Japanese; Scottish kill at a higher rate than Canadians; and Americans kill at a higher rate than Scottish (Fingerhut & Kleinman, 1990). Assuming that genetic differences are not responsible for these rate differences, it is not unreasonable to propose that cultural or ecological factors influence homicide rates, even if we don't know precisely what those factors are. Even within a single country, such as America, homicide rates vary—generally they are higher in cities than in rural areas, higher in the south than in the north, and higher in large states such as California and Texas than in smaller states such as Rhode Island.

It would be surprising, to take a common theoretical perspective, if socialization and social learning played no part in the causal chain leading to homicide (Berkowitz, 1993). Parents who have guns in the home, peers who model violent behavior, and media messages that portray killing as a glamorous activity can all be expected to influence young, impressionable minds. And some empirical evidence is consistent with these ideas (e.g., Smith & Zahn, 1999). There is also some evidence that males born with an extra Y chromosome are more prone to violence (Hoffman, 1977), as are boxers who have sustained frontal lobe damage (Johnson, 1969). Without denying the merits of these theories, we would like to suggest that an evolutionary perspective also might be useful in shedding some light on some links in the causal chain leading to homicide.

## THE EVOLUTIONARY PROCESS

It is widely recognized that natural selection is the principle causal force responsible for complex organic design. Differential reproduction, occurring because of differences in design, is the essence of natural selection. Variants that lead their bearers to increased relative reproductive success will be represented in succeeding generations more than variants that do not. Natural selection is a ruthless executioner. The sole criterion preventing evolutionary oblivion is successful gene replication. Variants that fail to have effects that increase their replicative success are mercilessly weeded out. This execution process occurs relentlessly, generation after generation, acting like a genotypic sieve.

Those design features that succeed in passing through the extraordinarily long succession of selective filters tend to have remarkable properties. The most central property is that they have phenotypic effects that lead to their own propagation. But in complex multicellular species such as humans, they must also generally interact well with other properties of the organism. Renegade genes, lawless alleles, mutants that insert sand into the genotypic machinery, with some exceptions, tend to lead to organismic collapse and reproductive failure. Those that coordinate well with their fellow organismic travelers, that facilitate their functioning, tend to lead to reproductive success.

All living humans are remarkable collections of genes that have leaped over the successive hurtles generation after generation, surviving the gauntlet of hazards to survival, vagaries of reproduction, and interacting reasonably well with their traveling companions. They have been designed to interact with recurrent physical, social, or internal environments in ways that promote the reproduction of the individuals who possess them, or their genetic relatives (Buss et al., 1998; Hamilton, 1964; Tooby & Cosmides, 1990; Williams, 1966). They are all products of selection, or rather multiple selections, operating ruthlessly over hundreds, thousands, millions, even billions of years.

The process of natural selection gives rise to three products—adaptations, by-products of adaptations, and noise (Tooby & Cosmides, 1990; Williams, 1966). An adaptation may be defined as "an inherited and reliably developing characteristic that came into existence as a feature of a species through natural selection because it help to directly or indirectly facilitate reproduction during the period of its evolution" (Buss et al., 1998, p. 535). Each adaptation evolved in response to a unique set of selection pressures over the course of its evolutionary history. This is the environment of evolutionary adaptedness (EEA) of an adaptation. The EEA is best described as the statistical aggregate of selection pressures responsible for the evolution and maintenance of an adaptation. Each adaptation has its unique EEA—an individualized time frame and corresponding aggregate of unique selective events that led to its evolution. The EEA of the human eye, for example, stretches back more generations and is an aggregate of different selection pressures than the EEA of bipedal locomotion or the EEA of human language.

Adaptive problems are features of an organism's environment, including the physical, social, and intraorganismic environment, which affect its reproduction. These range from finding food, combating predators, choosing mates, defending against aggressive rivals, and prioritizing and coordinating the activation of different body mechanisms. When adaptive problems recur generation after generation, they become the selection pressures that shape the genotype of an organism through the differential reproduction of the bearers of different alleles that reliably code for the development of even slightly different phenotypic characteristics. When a phenotypic characteristic is successful enough that it leads to more reproductive success in its bearers than nonbearers over a number of generations, leading to its eventual spread to all or most members of a species, it is considered to be an adaptation. Solving an adaptive problem then, that is, in the manner in which a feature contributes to reproduction, is the proper function of an adaptation. And each adaptation has its own unique function. Callus-producing mechanisms function to protect physiological structures beneath the skin; eye blink reflexes protect the eyes from physical threats; specialized fear of snakes, darkness, heights, and strangers each serve unique protective functions. The functions of adaptations, of course, need not lead directly to reproduction, but they must ultimately be tributary to reproduction. A motive to strive for status, for example, may have evolved through a tortuously long causal chain, involving (a) propulsion up the social ladder, (b) the consequent gaining of greater access to certain resources, (c) rendering the bearer more attractive to the opposite sex, (d) producing more bountiful mating opportunities, (e) eventually leading to being chosen as a mate, and (f) which in turn leads to sexual behavior that produces offspring. One of the central goals of evolutionary psychology is to identify adaptations and their proper functions, which require a description of the specific manner in which it historically has contributed to reproductive success.

Adaptations, of course, are not the only product of selection. The process of selection also produces by-products and a residue of noise. By-products are best regarded as reliably developing, incidental effects of adaptations. Reading lamps, for example, are designed to produce light, but they tend to produce heat as well. Heat is an incidental by-product of light production, and not part of its function (except in those cases where lights are intentionally designed to produce heat, as in the case of lamps that keep french fries warm in fast-food restaurants). Analogously, the human belly button is a by-product of what was formerly an adaptation—the umbilical cord. As far as we can tell, the belly button per se has no function. It's not good at collecting food, fending off predators, or provisioning children. But the adaptation of which it is a by-product, the umbilical cord, is an astonishingly important and well-designed adaptation, without which the growing embryo would not gain the sustenance needed for its viability.

The hypothesis that something is a by-product carries with it the theoretical burden of specifying the adaptation of which the incidental effect is a part. Mere assertions of this or that characteristic being a by-product are theoretically vacuous without the proper specification of the adaptation it is proposed to be a by-product of. Both sets of hypotheses—those about adaptations and those about by-products—are most useful scientifically when they generate precise, testable predictions and can simultaneously account for known observations in a parsimonious manner.

## AN EVOLUTIONARY PERSPECTIVE ON AGGRESSION

Common stereotypes of the evolutionary process depict it as "nature red in tooth and claw," with individuals fighting viciously for survival. As a sole depiction, this view is wildly misleading. The evolutionary process produces many adaptations designed to deliver benefits to others. Parental love, a motive that produces many benefits to children, is one example. But it's not the only one. Benefit delivering adaptations are also predicted to evolve when the recipients are other members of one's kin group, such as sisters, brothers, nephews, nieces, aunts, uncles, parents, grandparents, grandchildren, and even great grandchildren (Hamilton, 1964).

Furthermore, there are other evolutionary processes that result in various forms of altruism, cooperation, and mutualism. One is reciprocal altruism, whereby two cooperative individuals can both benefit by bestowing help on the other, resulting in "gains in trade" (Trivers, 1971). Hunting, for example, is a high-variance activity. In any given week, one hunter might be successful, the other hunter unsuccessful. If I share my meat with you when I am successful, and you share your meat with me when you are successful, we both benefit. Selection favors adaptations that exploit these opportunities for gains in trade, resulting in the evolution of cooperation through reciprocal altruism that can extend for years, decades, or even a lifetime (Axelrod & Hamilton, 1981). And natural selection can favor other forms of benefit-delivering adaptations, such as those involved when close friends become irreplaceable to each other (Tooby & Cosmides, 1996) and when the interests of a married couple become deeply intertwined (Buss, in press). The evolutionary process, in short, can result in many adaptations that are rightly regarded as nice, kind, cooperative, altruistic, and benefit bestowing.

Nonetheless, it is also true that evolution by selection is fundamentally a competitive process. Alleles for adaptations can evolve only if they succeed in out-propagating other competing alleles that happen to be present in the population at the same time. At the most general level of abstraction, this competitive process can take two forms. The first form is competition for the acquisition of reproductively relevant resources—for example, more efficiently acquiring food or more reliably acquiring reproductively valuable mates. This process can be called "competitive" even if the competing organisms never encounter each other. In "scramble food competition," for example, organisms are merely struggling as best they can to secure far-flung food that happens to exist in the local environment. Individuals with adaptations or design features that facilitate success at scrambling for food are favored by selection at the expense of those that are less adept at scrambling for food.

In addition to acquiring reproductive resources for self, however, a second general means of reproductive competition involves inflicting costs on competitors. Holding one's own resource acquisition constant, for example, one can increase one's *relative* reproductive success by depriving rivals of access to those same resources. The stealing of resources from a rival, for example, can simultaneously decrease the competitor's reproduction while increasing the resources available for one's own reproduction. When resources are limited, finite, or scarce, inflicting costs on competitors can be an extraordinarily effective means of increasing one's own relative reproductive success.

This theoretical perspective suggests that, in addition to whatever cooperative and benefit-bestowing adaptations have evolved, selection has also likely produced adaptations in humans whose proper function is to inflict costs on competitors. Stated differently, aggression can be an evolved solution to a number of specific adaptive problems (Buss & Shackelford, 1997a, 1997b). Aggression can function to co-opt the reproductively relevant resources of others, such as food, tools, weapons, or territory. It can be used to defend against incursion on one's own resources from others. It can be used to inflict costs on rivals through physical injury or reputational damage, hindering a rival's ability to compete for resources. Aggression can be used to negotiate status or dominance hierarchies by displacing a higher-ranking rival or preventing a lower-ranking rival from ascending in rank. Aggression can be used to cultivate a social reputation that deters others from inflicting costs. When choosing a victim, most people would think twice about stealing from a Mafia hit man, tangling with a professional boxer, or flirting with the girlfriend of a member of the Hell's Angels motorcycle gang. Aggression can be used to deter long-term mates from sexual infidelity (Buss & Shackelford, 1997b; Daly & Wilson, 1988). And aggression can be used to reduce the resources expended on genetically unrelated children, as when a stepfather drives a stepson away from the home. In sum, although aggression is commonly viewed as repugnant under many circumstances, it is clear that adaptations designed to inflict costs on other humans can evolve, have evolved, and can be designed to solve a large array of diverse adaptive problems.

It's important to bear in mind that adaptations for aggression do not operate as "blind instincts" that robotically drive a person to inflict costs on other humans in a manner oblivious to circumstances; quite the opposite. Blind, robotic, aggressive impulses would be ruthlessly selected against, compared with a more advantageous alternative: Having aggression as one strategy within a menu of strategies, activated only under a highly specific sets of co-occurring conditions. A simple example will illustrate this point. Other humans vary in physical formidability. Attacking a highly formidable human is far more risky than attacking a weak and vulnerable one. Selection should have favored information-processing devices that calculate relative formidability and decision rules to aggress or not to aggress depending on the outcome of this calculation. Adaptations to aggress blindly would have been mercilessly selected against in comparison to highly situation-contingent aggression adaptations.

Assessment of relative physical formidability, of course, is only one among many features of contexts that decision-rules for aggression should be selected to be contingent on. Others include the extensity and formidability of the victim's kin group and coalition, the reputational consequences of enacting an aggressive strategy, the risk of future retaliation, the availability of alternative means of solving the particular adaptive problem, the costs and benefits of those alternatives, and many others. The key point is that adaptations for aggression are not blind or oblivious to context; they are expected, on theoretical grounds, to be exquisitely sensitive to individual and social circumstances.

It is also important to note that it is exceedingly unlikely that there evolved a gene for aggressive behavior in context A, and another gene for aggressive behavior in context B, and so on. It is more likely that numerous genes interact, leading to the reliable development of information-processing mechanisms in the brain. These mechanisms form sets of decision rules that (a) recognize adaptive problems, (b) evaluate multiple contextual features historically important to the solution of the adaptive problem, and (c) adopt the behavioral solution determined by historical contingency to yield the greatest benefit at the lowest cost. The solution adopted may or may not be the optimal solution in any given situation. Its adoption, because it is based on extant information as it relates to historical contingency, may be suboptimal because of (a) contextual features overlooked in the evaluation of the situation and other forms of uncertainty, such as having no knowledge of the fact that a rival has a large, socially powerful kin network; (b) experiential calibration of decision rules in contexts sharply different from those encountered in another context, such as having been in numerous relationships in which one's romantic partners were unfaithful and starting a new relationship with a faithful mate; (c) incorrect identification of a context as would occur if decision rules were "tricked" into adopting a behavioral strategy in light of novel circumstances that resembled historical contingency, but actually were not historically contingent, or (d) selection for decision rules that work well on average, but are not perfectly matched to all of the specific features of a context required to render an optimal solution 100% of the time.

Understanding that evolved aggression adaptations are designed to be highly sensitive to context helps to clarify a common misunderstanding about evolutionary perspectives on aggression. Some social scientists erroneously believe that findings of individual differences within culture or variations across cultures in the rates of aggression somehow contradict an evolutionary explanation. They don't. A physiological analogy will help to show why. Although callus-producing mechanisms are universal across humans, there are tremendous individual differences within cultures and between cultures in the thickness and distribution of calluses. These differences occur because different individuals and different groups of individuals experience different rates and types of repeated friction to their skin. American academics tend to have few calluses; tennis players develop them on their favored hands; construction workers develop them on their arms; and Yanomamo Indians develop them on their feet. These variations, of course, do not falsify the hypothesis that humans universally have evolved callus-producing mechanisms. Instead, they illustrate that evolved callus-producing mechanisms are designed to be highly sensitive to contextual variations—universal adaptations that are required to explain the variability. The same applies to hypothesized aggression adaptations. Universality or species-typicality is sought at the level of underlying psychological design, not at the level of manifest behavior. Confusion about this key issue is largely responsible for misunderstandings about the evolutionary psychology of aggression and other psychological adaptations, including those that might be designed to kill other humans.

## THE EVOLUTION OF HOMICIDE

Killing may be regarded as the ultimate form of aggression, even though it is a very unique kind of act. Killing members of one's own species, contrary to widely held beliefs by many, turns out to be widespread in insect species, mammalian species, and primate species (Buss & Duntley, under review). It occurs in stingless bees, scorpions, spotted hyenas, lions, langur monkeys, and chimpanzees. Male lions, when they usurp a resident male, routinely kill (or attempt to kill) the lion cubs sired by the displaced male. The killing causes the female lion to enter estrus, at which time the new reigning male reinseminates her. No animal biologist, to our knowledge, doubts that male lions have evolved adaptations designed to perform these kinds of killings.

When it comes to humans, however, even evolutionists get leery about invoking adaptations for homicide, even when confronted with killings that occur in contexts remarkably similar to those witnessed in other species. Infanticides, for example, are attributed by some evolutionists to "failures of engagement of the normal mechanisms of parental love" (Daly & Wilson, 1998). Killings of rivals are attributed to "maladaptive byproducts of mechanisms that evolved for non-lethal functions." The idea that humans might have evolved adaptations whose dedicated function is to murder other humans seems to be so abhorrent that it has not been seriously entertained, scrutinized, or examined. In contrast, we have proposed a theory that appears to be radical in this context—that humans have evolved not one, but many adaptations whose proper function is to produce the death of other humans (Buss & Duntley, under review; Duntley & Buss, 1998; see also Ghiglieri, 1999; Tooby & Cosmides, 1988; Wrangham, 1999).

There are many potential benefits, evolutionarily speaking, to killing conspecifics, given the right set of contextual features. These include eliminating intrasexual competitors; gaining access to a rival's material resources; gaining access to a rival's fertile mates; cultivating a reputation that deters exploitation from others; protecting oneself from injury, rape, or death (self-defense function); protecting one's kin from injury, rape, or death; protecting one's mate from injury, rape, or death; eliminating resource-absorbing infants or children who have poor prospects for survival or reproduction; eliminating resource-absorbing infants or children who are genetically unrelated to oneself; and eliminating infants or children who interfere with investments in vehicles better able to translate finite investments into fitness (Buss & Duntley, under review).

In fact, viewed dispassionately from an evolutionary perspective, the surprise is not why killing occurs. Because the fitness benefits of killing can be so large and manifold, the surprise is that killing is not more common. And to explain that, we must explain another facet of our theory of "Murder by Design," which invokes the principle of antagonistic coevolution.

Coevolution is a principle that is commonly invoked to explain reciprocal evolutionary changes in interacting species. Predators and prey are prototypical examples of antagonistic coevolution. Prey animals that are slow and less agile than their conspecifics tend to be dinner for predators. In succeeding generations, those prey animals who survived and reproduced tend to be slightly more agile and fleet of foot. This greater agility imposes selection pressure on predators; the slow and clumsy predators fail to eat and so starve to death, compared with their more agile contemporaries. Each increment in the speed and evasive ability of prey selects for corresponding increments in the speed and counter-evasion tactics of predators. In this manner, reciprocal evolutionary changes occur in predators and prey, as each evolves in response to the adaptations in the other. Analogous coevolutionary arms races occur among parasites and hosts.

Although rarely invoked, analogous coevolutionary arms races can occur within members of the same species. They can occur between the sexes, as when deception by men selects for deception-detection mechanisms in women in certain mating contexts (Buss, in press). As another example, if infidelity is

advantageous for women, but not for their husbands, it will produce a coevolutionary arms race in which male sexual jealousy will evolve as a defense
against infidelity, which will cause women to evolve mechanisms that mute
signals of its occurrence, which in turn will select for more sensitive infidelity-
detection devices in men. These kinds of antagonistic coevolutionary arms races
are probably widespread in humans, and can spiral endlessly as adaptations and
counteradaptations become more and more sophisticated.

Our theory of "Murder by Design" invokes the principle of antagonistic
coevolution. Although killing is sometimes advantageous to the killer, it is
usually markedly costly to the victim (Buss & Duntley, under review). It ter-
minates all future reproductive opportunities of the victim. The victim's mates
may become reproductively valuable resources available to rivals. The victim's
children may become more vulnerable and potentially exploitable without the
victim around to protect them. The entire lineage of the victim can be jeop-
ardized by his or her death, producing cascading fitness costs down successive
generations. For these and other reasons, it's very bad for one's fitness to be
killed.

Because of the manifold costs of getting killed, as soon as killing entered the
human population as a strategy, coevolutionary forces would have immediately
begun to prevent its occurrence. Any mutation that favored the prevention of
being killed would have enjoyed an enormous fitness advantage. Just as selection favored specialized fears to prevent dying from snakebites, selection would
have favored the evolution of antihomicide mechanisms to avoid becoming a
victim of homicide. Antihomicide strategies, including killing to prevent being
killed, would then have had two effects on the evolution of homicide adaptations. First and most obvious, they would have made it more risky and costly
to attempt to kill other humans. This would have driven the homicide rate
down, because the net fitness benefits of killer strategies would have become
sharply reduced.

The second effect is more insidious and involves a further iteration in the
coevolutionary cycle. The design of evolved killing strategies would have become more sophisticated. Design features would have evolved to allow killers
to escape the costs imposed by antihomicide mechanisms. Tactics would have
evolved to evade defense mechanisms. Contexts would have been chosen in
which the risks of killing would have been minimized or the net benefits maximized. The psychology of killers would have evolved to choose victims selec-
tively, deceive victims by masking homicidal intent, choose killing in conditions
of anonymity, and many others (Buss & Duntley, under review). Of course,
further iterations in the coevolutionary spiral would have produced increasingly refined antihomicide defenses, such as deception-detection devices, avoidance of contexts in which one's life might be vulnerable, producing armaments
and fortifications, and many others (see Duntley & Buss, in preparation). The
coevolutionary arms race between killer and antikiller strategies continues to
spiral with no end in sight.

At this single slice in time, we believe that humans have already gone through multiple iterations of the coevolutionary process and currently possess a highly elaborate and complex psychology of killing, as well as a correspondingly elaborate and complex antihomicide psychology. Dozens of specific predictions deriving from this theory of evolved murder mechanisms have been, and are being, confirmed empirically (e.g., Buss & Duntley, under review; Buss & Duntley, 2002; Shackelford et al., 2000; Shackelford, Buss, & Weekes-Shackelford, in press).

## PUBLIC POLICY IMPLICATIONS

More than 563,000 homicides occur worldwide each year, representing a global rate of roughly 10.7 for every 100,000 individuals (Mercy & Hammond, 1999). The United States shows homicide rates almost exactly at the average for countries worldwide, logging a rate of 10 per 100,000 per year. Some countries, such as those in Sub-Saharan Africa show rates four times as high. Other countries, such as China, show rates only half as high as those in the United States.

These global figures, however, mask the types of individuals who are especially likely to be victims of murder. The rates of homicide are 3.5 times as high for males as they are for females, suggesting high sex linkage in patterns of victimization. The age distribution of homicides also differs sharply between the sexes. Whereas the risk of a female being killed is highest in infancy, the risk of a male being killed peaks in the 15 to 29 year age group—precisely the ages at which males engage in the most intrasexual competition. Indeed, homicide is the third leading cause of death for men worldwide in the 15–44 year-old age bracket, accounting for nearly 9% of all deaths (Mercy & Hammond, 1999).

Policies aimed at solving these problems range from efforts at gun control to attempts to impose deterrents to murder, such as capital punishment. As two authors recently noted, however, "the development and implementation of effective policies and programs for preventing violence must be firmly grounded in science" (Mercy & Hammond, 1999, p. 298). To cite another author, one can view the law as a "lever" designed to move human behavior in certain directions deemed desirable—to prevent people from committing some types of acts (e.g., murder), and to encourage them to perform other types of acts (e.g., provision their children) (Jones, 1999). The effectiveness of the law, or any other form of public policy, hinges on the accuracy of the psychological model on which laws and policies are based. Inaccurate, ill-informed, or scientifically inaccurate models will lead to policies that are ineffective in producing the desired changes in human behavior.

Although our evolution-based theory of homicide was developed to explain the causal origins of homicide and the specific contexts in which it occurs, not specifically as a tool to be used in the service of public policy, we believe none-theless that it might be used to good effect to offer some novel suggestions, albeit quite provisional and preliminary, that might inform efforts at shaping public policy.

We start with the premise that everyone has the capacity to commit homicide—we all have inherited specialized adaptations designed to murder other humans. Our studies have shown, for example, that most people state, at a minimum, that they would be willing to kill to prevent themselves from being killed, and also would be willing to kill to prevent their children from being killed. Whether these and other homicide mechanisms are engaged or activated depends critically on contextual circumstances. Our theory offers a specification of what those circumstances are likely to be for each type of homicide, thus offering a set of contexts toward which policy efforts might be specially directed.

Infanticide offers an obvious illustration. Evolutionary analyses of infanticide have revealed several distinct contexts in which children's lives are in danger—factors missed by nonevolutionary approaches. One of the greatest risk factors, for example, is having a stepparent in the home. Compared with residing with both genetic parents, preschool children who reside with a stepparent are 100 times more likely to be killed (Daly & Wilson, 1988). Although it has not been conclusively shown that this effect occurs because of evolved infanticide adaptations, as we argue (Buss & Duntley, under review), or because it is an incidental by-product of the failure to engage the normal evolved mechanisms of parental love, as others have argued (Daly & Wilson, 1998), evolutionary thinking clearly is what led to this important discovery. It is important to bear in mind that most stepparents do not kill their stepchildren, and there is the risk of inflicting reputational damage to stepparents by overgeneralizing these results. Nonetheless, it is clear that having a stepparent in the home is the single largest homicide risk factor for preschool children, dwarfing all other risk factors. Perhaps public policy could be aimed at educating stepparents on the special risks that they face as a consequence of being in this social situation. Additional risk factors to infants discovered by evolutionary psychologists include when the woman giving birth is young, unmarried, and lacks an investing father and when the infant is premature, unhealthy, or deformed, which may render investment in the child a potentially fruitless effort in terms of fitness (Daly & Wilson, 1988).

A second example pertains to women who are at risk of being killed by their romantic partners, those who presumably love them. According to our theory, men have evolved specific mate killing mechanisms that are engaged in specialized circumstances—when they are discovered committing a sexual infidelity and when they unceremoniously "dump" the man. Indeed, our empirical studies of homicidal fantasies reveal that rejected men frequently contemplate killing the woman who has spurned them, even though they do not act on these fantasies (Buss & Duntley, under review). Many men in this situation have the recurrent thought: "If I can't have her, no one can." Some state that "If she won't live with me, then she won't live at all." And empirically, sexual infidelities and breaking up with a husband or de facto spouse who wants to continue the relationship are the strongest risk factors for adult women being killed (Daly & Wilson, 1988; Shackelford et al., in press), especially if they are young and hence highly reproductively valuable (Shackelford et al., 2000). Furthermore, the first six months of the breakup are the most dangerous for the woman. Many women agree to meet with a potentially homicidal ex-mate "just one last time," failing to realize the special dangers of this time and circumstance.

In summary, one implication of our theory for public policy is to identify the circumstances in which evolved homicide mechanisms are most likely to be activated and to direct special efforts at educating people about these circumstances.

A second approach would be to capitalize on the evolved antihomicide mechanisms that humans naturally possess (Duntley & Buss, in preparation). Many approaches to modern psychology treat "emotions" as somehow opposed to "rationality" (Buss, 2001). Emotions are presumed to cloud thinking, preventing logical thought. As a consequence, people are sometimes encouraged to get rid of their fears or to ignore them as irrational, instinctual baggage from a past long forgotten. If our theory is correct, and some of these fears are actually activated antihomicide mechanisms, then ignoring the danger signals they provide may prove lethal. Identifying with greater precision the nature of these emotion-based antihomicide defenses and training people to attend to their signals may provide a second avenue for decreasing the risk of being killed.

Clearly, at this early stage in our evolutionary homicide theory, it would be premature to base any sweeping public policy on its tenets. Nonetheless, we believe that the theory is the most comprehensive and scientifically accurate theory of homicide yet proposed, and that exploring the insights it provides might ultimately give us tools to reduce the incidence of homicide.

## REFERENCES

Axelrod, R., & Hamilton, W.D. (1981). The evolution of cooperation. *Science, 211,* 1390–1396.

Berkowitz, L. (1993). *Aggression: Its causes, consequences, and control.* New York: McGraw Hill.

Buss, D.M. (in press). *The evolution of desire: Strategies of human mating* (Revised ed.). New York: Basic Books.

Buss, D.M. (2001). Cognitive biases and emotional wisdom in the evolution of conflict between the sexes. *Current Directions in Psychological Sciences, 10,* 219–223.

Buss, D.M., & Duntley, J.D. (1998). *Evolved homicide modules.* Paper presented to the Annual Meeting of the Human Behavior and Evolution Society, Davis, California.

Buss, D.M., & Duntley, J.D. (2002). *Mating motives for murder.* Paper presented to the Annual Meeting of the Human Behavior and Evolution Society, Rutgers University, New Brunswick, New Jersey.

Buss, D.M., & Duntley, J.D. (under review). Murder by design: The evolutionary psychology of homicide. *Behavioral and Brain Sciences.*

Buss, D.M., Haselton, M.G., Shackelford, T.K., Bleske, A.L., & Wakefield, J.C. (1998). Adaptations, exaptations, and spandrels. *American Psychologist, 53,* 533–548.

Buss, D.M., & Shackelford, T.K. (1997a). Human aggression in evolutionary psychological perspective. *Clinical Psychology Review, 17,* 605–619.

Buss, D.M., & Shackelford, T.K. (1997b). From vigilance to violence: Mate retention tactics in married couples. *Journal of Personality and Social Psychology, 72,* 346–361.

Daly, M., & Wilson, M. (1988). *Homicide.* Hawthorn: Aldine de Gruyter.

Daly, M., & Wilson, M. (1998). *The truth about Cinderella: A Darwinian view of parental love.* London: Weidenfeld & Nicolson.

Duntley, J., & Buss, D.M. (1998). *Evolved anti-homicide modules.* Paper presented to the Annual Meeting of the Human Behavior and Evolution Society, Davis, California.

Duntley, J.D., & Buss, D.M. (in preparation). *The evolution of anti-homicide mechanisms.* Austin: Department of Psychology, University of Texas.

Fingerhut, L.A., & Kleinman, J.C. (1990). International and interstate comparisons of homicide among young males. *Journal of the American Medical Association, 263,* 3292–3295.

Ghiglieri, M.P. (1999). *The dark side of man: Tracing the origins of violence.* Reading, MA: Perseus Books.

Hamilton, W.D. (1964). The genetical evolution of social behavior. I and II. *Journal of Theoretical Biology, 7,* 1–52.

Johnson, J. (1969). Organic psychosyndromes due to boxing. *British Journal of Psychiatry, 115,* 45–53.

Mercy, J.A., & Hammond, W.R. (1999). Combining action and analysis to prevent homicide. In M.D. Smith & M.A. Zahn (Eds.), *Homicide: A sourcebook of social research* (pp. 297–310). Thousand Oaks, CA: Sage.

Shackelford, T.K., Buss, D.M., & Peters, J. (2000). Wife killing: Risk to women as a function of age. *Violence & Victims, 15,* 273–282.

Shackelford, T.K., Buss, D.M., & Weeks-Shackelford, V. (in press). Wife-killings committed in the context of a "lovers triangle." *Journal of Basic and Applied Social Psychology.*

Smith, M.D., & Zahn, M.A. (Eds.). (1999). *Homicide: A sourcebook of social research.* Thousand Oaks, CA: Sage.

Tooby, J., & Cosmides, L. (1988). *The evolution of war and its cognitive foundations.* Institute for Evolutionary Studies, Technical Report #88–1.

Tooby, J., & Cosmides, L. (1990). On the universality of human nature and the uniqueness of the individual: The role of genetics and adaptation. *Journal of Personality, 58,* 17–68.

Trivers, R.L. (1971). The evolution of reciprocal altruism. *Quarterly Review of Biology,* *46,* 35–57.

Williams, G.C. (1966). *Adaptation and natural selection.* Princeton, NJ: Princeton University Press.

Wrangham, R. (1999). Evolution of coalitionary killing. *Yearbook of Physical Anthropology, 42,* 1–30.

6

# Fear of Death and Social Behavior
## *The Anatomy of Human Destructiveness*[1]

*Sheldon Solomon, Jeff Greenberg, and Tom Pyszczynski*

> Intensified progress seems to be bound up with intensified unfreedom. Throughout
> the world industrial civilization, the domination of man by man is growing in scope
> and efficiency. Nor does this trend appear as an incidental, transitory regression on
> the road to progress. Concentration camps, mass exterminations, world wars, and
> atom bombs are no "relapse into barbarism," but the unrepressed implementation of
> the achievements of modern science, technology, and domination. And the most
> effective subjugation and destruction of man by man takes place at the height of
> civilization, when the material and intellectual attainments of mankind seem to allow
> the creation of a truly free world.
>
> Herbert Marcuse, *Eros and Civilization*

We are at a crossroads of human existence: We possess the technical knowledge
required to provide for the material needs of all of humanity without systematic plunder and extermination of others; yet, systematic plunder and genocidal
extermination continue to thrive. The United Nations Department of Public
Information reports that UN peacekeeping forces are currently active in India
and Pakistan, Cyprus, Lebanon, Iraq and Kuwait, Western Sahara, Georgia,
Bosnia and Herzegovina, Prevlaka, Kosovo, Sierra Leone, East Timor, the Democratic Republic of Congo, and Eritrea. In other locations, for example, the
most recent round of atrocities in and around Israel, the conflicts are too bloody
and violent for peacekeepers to risk their presence there.

Closer to home, in 1995 Timothy McVeigh and Terry Nichols expressed their
displeasure with the U.S. government by blowing up the Oklahoma City Federal Building and 167 people in it (on June 11, 2001, we expressed our displeasure with Timothy McVeigh by exterminating him). In 1998, Aaron
McKinney and Russell Henderson lured University of Wyoming student Mat-
thew Shepard from a Laramie bar, lashed him to a fence, bludgeoned his head
with a gun, and left him to die because he was gay; and, Jasper Texans Lawrence
Brewer, John King, and Shawn Berry launched their hate group, the Texas
Rebel Soldiers, by beating and decapitating James Byrd Jr. by dragging him by
a chain wrapped around his ankles tied to a pickup truck. In 1999, Buford O.

Furrow sent "a wake-up call to America to kill Jews" by a shooting rampage at a Jewish Community Center in Los Angeles, topped off with the murder of a postal worker because he was Filipino.

Easy access to increasingly sophisticated weapons makes every individual a potential mass murderer and every country the potential site of the next genocidal holocaust. Although public concerns about the prospect of a nuclear holocaust resulting in the extinction of our species have subsided since the Cold War ended, it remains a very real possibility. Understanding the psychological underpinnings of human violence, in hope of ameliorating or at least attenuating human cruelty and destruction, should thus be one of the most important priorities of the natural and social sciences; and public policy should be forged in light of this knowledge.

For almost two decades, we have been developing, testing, and refining a theoretical account of human behavior that we believe offers some important insights about human violence. In this chapter, we present the tenets and evidence for *terror management theory* and discuss the implications of these ideas for understanding and ameliorating the viciousness that has characterized so much of our species' history to date.

## AN EVOLUTIONARY, EXISTENTIAL, AND PSYCHODYNAMIC ACCOUNT OF HUMAN BEHAVIOR

This section comprises a review of the intellectual roots and core propositions of terror management theory and the large body of empirical evidence supporting it.

### Terror Management Theory

Terror management theory (Greenberg et al., 1986; Solomon et al., 1991) is largely based on the work of the late cultural anthropologist Ernest Becker (1929–1974). In works such as *The Birth and Death of Meaning* (1962, 1971), *The Denial of Death* (1973), and *Escape from Evil* (1975), Becker attempted to integrate ideas from a wide range of academic disciplines in order to synthesize a scientific—in the sense of being empirically assessable—account of human behavior that could serve to illuminate the psychological underpinnings of human evil and, following the Enlightenment tradition, in so doing, provide insightful direction for constructive individual and social change.

. . . man's destructiveness and cruelty cannot be explained in terms of animal heredity or in terms of a destructive instinct, but must be understood on the basis of those factors by which man *differs* from his animal ancestors. The problem is to examine *in*

*what manner and to what degree the specific conditions of human existence are re-*
*sponsible for the quality and intensity of man's lust for killing and torturing.* (Eric
Fromm, *The Anatomy of Human Destructiveness*, 1973, p. 186)

Becker's analysis of human affairs begins from an evolutionary perspective
by considering how human beings are similar to as well as uniquely different
from all other forms of life. Humans share with all life forms a biological
predisposition toward self-preservation in the service of survival and reproduction. However, various forms of life differ in the terms of the specific morphological, physiological, behavioral, and psychological adaptations they have
made in order to exist in the particular environmental niches they inhabit. For
example, the cactus stores large amounts of generally very scarce water internally, and wards off predators' access to this precious fluid with rather sharp
thorns, rendering it perfectly suited for life in the desert; the tapeworm leads
a much different life fastened to the interior of a host animal's digestive tract;
an eagle employs keen eyesight to procure its dinner, while the nocturnal bat
accomplishes the same task with equally keen audition; and bees scan their
visual surroundings as they fly from food sources to their hives, and then dance
to communicate the whereabouts of the victuals to their mates.

Human beings are not especially well suited to survive individually on the
basis of our physical attributes (although upright bipedalism, the prehensile
thumb, and stereoscopic vision have been quite useful): They are not very large
or fast and their senses lack in acuity relative to the eyesight of the eagle, the
hearing of the bat, or the olfactory prowess of the dog. Instead of, or rather in
addition to, our physical attributes, humans have adapted to their surroundings
by sociability and intelligence. Our highly social nature fosters cooperation in
the service of tool making, hunting/gathering, agricultural pursuits, and (subsequently) the development of a host of elaborate political, economic, and religious institutions (e.g., the state, the marketplace, schools, grocery stores,
hospitals) that facilitate our collective survival; all these activities in turn require a high degree of intelligence made possible by increases in cranial capacity:

[I]n hominids evidence of radical cultural change has tended to correlate with increases
in brain size. *Homo erectus* was characterized by major cultural innovation as well as
a larger brain: *erectus* produced tools of great refinement, eventually domesticated fire,
and migrated over much of the globe. *Homo sapiens*, with the largest hominid brain,
produced the exponential rate of cultural change that characterizes modern human
society. (Merlin Donald, *Origins of the Modern Mind*, 1991, p. 100)

Especially adaptive hominid cognitive skills include the ability to delay behavior in novel and uncertain situations in order to ponder existing alternatives, reflect on past experiences and consider future possibilities, impute
mental states to others and make inferences about the nature of others' mental
states, impute mental states to one's "self" and make inferences about one's

own mental states (self-awareness), and imagine things that do not yet exist (e.g., tools) and then create objects in accordance with those images.

Following Kierkegaard, Becker argues that self-awareness in humans, when juxtaposed with the capacity to reflect on the past and, more important, to envision the future, inevitably produces a uniquely human existential condition that is both awesome and dreadful. Only human beings, by virtue of consciousness, are simultaneously alive and aware that they are alive; they are, in Otto Rank's (1936/1978, p. 4) lovely phrase, "the temporal representative of the cosmic primal force," that is, directly descended from, and consequently related to, the first living organism, as well as everything that has ever been alive, is currently living, and will live in the future. What a joy to be alive and know it. "Whether it be the fresh and spontaneous perception of a landscape, or the dawning of some truth as the result of our thinking, or a sensuous pleasure that is not stereotyped, or the welling up of love for another person" (Fromm, 1941/1965, p. 286), human beings have a unique capacity for awe, wonder, and delight.

Life, then—especially for those aware of being alive—rules! But here's the rub: The natural conclusion of every life is death, and only human beings are explicitly aware that this is the case. What an outrageous and terrifying affront to a finely crafted survival machine designed by billions of years of evolution to stay alive at all costs, to learn as an unexpected by-product of self-awareness (otherwise an incredibly powerful evolutionary adaptation) of the ultimate futility of this most basic biological imperative:

Ay, but to die, and go we know not where;
To lie in cold obstruction, and to rot;
This sensible warm motion to become
A kneaded clod; and the delighted spirit
To bathe in fiery floods or to reside
In thrilling regions of thick-ribbed ice;
To be imprison'd in the viewless winds,
And blown with restless violence round about
The pendent world; or to be worse than worst
Of those that lawless and incertain thoughts
Imagine howling!—'tis too horrible!
The weariest and most loathed worldly life
That age, ache, penury, and imprisonment
Can lay on nature is a paradise
To what we fear of death.
             Shakespeare, *Measure for Measure*

Potentially paralyzing dread of death is thus the inevitable result of a self-conscious organism predisposed toward self-preservation. And this horror is exponentially compounded by the concurrent realization of the profound vulnerability of every human being. Death can occur at any time for reasons that often cannot be anticipated or controlled. For every person that dies in the night at a ripe old age with their family members crowded around keeping a loving vigil, others perish alone from disease; others in the stomachs of hungry predators, others by the hands of their enemies; and still others in tidal waves, earthquakes, hurricanes, or countless other potentially life-terminating mishaps that befall every living creature on a regular basis. And this horror and dread of death becomes amalgamated into unmitigated terror when combined with the recognition that humans are animals: sentient pieces of breathing, defecating, menstruating, fornicating, expectorating, ejaculating meat—no more fundamentally significant or enduring than a fly hovering over a fresh pile of teacup poodle feces or the poodle that produced it.

Following Otto Rank (1936/1978) and Norman Brown (1959), Becker posits that the explicit awareness of death and the potential for debilitating terror engendered by this awareness is the most significant event in the evolutionary history of our species. Susanne Langer independently advances the same argument in *Mind: An Essay on Human Feeling* (1982, pp. 90, 91, 103):

And with the rise and gradual conception of the "self" as the source of personal autonomy comes, of course, the knowledge of its limit—the ultimate prospect of death. The effect of this intellectual advance is momentous. . . . It is in a fairly recent phase of that evolutionary course that the realization of death as the inevitable finale of every life has overtaken mankind . . . Its long preparation, however, has been as natural as the wholly unplanned developments which culminate in the peacock's ornamental tail or the beaver's landscape architecture.

Following Becker, Brown, Rank, Langer, and others (see, e.g., Spengler, 1926), terror management theory proposes that culture—humanly constructed beliefs about the nature of reality shared by individuals in groups—serves to assuage the terror engendered by the uniquely human awareness of death and, in so doing, to preserve consciousness (in its present form) as a viable form of mental organization. Only human beings embed themselves in a linguistically generated symbolic universe of their own creation that is nevertheless believed to be an absolute representation of reality by the average enculturated individual. Culture serves to reduce anxiety about death by providing the possibility for individuals to perceive themselves as persons of *value* in a world of *meaning*, and hence qualified for immortality. Accordingly, all cultures provide their constituents with an account of the origin of the universe, a prescription for acceptable conduct in the context of socially designated roles, and an explanation of what happens to people when they die that offers hope of immortality, symbolically through the performance of heroic deeds, the creation of enduring monuments or works of art, the production of large families, an identification with enduring institutions, or the personal amassing of large fortunes, and/or literally through the various kinds of afterlives promised by most organized religions.

For example, in the Judeo-Christian tradition with which most of us are familiar, God created the earth and all of its present inhabitants in six days; but this view is radically divergent from accounts of the origin of the universe and human beings subscribed to by other peoples. The Ainu, original inhabitants of Japan, believe that the earth was initially lifeless mud and water until a heavenly creator sent a bird to make earth and that humans are descended from the polar bear. The Bushmen of the Kalahari Desert in Southwest Africa believe that God created everything after assuming the form of a praying mantis. The Eskimos of Kukulik Island in the Bering Strait believe that a Creator-Raven made the world then, after a brief rest, turned pebbles into people who were subsequently instructed to throw pebbles into water that became whales. The earth was created by a dung beetle out of mud, according to the Negritos, pygmy people of Malaysia; and the Papua in New Guinea are quite certain that the first humans came out of a palm tree (all of these examples from Leeming & Leeming, 1994).

Despite the wide diversity of mutually exclusive accounts of the origin of the universe and humankind (mutually exclusive in the sense that veracity of any given account would almost certainly disconfirm all others), Leeming and Leeming (1994, p. viii) observe that:

[W]hen creation myths are compared, certain universal or archetypal patterns are discovered in them. Behind the many individual creation myths is a shadow myth that is the world culture's collective dream of differentiation (cosmos) in the face of the original and continuously threatening disorder (chaos).

The basic creation story then, is that of the process by which chaos becomes cosmos, no-thing becomes some-thing. In a real sense this is the only story we have to tell. . . . It lies behind our attempts to "make something" of our lives, that is, to make a difference in spite of the universal drive toward meaninglessness.

A primary function of culture is thus to provide a meaningful conception of reality; the fact that all culturally constructed conceptions of reality are problematic in terms of their likelihood of being true is psychologically immaterial. Psychologically, it is much more important to be certain than to be right.

Although confidence in a shared set of beliefs about the nature of reality, what we generally refer to as a *cultural worldview,* is a necessary component of human psychological equanimity, it is not sufficient. Also necessary is the sense that one is a uniquely significant, heroic in Becker's (borrowed from William James) words, member of the cultural drama to which one subscribes. We all want to "make something" of our lives. To accomplish this, all cultures have social roles with associated prescriptions of appropriate conduct, the satisfaction of which allows individuals to perceive themselves as persons of value in a world of meaning, and in so doing to acquire *self-esteem.*

Self-esteem, the belief that one is a valuable member of a meaningful universe, is thus the psychological mechanism by which culture performs its anxiety reducing function: The primary function of self-esteem is as an anxiety-buffer, especially with respect to concerns about death (of which one need not be aware). According to this analysis, the need for self-esteem is universal; however, the manner by which it is acquired is historically and culturally relative. This is because self-esteem is ultimately a cultural construction; the standards by which one judges one's self to be of value are almost invariably culturally inculcated (even if one is unaware that this is the case). Anthropologist Walter Goldschmidt (1990) describes the universal need for self-esteem as "affect hunger" that is satisfied through the pursuit of prestige in the community by meeting or exceeding culturally designated standards of value and/or achievement.

Standards of value and achievement, what it means to be good and/or right, vary considerably across cultures (similar to the diversity of views about the origin of the universe and human beings described earlier). For example (from Goldschmidt, 1990), a heroic accomplishment for a Crow Indian warrior is to gallop into an enemy camp and touch one of the enemy warriors without injuring him; Tlingit Indians are regarded in proportion to how many blankets and other objects they have accumulated, and then either given away or destroyed; Yurok Indians value ceremonial goods such as skins of albino deer and obsidian blades, but would be loathe to give them away and horrified at the prospect of destroying them; Dinka men are measured by the number of cattle they possess; and a Trobriand Island man is measured by the size of the pyramid of yams he builds in front of his sister's house and leaves to rot.

Perhaps these criteria for acquiring self-worth seem absurd, but consider some examples closer to home. In America, self-esteem can be acquired by: proficiently hitting a cow skin covered ball with a wooden stick (e.g., Ken Griffey Jr.); having silicon sacks surgically implanted in one's breasts (e.g., Pamela Anderson); having the right colored plastic cards in one's wallet (e.g., American Express: "Don't leave home without it."); pretending to engage in heroic actions (e.g., Bruce Willis); and, in at least one case, by imitating talking through one's own anus (i.e., Jim Carrey). And that's probably enough said about the arbitrary nature of bases of self-worth! There thus seems to be no limit to the socially sanctioned means by which a sense of value can be acquired and no absolute barometer of good and evil, in that just about every conceivable behavior or moral standard that is valued in one social milieu is disparaged or despised in another.

In sum, terror management theory posits that cultural worldviews developed as an evolutionary adaptation to the uniquely human awareness of death—an awareness that was most likely an unfortunate by-product of an otherwise very powerful and adaptive form of mental organization: self-awareness/consciousness. Cultural worldviews consist of humanly constructed beliefs about the nature of reality that people in a group share to acquire self-esteem: a sense of meaning and value that confers psychological equanimity via belief in symbolic and/or literal immortality. Human beings are thus cultural animals, and the essence of culture is death-denial.

## THE ARCHEOLOGICAL AND ANTHROPOLOGICAL EVIDENCE

A large body of archeological and anthropological evidence is consistent with the terror management perspective. For example, based on an evolutionary analysis of the archeological record, Donald (1991) proposed that the original purpose for the development of language was to enable our hominid ancestors to construct narrative accounts of the universe, rather than to facilitate communication, coordinate social activities, or foster creative alteration of the physical environment; for Donald, these obviously handy attributes of language were secondary manifestations after language use had already been established for constructing narratives. Whether pragmatic purposes preceded (see, e.g., Aiello & Dunbar, 1993) or followed the development of narrative accounts of the universe, such accounts were undoubtedly central to the development of language and the cultural worldviews these emerging languages were able to convey.

The archeological and anthropological records leave similarly little doubt that narrative accounts of the universe were not generated primarily to produce increasingly accurate accounts of the world, as often suggested by evolutionary psychologists (see, e.g., Tooby & Cosmides, 1992) but rather to make "the incredible credible" (Fromm, 1973), the "unreal real" (Rank, 1932), that is, to conceive of a predictable and orderly universe in which eternal life was the inevitable result of proper behavior. In accord with this claim, language, art, body ornamentation, and ritual burials appear suddenly and simultaneously as part of the Middle/Upper Paleolithic period (30,000–50,000 years ago; Mithen, 1996).

Concerns about death may also have contributed to the transition from small bands of seminomadic hunting/gathering peoples to larger, more sedentary communities 10,000 years ago. Evolutionary psychologists (e.g., Wilson, 1998) generally attribute this transition to the development of agriculture, but this account has been challenged by recent excavations in Turkey showing remains of large communities of people at least 1,000 years before the advent of agriculture (e.g., Balter, 1998). Although there was no evidence of agricultural activity at these sites, there was striking evidence of ritual burials, especially of children, under houses and in direct proximity to large murals of spectacular artwork depicting humans grappling with natural forces, for example, large predatory animals. Perhaps people came together in larger communities as particularly compelling worldviews began to spread throughout a specific area. Large-scale unifications under spiritually sanctioned authorities, often viewed as part-deities, may have provided the type of grandeur and displays of power likely to garner and sustain faith in such death-transcending ideologies.

"You have all the fears of mortals and all the desires of immortals" (Seneca, A.D. 49/1951, p. 295). From this point in history to the present, all civilizations are clearly different approaches to the same problem: how to satisfy human's insatiable immortal desires engendered by their seemingly inconsolable mortal fears. Ancient Chinese emperors took their families and staff with them to the grave by burying them alive in their tombs; subsequently this corporeal entourage was replaced by legions of more durable, life-size terra-cotta statues. In Egypt, pharaohs spent their lives in a frenzied effort to deny death through the construction of the magnificently durable pyramids and funerary techniques. The Judeo-Christian-Islamic tradition is originally derived from the previously noted ancient Sumarian text the Epic of Gilgamesh (May, 1991). In the story, Gilgamesh is overwhelmed with grief after the death of his best friend Enkidu, and becomes obsessed with the prospect of his own death: "When I die, shall I not be like unto Enkidu?" Gilgamesh then departs on a quest to obtain immortality; a quest that humans have been diligently pursuing to this day; see, for example, *Together Forever: An Invitation to Be Physically Immortal* (Brown, Strole, & Brown, 1990), *Talking to Heaven. A Medium's Message of Life after Death* (Van Praagh, 1997), and *Why Die? A Beginner's Guide to Living Forever* (Bowie, 1998).

## THE TERROR MANAGEMENT ANALYSIS OF HUMAN VIOLENCE

There is no doubt about the presence of aggressive and destructive tendencies in the human psyche which are of the nature of biological drives. However, the most pernicious phenomena of aggression, transcending self-preservation and self-destruction, are based upon a characteristic feature of man above the biological level, namely his capability of creating symbolic universes in thought, language and behavior. (L. von Bertalanffy, *Comments on Aggression* [1956; quoted in Fromm, 1973, pp. 186–187])

But how does a theory positing that culture serves to provide a sense of meaning and value to deny death help us understand our species' propensity for violence, cruelty, and destructiveness? According to the theory, cultural conceptions of reality always include many fictional elements that can only be sustained by social consensus; thus, the more people who adhere to a specific conception of reality the easier it is to sustain belief in a particular "illusion." Consequently, a substantial proportion of human activity is directed toward preserving faith in one's worldview and a sense that one is meeting or exceeding the standards of value associated with that worldview. Accordingly, anything that threatens the validity or integrity of one's worldview, or one's value in the context of their worldview, undermines the strength of the death-denying psychological apparatus. As individuals, we are therefore prone to lash out at anyone who threatens our sense of self-worth or the beliefs upon which our self-worth is based. Becker (1975, p. 5) put it this way:

What men have done is to shift the fear of death onto the higher level of cultural perpetuity; and this very triumph ushers in an ominous new problem. Since men must now hold for dear life onto the self-transcending meanings of the society in which they live, onto the immortality symbols which guarantee them indefinite duration of some kind, a new kind of instability and anxiety are created. And this anxiety is precisely what spills over into the affairs of men. In seeking to avoid evil, man is responsible for bringing more evil into the world than organisms could ever do merely by exercising their digestive tracts.

This simple insight can help explain interpersonal examples of violence ranging from lovers' quarrels and bar fights to jealousy fueled homicides and school shootings. However, this perspective is even more useful in explaining intergroup aggression. The most pervasive and salient threat to any cultural worldview is the existence of others who subscribe to different cultural worldviews, because accepting the validity of an alternative conception of reality necessarily (at least implicitly) undermines the confidence with which one subscribes to one's own worldview. This then exposes the individual to the potential anxiety that their worldview was originally constructed to contain, and instigates a host of compensatory reactions to restore psychological equanimity.

One response to encountering someone with a radically different cultural worldview is to dispose of one's own worldview and adopt the worldview of the other, as occasionally occurs in religious and political conversions. Yesterday's Christian is now Buddhist; yesterday's Vietnam War–protesting Students for a Democratic Society member is now a Republican Party shill. Consistent with this notion, research (see, e.g., Paloutzian, 1981; Ullman, 1982) has shown that just prior to conversion, self-esteem is low and fear of death is very high, but that self-esteem increases and fear of death declines immediately following conversion.

More often, however, people respond to the implicit threat of encountering a different Other in ways that bolster their confidence in their existing worldview in the service of retaining it (Berger & Luckmann, 1966/1967). The first line of psychological defense in light of alternative conceptions of reality is to derogate the people in possession of them. Sure, the Bushmen of the Kalahari Desert believe that God assumed the form of a praying mantis in order to create the universe; but then again these are half-naked preliterate, barely transcending-the-monosyllable, not-quite-human savages. If they had running water, cable television, designer jeans, and e-mail like we do, surely they would understand the error of their ways and see that God cannot be some giant bug; everyone who knows anything knows that God created the earth in six days and created us (well, men at least!) in His image.

At the same time that we derogate people who do not share our cultural worldviews, we make implicit and explicit efforts to divest people of their worldviews and go to great lengths to convince them (generally with tremendous displays of political, economic, and military power) to adopt our own culturally constructed conception of reality. Missionary activity is the most obvious example of this phenomenon in the religious domain, as well as the Cold War in the political arena. Christian missionaries have played a large role in the colonization of scores of indigenous cultures around the world. Similarly, the United States and the Soviet Union spent enormous time and energy in the latter part of the twentieth century to convince Third World countries to adopt a capitalist or communist ideological approach to life. And although there are obviously enormous physical resources at stake here, the major payoff for wholesale religious, political, and/or economic conversions is blatantly psychological. All cultures are fragile social constructions sustained by social consensus; consequently, the more people who adhere to a particular conception of reality, the easier it is for people to be confident that their vision of reality is "true."

However, there will always be headstrong peoples who tenaciously adhere to their ways of life despite our withering condemnation and heavy-handed invitations to dispose of their heritages and assume ours: *These* people must of course be exterminated in order to demonstrate (to them and ourselves) that our vision of reality and our way of life is indeed more "true" than theirs. Hence, the many "holy wars" throughout history: *"My God is better than your God and we'll kick your ass to prove it."* Thus, according to this analysis, the ultimate cause of most if not all protracted armed conflicts is psychological, and stems from humankind's fundamental inability to tolerate those with different death-denying visions of reality. This is not to suggest that political and material issues are irrelevant; of course they often play a large role in wars. What we are claiming, however, is that wars are ultimately battles for ideological supremacy: "[W]ars and persecutions are, at bottom, expressions of rivalry between contending claims to immortality and ultimate spiritual power" (Lifton, 1983, p. 315). The Middle East, Ireland, India/Pakistan, Rwanda, and the country formerly known as Yugoslavia are host to just a few of the many seemingly intractable (often going back thousands of years) conflicts where each side denies the right of the other to exist. For example, the official policy of the Palestine Liberation Organization for many years was to push all Israelis into the ocean; the Israelis countered with the quaint slogan "The only good Arab is a dead Arab." Former President Ronald Reagan fueled Cold War animosity by continual reference to the Soviet Union as the "Evil Empire," whereas the Soviet-supported Iranian fundamentalists countered by designating the United States as the "Great Satan."

Clearly, this is not the rhetoric of rational political and economic disagreement; it is the histrionic and terrified defense of death-denying ideologies unable to bear the psychological brunt of alternative conceptions of reality. And human history has been replete with a succession of unspeakable horrors as a result, that is, oceans of blood, mountains of misery, and as Marcuse (1955) observed decades ago, few signs of abatement have appeared despite physical resources and technological development that make the prospect of a peaceful planet a practical possibility. Instead, obscene amounts of energy and resources are currently devoted to development and deployment of increasingly lethal biological and nuclear weapons that make it quite possible that human beings will be the first form of life to become extinct via self-extermination.

The idea that cultural worldviews serve to deny death by providing people with a sense that they are valuable members of a meaningful universe, and that consequently the mere existence of people with different worldviews is threatening and provokes a host of unfortunate responses, for example, nationalism, racism, religious fanaticism, militarism, culminating in violent efforts to annihilate them. Sounds bleak indeed, but it gets worse! Because cultural worldviews are symbolic (although they have very physical manifestations, e.g., flags, monuments, and other cultural icons that render the culture more tangible and convincing), and death is quite physical, no culturally constructed symbol is capable of completely eliminating human beings' terror of death. Thus, a panic constantly lingers on the threshold of consciousness, one that can at any time burst into awareness and instigate a state of unmitigated terror. According to Becker (1975), this dread is repressed, and then projected onto a person or group of people who become scapegoats and subsequently deemed the all-encompassing repositories of evil whose eradication would make life on earth as it is in heaven. In other words, even if there weren't ethnically or ideologically different people to disparage and destroy to restore our psychological equanimity when our death-denying illusions are threatened, we would designate scapegoats based on subtle differences to berate and batter as a conduit to siphon off the residual fear of death that our cultural worldviews are incapable of completely eliminating. Constant ethnic strife, and harassment of, and hostility toward, culturally designated scapegoats is thus the sad price that human beings pay for being creatures with mortal fears and immortal aspirations.

## An Historical Example: The Rise of Hitler

One aspect of Becker's analysis of human evil we find most convincing is the insight it provides into the phenomenon of Nazi Germany. This brief example, although an oversimplification, illustrates the power of this perspective. Following World War I, the German people lost faith in their government and their sense of self-worth as Germans; they were riddled with reminders of their own mortality These problems were further exacerbated by the economic depression that leveled the country before Hitler took power. In *Mein Kampf*, written while serving a light prison sentence for treason (in perhaps the most tragic and ironic error in judgment in recorded history, the government did not want to make him a martyr) and in many rousing speeches after his release, Hitler offered a vision of a new Germany asserting the superiority of Germans over the impure animal races, and their inevitable rise under his leadership once the tainted vermin such as Gypsies and Jews were purged from German society. With continuous references to a divine will and a glorious national movement that would live on long beyond his individual death, Hitler confidently offered the German people a worldview built upon ancient Germanic traditions which could both blame past and current problems on outsiders and provide deep feelings of self-worth to the only true humans, the Aryan majority. Hitler thus succeeded in becoming the transference object, or source of security and self-worth, for enough German people to seize control and spiral toward holocaust and destruction (Becker, 1973, 1975).

## Experimental Evidence Assessing Terror Management Theory

By simplifying, formalizing, and extending the analysis of Becker, his intellectual forebearers, and like-minded contemporaries, terror management theory provides connections to contemporary discourse in psychology and the other social sciences. Equally important, the theory has generated a host of testable hypotheses, which have in turn produced a large body of research that has supported the basic tenets of the theory and stimulated further refinements of it. Although we initially found these ideas compelling because of their logical coherence and their consistency with archeological and anthropological evidence and historical events, we believe the experimental evidence further attests to their validity.

### Self-esteem as anxiety-buffer.

An initial line of research was directed toward investigating the anxiety-buffering properties of self-esteem. A large literature (reviewed in Solomon et al., 1991) has established a negative correlation between self-esteem and anxiety. However, these findings could not establish a causal connection between heightened self-esteem and reduced anxiety because it is also possible that this correlation results from chronic anxiety, causing people to have low self-esteem. Consequently, Greenberg, Solomon, Pyszczynski, Rosenblatt, Burling, Lyon, and Simon (1992) conducted a series of experiments in which participants were exposed to threatening situations after self-esteem was momentarily elevated or left unaltered, and anxiety was subsequently assessed. In one study, participants were given either positive or neutral false feedback on a bogus personality assessment (a manipulation check indicated that we were successful in this regard) and then asked to watch some gory scenes of an electrocution and autopsy (or benign scenes of comparable length in a control condition); afterward they reported their anxiety on a state anxiety scale. In support of our predictions, for participants in the neutral self-esteem condition, watching the gory death video produced higher self-reported anxiety relative to the benign control group; but heightened anxiety in response to the death video was eliminated when participants' self-esteem was momentarily raised prior to watching it.

Two additional studies replicated the finding that self-esteem serves an anxiety-buffering function, including one using a different manipulation of self-esteem (bogus feedback on a supposed intelligence test). Both studies used a different, more direct physical threat (anticipation of electrical shocks) and a more direct physiological assessment of anxiety (skin conductance). Participants in the neutral self-esteem condition were (not surprisingly) quite aroused (had high skin conductance scores) while expecting electrical shocks relative to control group participants expecting to observe some colored lights; however, this heightened arousal in anticipation of electrical shocks was eliminated when self-esteem was temporarily increased.

Greenberg, Pyszczynski, Solomon, Pinel, Simon, and Jordan (1993) subsequently demonstrated that momentarily elevated or dispositionally high self-esteem reduced vulnerability to denying defensive distortions. The participants were told that emotional people either live long or die young and were then asked to report how emotional they were. If self-esteem was unaltered or dispositionally modest, participants told that emotionality was associated with a long life reported high emotionality, whereas those told that emotionality was associated with a short life reported low emotionality. Thus, they biased their reports of emotionality to support the likelihood that they would live a long life. However, these biased assessments of emotionality were eliminated when self-esteem was elevated (by bogus feedback on a personality inventory) or dispositionally high. High or bolstered self-esteem thus at least temporarily eliminated the participants' need to bias their self-perceived emotionality to make them feel like they would live especially long lives. Collectively, this research provides compelling convergent evidence that self-esteem serves an important anxiety buffering function.

### Mortality salience paradigm.

A second line of research has explored the effects of subtle reminders of death on a host of interpersonal behaviors. We reasoned that if cultural worldviews serve a death-denying function, then asking people to think about their own death (*mortality salience*) should increase their need for the protection normally afforded by the cultural worldview and consequently provoke more favorable reactions to anyone who upholds the worldview, as well as more unfavorable reactions to anyone who threatens the worldview. Theory-consistent mortality salience effects have been obtained in over 100 studies investigating a wide range of social behavior, including risk-taking, creativity and guilt, depression and anxiety-disorders, self-esteem defense, attitudes toward the human body and the natural world, perceptions of similarity to self and others, identification with in-groups, and reactions to similar and dissimilar others. Because the effects of mortality salience on reactions to similar and dissimilar others are most pertinent to the issue of human aggression, we focus primarily on them here.

In a typical study, we tell participants entering the lab we are studying personality traits and that they consequently would complete some standard personality assessments. Embedded in several personality scales (e.g., neuroticism scale, social desirability scale) is what is described as a new projective measure consisting of two open-ended questions to render mortality momentarily salient: *"Please briefly describe the emotions that the thought of your own death arouse in you"* and, *"Jot down, as specifically as you can, what you think will happen to you as you physically die."* Participants in control conditions complete parallel questions about other topics (e.g., eating a meal, watching television, dental pain, social rejection). Then, in what is often portrayed as a completely different experiment, participants are given an opportunity to evaluate others who either share or differ from their cultural worldviews and/or dominant cultural values: this constitutes the primary dependent measure.

Greenberg, Pyszczynski, Solomon, Rosenblatt, Veeder, Kirkland, and Lyon (1990, Study 1) had Christian participants rate Christian and Jewish targets (who were portrayed as quite similar except for religious background) after a mortality salience or control induction. In the control condition, there were no differences in participants' evaluations of the targets; however, a subtle reminder of death in the experimental condition produced increased affection for the fellow Christian target and exaggerated hostility for the Jewish target. Greenberg et al. (1990, Study 3) then exposed American college students to essays supposedly written by an author who either praised or condemned the American way of life following a mortality salience or control induction. Participants rated the author of the pro-U.S. essay more favorably than the author of the anti-U.S. essay in the control condition; however, in response to mortality salience this tendency was exaggerated in both directions (i.e., more positive and negative reactions to pro- and anti-U.S. authors, respectively).

The role of in-group identity in assuaging concerns about mortality also has been demonstrated in the domain of domestic race relations. Specifically, mortality salience leads white Americans to react sympathetically to a white racist (Greenberg, Schimel, Martens, Solomon, & Pyszczynski, in press) and to react negatively to an African American individual who violates the negative stereotype of African Americans—specifically, a studious chess-playing male African American college student (Schimel et al., 1999).

These results support the notion that religious, political, and ethnic identities and beliefs serve a death-denying function, in that people respond to momentary reminders of death by increasing their affection for similar others and disdain for dissimilar others. But earlier we argued that even in the absence of others who differ in these salient ways, people would designate others as a scapegoat to serve a terror assuaging function. Harmon-Jones, Greenberg, Solomon, and Simon (1995) examined this notion empirically by assigning previously unacquainted people to different groups on the basis of their preference for abstract art works by Paul Klee or Wasily Kandinsky (the minimal group paradigm; Tajfel, Billig, Bundy, & Flament, 1971). Participants then rated themselves and fellow in-group members and members of the other group after a mortality salience or control induction. Thinking about death resulted in exaggerated regard for one's own group and disparagement of those who preferred a different kind of art, despite the fact that the group had just been formed minutes ago, participants did not know anyone in their group directly, and membership in the group was based on a relatively unimportant preference for abstract art.

One possible shortcoming of these findings is that they are all based on attitudinal measures. Thinking about death may engender more positive and negative attitudes toward similar and dissimilar others respectively but without leading people to behave accordingly. Additional research has, however, demonstrated the effects of mortality salience on actual behavior. After completing a mortality salience or control induction, Ochsmann and Mathy (1994) told German university students that the experiment was over and had them sit in a reception area, presumably to be paid for participating in the study. There was a row of chairs in the reception area, and in the center of the row was another student who was actually a confederate of the experimenters. The confederate appeared to be a German student for half of the participants; for the other half, the confederate appeared to be a Turkish student (currently a despised minority in Germany). The investigators were interested in how close to or far way from the confederate each participant would sit as a function of his appearance (German or Turkish) after thinking about death or a benign control topic. Although physical distance did not differ as a function of the confederate's appearance in the control condition, mortality salient participants sat closer to the fellow German and further away from the Turkish infidel. This finding establishes that mortality salience influences actual behavior above and beyond changes in attitudes.

More recently, McGregor et al. (1998) demonstrated that subtle reminders of death produce actual physical aggression toward those who threaten deeply cherished beliefs. Liberal or conservative college students read an essay they believed was written by another student in the study that condemned either liberals or conservatives (e.g., "Liberals are the cause of so many problems in this country. . . . The bleeding heart stance they take, of trying to help everyone is a joke and incredibly stupid. How can they help the world when they can't even help themselves?" or "Conservatives are the cause of so many problems in this country. . . . The cold-hearted stance they take, of trying to help only themselves is a joke and incredibly stupid. They are too busy thinking of themselves, and don't care about anyone else."). Then, after a mortality salience or control induction in what they believed to be a separate study, participants were given an opportunity to administer a quantity of their choosing of very hot salsa to the student who wrote the essay in the "first study" and who claimed to dislike spicy foods. We used hot sauce administration as a direct measure of physical aggression because of some highly publicized incidents of hot sauce being used malevolently to harm others (e.g., police officers assaulted by a cook at Denny's; children being abused by being forced to drink hot sauce). Results indicated no differences in hot sauce allocation for similar and dissimilar others in the control condition; however, following mortality salience, participants administered twice the amount of hot sauce to different others than they did to similar others. Two additional studies replicated these effects. Reminders of death thus produced direct aggression toward those who challenge cherished aspects of cultural worldviews.

The general finding that mortality salience produces *worldview defense* (i.e., exaggerated positive and negative responses to similar and dissimilar others, respectively) is thus quite robust, and extends beyond attitudinal preferences to behavior and direct acts of physical aggression. Mortality salience effects have been independently obtained in labs in the United States, Canada, Germany, Israel, Italy, the Netherlands, and Australia, using a variety of mortality salience manipulations, including fear of death scales (instead of our typical open-ended questions) and films of gory automobile accidents. Mortality salience effects are also apparently unique to thoughts of death: asking people to ponder unpleasant but nonlethal matters (e.g., failing an exam, giving a speech in public, being socially ostracized, being paralyzed, being in pain at the dentist) often results in self-reported anxiety and negative affect, but does not engender worldview defense (see Greenberg et al., 1997, for a review of this research). Additionally, mortality salience effects have been obtained in natural settings, for example, when people are interviewed in front of a funeral parlor as opposed to 100 meters away from the funeral parlor (Pyszczynski et al., 1996).

Thus, subtle reminders of mortality are sufficient to arouse these effects. In fact, mortality salience effects do not even require a conscious confrontation with reminders of death at all! In three studies, Arndt et al. (1997) found exaggerated reactions to pro- and anti-U.S. essay authors following subliminal reminders of death (specifically, 28 millisecond exposures to the word "death" vs. "field" or "pain"). This work, along with other findings (for a review, see Pyszczynski et al., 1999), has shown that worldview defense is intensified whenever death-related thought is on the fringes of consciousness (i.e., high in accessibility).

### Moderating factors.

Subsequent research has attempted to identify variables that moderate mortality salience effects. Greenberg, Simon, Pyszczynski, Solomon, and Chatel (1992) studied the effects of mortality salience on worldview defense as a function of political orientation. It is fairly well established that Americans with liberal political orientations are more tolerant and open-minded than conservatives (see, e.g., Stone, 1980). Indeed, liberal is defined as "tolerant of views differing from one's own; broad-minded" in *Webster's New World Dictionary*, Third Edition (1991). Therefore, we predicted and found that liberals and conservatives would react very differently to dissimilar others following subtle reminders of death. Specifically, and consistent with prior research, conservative participants rated fellow conservatives more positively and liberal targets more negatively after mortality salience; however, liberal participants did not derogate conservative targets after mortality salience. Presumably, this is because the liberal value of tolerance becomes especially salient and important after thinking about death; consequently, different others (in this case, conservatives) are not derogated. In support of this explanation, a second study eliminated derogation of dissimilar others following mortality salience by first priming the value of tolerance by reminding participants that an important aspect of the American way of life is respect for all others, regardless of how different they may be.

Another line of research was undertaken by Harmon-Jones et al. (1997) to examine the effects of momentarily elevated and dispositionally high self-esteem on worldview defense in response to mortality salience. We reasoned that if self-esteem serves as an anxiety buffer and death is the ultimate anxiety, high self-esteem (situational or dispositional) should attenuate worldview defense after reminders of death. In other words, people with high self-esteem should be less likely to derogate dissimilar others and venerate similar others in response to mortality salience. This is precisely what we found. Specifically, American participants with dispositionally low self-esteem (or people who received neutral personality feedback) showed exaggerated positive and negative reactions to pro- and anti-American targets, respectively; however, these exaggerated responses to mortality salience were reduced when self-esteem was dispositionally high or momentarily elevated by bogus positive personality feedback.

## PUBLIC POLICY IMPLICATIONS

According to terror management theory, the uniquely human awareness of death gives rise to paralyzing terror that is managed through the development of cultural worldviews. Culture provides a sense of meaning and a blueprint of action for acquiring self-esteem. Self-esteem, the belief that one is a valuable member of a meaningful universe, confers a sense of psychological equanimity through death transcendence via symbolic and/or literal immortality.

From this perspective, this form of death-denying mental organization plays a significant role in human violence, destruction, and cruelty. To the extent that cultural worldviews serve a death-denying function, the mere existence of different others is psychologically threatening, and results in efforts to belittle, convert, and annihilate people with alternative conceptions of reality. To the extent that culture is symbolic and ephemeral and death is physical and permanent, there will always be residual anxiety concerning death that is re-pressed and projected on to scapegoats; hence the motivation for every culture to designate its own in-house inferiors or external enemies to loathe and op-press.

What implications do these notions have for public policy? We should pref-ace our answers to this question with two important points. First, we think it is important to avoid simple and unidimensional thinking (even ours!) about the underlying causes of violence, cruelty, and destruction; these are surely complex and multidimensional problems. There is ample evidence, for example, that these unsavory aspects of human behavior are exacerbated by easy access to firearms; poverty; crowding; hot weather; alcohol and other drugs; physical, sexual, and/or emotional abuse; sociopathic personality; realistic conflict over resources; and excessive exposure to, and veneration of, violence in the media. Public policy should be forged, and legislative action initiated, in light of this knowledge.

Second, legislative and educational interventions based on knowledge ac-quired by the social sciences often encounter powerful resistance because they are incompatible with prevailing political ideologies and/or economic interests. For example, restricting easy access to handguns and assault rifles would ex-ponentially reduce the number of people murdered each year in America; but legislation to do so is summarily dismissed as incompatible with our consti-tutional right to bear arms. Graphic depiction of violence in movies and chil-dren's television programming clearly engenders destructive behavior (see, e.g., Bushman & Anderson, 2001), but efforts to limit exposure to graphic violence are generally opposed by the multinational corporations who reap gargantuan profits from such ventures under the guise of protecting our First Amendment right to free speech. Consequently, all of our broad recommendations need to be supplemented by effective strategies for implementation.

With these significant qualifications in mind, based on terror management theory and research, we offer the following suggestions.

## Broad Public Dissemination

We agree with E.O. Wilson (1978, p. 120): "With pacifism as a goal, scholars and political leaders will find it useful to deepen studies in anthropology and social psychology, and to express this technical knowledge openly as part of political science and daily diplomatic procedure." Thus, we believe that politi-cians and political scientists, as well as the general public, need to become intimately familiar with the notion that the awareness of death engenders the need for cultural belief systems which, in turn, produces animosity toward those with different cultural worldviews and an inclination to dispose of resid-ual anxiety via scapegoating for two reasons. First, from a purely pragmatic (in the tradition of Peirce and Dewey) perspective, human beings have historically been successful in solving problems in direct proportion to our understanding of the underlying dynamics of them. For example, treatment of a variety of diseases was vastly facilitated when we learned they were caused by bacteria, and the Wright brothers were able to get a plane off the ground because of what they learned from their detailed study of aerodynamics in a wind tunnel. Understanding underlying causes has thus served us well in the physical domain, and there is no reason to suspect it may not do the same psychologically.

Second, wholesale public awareness of the role of death-denial in the production of human evil may be therapeutic in the psychoanalytic sense of making the unconscious conscious (e.g., Freud, 1917/1989). If human animosities and violence are (even in part) the result of repression of the fear of death projected onto designated objects of evil, then this form of defense, like other Freudian defenses, can remain in place only to the extent that people remain unaware of what they are repressing. In fact, our work suggests that death is primarily a problem when it is outside of conscious attention (Pyszczynski et al., 1999). By making people recognize the nature of their repression, they will have to find other means to assuage their terror, just as hysteria disappeared as a widespread disorder when its psychosomatic underpinnings became common knowledge. Of course the problem of death will still be there, which raises the question of how to dispose of the terror formerly reduced by ethnic conflicts and in-house cultural caste systems. Interestingly, Becker (1975) recognized that while we may not be able to eliminate terror driven hatred, perhaps we can use our capacities for symbolic abstract thought to direct such animosities toward more legitimate and inanimate targets, e.g., poverty, illness, or ignorance.

## Foster Development of Worldviews Emphasizing Our Similarity to Other Humans

In *Why War*, the famous exchange between Freud and Einstein (Einstein, 1960), Freud (like Becker above), although not optimistic about the prospect of banishing human aggression, was hopeful that the human propensity to love those with whom we identify could be utilized to offset our aggressive inclinations. E.O. Wilson (1978, p. 120) comes to similar conclusions in *On Human Nature* when he prescribes "cross-binding loyalties. . . . To provide a more durable foundation for peace, political and cultural ties can be promoted . . . it will become discouragingly difficult for future populations to regard each other as completely discrete on the basis of congruent distinctions in race, language, nationhood, religion, ideology, and economic interest."

In other words, we need to remind people (and ourselves) that human beings from all corners of the planet have much more in common than we have differences and that historical distinctions between humans in race, language, nationhood, religion, and politics are social constructions of relatively recent origin and do not in any way reflect underlying genetic differences:

Fewer than 10,000 generations separate everyone alive today from the small group of Africans who are our common ancestors. That's much more than the twenty or so generations mentioned in Genesis, but it's the blink of an eye in evolutionary terms. Even over thousands of generations human groups have not differentiated in any substantial way. Rather, the genetic evidence indicates that modern human beings have expanded as a single, relatively well mixed population without subsequent genetic bottlenecks. . . . Our comparative youth as a species account for our extreme genetic homogeneity. The chimpanzees living on a single hillside in Africa have twice as much variety in their DNA as do the six billion people scattered across the globe. (Steve Olson, *The Genetic Archaeology of Race*, 2001, p. 76)

Thus, when we kill another human being we are killing a close member of our own family. The question then becomes how to shift people toward a focus on our deeply shared humanness rather than our more superficial but highly salient political and cultural differences.

## Foster Development of "Liberal" Worldviews Encouraging Acceptance of Diversity

Despite our genetic homogeneity, humans still vary substantially along culturally constructed cosmological, linguistic, religious, political, and economic dimensions that reflect the unique history and environmental circumstances of different groups of people. These differences, just like variation in a population's gene pool, should be cherished; otherwise we become a homogenized unidimensional species of "inbred" creatures unable to adapt to abrupt changes in our surroundings. But cherishing diversity requires the development of worldviews that accept and respect those who are different. Recall that whereas conservative American participants responded to mortality salience with exaggerated hostility to a liberal target, this was not the case for liberals evaluating conservative targets. Thus, if an important aspect of a cultural worldview includes the acceptance and respect for others (e.g., the hippies in the United States of the 1960s and social democrats in many European countries today), then reminders of mortality should not engender hostility toward others who do not share similar beliefs (as opposed to terror-driven hatred of different people characteristic of fundamentalists of all stripes in all times and places, e.g., German Nazis during World War II, the Taliban in Afghanistan, and some conservative Republicans in the United States today).

## Foster Development of Worldviews Providing Self-esteem

We have argued that self-esteem, the belief that one is a person of value in a world of meaning, is an anxiety buffer that serves to assuage concerns about mortality. In support of this proposition, we demonstrated that elevated self-esteem reduces anxiety (self-report and physiological arousal) and defensive cognitive distortions and, more important, that heightened or dispositionally high self-esteem reduces the derogation of dissimilar others typically engendered by subtle reminders of death. Self-esteem thus seems to be an excellent antidote to terror-driven hatred of, and violence toward, people with different cultural worldviews.

Given our argument that self-esteem is a social construction to the extent that the standards by which people judge themselves to be of value are generally acquired by the culture in the course of socialization, it follows that there is a historical and cultural aspect to self-esteem acquisition and maintenance: Times change and standards vary in terms of what is valued by a specific culture at a particular moment in time relative to the character of given individuals. The same person who would lead a healthy and happy life in one time and place might be a miserable (and dead) outcast in another, and some periods in human history may be especially fertile spawning grounds for epidemic levels of violence and destruction when opportunities to procure self-esteem become generally inaccessible to substantial proportions of a given population.

For example, a homosexually inclined boy might have had no problem acquiring meaning and value in ancient Greece, but would not fare as well in Wyoming in the 1990s; a Maasai man today is venerated in proportion to the number of cows in his possession, but this would do little to enhance his reputation as a stockbroker on Wall Street. And there will be certain historical moments when self-esteem is in especially short supply—specifically, when dominant cultural worldviews begin to lose their credibility, and/or when the standards of value espoused by a culture become difficult or impossible for the average individual successfully adhere to.

This is an especially difficult historical moment to acquire self-esteem in America, in that traits that we used to value—responsibility, decency, sincerity, generosity, concern for others—are now considered irredeemable character flaws or at least the stuff that fools are made of. In America in the new millennium, we value infinite wealth, eternal youth, sexual potency, and provocative beauty (at progressively earlier ages). The problem of course is that the average American will never be infinitely wealthy, forever young, or look like the people on the covers of *People*, *Playboy*, and *Cosmopolitan* magazines. Truth be told, not even the people on the covers of those magazines actually look like that—even beauty queens and kings are no longer pretty enough to appear as they really are! The difficulty of sustaining self-worth over the life span arises when the vast majority of us figure this out as we settle into our lives of (in Thoreau's words) "quiet desperation" in our typically dead-end jobs.

Consequently, we live in a culture in which most people are apt to perceive themselves as failures and suffer the psychic consequences accordingly. The well-publicized tragedy at Columbine High School in 1999 when Eric Harris and Dylan Klebold rampaged through their school, reenacting a video game killing fellow students before killing themselves, provides an excellent example (and one of many, distinguished only by its heinousness) of how culturally induced deficits in self-worth can provoke destructive outbursts.

Although blessed with physical health and more than ample material resources, Klebold and Harris were deemed pathetic misfits in a vicious social universe that exclusively valued good looks and athletic prowess. Eric and Dylan were routinely tormented by the popular guys, taunted as "losers" and "faggots," and were ignored and/or scorned by the girls whose attention they solicited. In their journals, Harris and Klebold wrote of being socially rejected and their consequent lack of self-esteem. That this was the impetus for their brutal outburst is manifestly evident from the suicide note left by Eric Harris:

By now, it's over. If you are reading this, my mission is complete. I have finished revolutionizing the neoeuphoric infliction of my internal terror. Your children who have ridiculed me, who have chosen not to accept me, who have treated me like I am not worth their time are dead. THEY ARE FUCKING DEAD.

I may have taken their lives and my own—but it was your doing. Teachers, parents, LET THIS MASSACRE BE ON YOUR SHOULDERS UNTIL THE DAY YOU DIE.

Without absolving Harris and Klebold of a substantial proportion of the responsibility for their malicious and self-destructive behavior, perhaps this would not have happened if they were embedded in a more benevolent social environment where self-esteem was attainable for not only sports stars and beauty queens. After the massacre, classmates revealed that Dylan and Eric both loved to go bowling and even took a bowling class that met at 6:15 A.M. As a bowling classmate observed in the June 10, 1999, issue of *Rolling Stone:* "It was a sport that wasn't so physical. It was cool because even if you weren't good at other sports, you could still be good at bowling. It was a way to make yourself feel better."

Accordingly, we need to seriously reconsider and modify the dominant values of our culture in order to provide opportunities for more individuals to perceive that they are persons of value in a world of meaning. This will not be easy in a massive economic pyramid in which most people have to spend 50 workweeks a year engaged in low-paying occupations involving activities such as hauling garbage, gutting chickens, and working assembly lines for the convenience of everyone else. But we need to work toward this goal because people with a secure sense of self-worth that they can sustain over their life span will be far less likely to belittle, ostracize, and kill dissimilar others to quell their dread.

Or will they? The notion that high self-esteem reduces violent behavior has recently been challenged by Baumeister and his colleagues (see, e.g., Baumeister, 2001; Baumeister et al., 1996), who argued that high self-esteem is associated with violent behavior and that people with low self-esteem are in fact less violent. Although this claim has received a large amount of attention in the scientific journals as well as the media and popular press, it is unequivocally incorrect.[2]

First, Baumeister and colleagues ignored a massive literature (see, e.g., reviews by Crocker & Wolfe, 2001; Harter, 1999; Solomon et al., 1991; Tesser, 1988) demonstrating in many ways that high self-esteem people are generally better adjusted and less prone to anxiety, shame, and hostility than their lower self-esteem counterparts. They made no serious attempt to address this literature, including our evidence that people with momentarily elevated or dispositionally high self-esteem do not berate dissimilar others in response to mortality salience.

Second, Baumeister often conflates (and in so doing confuses) self-esteem with narcissism. Most psychologists recognize the difference between genuine self-esteem and narcissistic self-inflation. For example, Karen Horney (1950) made a distinction between genuine self-esteem and neurotic pride. Genuine self-esteem is characterized by humility, the ability to accept constructive criticism and respect the achievements of superior others, and seeking new experiences in the service of continued growth and development. Neurotic pride is characterized by arrogance, an inability to accept constructive criticism, and avoidance of experiences that might disconfirm the overblown image of one self that is harbored for defensive purposes. According to Horney, people with neurotic pride (an overblown sense of self that masks incredibly low self-esteem) are especially hostile to superior others, or anyone who threatens their glorified self-image; and they react to such threats with vindictiveness, hostility, and aggression.

A considerable empirical literature supports this distinction between genuine self-esteem and defensive egotism, and its importance for differentiating between violent and nonviolent individuals. For example, Kernis et al. (1989) showed that stable high self-esteem people are particularly low in hostility and defensiveness, whereas those with unstable high self-esteem are especially prone to these tendencies. Similarly, in studies of bullying, Salmivalli et al. (1999) found that high self-esteem children are least likely to contribute to bullying, and most likely to stick up for victims of bullying and that defensive egotists are the bullying types. Existing theory and research thus supports our claim that genuinely high self-esteem effectively reduces hostile and destructive behaviors.

Albert Camus observed, "There is only one liberty, to come to terms with death. After which, everything is possible" (cited by Beaver, 1986). Finally, we need to, as a society and as individuals, accept the reality of the finite nature of life. As Seneca suggested some 2,000 years ago, humans are creatures with mortal fears and immortal desires. But only small children and narcissistic megalomaniacs insist on having everything they want, even what they cannot have, turning purple with rage and lashing out at innocents when their unrealistic desires go unfulfilled. We need to become mortal creatures with mortal desires, and for this, a great deal of imagination, courage, humility, and ultimately faith will be required. Perhaps personal forms of spirituality and courses in death awareness can aid us in progressing toward a true state of enlightenment Becker (1975, p. 145) envisioned when, based on Camus's *The Plague*, he pointed to "a day when each person would proclaim in his own fashion the superiority of being wrong without killing than being right in the quiet of the charnel house."

## NOTES

1. The authors share equal responsibility for this work, which was generously supported by grants from the National Science Foundation and The Ernest Becker Foundation. Correspondence concerning this chapter can be addressed to Sheldon Solomon, Department of Psychology, Skidmore College, Saratoga Springs, New York, 12866; e-mail: ssolomon@skidmore.edu.

2. After an unfortunate wave of publicity, and because of the weight of the evidence, Baumeister essentially retreated from his own position, acknowledging that in fact those prone to violence do not have high self-esteem, but rather are narcissists lacking genuine self-esteem but desperately desiring it (Bushman & Baumeister, 1998).

## REFERENCES

Aiello, L., & Dunbar, R.I.M. (1993). Neocortex size, group size and the evolution of language. *Current Anthropology, 36,* 199–221.

Arndt, J., Greenberg, J., Pyszczynski, T., & Solomon, S. (1997). Subliminal presentation of death reminders leads to increased defense of the cultural worldview. *Psychological Science, 8,* 379–385.

Balter, M. (1998). Why settle down? The mystery of communities. *Science, 282,* 1442–1445.

Baumeister, R. (2001). Violent pride. *Scientific American, 284,* 96–101.

Baumeister, R., Smart, L., & Boden, J. (1996). Relation of threatened egotism to violence and aggression: The dark side of high self-esteem. *Psychological Review, 103,* 5–33.

Beaver, H. (1986). Commentary. In H. Melville, *Moby-Dick; or, The Whale.* (p. 799). London: Penguin Classics.

Becker, E. (1962/1971). *The birth and death of meaning.* New York: Free Press.

Becker, E. (1973). *The denial of death.* New York: Free Press.

Becker, E. (1975). *Escape from evil.* New York: Free Press.

Berger, P.L., & Luckmann, T. (1966/1967). *The social construction of reality: A treatise in the sociology of knowledge.* Garden City, NY: Anchor Books.

Bowie, H. (1998). *Why die? A beginner's guide to living forever.* Scotsdale, AZ: PowerSurge Publishing.

Brown, C.P., Strole, J.R., & Brown, B. (1990). *Together forever: An invitation to be physically immortal.* Scotsdale, AZ: PowerSurge Publishing.

Brown, N.O. (1959). *Life against death: The psychoanalytical meaning of history.* Middletown, CT: Wesleyan University Press.

Bushman, B., & Anderson, C. (2001). Media violence and the American public: Scientific facts versus media misinformation. *American Psychologist, 56,* 477–489.

Bushman, B., & Baumeister, R. (1998). Threatened egotism, narcissism, self-esteem, and direct and displaced aggression: Does self-love or self-hate lead to violence? *Journal of Personality and Social Psychology, 75,* 219–229.

Crocker, J., & Wolfe, C. (2001). Contingencies of self-worth. *Psychological Review, 108,* 593–623.

Donald, M. (1991). *The origins of the modern mind: Three stages in the evolution of culture and cognition.* Cambridge, MA: Harvard University Press.

Einstein, A. (1960). Why war? In O. Nathan & H. Norden (Eds.), *Einstein on peace.* New York: Schocken Books, 1960.

Freud, S. (1917/1989). *Introductory lectures on psychoanalysis.* New York: W.W. Norton and Company.

Fromm, E. (1941/1965). *Escape from freedom.* New York: Avon Books.

Fromm, E. (1973). *The anatomy of human destructiveness.* New York: Holt, Rinehart and Winston.

Goldschmidt, W. (1990). *The human career: The self in the symbolic world.* Cambridge, MA: Basil Blackwell, Inc.

Greenberg, J., Pyszczynski, T., & Solomon, S. (1986). The causes and consequences of a need for self-esteem: A terror management theory. In R.F. Baumeister (Ed.), *Public self and private self* (pp. 189–212). New York: Springer-Verlag.

Greenberg, J., Pyszczynski, T., Solomon, S., Pinel, E., Simon, L., & Jordan, K. (1993). Effects of self-esteem on vulnerability-denying defensive distortions: Further evidence of an anxiety-buffering function of self-esteem. *Journal of Experimental Social Psychology, 29,* 229–251.

Greenberg, J., Pyszczynski, T., Solomon S., Rosenblatt, A., Veeder, M., Kirkland, S., & Lyon, D. (1990). Evidence for terror management theory II: The effects of mortality salience on reactions to those who threaten or bolster the cultural worldview. *Journal of Personality and Social Psychology, 58,* 308–318.

Greenberg, J., Schimel, J., Martens, A., Solomon, S., & Pyszcznyski, T. (2001). Sympathy for the devil: Evidence that reminding whites of their mortality promotes more favorable reactions to white racists. *Motivation and Emotion, 25,* 113–133.

Greenberg, J., Simon, L., Pyszczynski, T., Solomon, S., & Chatel, D. (1992). Terror management and tolerance: Does mortality salience always intensify negative reactions to others who threaten one's worldview? *Journal of Personality and Social Psychology, 63,* 212–220.

Greenberg, J., Solomon, S., & Pyszczynski, T. (1997). Terror management theory of self-esteem and cultural worldviews: Empirical assessments and conceptual refinements. In M. Zanna (Ed.), *Advances in experimental social psychology* (Vol. 29, pp. 61–139). Orlando, FL: Academic Press.

Greenberg, J., Solomon, S., Pyszczynski, T., Rosenblatt, A., Burling, J., Lyon, D., & Simon, L. (1992). Assessing the terror management analysis of self-esteem: Converging evidence of an anxiety-buffering function. *Journal of Personality and Social Psychology, 63,* 913–922.

Harmon-Jones, E., Greenberg, J., Solomon, S., & Simon, L. (1996). The effects of mortality salience on intergroup bias between minimal groups. *European Journal of Social Psychology, 26,* 677–681.

Harmon-Jones, E., Simon, L., Greenberg, J., Pyszczynski, T., Solomon, S., & McGregor, H. (1997). Self-esteem, mortality salience, and defense of the cultural worldview. *Journal of Personality and Social Psychology, 72*, 24–36.

Harter, S. (1999). *The construction of the self: A developmental perspective.* New York: Guilford.

Horney, K. (1950). *Neurosis and human growth: The struggle toward self-realization.* New York: W.W. Norton.

Kernis, M., Grannemann, B., & Barclay, L. (1989). Stability and level of self-esteem as predictors of anger arousal and hostility. *Journal of Personality and Social Psychology, 56*, 1013–1022

Langer, S.K. (1982). *Mind: An essay on human feeling,* Vol. 3. Baltimore, MD: Johns Hopkins Press.

Leeming, D.A., & Leeming, M.A. (1994). *Encyclopedia of creation myths.* Santa Barbara, CA: ABC-CLIO, Inc.

Lifton, R.J. (1983). *The broken connection: On death and the continuity of life.* New York: Basic Books.

Marcuse, H. (1955). *Eros and civilization.* Boston, MA: Beacon Press.

May, R. (1991). *The cry for myth.* New York: Dell Publishing.

McGregor, H., Lieberman, J.D., Greenberg, J., Solomon, S., Arndt, J., Simon, L., & Pyszczynski, T. (1998). Terror management and aggression: Evidence that mortality salience motivates aggression toward worldview threatening individuals. *Journal of Personality and Social Psychology, 74*, 590–605.

Mithen, S. (1996). *The Prehistory of the mind: The cognitive origins of art, religion and science.* London, UK: Thames and Hudson.

Ochsmann, R., & Mathy, M. (1994). *Depreciating of and distancing from foreigners: Effects of mortality salience.* Unpublished manuscript, Universitat Mainz, Mainz, Germany.

Olson, S. (2001) The genetic archaeology of race. *Atlantic Monthly, 287*, 69–80.

Paloutzian, R.F. (1981). Purpose in life and value changes following conversion. *Journal of Personality and Social Psychology, 41*, 1153–1160.

Pyszczynski, T., Greenberg, J., & Solomon, S. (1999). A dual process model of defense against conscious and unconscious death-related thoughts: An extension of terror management theory. *Psychological Review, 106*, 835–845.

Pyszczynski, T., Wicklund, R., Floresku, S., Koch, H., Gauch, G., Solomon, S., & Greenberg, J. (1996). Whistling in the dark: Exaggerated consensus estimates in response to incidental reminders of mortality. *Psychological Science, 7*, 332–336.

Rank, O. (1932). *Art and artist: Creative urge and personality development.* New York: Alfred A. Knopf.

Rank, O. (1936/1978). *Truth and reality.* New York: Norton.

Salmivalli, C., Kaukianinen, A., Kaistaniemi, L., & Lagerspetz, K. (1999). Self-evaluated self-esteem, peer-evaluated self-esteem, and defensive egotism as predictors of adolescents' participation in bullying situations. *Personality and Social Psychology Bulletin, 25*, 1268–1278.

Schimel, J., Simon, L., Greenberg, J., Pyszczynski, T., Solomon, S., Waxmonsky, J., & Arndt, J. (1999). Stereotypes and terror management: Evidence that mortality salience enhances stereotypic thinking and preferences. *Journal of Personality and Social Psychology, 77*, 905–926.

Seneca. (A.D. 49/1951). On the shortness of life. In J.W. Basore (Trans.), *Moral Essays*, Volume II Cambridge, MA: Harvard University Press.

Solomon, S., Greenberg, J., & Pyszczynski, T. (1991). A terror management theory of social behavior: The psychological functions of self-esteem and cultural worldviews. In M. Zanna (Ed.), *Advances in experimental social psychology* (Vol. 24, pp. 91–159). Orlando, FL: Academic Press.

Spengler, O. (1926). *The decline of the west*. Volume 1: *Form and actuality*. New York: Alfred A. Knopf.

Stone, W.F. (1980). The myth of left-wing authoritarianism. *Political Psychology, 2,* 3–20.

Tajfel, H., Billig, M.G., Bundy, R.P., & Flament, C. (1971). Social categorization and intergroup behavior. *European Journal of Social Psychology, 1,* 149–178.

Tesser. A. (1988). Toward a self-evaluation maintenance model of social behavior. In L. Berkowitz (Ed.), *Advances in experimental social psychology* (Vol. 21, pp. 181–227). San Diego, CA: Academic Press.

Tooby, J., & Cosmides, L. (1992). The psychological foundations of culture. In J.H. Barkow, L. Cosmides, & J. Tooby (Eds.), *The adapted mind*. New York: Oxford University Press.

Ullman, C. (1982). Cognitive and emotional antecedents of religious concern. *Journal of Personality and Social Psychology, 43,* 183–192.

Van Praagh, J. (1997). *Talking to heaven: A medium's message of life after death*. New York: Dutton.

Wilson, E.O. (1978). *On human nature*. Cambridge, MA: Harvard University Press.

Wilson, E.O. (1998). *Consilience: The unity of knowledge*. New York: Alfred A. Knopf.

# 7

# An Evolutionary Perspective on Intercultural Conflict
## Basic Mechanisms and Implications for Immigration Policy[1]

Harold D. Fishbein and Nancy Dess

If humankind is one big extended family, family fights are standard fare. The briefest reflection brings to mind intercultural violence around the globe in the twentieth century. Hitler's "Final Solution," Japan's brutal 30-year occupation of the Korean peninsula, 50 years of tension between India and Pakistan, 2 million casualties in a decades-old conflict between northern and southern Sudan and neighboring states, the killing and displacement of indigenous people in Chiapas by the Mexican Army since 1994, and the "ethnic cleansing" of Kosovars by Serbs in the late 1990s are just a few examples. The United States has been no bystander: It has been party to two world wars, two Asian wars, a 40-year Cold War with the former Soviet Union, a Desert Storm, bloody campaigns in Central and South America, and "peace missions" in Africa and the Balkans; it has used nuclear weapons against civilians yet is heading up the "war on terrorism." Millions of lives have been lost, millions more shattered.

Borders shift, conflicts wax and wane, and cultural groups vary in the extent to which relations with neighbors are governed by hostility or peace. None-theless, viewed globally and in deep time, intercultural conflict is characteristic of our species. What sort of light does an evolutionary perspective shed on this phenomenon? And what steps does this perspective suggest might be useful in avoiding or resolving these conflicts?

## OVERVIEW

This chapter deals with an evolutionary analysis of intercultural conflict. The core assumption is that genes determine some aspects of human social behavior. Our genes make *all* of our social behavior possible, but because of our evolutionary design—as social primates and, later, as tribally organized hunters and gatherers—we have inherited a genetic structure that makes certain kinds of attitudes and social behavior inevitable. Further, the occurrence of some of these attitudes and behaviors makes the development of prejudice and discrimination toward members of other cultures highly likely. These attitudes and behaviors constitute an "us versus them" psychology that is genetically determined.

On the basis of the current state of knowledge, it is highly likely that particular processes are genetically coded that normally ensure that the evolved social behaviors (phenotypic characteristics) will develop. For example, neither English nor Spanish is coded in the genes, but language-inducing processes are. If a child is reared in an English-speaking community, she'll learn English. If she's reared in an American Sign Language (ASL) community, she'll learn ASL. Either outcome can occur because language-inducing processes that have evolved in the species have developed in the individual. Although debate continues over whether these processes are modular or generic and about exactly how human communication is unique, that children's great facility for learning human language is an evolutionary legacy is clear.

Intercultural conflict depends on comparable processes. Because the processes are deeply embedded in our genetic/evolutionary heritage, attempts to modify prejudice and discrimination will have to deal with these processes and find ways to accommodate to them, or use them to attain different goals. One of the processes, authority acceptance, is often used to encourage prejudice and discrimination, but can be employed to combat it. Another process, out-group attractiveness, evolved to maintain an adequate level of genetic variability within the tribe, and may very well be used to combat prejudice and discrimination.

Exactly what "genetically determined" means will be developed throughout the chapter. What it does *not* mean merits a preview. Genetic determination of complex behavioral processes does not imply insensitivity to learning or context. To the contrary, the developmental elaboration of the processes treated here and their behavioral expression depend critically on the environment. The specific targets of the prejudice and discrimination, for example, are acquired through enculturation. It is not in the genes that African Americans and European Americans will be mutually prejudiced and discriminatory, or that white Americans will demonize Americans of Japanese descent. Knowledge of who is "in" and who is "out" and intergroup behavior are shaped through experience.

Similarly, whether intergroup prejudices escalate into violence depends on proximate political, economic, and environmental circumstances. For instance, Hutus and Tutsis share a language and religion, have intermarried extensively, and have engaged in complex sociopolitical relations for hundreds of years. Tribal identities did not make the massacres of the mid-1990s inevitable. Rather, the exaggeration of power and status differentials during Belgian colonialism and postindependence instability galvanized tribal allegiance and fanned mutual hostility, forming the fuse that was lit by the 1994 airplane crash in which the presidents of Rwanda and Burundi perished. Thus, "tribal rivalry" does not adequately explain this tragedy. It is not, however, irrelevant: "Hutu" scrawled on a Rwandan home often meant the difference between life and death. In summary, the strong predisposition to identify with and prefer an in-group and to be wary or hostile toward out-groups does not compel violence. It is a substrate that can be catalyzed into violence by political exploitation, recession, ecological degradation, and so on.

Finally, that certain psychological processes are genetically determined does not mean that the attitudes and behaviors arising from those processes are morally correct. Whether moral rectitude can be derived from evolutionary reasoning is beyond the scope of this chapter. However, even scholars who argue that inquiry into human evolution is morally informative (e.g., Arnhart, 1998) do not suggest that a genomic basis, ancestral adaptive advantage, or specieswide inclination constitutes moral justification, and no such suggestion is made here. The issue is whether the psychological processes underlying intercultural conflict are illuminated by understanding our species' natural history and, if so, how this understanding might inform attempts to modify or redirect them in ways deemed socially useful through legitimate means. Specifically, we assume here that reducing violence and increasing intergroup harmony will be socially useful, and that influencing public policy is a legitimate means of advancing this agenda.

The chapter reviews key concepts in developmental and evolutionary theory and proposes specific mechanisms central to the epigenesis and evolution of intercultural conflict. It ends with a "case study" of immigrants' entry into a society. Lessons learned from the mutual accommodation of immigrants and the host society may help us understand and improve upon policies bearing on conflict that arises at the interface of different societies.

## KEY EPIGENETIC CONCEPTS

### Canalization

A likely genetic process controlling the species-specific developmental aspect of an evolutionary design is "canalization" (Waddington, 1957). Gottlieb (1991) synthesized theoretical and empirical research on this topic, which he refers to as "experiential canalization of behavior." In this view, behavioral development involves a hierarchical system of four mutually interacting components: genetic activity, neural activity, behavior, and environment. Genetic activity influences neural development, but the activity of the nervous system influences genetic activity by determining which genes will be turned on or shut off. There is a similar bidirectional effect between behavior and neural activity and, indeed, for all other combinations of the four components. Thus, it is not merely genes that ensure that any infant or child attains a species-specific characteristic, such as language, but rather the effect of all four components working together. The developmental target is coded in the genes in the sense that for normal rearing environments, the genes produce nervous systems that activate behavioral processes which determine that the species-specific behavioral characteristic will be acquired. The genes, the nervous system, the behavior, and the environment all work together to canalize the developing behavior. This process is called *epigenesis*. Thus, as children start to speak English in normal English-speaking environments, their English speech is reinforced by others in the environment, who continue to speak English to them. And their nervous systems continue to develop the necessary connections to sustain and enhance spoken English.

When the genes and the various environments—intracellular, extracellular, family social interactions, atmospheric pollution levels—are in a normal range for the species, then the developmental targets will be attained. Infants will nurse, crawl, walk, and talk, according to the *epigenetic* timetable coded in the genes. Moreover, canalization processes are self-correcting in addition to being self-directing. Epigenesis works to put back on the evolutionarily designed developmental track any deviations from the species-specific targets. For example, infants will learn to walk at about one year of age even if they've had very little opportunity to crawl as is the case with Hopi infants. As another example, hearing infants reared by deaf, ASL-using parents learn to speak normally provided that they are also involved with a vocal-speaking community.

### Genes, Mind, and Culture

All humans are reared in and live in cultures. These cultures resemble each other in many ways, and yet differ in important ways, such as language and religious practices. Infants and children need to learn the practices of the culture they are reared in, and canalization processes ensure that they will learn some of them. The process of socializing children into their culture is called enculturation. Enculturation makes us uniquely American or English or Mexican. From a genetic/evolutionary view, how might this enculturation come about?

In the 1981 book *Genes, Mind, and Culture*, Lumsden and Wilson provide a convincing model as an answer. They distinguish three kinds of culturally learned behavior. The first is species-specific patterns that are seen in all cultures, such as nursing by infants, walking, and the coordinated use of two hands. The second is variants of species-specific patterns that distinguish cultures from each other, such as particular languages, religious practices, rules for sharing, tool manufacture, whether the bride or the bridegroom leaves the family of origin. Both the first and second kinds are thus universal aspects of human behavior. The third is the relatively unique practices that are cultural specific, such as driving on the left side of the road. All three kinds of learning are possible because humans evolved as cultural animals. In a sense, culture is encoded in our genes.

Lumsden and Wilson (1981) maintain that genes and culture coevolved—that systematic changes in human genetic structure led to systematic changes in the nature of human culture and vice versa. In their model the four principal levels of biological organization are molecular, cellular, organismic, and populational. The first three of these levels constitute the details of epigenesis, as described earlier. The connections between these levels follow a particular direction, from the least to the most complex. This directionality implies that there is systematic change in each of the levels, as opposed to the maintenance of stable canalized characteristics.

At the molecular level, the genes, which are groups of DNA molecules, produce proteins. These proteins bond together to form all the varied cells in the body. Of particular interest are the brain cells (neurons). The structure and functioning of these neurons produce epigenetic rules for acquiring cultural characteristics and for developing individual cognitions and behavior, for example, the names of colors, the qualities of apples. The epigenetic rules are canalized, and if the external environment is highly similar for all individuals, then their cognitions and behavior will be similar. The population of individuals who reside and interact in a given region form a culture and share a language. The linkage between the organismic and populational levels reflects the translation of genes into culture. The linkage of the populational and molecular levels reflects how evolutionary processes operating on a population of individuals influence gene frequencies.

These latter two linkages are especially important in the present context. Lumsden and Wilson (1981) identify two broad classes of epigenetic rules: those that transform cultural inputs, for example, socialization experiences, into "knowledge structures," and those that transform knowledge structures into behavior. Knowledge structures primarily consist of memory and cognitive processes. Behavior is what individuals do in their social and physical environments. The consequences of behavior are different levels of "genetic fitness," that is, survival and reproduction. If certain types of epigenetic rules lead to behaviors with high genetic fitness within a given population, then those rules ultimately will become the norm for that population. If certain epigenetic rules lead to behaviors with low genetic fitness, then the genes supporting those rules will disappear. Perhaps the clearest example of this gene-culture coevolution is spoken language. Individuals in a population whose anatomical structure and epigenetic rules led to language behavior had higher genetic fitness than those who lacked these rules. Language is cultural, but language use produced the genetic changes in a population that made language development inevitable.

The distinction between cultural-specific from species-specific canalized characteristics is important. All canalized characteristics started at the cultural-specific level. If they spread to other cultures through "intermarriage" and had high genetic fitness in the new cultures, then ultimately those characteristics became canalized in the new cultures. The only reasonable way that a character could become canalized for all members of the species is if it had high genetic fitness in every culture on earth. Based on the paleoanthropological record, modern humans emerged at least 40,000 years ago, and probably considerably earlier (Fishbein, 1976, 1984). It is thus highly likely that any cultural changes that have occurred in human populations since then were either purely cultural, that is, not genetic, or were coevolved cultural-specific changes.

Research by Greenfield and Childs (1991) among the Zinacantecos, a Maya Indian culture, supports the Lumsden and Wilson (1981) model. The Zinacantecos have a culture that distinguishes them from neighboring groups—and, of course, from all non-Mayan cultures. Moreover, they have a distinctive population genetic structure because marriage is largely restricted to other members of their culture. Greenfield and Childs (1991) asked two questions within a cultural/genetic framework. First, do Zinacanteco infants and children show patterns of psychological development characteristic of non-Mayan cultures? Second, do they show culture-specific patterns that have continuity into adulthood? An affirmative answer to the first question provides support for the existence of universal species-specific gene/culture coevolution. An affirmative answer to the second question provides support for culture-specific coevolution.

The data are based on four years of fieldwork carried out in the native language of Tzotzil, but also 30 years of multidisciplinary studies carried out by other colleagues. Regarding universal species-specific capabilities, the following results were obtained:

- On mental and motor tests carried out with babies, the sequence of behavioral milestones was the same as for babies in the United States.

- In a study with young Zinacanteco children who had no familiarity with "nesting cup" toys, Zinacanteco children and U.S. children showed the same developmental sequence of strategies for combining the cups.

- In several studies using different materials and requiring different cognitive activities, Zinacanteco children between the ages of 4 and 18 showed the same sequences of abilities, at the same ages, as U.S. children, for example, the ability to classify different objects in a variety of ways. In some of these tasks, the cognitive abilities tapped for the Zinacantecos were quite novel and on the surface, inconsistent with cultural learning.

Greenfield and Childs (1991) conclude that the above pattern of results supports a universal species-specific developmental sequence.

Regarding culture-specific behavior, Zinacanteco babies show very low levels of physical activity. This "restrained" motor activity is also found among Chinese American, Navajo, and Japanese babies, but not in European American babies. The four groups who are "restrained" all have different diets and pre-natal care from each other, which rules out common socialization practices as the bases for similarity. The findings suggest the existence of a genetic basis for the restraint. Given that these groups also have Asian roots, the assumed genetic basis makes sense. Focusing on the Zinacantecos, the behavior of moth-ers reinforces infants' low activity levels: The babies are swaddled (wrapped) and are nursed at the slightest movement. European American babies rarely receive this kind of treatment. As a consequence of different starting activity levels and different maternal treatment, the activity levels of the two groups of babies become even more divergent during the first week of life. Moreover, relative to European Americans, this pattern of Zinacanteco motor restraint is observed at all developmental levels, including adulthood. It is not the case that Zinacanteco babies are more listless than European Americans. In fact, the opposite may be the case. Research has found them to be more attentive to their surroundings, for longer time periods, than European American babies.

Greenfield and Childs (1991) discuss these results from cultural and genetic/evolutionary points of view. They conclude that in the Zinacanteco culture, motor restraint has an adaptive advantage. Given the apparent long-term sta-bility of their cultural practices, this motor restraint likely was a coevolved behavior characteristic.

## Hunter-Gatherer Minds in Postindustrial Bodies

Alice Rossi (1977) has written:

[T]he two hundred years in which industrial societies have existed is a short time, indeed, to say nothing of the twenty years in which a few of the most advanced in-dustrial societies have been undergoing the painful transition to a post-industrial stage. Our most recent genes derive from that largest segment of human history during which men and women lived in hunting and gathering societies; in other words, Westernized human beings now living in a technological world are still genetically equipped only with an ancient mammalian heritage that evolved largely through adaptations appro-priate to much earlier times. (p. 3)

As noted in a previous section, the universal species-specific canalizations appear to have been in place at least 40,000 years ago, and evolutionary changes since then probably have been either purely cultural or genetically culture specific. We described an example of the latter with motor restraint in the Zinacantecos. There is no evidence of species-specific genetic changes in the past 40,000 years. As a consequence, the assumption being made here is that humans are currently operating with hunter-gatherer epigenetic systems. These systems evolved and supported cultures that were tribal, consisting of approximately 500 men, women, and children. The systems were sufficiently flexible to allow the development of agricultural societies, which have been in existence for about 10,000 years. They also permitted the very recent cultural evolution of industrial and postindustrial societies. The fate of the latter is questionable as can been seen in the destruction of the habitat and of each other in which many societies are engaged.

As Rossi (1977) noted, much of our genetic equipment is based on "an ancient mammalian heritage." Although that is certainly true, a more profitable approach for the present purposes is to focus on our more recent primate and hunter-gatherer heritages. In this ancestry lie the keys to understanding the genetic/evolutionary bases of the development of prejudice and discrimination.

### The Primate Heritage.

Primates evolved about 60 million years ago from mammalian ancestors probably resembling contemporary tree shrews (Andrews, 1985). Four major events occurred within that time span:

- The New World and Old World primates were separated about 50 million years ago.
- The Old World monkey-ape split occurred about 40 million years ago.
- The common Old World ancestors of gorillas, chimpanzees, and humans emerged about 12–16 million years ago.
- The evolutionary lines leading to distinct gorilla, chimpanzee, and human species appeared about 6–10 million years ago.

There are two chimpanzee species, *Pan troglodytes*, known as the common chimpanzee, and *Pan paniscus*, known as the pygmy chimpanzee or bonobo. Of the four species—humans, gorillas, bonobo, and common chimpanzees— the bonobo and common chimpanzee have the highest degree of genetic relatedness. Among the primates these four species apparently are more closely related to each other than they are to any other species (Wrangham, 1987).

Evolution is an ongoing experiment in design. What is the nature of the human design? In that the focus here is the evolutionary basis of prejudice and discrimination, the social aspects of the design are of greatest interest. The design has three major components: the heritage we share with the Old World monkeys and apes, that which we share with the chimpanzees and gorillas, and our hunter-gatherer heritage. The emphasis here will be on those social/behavioral elements that are commonly found among Old World primates and those social/behavioral elements that characterize hunter-gatherer groups. The monkey-ape split occurred approximately 40 million years ago, and the ape-human species have had 6–10 million years of independent evolutionary history. All living species are different than the common ancestor. Any social/ behavior commonalities that exist among the monkeys and apes, or among the apes and humans, are assumed to be part of the design of the common ancestors and continue to be part of the current human design.

### Old World Monkeys and Apes.

The primary adaptation of nearly all the Old World (African and Asian) primate species, including humans, is for life as a member of a group (Fishbein,

1976, 1984; Tooby & DeVore, 1987). These species have evolved so that the group provides the framework for subsistence activities, protection, reproduction, and socialization of the young. All are political creatures. In these species there is a frequent association of members of all ages and both sexes throughout the lifetime of each individual. In all cases the offspring are typically born singly and are relatively helpless at birth, and they are highly dependent on the adults for a considerable period thereafter. Socialization starts shortly after birth, and occurs primarily through play, observation, imitation, and interactions with group members. The major task of preadults is to learn to fit into and contribute to the stability of the social group. In order to accomplish this task, they have to develop:

- knowledge of who are group members
- a set of social skills important to the group
- an enduring set of social relationships with many, if not most, members
- knowledge of the rules of interaction and of the roles appropriate to self and others

These rules and roles are both age and sex related. What is tolerated in infants, for example, tugging on the hair of adults, is often treated harshly in juveniles.

If the social development of certain maturing members of the group deviates significantly from the norm, then as adults their ability to contribute to the vital functions of the social group to which they belong may be compromised. Natural selection has operated and continues to operate in such a way that individuals who undergo relatively normative social development contribute to all four vital functions of the group, whereas those who do not become peripheral members. The latter face a less certain reproductive future than do more central members. This is a negative feedback system involving genes and behaviors. In a stable environment, individuals who have a genetic structure such that key social competencies develop will be able to reproduce (or get their close relatives to do so), thus continuing their genes in the population gene distribution. Those whose genetic structure is such that they do not develop those key competencies will have low fitness; their genes' representation in the gene distribution will diminish (Fishbein, 1976, 1984).

For the present purposes, one of the most significant social aspects of primate groups is the existence of dominance hierarchies. Dominance refers to the ability of one group member to "supplant" another in order to gain access to preferred or scarce resources, such as particular foods, shade, water, close proximity to certain other group members, and sex with specific individuals. A group member typically gains dominance over another in one of three ways: defeating the other in a fight, or giving the appearance of being able to do so; forming a coalition with another group member against some or all other group members; or being the son or daughter of a mother who is high in the dominance hierarchy. The latter characteristic typically has importance among the

Old World monkeys, and not among the apes. The critical factor here is that in monkey and baboon species, males typically leave their natal groups at adolescence, whereas females remain with their group throughout their lives. These females form dominance hierarchies, but the males do not (Hinde, 1983).

Primates do not retain their dominance status by constantly fighting with or threatening others. Rather, other group members with whom they do not have close positive relations simply avoid them, or move away when they approach. Two markers for highly dominant individuals are that other group members pay attention to them or try to gain their attention (Chance, 1975) and other group members attempt to "groom," that is, to tactually search through another's fur for parasites (Seyfarth, 1983), or be groomed by them. Strum (1987) and others have shown that one of the consequences of grooming relationships is the development of alliances. These alliances increase one's effectiveness in accomplishing goals within the group.

Thus, the picture that has emerged in recent years concerning dominance hierarchies is that the most dominant individuals are not only to be feared but also to be favored. Others want to be allied with them and to be responded to affectionately by them. Although there is no evidence that in nonhuman primate groups highly dominant individuals become role models for younger group members, we will see this characteristic emerge in human groups.

### The Hunter-Gatherer Heritage.

Ernst Mayr (1997) makes a useful distinction between "ultimate" and "proximate" evolutionary causes. Ultimate causes are closely tied to the evolutionary history of a species and get manifested in the genotype of that species. The ultimate causes exist in part due to adaptation through natural selection. In the social and physical environments in which the genetically based processes were expressed, the individuals manifesting the underlying genotype were reproductively successful. Other nonselective processes, such as geographic isolation (genetic "drift") and chromosomal linkages or crossovers, also shape the genome. Ultimate causes enable the development of genetically specified processes (e.g., memory, language acquisition) in the phenotypes of members of the species. Proximate causes orchestrate the playing out of those processes in the here and now, in any environments in which they are triggered, even if these environments and the consequences of the phenotype expression differ substantially from those in which the genotype evolved.

As indicated above, the evolutionary line leading to the hunter-gatherer design is 6 to 10 million years beyond the emergence of the common ancestor of humans, gorillas, and chimpanzees. The hunter-gatherer subsistence mode and social structure has been a relatively constant human feature for 99% of our existence. What are the major aspects of this design that differentiate us from the African monkeys and apes? This summary draws on Fishbein (1976, 1984), Irwin (1987), Tooby and DeVore (1987), and Wrangham (1987).

At the broadest level, nearly all hunter-gatherer societies consist of a set of genetically related subsistence groups that collectively form a tribe. Each subsistence group resides in a certain region and generally has limited contact with other tribal groups throughout the year. Members of the various groups are often closely related in that sisters and daughters move to other groups for marriage. Their offspring are cousins, nephews, and nieces of members of the natal group. Female departure is the norm; however, in some societies the males usually leave the natal group, and in others males or females may leave. Unlike the African apes, humans maintain bonds between family members in different groups that continue over time and space. Thus, all members develop strong identifications with the tribe as a whole.

Unlike the African apes, subsistence groups are comprised of families. The family is the basic social unit, typically consisting of a married adult male and female, their preadolescent male and female offspring, unmarried adolescent and adult sons, and, often, parents of the father. Polygamy and polyandry occur but are infrequent. Marriages are relatively permanent. In primate terms, the couple is socially pair-bonded, a characteristic rare in the African apes. Depending on rate of survival, family size may be small or large, which obviously will affect size of the subsistence group. In times of limited availability of food, which is usually seasonal, the group may split into its family components, each moving to an area with enough food to support it.

Unlike the African apes, fathers identify their wife's offspring as their own. Extramarital couplings notwithstanding, a wife's offspring are more likely than not to be her husband's sons and daughters. Corresponding to this paternal likelihood, fathers invest time and energy in helping to raise their children to a far greater extent than do the African apes.[2] In addition to mutual involvement in child rearing, husbands and wives have extensive reciprocal and cooperative relationships with each other. Food sharing is an integral part of this collaboration.

Hunter-gatherer groups, as groups, share many goals and activities above and beyond those at the family level of organization. Socialization of children is a group responsibility, as are the division of labor, protection, and food sharing along gender lines. In some societies, hunters are not even permitted to eat their own "kills," but must give them to other group members. They, of course, benefit from the successes of their compatriots. Related to food sharing and group organization, there is extensive male-male cooperation, and relative to most primates, less aggression and competition. The principal group ethics are sharing and reciprocity. These both produce and require extensive interpersonal interdependencies and social cohesion—even more so than in the African apes.

Finally, relative to the African primates, there are very marked cultural differences between tribes, especially those separated by substantial geographic distance. The term "culture" emphasizes here language, dialect, religious practices, moral rules, belief systems, dress, art, tool decoration, and any or all activities that characterize a given tribe, such as offering particular food or drink to visitors. A good case has been made for functionally significant cultural transmission in other African primates (de Waal, 2001), but our species is distinctive in its cultural complexity and symbolic richness.

Thus, humans and nonhuman primates evolved as members of closely knit subsistence groups. One uniquely human characteristic is that these groups were additionally strongly interconnected through tribal identifications. Members of the same tribe were relatively safe with and could count on nurturance from same-tribe members, even if those members were unknown. Other-tribe strangers, however, were potentially dangerous, especially during the regularly recurring periods of scarce resources. Given that the hunter-gatherer tribal mode of living for the genus, *Homo*, has been in existence for more than 1 million years, genetic/evolutionary processes presumably emerged that led to sustaining tribal autonomy and continuity against neighboring tribes. These processes would have become incorporated into human epigenetic systems, making it nearly inevitable that individuals would be prejudiced toward and discriminate against members of other tribes (ultimate causes). The recent, rapid emergence of new social structures (states) and modes of subsistence (e.g., industrial) was not matched by a shift in epigenetic systems. As a consequence, mechanisms that evolved for regulating intertribal contacts became inappropriately applied to within-culture relationships (proximate causes). In other words, humans are predisposed to treat out-group members of their own cultures as if they were members of different tribes.

## DARWINIAN PROCESSES IN INTERCULTURAL CONFLICT

At least three genetic/evolutionary factors emerged to sustain tribal autonomy and continuity against neighboring tribes. They arose from:

- The inherent nature of Darwinian selection processes on relatively closed breeding populations (*inclusive fitness*)
- The evolutionary basis of *intergroup hostility* among the common ancestors of human hunter-gatherers
- The evolutionary design of *authority-bearing systems* in human cultures

Each of these factors is discussed, after which a fourth factor that can moderate prejudice—*out-group attractiveness*—is introduced.

### Inclusive Fitness

One of the major innovations in evolutionary theory is the elaboration of the concept of *inclusive fitness* (Hamilton, 1964, 1975) and its relationship to social behavior (Wilson, 1980). Inclusive fitness refers to the extent to which an individual and his or her close relatives have surviving offspring. Individuals with high inclusive fitness are those who transmit relatively many genes to the next generation. Those with low fitness (individuals and close relatives) transmit relatively few genes to the next generation. One implication of inclusive fitness is that individuals (whether insects or humans) consciously or unconsciously attempt to get their genes into the next generation in basically two ways: reproduce a great deal, or act in ways to get their close relatives to reproduce a great deal. For example, assuming that two siblings have in common one-half of their genes, Sibling A's inclusive fitness would be higher by Sibling B's having five surviving offspring and Sibling A none, than by Sibling A having two surviving offspring and Sibling B none. Another implication is that when resources important for survival are limited, individuals will show preferences to relatives and act in ways to decrease the likelihood that nonrelatives will successfully reproduce or survive. They may prevent nonrelatives from mating, withhold food or shelter from them, or kill their offspring. The latter is a strategy that male langur monkeys usually perform (Hrdy, 1999), but also is seen in other primates, including humans.

The most obvious reproductive strategy for getting one's genes into the next generation is to mate with siblings or the opposite-sex parent—engage in incest. Extreme inbreeding has the negative consequence of "inbreeding depression": Closely related mating partners are more likely to have offspring that are stillborn, die early, or have mental or physical defects (see Gene Flow and Outgroup Attractiveness, below). These all decrease the likelihood that one's genes will survive beyond the next generation.

Another important implication of this line of reasoning is that we should prefer that our siblings marry second cousins rather than unrelated persons. Our siblings share on average 50% of our genes, our second cousins share about 6% of our genes, and unrelated persons share close to 0% of our genes. Thus, more of our genes get transmitted to the next generation when our siblings marry a second cousin than when they marry an unrelated person. There are some recent historical data consistent with this analysis. Irwin (1987) has analyzed marriage patterns for the Netsilik Eskimos of Canada. They were more likely to marry within the local community than with a member of a nearby Netsilik community, and relatively unlikely to marry a member of another tribe. This pattern of marriages leads to relatively high genetic relatedness in members of the local community.

Other important genetic as well as social consequences of this analysis have been described by Hamilton (1964, 1975). In short, he shows mathematically that natural selection could operate in such a fashion that, given the opportunity, individuals would behave altruistically toward their relatives. Altruism refers to the performance of some act that benefits another at some expense to one's self, for example, giving food to a cousin. His analysis demonstrates that behaving altruistically toward relatives (and their reciprocating) increases the Darwinian fitness of both parties. Hence, over many generations the genes of both parties, including those influencing altruism, would become widespread in any breeding population.

In Hamilton's analysis, the Darwinian success of altruistic behavior depends on being able to direct it toward relatives as opposed to nonrelatives. How would kin be recognized? In small inbreeding communities like that of the Netsiliks, everyone is a relative, so identifying them would not have been a problem. However, communities that insular are not the norm among primates, so psychological proxies for relatedness—familiarity from early in life, knowing who shares food, is a grooming partner, and so on—would have served as selection phenotypes.

From the point of view of prejudice and discrimination, the direct implication of Hamilton's analysis is that we are essentially designed to be ethnocentric—to favor our own group as opposed to others. A consequence of the psychological nature of kin recognition is that nonkin will be treated like kin when circumstances permit no distinction. Thus, selection for behaviors that increase inclusive fitness is a means by which individuals will favor an in-group comprised of nonrelatives as well as relatives. A dramatic example to which this mechanism may be applied is the kamikaze pilot or suicide bomber. Although dying may seem to belie an evolutionary struggle to "survive," it actually increases fitness if benefits to the in-group exceed the viability of the individual's potential offspring. The sum of material and status gains for suicide attackers' families and damage to enemy out-groups may exceed an attacker's likely reproductive success. This is the case for the typical young, oppressed, male Palestinian bomber, as it is for a Tamil Tigress in Sri Lanka where, "acting as a human bomb is an understood and accepted offering for a woman who will never be a mother" (Pearson, 2002).[3]

## Intergroup Hostility: Heritage from the Common Ancestor of Apes and Humans

Harming an out-group can be an indirect result of preferential treatment of the in-group (Brewer, 1999). Thus, intergroup hostility can be explained partly in terms of the inclusive fitness benefits of in-group favoritism. Some writers have suggested that antagonism toward nongroup members also was directly selected for, as protecting the in-group from intruders and competitors would further enhance inclusive fitness (e.g., Irwin, 1987; Reynolds, 1987). Although in-group favoritism and out-group hostility do appear to be separable phenomena, coevolution of these two intergroup biases seems likely: Both are rooted in the distinction between in- and out-groups, and both rise as mortality salience increases (see Solomon et al., this volume). Consistent with the epigenetic model described above, early childhood development of in-group positivity may be preparatory to the context-sensitive development of out-group derogation (Cameron et al., 2001).

Comparative data support a coevolutionary view of intergroup biases. Wrangham (1987) has provided an enormously useful integration of research concerned with the social organization of the African apes (both chimpanzee species and gorillas) and human hunter-gatherers. These four species share a common ancestor that lived 6 to 10 million years ago. It is assumed that if the common ancestor possessed a given social characteristic, then there is a 6- to 10-million-year genetic/evolutionary continuity of that phenotype. We infer this possession if all of the descendants—all four of these species—share the given social characteristic.

All long term (two or more years) major field studies of apes formed the basis of Wrangham's analysis. Only 10 such studies exist, two each for the gorilla and bonobo, and six for the common chimpanzee. Thus there may be serious problems with sampling, but this is what we have, and Wrangham's comparative analysis seems to be the most complete available. For the hunter-gatherer data, Wrangham reviewed several sources that dealt with their social organization. These include well over 150 ethnographic analyses of different hunter-gatherer societies. Sampling does not seem to be a problem here.

According to Wrangham, 14 characteristics of social organization capture the essence of the structure and functioning of the groups formed by the four species. Six of these characteristics vary considerably across all four species, and no conclusions could be made. For six of the remaining characteristics, he concludes that the common ancestor of all four species had the characteristic being considered, and for another two, he concludes that the common ancestor did not have the characteristic. The eight "conclusive" characteristics were arrayed as follows:

### Social Network.

"Social network" refers to whether the subsistence group is relatively closed or relatively open to outsiders. The critical observation involves whether nongroup members are excluded from the activities of the in-group. As a point of reference, subsistence group size averages about 25 for hunter-gatherers, 13 for gorillas, 60 for common chimpanzees (Jolly, 1972), and probably about 60 for bonobos (inferred from Wrangham's discussion). A distinguishing feature of hunter-gatherers is that they typically are members of a "tribe," averaging about 500 members and consisting of many subsistence groups. All three African ape species have closed social networks, and hunter-gatherers are closed with respect to the tribe and semiclosed with respect to the subsistence group. Wrangham concludes that the common ancestor formed groups with closed social networks.

### Lone Males.

"Lone males" refers to whether males ever travel alone. Traveling alone is potentially dangerous in that it may put one in contact with neighboring

groups. This occurs with all four species. As a consequence, Wrangham concludes that this activity occurred for the common ancestor.

### Female / Male Dispersion.

The third characteristic deals with whether females breed in their natal group
(the group they were born into). In all four species, females generally leave
the natal group, join another nearby subsistence group, and mate therein. This
is a different pattern than is seen in African monkeys and baboons, where the
females generally stay in the natal group from birth to death (Hinde, 1983).
Wrangham (1987) concludes that in the common ancestor, females rarely bred
in their natal group. By contrast, the fourth characteristic, which is common
to both chimpanzee species and hunter-gatherers, is that males generally remain in the natal group. The picture is unclear for gorillas.

The remaining characteristics, which are perhaps the most important in
terms of the development of prejudice and discrimination, deal with "intergroup relationships." These are concerned with how adult members of one
social network react to members of other social networks. For the apes, there
is one subsistence group in relation to outsiders, and for the hunter-gathers,
there is one tribe in relation to outsiders.

### Interaction Quality.

"Quality of the interaction" involves the dimension of hostility. For the
gorilla, common chimpanzee, and hunter-gatherer tribes, reactions to outsiders
typically are hostile. Violent attacks, occasionally leading to killings, have been
observed. In one study of 50 hunter-gatherer societies, tribal warfare typically
occurred on average every two years. The major function of hostility toward
outsiders is to protect group members from attack or capture. An important
secondary function is the protection of scarce resources. Few observations have
been made of the bonobo, but these indicate at least tense interactions with
outsiders. Wrangham (1987) concludes that hostile intergroup relations were
the norm for our common ancestor.

### Parties to Out-group Hostility.

This characteristic concerns the identity of the active participants in hostile
interactions. Insufficient data are available for the relatively pacifistic bonobos,
but for the other three species, the adult males and occasionally adolescent
males are the usual interactants. In the Old World monkeys, by contrast, adult
females often participate in the violence. Wrangham concludes that "males
only" was the pattern for the common ancestor.

### Stalk / Attack.

"Stalk/attack" refers to whether the adult and adolescent males of a group
will actively seek out, stalk, and attack outsiders, in addition to reacting with

hostility during chance encounters. Again, limited data are available for the bonobo, but stalking and attacking have been observed for the other species. In one study a group of male chimpanzees were observed stalking and killing a female chimpanzee who had formerly been a member of their group (Goodall et al., 1979). Thus, violence is not only directed toward strangers, or toward adult males. Wrangham concludes that these activities characterized the common ancestor.

### Territorial Defense.

"Territorial defense" refers to whether these species stake out a particular group territory and attempt to prevent outsiders from entering it. The most common observation is that they occupy a home range that overlaps with that of neighboring groups. It is rare for any of them to patrol the perimeter to prevent incursions of outsiders. When outsiders penetrate too deeply into the home range, they will be repelled. Wrangham (1987) concludes that the common ancestor did not engage in territorial defense.

According to this pattern of characteristics, the human evolutionary social heritage from the common ancestor of bonobo, common chimpanzee, gorillas, and human hunter-gatherers is a design as members of relatively closed subsistence groups. The permanent members of these groups are typically the males who defend the group against outsiders. These encounters are usually hostile and occasionally violent. Males periodically travel alone, and when with other males may stalk and attack nongroup members. Females migrate out of their natal group and join other nearby groups. When they do so, they are vulnerable to attack by stalking adult males.

These observations suggest that the evolutionary basis for prejudice and discrimination differs for males and females. The key data are these: Males usually stay with their natal group, whereas females leave at adolescence and join another group; adolescent and adult males, but not females, defend the group against outsiders, and even stalk and attack them. These behavior patterns show that males are more hostile to nongroup members than are females, and adult males more so than immature ones. The observations may mean that males are more predisposed than females to form a strong group identification and to develop commitments to many group members, and older males more so than younger ones. Adult females form close bonds with their offspring and with only a small number of adult males and/or females. Using evidence consistent with the above, Lever (1978) has shown that boys in Western cultures are more likely than girls both to be members of large groups and to play in competitive games. Preadolescent and adolescent females appear to have a more tenuous identification with the natal group than same-age males—that is, one more readily overcome by attractions beyond it (see Outsider Attractiveness, below)—in that they eventually leave to join another group. Perhaps more flexible group identification on the part of females is a necessary condition for their permanent departure. The stronger group identification of males could lead to more hostility toward outsiders through mechanisms such as outsider salience, sensitivity to perceived group threats, social contagion, and reduced exposure to aggression-moderating influences. These factors could operate on attitudes, behavior, or both (Franco & Maass, 1996).

The notion that human females display less in-group favoritism and more acceptance of different others than do males is supported by studies with American high school and college samples (Eisikovits, 2000; Hoover & Fishbein, 1999; Johnson & Marini, 1998; Mills et al., 1995; Quails et al., 1992) as well as in a large multinational study (Glick et al., 2000). Not surprisingly, these gender differences are complex, varying, for instance, as a function of whether measures tap implicit versus explicit attitudes (Rudman & Kilianski, 2000) or social versus sexual distance (Hoxter & Lester, 1994). Although the precise nature and mechanisms of gender differences in prejudice is unclear, evidence from many primate species and diverse human cultures makes rootedness in human evolution a plausible concept.

## Authority-Bearing Systems

As noted in a previous section (The Hunter-Gatherer Heritage), one of the most dramatic shifts human evolution took relative to that of the African apes was in the area of culture. The prominent evolutionary theorist C.H. Waddington (1960) has referred to this human characteristic as a "cultural sociogenetic system" (abbreviated CS-G system). CS-G systems are built on biological hereditary systems and, like the biological systems, are fundamentally involved with transmitting information from one generation to the next. The primary processes of doing this are social teaching and learning. CS-G systems evolve over time, but the mechanisms are different than those of biological evolution in that no genetic changes occur.

CS-G systems involve the transmission of an enormous amount of information. This is made possible by our highly evolved symbolic and communication abilities and, Waddington argues, by the evolution of "authority-bearing systems." The essence of these systems is that the receivers of information are designed to accept as true or valid the messages transmitted to them by authorities. Human cultures are so complex that individuals do not have the time or means to independently test out or evaluate each piece of new information. The mechanism evolution "selected" for overcoming this problem was authority acceptance. Waddington suggests that authority acceptance has its roots in "model-mimic" or "leader-follower" patterns of interaction seen in other animals, but it is dramatically extended to encompass conceptual or symbolic materials.

The notion of "authority" is a relative one. A sister or brother may take on the role of authority relative to a younger sibling, but the mother is an authority to them all. In general, an authority is a person who has greater legitimate status or power than another person. As noted in the discussion of monkey dominance hierarchies, high-status individuals are attended to and sought out for grooming more than others. They hold privileged positions in the social group and others follow their lead and respect their desires. These primate characteristics form the bases for authority acceptance. The principle shift is from the behavioral (nonhuman primates) to the conceptual (humans).

Waddington maintains that much of the information transmitted in a CS-G system is "value-laden" or "ethical" and takes the form of beliefs. Thus, not only do children have to know what items not to eat because they are poisonous and what locations to avoid because snakes or leopards reside there (and not personally test out the validity of this information), but also they are required to know and accept beliefs and behaviors concerned with other persons and spiritual entities. There are "right" and "wrong" beliefs and courses of action, and these are often highly cultural-specific, for example, wearing veils, not eating pork, aiding the poor, facing East while praying.

Waddington argues that one essential component of authority acceptance is the psychological internalization of what authorities tell us. We personally take on (take in) the beliefs and values of authorities; this gives these ideas an obligatory character. We eventually come to extol their values and, in turn, transmit these to others over whom we have authority. Thus, we not only accept as valid what authorities tell us, but also, in a sense, come to maintain that the ideas are what they *should* be.

Waddington indicates, following psychoanalytic and Piagetian research, that authority acceptance has a developmental path. It appears to peak between the ages of 4 and 7 years, and to decline somewhat as children mature. One reason for the decline is the growing influence of peers on our thoughts and actions. In Piaget's (1932/1948) research, for example, children under age 7 usually say that game rules can't be changed because the rules were handed down by the elders. After age 7, children start to say that they can change the rules if their playmates agree to it. Although authority acceptance might decline after age 7, it remains a potent force throughout the human lifetime. As an example, young men and women go to war and risk their lives (often zealously) because their leaders tell them that doing so is based on a just cause.

At least three types of evidence support the concept that humans are authority acceptors. The first involves children's ideas about obedience to authority. The literature indicates that there is little change between the ages of 4 and 11 years in children's willingness to obey legitimate authorities, provided that immoral acts are not requested or that the authorities are not intruding in areas of the child's jurisdiction (Braine et al., 1991; Damon, 1977; Turiel, 1983). This research shows that some of the reasons children give for obedience change with age. Other research (Smetana, 1986) finds that during adolescence, the area of a child's jurisdiction increases, which has the consequence of narrowing the range of others' legitimate authority.

In Braine et al.'s (1991) study, boys and girls between the ages of 6 and 11 years were read stories about children's conflicts with six types of legitimate authority, and two types of nonsanctioned authority: a power move by an older sibling and stealing by armed robbers from a store. After each story was read, the subjects were asked how the child in the story felt, what he (or she) should do, why, and how the authority figure would react if the child were not obedient. The five major results were:

- Although children indicated different levels of obedience to different types of legitimate authority figures, there were essentially no age differences in extent of compliance.

- In nearly all cases, children of all ages stated that there would be negative consequences, for example, punishment, for noncompliance. This suggests that compliance is largely based on avoidance of these bad outcomes.

- As age increased, there was a decrease in the frequency with which the subjects believed that the children in the stories would feel "sad" when placed in conflict. Older subjects were more likely than younger ones to attribute angry feelings to the children.

- Older subjects gave more varied reasons for complying with legitimate authorities than younger ones, reflecting greater social knowledge.

- There were marked differences between older and younger subjects to the robber story, but not to the older sibling story. These differences were based on the relative values the subjects placed on avoiding physical harm and protecting one's money.

The second line of evidence supporting the idea that humans are authority acceptors involves children's modeling behavior. The assumption made regarding authority acceptance is that children will not only accept as valid what authorities tell them, but also what authorities show them. Thus, children should be more likely to model their own behavior after high-status than low-status models. A number of studies support this conclusion. In Hetherington's (1965) experiment, groups of 4½-, 7-, and 10-year-old boys and girls and their parents were the subjects. The relative dominance of each parent was assessed through measuring which parent had the most influence in solving hypothetical child care problems. Two measures of children's identification with their mothers and fathers, respectively, and one measure of imitation of each parent were taken. The identification measures involved strength of masculine and feminine sex roles and similarity of personality characteristics with parents. The imitation measure involved judgments of the prettiness of pictures, as modeled by each parent. In general, the results strongly support the importance of parental status in identification and imitation. Both boys and girls were more likely to identify with and imitate the more dominant parent; however, girls were relatively less susceptible to variations in mother-dominance than boys were to variations in father-dominance.

In Grusec's (1971) research the subjects were 7- and 11-year-old boys and girls who were given opportunities to imitate a same-sex adult with either high or low "power." In the high-power condition, the adult was introduced as a person who was going to select children for an interesting trip. Moreover, after the adult and child finished their tasks, the adult was going to interview the child for possible trip selection. In the low-power condition, the same adults were given no special status or relationship with the children. While the children watched, the adults in both conditions played a bowling game and either conspicuously gave some of their winnings to charity (Experiment 1) or used very stringent performance criteria for rewarding themselves (Experiment 2). The adults left the room, and the children played the same game. In both experiments, children were found to imitate the high-power models to a greater extent than the low-power ones.

Finally, children are more likely to imitate high-status than low-status persons. In experiments with children by Brody and Stoneman (1981, 1985), second- or third-grade boys and girls watched a same-sex "model" child choose his or her favorite foods from pairs of pictures. The model was either older (high status), the same age, or younger (low status) than the subjects, who were informed about the model's age. After the models made their choices, the subjects selected their favorite foods. In both studies, the subjects imitated the choices of the same age or older children much more frequently than they did the younger ones.

The third line of supporting evidence deals with the general question of the relationship between understanding ideas and either believing or disbelieving them (Gilbert, 1991). Gilbert has reviewed and integrated a large number of empirical and theoretical papers concerned with this issue. Interestingly, the framework of his study is philosophical, contrasting Rene Descartes's view that a person's decision to believe or disbelieve an idea occurs after he or she has attempted to understand it, with Baruch Spinoza's view that believing an idea and understanding it occur at the same time. Spinoza thought that disbelieving an idea requires additional mental processing. Authority acceptance is highly consistent with Spinoza's view, although neither Descartes nor Spinoza qualify their positions regarding the status of the person who transmits the information. Simply put, Spinoza says that we believe what others tell us. Gilbert concludes that Spinoza's view, or one similar to it, is correct. At a minimum, belief of ideas precedes disbelief.

The connection between authority acceptance and the development of prejudice and discrimination is fairly obvious. Children believe what their parents and other authorities—for example, teachers, political figures, athletes, actors, older siblings—tell them. They also believe what they read in books, magazines, and newspapers, and what they hear and see on television. Much of what they learn conveys consistent messages as to the characteristics and status of in- and out-groups, including those based on race/ethnicity, gender, mental status, and other variables. Children not only believe these messages but also incorporate them into their own value systems. Adults (and presumably children) may hold beliefs that are not readily modified by particular counterexamples. Thus a black child may have a white child as a best friend and still believe, as his peers, parents, and other family members have instructed him, that whites are not trustworthy. If this same black child develops a large number of friendships with whites, however, these experiences may transform the beliefs he has acquired from his family and friends.

## Gene Flow and Out-group Attractiveness

The genetic analyses in this section come primarily from six sources: Cavalli-Sforza and Bodmer (1971), Dobzhansky (1962), Gagneux et al. (1999), Lamb (2000), Thompson (1999), and Thrall et al. (1998). The concept of out-group attractiveness based on these analyses is one of the author's (Fishbein).

In nonhuman primates, mating rarely occurs between individuals that have been reared together. At sexual maturity, depending on the species and ecological conditions, adolescent males or females leave the natal group and migrate to another subsistence group. In turn, each subsistence group accepts migrants from other groups. For example, adolescents from Group A generally migrate to B or C, those from B generally migrate to A or D, and so on. Extragroup matings also occur through females' seeking mating partners outside of their group without leaving it. In that these subsistence groups are relatively small, mating outside of the group has both the short- and long-term effect of decreasing the likelihood of incest and inbreeding. It also has the long-term effect of keeping within group genetic variability at a sufficiently high level to accommodate environmental changes that inevitably occur, such as the introduction of new diseases and long-term drought.

In human hunter-gatherers, mating nearly always occurs outside the subsistence group, but within the tribe. Assuming that at any one time no more than half the tribal members can reproduce, a tribe consists of about 125 mating couples. A relatively small mating population presents at least three potential problems. The first is "inbreeding depression." Inbreeding depression is a phenomenon seen in a wide variety of animal and plant species. It is a loss of Darwinian fitness in populations that have increased homozygosity for many genes, that is, both alleles for a given gene location are identical. Sometimes this homozygosity leads to valued phenotypic outcomes, as plant and animal breeders can attest to. But this homozygosity also leads to increased recessive genetic diseases that are deleterious to survival or reproduction. The problem with homozygosity is that many recessive alleles are lethal or deleterious, but are not problematical when paired with another allele that is dominant and not deleterious. Hundreds of known genetic diseases are caused by recessive alleles in a homozygous state, for example, sickle cell anemia, Tay Sachs, cystic fibrosis, phenylketonuria (PKU), and hypothyroidism. It is believed that the average human carries three or more lethal recessive alleles. Thus, close relatives who mate are at increased risk for homozygosity of these harmful alleles among their offspring.

Let us assume that mating with very close relatives (e.g., brother-sister, mother-son) was forbidden in ancestral hunter-gatherer groups, as it is in essentially all contemporary societies (some allow first cousin marriages, but in the United States about one-half of the states prohibit it). Because of the small size of the mating population, if mating only occurred within the tribe, and if first- or second-cousin marriage was the preferred norm, as it is in some aboriginal tribes (Tinsdale, 1974) this would lead, over time, to population increases in homozygosity at numerous gene loci. Because some of these alleles would be deleterious, this would lead to a loss of Darwinian fitness. Although we have no studies of the effects of increases in homozygosity in hunter-gatherer tribes, careful large-scale studies in France and Japan after the Second World War comparing offspring of genetically related (primarily first and second cousins) versus unrelated parents showed that the rates of stillborns, neonatal, and early infancy deaths were much greater for related parents.

What can be done to prevent the inbreeding problem? The answer is simple—gene flow. Gene flow is the introduction of new genetic material from members of outside groups. The usual way this occurs is through migration of some outsiders to the host tribe, where they set up residence and mate with one or more members of the tribe. Computer simulations of the process indicate that the numbers of outsiders need not be large in order to accomplish the goal of maintaining genetic heterozygosity both within and among members of the population.

The second problem with small mating populations is genetic drift. Even assuming random mating in the population, as contrasted with first- and second-cousin preferences, one or more alleles at various particular genetic loci will be lost over generations due to the random effects of small population size. Thus other alleles will become fixed in the population, increasing homozygosity. Because this is a random process, the alleles affected were probably at a low frequency in the population to begin with and can never get passed on to the offspring. If this random loss of some alleles occurs most generations, then many of them will eventually become eliminated from the population. Again, the fixing of other alleles in the population means homozygosity at a number of genetic loci in the population. This occurrence may have no noticeable short-term effect. However, the population gene pool loses variability and many, perhaps most, individuals become less able to adapt to environmental changes. What can be done to prevent the genetic drift problem? The answer is, again, simple—gene flow. Immigrants bring in new genetic material, perhaps the lost alleles but certainly different alleles, and this increases genetic variability in the host tribe.

The third problem has already been noted in the cases of inbreeding depression and genetic drift—reduced genetic variability associated with small mating populations. Small populations with limited variability in the gene pool may be well adapted to the normal range of environments to which they are immediately exposed. However, due to both genetic drift and previous Darwinian selection in response to environmental change, the loss of significant number of alleles probably occurred. Indeed evolution itself involves the weeding out of maladaptive or nonadaptive alleles and their replacement by alleles that are more adaptive. But as noted earlier, once those alleles are lost, their potential for future adaptation is also lost. They may be maladaptive in the present environment, but highly adaptive in other environments. An important balance has to be struck between the weeding out of currently nonadaptive alleles and their retention as a hedge against future environmental changes.

The obvious answer to the problem of limited genetic variability is gene flow. Outsiders bring in additional genetic variation that increases genetic variability of the host tribe. This process also has the advantage that it brings in some "tested" variation—some different genes that already have some selective value in the out-group population. However, too much gene flow, especially from out-groups operating under different selection pressures than the host tribe, can be problematic in that it may disrupt the existing genetic adaptation to local ecology that the host tribe has attained (outbreeding depression). Thus, dual selection pressures—on admitting new genes into the pool and on retaining the existing pool—would operate on phenotypes expressed at the in-group/out-group interface.

To summarize, there are two significant and interrelated problems associated with small populations, which have different effects. The first is an increase in homozygosity brought about by inbreeding, leading to the expression of deleterious genes. The second is the loss of genetic variation brought about by genetic drift, leading to the reduced ability of members of the population to adapt to new environments. Adequate gene flow from migrants will counter both negative effects.

Similar to the argument in the discussion of inclusive fitness, the adaptive advantage of gene flow is presumed to have psychological consequences. To accept migrants into the host tribe, members of the host tribe must overcome the wariness and hostility they feel toward outsiders and want to bring one or more of them into the group. As is discussed in the next section, each of us carries "badging" mechanisms, psychological processes that lead us to notice characteristics that mark group membership and make it possible to distinguish in-group and out-group members. Where differences are perceived, psychological processes are assumed to exist that evaluate these differences. Importantly, the tendency toward negative evaluation of salient differences emphasized above is complemented by a capacity for positive evaluations. Like many species from crows to chimpanzees, humans are attracted by novelty (neophilia) as well as put off by it (neophobia), and curiosity opens the door to other favorable assessments of utility or aesthetic value. These positive evaluations can, in turn, lead to a decision to either include the outsiders in the in-group or to incorporate some of their different characteristics into the in-group.

Out-group attraction occurs even between warring societies, where some members of opposing groups marry and have children. And certainly this mutual attraction occurs between in-group and out-group members who are not at war or in a state of conflict. In addition, when some out-group characteristics such as new tools, techniques, or other cultural artifacts are valued, the host tribe may adopt them. Adoption of out-group characteristics makes the host tribe and the out-group more similar to each other, further breaking down barriers to friendship and intermarriage. Thus, phenotypic plasticity and intermarriage resulting from out-group attractiveness act in concert to change the culture.

The long-term outcome of incorporating outsiders into the tribe is increased gene flow, which has the effect of maintaining adequate genetic variability and reducing homozygosity. But the psychological mechanisms produced by the adaptive need for gene flow—out-group attraction—are opposed to those produced by inclusive fitness and intergroup hostility—bigotry and discrimination directed toward the out-group. Scholars from psychoanalysts (e.g., Guarton, 1999) to evolutionary psychologists (e.g., Guisinger & Blatt, 1994) agree that conflicting unconscious motives can coexist in a dialectical relationship. Emotional, behavioral, and cognitive building blocks of the outsider attraction/ bigotry dialectic include neophilia/neophobia, approach/avoidance, and "benevolent" and hostile stereotypes (Glick et al., 2000), such as Asians being good at math but sneaky or Jews being gifted in medicine but greedy. Depending on the relative strength of out-group attraction and hostility, our moral values, and external reality, one or the other of these motives will prevail in conscious thought or action. Based on the widespread prevalence of intercultural conflict, the psychological forces underlying prejudice and discrimination appear generally to be stronger than those underlying outsider attraction. However, gene flow does not depend on every tribal member mating with outsiders. It only takes a few persons each generation to ensure adequate gene flow for maintaining genetic variability and keeping homozygosity at an acceptable level. Whether out-group attraction evolved through selection at the group or individual level (see Wilson & Sober, 1994), it would only have needed to govern the behavior of a small number of individuals under certain circumstances to have earned a place in our species' social-psychological repertoire.

## Identification of Tribe Members and Multigroup Membership

From the perspective of the development of prejudice and discrimination in contemporary society, two related issues must be addressed: identification of tribe members (or, conversely, outsiders) and multigroup memberships. The issue of identification of tribe members relates to two of the four evolutionary factors discussed in this chapter: inclusive fitness and intertribal hostility. Preadolescent hunter-gatherers are assumed to know relatively few members of the tribe outside their primary subsistence group. How can the young identify strangers who are tribal members (and thus safe) as opposed to outsiders of nearby tribes, who are potentially dangerous? Irwin (1987) suggests that this is accomplished through the evolutionary mechanism known as "badging." Certain groups of birds, for example, identify potential mates through identification of a particular song that only members of their breeding population have learned. Irwin plausibly argues that the young in any tribe readily learn to identify and differentiate most, if not all, of the cultural characteristics that they and fellow tribesmen share. If the stranger speaks the same language, with the same dialect, dresses the same, carries the same tools, and so on as do members of the subsistence group, then the stranger is not seen as an outsider, but rather a tribesman. The issue of tribal member identification and inclusive fitness has been extensively examined by Van den Berghe (1981) in the context of ethnic prejudice. Van den Berghe discusses three categories of "ethnic markers" which potentially serve to determine group membership:

- Genetically transmitted "racial" characteristics such as skin color, stature, facial features
- Human-made artifacts that are "worn" such as clothing, body painting, tattooing, circumcision
- Behavioral characteristics such as speech, manners, knowledge of particular myths or histories

Many of these are similar to Irwin's (1987) "badges." The most blatant markers are genetically transmitted differences that, clustered in a particular way, are treated categorically as "racial." As Van den Berghe (1981) points out, from a genetic/evolutionary view, dramatic differences in "racial" characteristics between neighboring tribes were rare occurrences and could not have been the basis for inclusive fitness choices. Members of nearby tribes are usually similar with respect to these characteristics, primarily because they evolved in essentially the same environment and because tribal intermarriage (forced or voluntary) occasionally occurred. For example, there is a gradient in Europe from North to South, of eye and hair color. Residents of neighboring territories show essentially the same pattern, but Scandinavian (blue and blond) and Southern Italy (brown and brown) are very different. Inclusive fitness choices occurred in relation to the nearby tribes, not between "Scandinavians" and "Italians."

Racial differences as tribal markers only became important during the postagricultural period, when city-states were founded, armies were formed, and territorial expansion occurred. Hostile encounters between white Europeans and black Africans are even more recent, perhaps only about 500 years. Van den Berghe (1981) indicates, however, that with few exceptions such as in South Africa and the United States, where there are strong barriers to interracial marriage, race as a basis for ethnic identity was short-lived. Typically, within several generations, enough intermarriage occurs in a society to obscure racial bases of ethnicity. As a related aside, in historical times the first contacts between members of different races were occasionally friendly, at least in the New World. The Pilgrims in Massachusetts, and the Spaniards in Mexico and Peru, were initially met with curiosity and not hostility by the various indigenous groups. The Pilgrim stories even indicate that the Wampanoag were friendly and saved the lives of those colonists. It was only when the Europeans waged war that the Native Americans became hostile. Thus, it appears that racial differences as a basis for prejudice is purely cultural/historical and not genetic/evolutionary. This conclusion is consistent with the consensus in fields ranging from genetics to cultural anthropology that "race" is socially constructed.

In his discussion of the "worn" and behavioral ethnic markers, Van den Berghe (1981) argues that the behavioral differences were the most reliable and most difficult to fake. By donning the clothes, hairstyle, and body paint of a neighboring tribe, it was easy to look like a member of that tribe. But to affect the mannerisms of the neighboring tribe, especially their language dialect, was often very difficult. Thus, language differences and similarities probably were the primary ways that tribal membership was assessed. This suggests that there is a genetic/evolutionary basis for strong sensitivities to and responses to speech.

Hunter-gatherers are simultaneously members of a number of groups: a tribe, a subsistence group, an extended family, an immediate family, an age-related group of peers (Eisenstadt, 1956), and a same-sex group ("We are boys," "We are girls"). Multigroup membership is much more extensive in hunter-gatherers than in the African apes, perhaps even greater among urban humans than hunter-gatherers. The existence of multigroup membership raises two problems. First, how are children able to understand and act on multigroup membership? Second, what happens when conflict occurs between groups of which one is a member? Regarding the first, it is likely that the tremendous growth in cognitive abilities, especially symbolic ones, relative to the African apes, permits humans to simultaneously identify with several groups. Symbolic labeling is a powerful social and intellectual tool, especially if it is reinforced by the behavior of other persons.

Regarding the second question, children and adults form a hierarchy of preferred groups, or a rank ordering of group allegiances. If the groups are in frequent conflict, a person may have to choose to disaffiliate from one or more of the groups, and thus become an outsider to them. In hunter-gatherer societies, which are relatively closed to people outside the tribe and where there is a strong need for social cohesion, these intergroup conflicts are probably infrequent. But in urban societies they are more common. Tonnesmann (1987) suggests that group identity is stronger when multiple memberships are not possible or permitted (i.e., the barrier could be cultural). Examples are discrete gender and racial identities in cultures in which a person must be male *or* female, black *or* white. From an evolutionary perspective, current challenges to rigid group boundaries (e.g., critical theory, transgender and multiracial activism) reflect ancient epigenetic processes playing out on a contemporary, heterogeneous, urban stage to which they were not specifically adapted. As such, these movements and responses to them are a laboratory for the study of the interplay between the "us/them" substrate and proximate conditions that shape social identities, intergroup relations, and political action.

## IMMIGRATION: A CASE STUDY IN PUBLIC POLICY

Immigration—leaving one group to join another—is an interesting "case" with which to explore the policy implications of the foregoing analysis. This attempt to do so draws on work in primatology, anthropology, sociology, political science, history, and psychology. Basic underlying assumptions, however, follow from evolutionary reasoning: human immigration has a natural history; it will share some key features with immigration in other primates, especially apes, but also will have unique features arising from factors that distinguish humans from our closest relatives.

### Immigration as a "Hybrid" Social Phenomenon

Immigration is a hybrid phenomenon in the sense that it engages both intergroup and within-group dynamics. Both types of encounter can be aggressive or peaceful; either can end in death or in rapprochement. Generally, though, intergroup primate encounters elicit wariness, threats, mutual rebuff, and/or fighting. Chimpanzees and gorillas usually are hostile toward intruders within group boundaries, particularly females and their infants (Goodall, 1986; Hasegawa, 1989; Sicotte, 2000). In a notorious display of similar behavior, Cuba, the United States, and Canada refused refuge from Nazi persecution to more than 900 Jews aboard the *St. Louis*, nearly 70% of them women and children; half later died in the Holocaust.

Encounters within primate groups also can be hostile, but group life generates mitigating factors. Long-term exposure to group members reduces xenophobia, lowering the odds of a quick escape or violent outburst and opening a window of opportunity for the subtler, up-close interactions critical to social cohesion. In-group dynamics also draw on established relationships and shared group knowledge. Knowledge about individuals' status, strength, and temperament, about allies and peacemakers, and about ritualized greetings and rules of engagement can moderate aggression and promote reconciliation toward in-group members (Aureli & de Waal, 2000).

Interactions between immigrants and members of a host group are a dance with elements of both intergroup and in-group encounters. How is an immigrant transformed from intruder to in-group member? What are the consequences of multigroup membership in natal and host societies? How does immigration transform the host society? These questions are explored below in terms of the natural history humans share with other primates and the ways in which the human story is unique, including the role of public policy.

## Natural History of Immigration

As noted earlier, movement from natal to other groups is common among primates. A particular pattern may be normative for a species, but deviation from the norm also occurs as a function of factors such as group size fluctuation, status hierarchy stability, and resource availability. For example, the general pattern for chimpanzees is for females to leave the natal group, but in a 21-year study in Bossou, Guinea, male dispersion matched that of females, perhaps due to intragroup competition and local ecology (Sugiyama, 1999). Similar themes and variations occur for humans.

In most circumstances, immigration is risky and stressful for the immigrant as well as the host group. Immigrants seek the benefits the host community has to offer but have no guarantee that they will be accepted or, once accepted, that life in the group will be good. Indeed, acceptance can be slow and grudging. Chimpanzees or gorillas accepted into a group may endure protracted harassment and wounding. Human immigrants similarly endure persecution, expressed in some forms like that seen in apes (e.g., physical violence) and in others with a human twist, such as name calling and institutionalized discrimination. Likewise, hosts may stand to gain much from newcomers but have no guarantee that they will not be harmed. Groups that admit immigrants are in fact vulnerable to "Trojan horses" such as coups, disease, and the stress of persistent instability. Social transitions are unsettling. Ambivalence on both sides of the immigration equation is characteristic of humans and our closest relatives.

The hopeful vision of immigration to be gleaned from natural history is that primates' social repertoire clearly includes acceptance of strangers into the group. It is not rare but common. Given the benefits of gene flow in small breeding groups, it is likely that immigration was a vital force in the evolution of our species and that mechanisms of mutual accommodation were selected for ["selected for" is a specialized term in evolutionary biology referring to the process of natural selection; here, "mechanisms of mutual accommodation" were selected for.]. Immigrants into chimpanzee and gorilla troops can find acceptance, even high status, in their adopted group. Similarly, immigrants to the United States can be found among the elite, from community leaders to industry magnates to members of Congress. Effective, humane policy will take account of the bright side as well as the dark side of our evolutionary legacy.

## Emergent Features of Human Immigration

Although human immigration dynamics derive from a fundamentally primate us/them dialectic, unique features have emerged from two interrelated phenomena: cognitive evolution and the appearance of nation-states. This summary and application to immigration draw on Boehm (1999; this volume), Diamond (1997), Donald (1991), Dunbar (1996), and Solomon et al. (2000; this volume).

A key aspect of human cognitive evolution is a fantastically elaborated capacity for abstract thought. Conceiving of distant times gave life to progeny who would exist in the future and to ancestors who existed long ago; coupled with self-awareness, it brought awareness of one's own mortality. Conceiving of remote places from which immigrants came created unseen Others. Things with no physical referent—immortality, fairness, evil spirits—became psychologically real and thus available for association with cultural badging and other social processes. Meaning-making was accompanied by a growing ability to communicate through language. At the individual level, language added symbolic exchange at a distance to the communication repertoire. At the collective level, language permitted first mythic oral traditions and, later, graphic representations of theories about the earth and heavens.

As cognition changed, sociality grew less pragmatic and more ideological, relative to the African apes. A collective worldview regulated emotions and behavior, including the exquisite new torments and heroics of which humans were capable. Custom was no longer merely something routinely done but became something that *ought* to be done, that was justified and morally right. The authority-bearing system gave leaders new means of influence, such as relaying missives from the spirit world and casting problems and solutions in terms of cosmologies. Concurrently, all adult group members could engage in politics in an unprecedented manner: They could question the legitimacy and wisdom of leaders. Thus, humans formed stable egalitarian societies in which leaders led with the group's consent. Finally, human cognitive evolution made possible "public policy" consisting of explicitly articulated rules, principles of collective action, and efforts after problem solving. Divisions of labor, dispute resolution, and practices related to eating, hygiene, child rearing, and mating no longer merely existed; they were prescribed by policies.

Policy specified how immigrants were to be regarded and treated. Whether Others were long-lost relatives, gods, or demons, whether greetings, warnings, or attack were in order, and whether a particular act by or toward Others was honorable or despicable were decided in principle and inculcated throughout the group. While diverse policies concerning in-group violence developed, a view of Others as dangerous—and thus to be approached cautiously, resisted, or killed—remained the norm.[4] This norm speaks not to an incapacity for peaceful intergroup relations but to the risk inherent to indiscriminately welcoming strangers. The slaughter of Moriori by invading Maori in Polynesia offers a poignant example of an encounter between related groups, separated by 1,000 years of cultural evolution, in which violent policies laid waste to pacifistic ones.

Immigration dynamics were altered within the last 15,000 years by dramatic changes in social organization. The key development was living in settled as opposed to nomadic communities, by hunter-gatherers engaged in intensive collecting or fishing and early agriculturalists. With settlement, group identity became linked to place; now, an "outside" existed literally, composed of the settled and unsettled land beyond the territorial border. The first "outsiders" with an identity as such to visit these early settlements were itinerant traders who came to exchange goods with residents. Traders were welcomed, or at least tolerated, because sedentary communities could use commodities unavailable in their territory and, more important, could articulate rules about the relationship with outsiders designed to benefit the group—that is, economic and foreign policies. Cultural badges signaling that traders were "just passing through" minimized the perceived threat they posed to territorial possession and way of life and, thus, provided a degree of protection. As signals of Otherness, the badges also would have elicited residents' wariness. Thus, badges both signaled outsiders' marginal status and ensured it.

As permanent settlements matured, they grew. Group sizes rose from tribes of hundreds to states of thousands. Initially, group sizes rose due to the population growth and longevity supported by intensive food production. As uninhabited land grew scarce, conquest and mergers in the face of external threat also occurred. The greater size and cultural heterogeneity of states transformed human politics. Not all of the changes derived from uniquely human processes. In marmosets, for instance, aggressiveness toward strangers increases as the breeding group grows larger (Schaffner & French, 1997). Nonetheless, human cognition did play out in entirely new ways in the state context. Belongingness was based more on "citizenship" and residency than on kinship or ageless custom; conflict resolution fell to courts rather than intimate acts of reconciliation; economic exchanges were redistributive instead of reciprocal. Power became more centralized and society more stratified. Badging incorporated symbols of government—coins, banners, seals, and the like.

Unlike bands or tribes, a state's viability required extensive cooperation between in-group members who would never meet in person and thus could only relate to each other symbolically, as citizens bound by allegiance to the same rulers, a shared worldview, and common policies. Immigrants threatened a citizenry by threatening the state; they posed consciously appraised and publicly discussed risks to citizens' rights to homeland, sovereignty, sacred ways of life, social stability, and economic security. As immigrants increasingly comprised groups of individuals displaced from other states, the perceived threat intensified while the attractions and benefits of mixing with outsiders remained relatively constant. Public policy assumed a more crucial role in immigration management. Within the centralized, hierarchical structure of states, policy formulation was the province of an elite whose interests—including retaining power and wealth—were foremost. How prominently the welfare and sentiments of the citizenry figured in policy varied as a function of how despotic or democratic the regime was. At either pole, many voices—the voices of immigrants along with women, children, and slaves—were disenfranchised whispers in policy debates. Where these groups' lots improved, changes were assessed as advantageous to the state and usually were accomplished through patronage and coalitions.

In this context, some aspects of modern immigration are understandable. The following characterization draws on the work of Booth et al. (1997), Daniels (1990), Fallers (1967), Shack and Skinner (1979), and Walzer (1997). The entry of immigrants into a society is remarkably common across historical time and place. When the immigrants arrive, whether in Africa, Asia, Europe, or North America, they seek out *landsmenn* (people from their natal community). Together they re-create important aspects of the original community. They reside in the same geographic area, form voluntary associations in which the home language is spoken, and start charitable and social institutions to help old and new immigrating *landsmenn*. They start schools in which instruction is in the native language, open markets specializing in familiar foods, and build churches, temples, or mosques where they can practice their religion and hospitals where they can be assured of sympathetic and competent treatment. The Chinatowns and Little Italys in many large U.S. cities are prototypes. Once these reconstructed "old country" communities are established, new immigrants readily assimilate into them.

The insularity of the immigrant community results from the pull of *landsmenn* toward each other as well as the repulsion of the host society. The pull reflects in-group favoritism, the security of being surrounded by kin and familiar, beloved cultural badges. The "social capital" that these established communities represent pays dividends in a range of domains, such as employment networking, psychological well-being, and mortality (e.g., Harker, 2001; Hummer et al., 1999; Nee & Sanders, 2001). Members of the host culture feed into the centripetal tendencies of the immigrants by excluding them from their in-groups. For example, in many large American cities for most of the twentieth century, Jews were not allowed to join any of the local country clubs and were essentially forced to form their own. Restrictive covenants excluding Poles, Southern Europeans, and Jews from renting or buying real estate were common through the 1950s.

Although immigrant insularity permits an easier initial transition, it also works against equal status. Insularity maintains the salience of the cultural boundary between immigrant and host groups and thus the members' respective in-group identities. Immigrant networks often ensure access only to low-paying, low-status jobs, reinforcing disparaging stereotypes about the group's ability, effort, and worth. Adherence to stereotypes minimizes the threat the group poses to the dominant group and thus, ironically, limits both intergroup conflict and immigrants' upward mobility. To the host society, the conflation of location and cultural badging increases the perceived homogeneity of the immigrant community, reducing individuation and further reinforcing stereo-types. Insularity also gives the appearance of immigrants having chosen to be a "them" rather than an "us." Whether the immigrant group actually desires assimilation (not all do), the *apparent* choice of insularity provides a convenient excuse for maintaining cultural barriers and status differentials by privileged groups in the host society. Separate, salient immigrant communities also are easier targets of prejudice and discrimination; attacks—verbal, physical, or po-litical—need only be directed at a part of town to hit their target.

Changes over time in the relation of the immigrant community to the host society are far less predictable than is initial entry. At one extreme, an immi-grant community remains marginalized across generations, as with the Bidun in Kuwait. In some cases, national identity, citizenship, and political power develop quickly. For example, the status of Irish-Catholic immigrants to the United States was transformed from intense derogation in the mid-nineteenth century to their domination of Boston politics and election of native son John Fitzgerald Kennedy as president less than a hundred years later. Accordingly, many assimilation models have been developed in attempts to characterize these patterns and their identity correlates (e.g., homogenizing linear versus ethnically segmented assimilation, "melting pot" versus "salad bowl" models, and so on; see Alba & Nee, 1997, and Keefe & Padilla, 1987).

The complex reasons for this variation are beyond the scope of this chapter. The key point here is that several recurrent themes in ongoing tension between immigrants and host societies follow directly from an evolutionary perspective. The first is the strong, persistent tendency of both groups to favor their in-group. Another is the ease with which members of the dominant host group leverage in-group favoritism into out-group hostility through the scapegoating of immigrants for every ill from disease and environmental destruction to crime and moral rot. A third is the prominent role in immigration policy de-bates of resource control, especially access to jobs, property and other capital, education, and health care. As noted by Papademetriou (1997—1998), "even in good economic times, most analyses look at immigration through the prism of 'adverse effects,'" a bias understandable in terms of in-group favoritism and out-group wariness.

A shameful chapter in U.S. history that illustrates these themes is the 1942 internment of more than 100,000 Japanese Americans, rendered suspect by the bombing of Pearl Harbor. Stereotypes infused public discourse and policy dis-cussions: The "Yellow Peril" was, by dint of genes, treacherous, hypersexual, unscrupulous, and "unassimilable." No matter that most internees were native-born citizens and functioning well in society, if not comprising a "model mi-nority." Upon threat to the state, they immediately reverted to Otherness. The testimony of General DeWitt of the Western Defense Command illustrates the depth of out-group wariness and the irrationality of the policy rationale it spawned:

[R]acial affinities are not severed by migration. The Japanese race is an enemy race and while many second and third generation Japanese born on United States soil, possessed of United States citizenship have become "Americanized," the racial strains are undiluted. . . . The very fact that no sabotage has taken place to date is a disturbing and confirming indication that such action will be taken. [*Final Report*, 1942]

Importantly, among those who lobbied hard for internment were white businessmen and farmers who had long resented the success of Japanese Americans in their economic sectors; they profited enormously when internees lost their businesses, homes, and farms. Although in-group favoritism, scapegoating Others, and competition for resources do not explain internment fully, they clearly propelled the government toward an imprudent but popular response to an attack on the homeland.[5] Governmental treatment of Arab Americans in the wake of September 11 may seem restrained by comparison, but Attorney General John Ashcroft's authorization of mass roundups of Arab citizens for "interviews" likely will be experienced as a sort of psychological internment by many of those citizens. As one Arab American poignantly remarked on the nightly news, were he to die in an airliner crash, he would be regarded by his government first as a suspect and only perhaps later as a victim. Similar contemporary cases abound elsewhere, in the lot of Asian nationals in England, Africans in France, Turks in Germany, and Latinos in the United States. These and other examples attest to the fragility of immigrant/host relations and the potential for policy to capitulate inappropriately to atavistic defenses rather than capitalizing on our capacity for prudential judgment.

## Human Nature and Immigration Policy

The emergent features of human immigration make immigration policy inherently complex. It obviously is not simply a matter of a resident group keeping outsiders out or outsiders wanting in. Institutionalized responses to, and the experience of, outsiders vary enormously. Consider, for instance, U.S. policy in the twentieth century: On the anti-immigrant side, it included establishment of an "Asiatic Barred Zone" early in the century (1917) and retroactive deportation for petty crimes, elimination of essential services for legal immigrants, and "denaturalization" authority for the Immigration and Naturalization Service at century's end (1996); in between—on the pro-immigrant side—were the War Brides Act of 1945, abolishment of the Asiatic Barred Zone (1952), the Refugee Relief Act of 1953, and a 1986 amnesty. Immigrant-host relations can even vary dramatically at a point in time in one host state and for immigrants from the same state, as with Thai policies toward Burmese immigrants in border camps versus in cities. The issue, then, is not how immigrants and people in a host society *can, must,* or *certainly will* behave, but rather what they are likely and unlikely to do in particular circumstances given their common evolutionary heritage. Simply put, given human nature, some cultural directives are an "easy sell," (e.g., eating birthday cake, helping kin), and some are a "hard sell" (e.g., lifetime celibacy, trusting strangers). Given the clear net benefit to society of immigration, the challenge is to develop policies that take our propensities into account and thus facilitate the mutual accommodation of immigrants and host society.

How can genetic/evolutionary and cultural/historical perspectives help us improve the process of mutual accommodation of immigrants and American culture? The policy suggestions below draw on common themes in resident/ immigrant interactions wherever they occur. They are generic and illustrative. Details important for policymakers to consider in the prudent development and implementation of specific policies are ignored. This necessary simplification is due to the practical limitations of this chapter, not to homogenization inherent to the evolutionary approach.

### Inclusive Fitness.

Inclusive fitness leads us to favor our own group over outsiders. This occurs for both the immigrants and members of the host community. Because social power and control reside with members of the host community, broad societal favors will aid the hosts. One key to social justice and harmony, then, is whom members of the host society identify as belonging to their group versus being outsiders. Although in-group favoritism cannot be eliminated, the substance of in-group identity and the strength of in-group favoritism are malleable. Suggestions for capitalizing on that malleability include:

1. *Fund and utilize research on in-group identity:* Experimental social psychologists have shown how readily people can adopt new, functional social identities. Ethnographic and survey research has illuminated how people reconcile ethnic, national, and other identities. Developmental research suggests that in-group positivity emerges early, so early childhood is a window of opportunity for shaping whom children identify with and favor. Research of this sort should be supported and used to develop educational and workplace policies that will yield in-group identities inclusive of a broader cross section of society.

2. *Incorporate "the human family" into national education standards:* Belongingness to the same species and having a place in the animal world can be a basis of a broadly shared identity that constrains nationalism. Children should learn how they are like people everywhere in age-appropriate, multidisciplinary ways. This agenda compels lessons about, for instance, the human genome and the United States as a "Nation of Immigrants"—a legacy not only of America's past but of the present and our primate heritage.[6] Facts are not sufficient: Merely providing information about human nature lends itself as well to maintaining the status quo or justifying evil as it does to positive social change. Lessons have to be explicitly directed toward the goal of an expansive and complex identity to achieve it.

3. *Make mixed race/ethnicity identification easy:* Multigroup identity can be facilitated by providing more alternatives to self-identification on official

documents. Some degree of categorization is necessary for pragmatic and, we think, psychological reasons. However, the categories needn't be few or mutually exclusive. Routinely confronting a long list of nested ethnic, racial, religion, and national identity choices with the direction to "check all that apply," along with an open-ended item, could shape notions of whom one's in-group is composed. It also subtly encourages people, as naïve statisticians, to appreciate their individuality and the heterogeneity of out-groups, both of which reduce simple categorical social reasoning (Brewer, 2000; Fishbein, 1996; Neuberg, 1992). The 2000 U.S. Census for the first time allowed respondents to choose more than one ethnic/racial category, a good start in this direction.

4. *Promote high-quality child care:* The vehemence with which one's cultural worldview and in-group are defended under threat (perceived or real) is inversely related to secure attachment style and self-esteem (Florian & Mikulincer, 1998; Mikulincer & Florian, 2000), both of which are rooted firmly in early relationships with caregivers (see Hrdy, 1999). The United States lags woefully behind other industrialized countries in its commitment to high-quality day care for all children. Federal and state governments should subsidize collective child care and parenting education. As in other primate societies, in every human culture men disproportionately engage in intergroup (and other) violence (Goldstein, 2001). Thus, special attention should be paid to how physical affection (Montagu, 1995), punishment alternatives (Milburn et al., 1995), and "emotional education" (Kindlon & Thompson, 2000) can be used to raise boys that more readily display prosocial behavior and are less prone to militant collective in-group defense or psychological postures that favor antiegalitarian political attitudes (right-wing authoritarianism, Altemeyer, 1996; social dominance orientation, Sidanius et al., 2000). Understanding the child care issue in terms of domestic security and prosperity may motivate change in this policy area.

### Out-group Prejudice and Discrimination.

As outsiders, immigrants usually will be treated with wariness, suspicion, derogation, and perhaps hostility. Notable large-scale exceptions to the rule, such as amnesties, asylum policies, and some immigrant groups' upward mobility, attest to the mutability of this response. Therefore, policymakers should be optimistic about their ability to attenuate out-group prejudice. Suggestions toward that end are as follows:

1. *Fund and utilize research on out-group prejudice:* Implicit attitudes toward out-groups express themselves as fast, unconscious responses to cues to out-group membership, or "badges." (Information and an attitude test are online at http://buster.cs.yale.edu/implicit/.) An impressive start has been made toward identifying manipulations that reduce the activation of these attitudes (Blair, 2001; Dovidio & Gaertner, 1999). Thus, out-group prejudice is not "automatically" elicited but can be controlled. Research on practical ways of controlling the development and elicitation of out-group prejudice should be used

to shape policy, especially that related to classroom practices, labor practices, law enforcement practices, and immigration screening.

2. *Facilitate naturalization:* About half of all legal immigrants to the United States become citizens through naturalization. The Constitution extends many but not all rights and privileges to noncitizens. Accordingly, one clear message from many presidents and congresses has been that as a nation we will favor citizens over noncitizens. Citizenship is no guarantee of fair treatment, to which Arab Americans escorted from airplanes and Sikh citizens attacked as "Arabs" after the World Trade Center and Pentagon tragedies can testify.[7] Naturalization does, however, confer legal standing as an insider and thus has advantages that permanent residency does not. Chief among these is the right to vote. Without the vote, the immigrant community must depend on the beneficence of citizens and their leadership—a risky proposition for members of our species. The legislative zeal of anti-immigrant forces over the last five years shows how risky it is.

After a 30-year decline, the naturalization rate began to climb in the 1990s. One reason for the upswing was facilitated application processing by the Immigration and Naturalization Service. Adequate resources should be made available to the INS for processing naturalization requests thoroughly and quickly. It is not inherently good to have more citizens, but it is a social good to give political voice to people who live legally in the United States and want to become citizens.

3. *Maintain and publicize rigorous immigration policies:* Every sensible review shows that the net impact of immigration on the United States in modern times has been extremely positive. The percentage of foreign-born citizens is far lower now than at the turn of the century, and self-selective factors in legal (and most illegal) immigration ensure that the majority of immigrants bring valuable skills and a strong work ethic with them or have family support available once they arrive.[8] Nonetheless, in the United States as elsewhere, much political rhetoric suggests that the country is being overrun by teeming hoards of criminal or otherwise unsavory characters (including, interestingly, pregnant young women) come to feed at the public trough.

This caricature is understandable in terms of the primal fear associated with arrival of strangers and the social changes they signal. The fear cannot be extinguished entirely, but it can be assuaged. First, current immigration criteria of nation-enhancing skills or a family support network must be strictly applied. Second, the empirically validated benefits to the nation of prudent immigration policy (also see Outsider Attractiveness, below) and reassurance that policies are being strictly applied should be well publicized. This information is an antidote to irrational xenophobia. Third, where demands related to immigration are a drain on a regional economy, the federal government should provide relief. Failure to do so becomes fodder for anti-immigrant rhetoric everywhere. Finally, when immigration is based on humanitarian concerns, the moral and legal rightness of the action should be unequivocally asserted by government officials. Appeals to the benevolence of the nation can be effective when cast in self-aggrandizing terms, such as American generosity and friendliness (see Authority-Bearing Systems, below).

4. *Beef up antidiscrimination laws:* In acknowledgment of the fact that immigrants are sometimes targeted as outsiders, federal and state laws offer protection to people on grounds of immigration status. Yet eight states still have no hate crime laws, and not all statutes mention immigration status per se as opposed to "nationality," which is ambiguous. These gaps in legal protection should be closed. This recommendation does not reflect confidence in criminal punishment as a deterrent; psychological and other research shows that it is not particularly effective. However, transgressions codified in law speak to a nation's values—to the acts it reproaches and to the groups it recognizes as vulnerable and worthy of protection. Uniform hate crime legislation naming immigrants as a protected group would be an important symbol of the public's obligation to defend them if need be.

### Authority-Bearing Systems.

Owing to authority bearing systems, we take the lead of authorities that give us direction concerning how to treat immigrants. This occurs through exhortation and legislation. If these directives are positive toward immigrants, then their acceptance will be aided; if negative, then it will be impeded. In this regard, policymakers play a critical role as setters of the nation's moral agenda. They accomplish this not only through the policy actually created but also by virtue of the values for which they advocate. Policy and the rhetoric surrounding it are a representation of authority, and it is human nature to be attentive and responsive to it. Just as the official rhetoric surrounding Japanese internment gave the public permission to support it, George W. Bush's admonishment to treat law-abiding Muslims with respect warned against untoward reactions to the September 11 attacks. Further suggestions are:

1. *Ensure basic human rights for immigrants:* Federal and international doctrine endorse certain inalienable rights to all people, in ways that can be interpreted as implying a right to asylum, education, and health care for immigrants. The devil, however, is in the details, and former President Clinton and Congress gave mixed messages on this count by, for instance, taking away funds for medical treatment of legal residents and placing five-year time limits on eligibility for other benefits. Although reducing these benefits does motivate some permanent residents to apply for citizenship, the net effect of such policies probably is negative: Reducing benefits sends the message that the legal residents are undeserving and unwelcome and thus reinforces anti-immigrant sentiment. A higher and more stable minimum standard of human rights should be articulated and applied.

2. *Closely monitor government response to external threats:* The nation did seem to learn a valuable lesson from the Japanese internment episode, which

culminated in a formal apology and reparations. Still, the treatment of Chinese scholars after alleged "spy" episodes in the 1990s and the harassment of Middle Eastern–looking men—including American citizens—after the tragic explosion of TWA 800 in 1996 and again in the wake of the World Trade Center/Pentagon disaster show that the potential for civil rights violations remains. To be sure, threats from abroad justify wariness and extreme caution. They also, however, can be used to erode important protections against individual rights and discrimination, such as racial profiling, and deprive the nation of important benefits, such as those brought by foreign artists and scholars.

3. *Support community building efforts:* In the end, a human being can have a close personal relationship with up to about 150 people. Harmonious intergroup relations are most easily and cheaply fostered in neighborhoods. For instance, the Orange Hats in Washington, D.C., have made progress in reducing crime, drug trafficking, and increasing neighborliness in deeply divided neighborhoods by holding large, y'all come picnics that start with a handshaking session (Anderson, 2000). It is hard to avoid speculating that the food sharing and intimate physical contact of handshaking played a crucial role in the spirit of cooperation that emerged, given that these are classic primate prosocial behaviors. State and federal governments would do well to provide modest incentives to community groups to coordinate inclusive, food-centered events to which immigrant and host society families with small children could get acquainted.

### Outsider Attractiveness.

Outsider attractiveness can be leveraged into highly desirable effects on a host culture and on intergroup relations. A key proximate mechanism is surveillance of out-groups for novel, appealing characteristics that can positively transform the host society. Immigrants admitted to the United States have brought with them myriad cultural goods that have been noticed and adopted by the host society, including new words, foods, clothing, arts, and religions. The groups' proximity also has stimulated intergroup romance and sexual contact. However, fully realizing the social potential of outsider attractiveness hinges on whether policies suppress or support it. The development and expression of outsider attractiveness are constrained by social-structural factors that limit contact with and the status of out-group members—for example, school, workplace, and neighborhood segregation, educational "tracking," workplace discrimination, exclusion from and negative stereotyping in the media, antimiscegenation laws. When, on the other hand, policy cultivates out-group attraction, rewards are reaped by individuals as well as the transfigured society. Past examples include skilled-worker and "extraordinary ability" visas, creation of integrated public magnet schools, and the repeal of antimiscegenation laws. The following suggestions build on this tradition:

1. *Revise social studies texts and standards:* Exposure to admired members of stigmatized out-groups can override preexisting biases against those groups

(Dasgupta & Greenwald, 2001). Similarly, liking for and approach toward strangers is greater when they are perceived as "winners," regardless of their gender or race (Lott & Lott, 1986). Too many histories taught to young children ignore or understate the accomplishments of remarkable individuals of other cultures and the contributions of minority groups to American culture. Curricular celebrations of what is fascinating about present or historical out-groups—their traditions, neighborhoods, cuisine, inventions, and so on—send constructive messages to children about treasures hidden in strangeness and encourage them to seek out what is valuable in differently lived lives.

2. *Create learning environments that support positive out-group evaluation:* Peer relations, especially during adolescence when key aspects of social identity develop, are a context in which outsider attractiveness can positively impact intergroup relations. A recent meta-analysis (Pettigrew & Tropp, 2000) shows that mere contact between groups increases out-group liking; the improvement is greater in tasks involving superordinate goals, cross-cutting group memberships, and equal status. These same conditions favor the development in school contexts of intergroup friendships (Hallinan & Teixeira, 1987) and out-group attraction (McKillip et al. 1977), in addition to reducing perceived threat (Stephan et al., 2000). Properly structured exchanges between diverse domestic and international school populations should increase the frequency with which students seek out further intercultural experience, through diverse colleges, workplaces, and social partners. Electronic technology could be used effectively in this regard.

3. *Promote women's leadership in intercultural outreach efforts:* Men and women are more alike than different, and both contribute to intergroup conflict and its resolution. Nonetheless, from chimpanzees at the Arnhem Zoo to bonobos in Congo to the human members of Women Waging Peace (www.womenwagingpeace.net), females are crucial to primate peaceableness. This penchant for peace complements the evidence that female apes and women in diverse cultures regard out-group members more favorably than do their male counterparts (see Intergroup Hostility, above). An additional bit of evidence of women's greater attraction toward out-groups is the fact that given the opportunity, college women choose to study abroad at twice the rate of men. The mechanisms of this gender difference—perceptual, emotional, cognitive, behavioral, social, and so on—are not clear. Whatever the mechanisms, it seems that when it comes to reaching across intercultural divides, women's motivation and leadership potential are greater than men's—and this potential stands in stark contrast to the global dominance of men in domestic and international policymaking. Preparing more women for this role, including training in how to draw men into peacemaking coalitions, may be a cost-effective way of capitalizing on out-group attraction. One policy mechanism is increased funding and mentoring to promote political leadership and diplomacy training among girls. Another is increased funding and academic credit for study abroad, so that more than the present 2% of U.S. college students can go abroad.

Enabling more students, especially women, to live in other cultures then to convey these positive experiences back to the United States would be wise.

## CONCLUDING COMMENTS

Now is a critical time in the struggle for intercultural rapprochement. Even before the September 11 attacks, the anti-immigrant climate in the United States was heating up, as evidenced by Save Our State initiatives in California and Florida, escalation of hate crimes directed at migrant workers and actual or presumed immigrants, and myriad other sorry events. The full benefits to society of moderating intergroup conflict and embracing the enriching attributes of out-groups have yet to be realized. As a special kind of primate, it is in us to be small, bigoted, insular, and backward looking. However, it also is in us to be expansive, wise, inclusive, and forward looking. For all their intransigence, primate societies do change. Let us use policy informed by an understanding of human nature to change our societies to the mutual benefit of hosts and others.

## NOTES

1. Portions of this chapter were adapted from Fishbein, H.D. (2002), *Peer Prejudice and Discrimination: Origins of Prejudice.* Mahwah, NJ: Lawrence Erlbaum Associates.

2. This is so even in societies whose cultural narrative does not include biological paternity, such as the Trobriand Islanders, and those endorsing partible paternity, such as the Canela in Brazil. Among the Islanders, and in the rare societies where marriage is uncommon (e.g., the Mosuo of China), men also hedge their genetic bets by investing significantly in their sisters' children.

3. Among humans, self-sacrifice is further enabled by the cognitive and cultural processes that deny death by creating a psychologically real afterlife (see Solomon et al., this volume).

4. An ironic example of the power of Other myths comes from the crew of the doomed whaling ship *Essex* who, in 1821, steered cleared of Tahiti due to a false belief that the residents would kill and eat them—then turned to cannibalism while adrift at sea.

5. It is impossible to overstate the essentialist hatred expressed toward Japanese Americans in 1942 through media (e.g., an *Los Angeles Times* editorial, "A viper is nonetheless a viper wherever the egg is hatched—so a Japanese American, born of Japanese parents, grows up to be a Japanese not an American") and genocidal threats from officials (DeWitt's assertion that "we must worry about the Japanese all the time until he is wiped off the map.").

6. Such a policy obviously faces challenges from creationists but, overall, educators and court decisions favor movement in this direction. In addition, rubrics other than evolution could be used where it is not politically viable.

7. A group's tenure does not ensure upward mobility. For groups with a long history of oppression (in the United States, Latinos and blacks), U.S.-born cohorts may suffer

by comparison to immigrants for a variety of reasons. The benefits of citizenship should not be confused for generational effects.

8. At 9.3%, the foreign-born population now is about twice the 1970 value but only two-thirds of the turn of the century value.

## REFERENCES

Alba, R., & Nee, V. (1997). Rethinking assimilation theory in a new era of immigration. *International Migration Review, 31,* 826–874.

Altemeyer, B. (1996). *The authoritarian specter.* Cambridge, MA: Harvard University Press.

Anderson, A. (2000, August). Orange Hats: Nonviolent community action in Washington, D.C.. Presented at the annual meetings of the American Psychological Association, Washington, D.C.

Andrews, P. (1985). Improved timing of homonoid evolution with a DNA clock. *Nature, 314,* 498–499.

Arnhart, L. (1998). *Darwinian natural right: The biological ethics of human nature.* Albany: State University of New York Press.

Aureli, F., & de Waal, F.B.M. (2000). *Natural conflict resolution.* Berkeley: University of California Press.

Blair, I.V. (2001). Implicit stereotypes and prejudice. In G.B. Moskowitz (Ed.), *Cognitive social psychology: The Princeton Symposium on the Legacy and Future of Social Cognition* (pp. 359–384). Mahwah, NJ: Lawrence Erlbaum.

Boehm, C. (1999). *Hierarchy in the forest: The evolution of egalitarian behavior.* Cambridge, MA: Harvard University Press.

Booth, A., Crouter, A.C., & Landale, N. (Eds.) (1997). *Immigration and the family.* Mahwah, NJ: Lawrence Erlbaum.

Braine, L.G., Pomerantz, E., Lorber, D., & Krantz, D. (1991). Conflicts with authority: Children's feelings, actions, and justifications. *Developmental Psychology, 27,* 829–840.

Brewer, M. (1999). The psychology of prejudice: Ingroup love or outgroup hate? *Journal of Social Issues, 55,* 429–444.

Brewer, M. (2000). Reducing prejudice through cross-categorization: Effects of multiple social identities. In S. Oskamp (Ed.), *Reducing prejudice and discrimination* (pp. 165–183). Mahwah, NJ: Lawrence Erlbaum.

Brody, G.H., & Stoneman, Z. (1981) Selective imitation of same-age, younger, and older peer models. *Child Development, 52,* 717–720.

Brody, G.H., & Stoneman, Z. (1985). Peer imitation: An examination of status and competence hypotheses. *Journal of Genetic Psychology, 146,* 161–170.

Cameron, J.A., Alvarez, J.M., Ruble, D.N., & Fuligni, A.J. (2001). Children's lay theories about ingroups and outgroups: Reconceptualizing research on prejudice. *Personality & Social Psychology Review, 5,* 118–128.

Cavalli-Sforza, L.L., & Bodmer, W.F. (1971). *The genetics of human populations.* San Francisco, CA: W.H. Freeman.

Chance, M.R.A. (1975). Social cohesion and the structure of attention. In R. Fox (Ed.), *Biosocial anthropology.* London: Malaby Press.

Damon, W. (1977). Measurement and social development. *Counseling Psychologist, 64,* 13–15.

Daniels, R. (1990) *Coming to America*. New York: HarperCollins.

Dasgupta, N., & Greenwald, A.G. (2001). On the malleability of automatic attitudes: Combating automatic prejudice with images of admired and disliked individuals. *Journal of Personality and Social Psychology, 81*, 800–814.

de Waal, F.B.M. (2001). *The ape and the sushi master: Cultural reflections of a primatologist*. New York: Basic Books.

Diamond, J. (1997). *Guns, germs, and steel: The fate of human societies*. New York: W.W. Norton.

Dobzhansky, T. (1962). *Mankind evolving*. New Haven, CT: Yale University Press.

Donald, M. (1991). *Origins of the modern mind: Three stages in the evolution of culture and cognition*. Cambridge, MA: Harvard University Press.

Dovidio, J.F., & Gaertner, S.L. (1999). Reducing prejudice: Combating intergroup biases. *Current Directions in Psychological Science, 8*, 101–105.

Dunbar, R. (1996). *Grooming, gossip, and the evolution of language*. Cambridge, MA: Harvard University Press.

Eisenstadt, D.N. (1956). *From generation to generation*. Glencoe, IL: Free Press.

Eisikovits, R.A. (2000). Gender differences in cross-cultural adaption styles of immigrant youths from the former U.S.S.R. in Israel. *Youth & Society, 31*, 310–331.

Fallers, L.A. (Ed.) (1967) *Immigrant and associations*. Paris: Mouton.

"Final report: Japanese evacuation from the West Coast, 1942, Headquarters Western Defense Command and Fourth Army, Office of the Commanding General, Presidio of San Francisco, California." (1943). Chapters 1 and 2. Washington, DC: U.S. Government Printing Office.

Fishbein, H.D. (1976). *Evolution, development, and children's learning*. Pacific Palisades, CA: Goodyear Publishing.

Fishbein, H.D. (1984). *The psychology of infancy and childhood*. Hillsdale, NJ: Lawrence Erlbaum.

Fishbein, H.D. (1996). *Peer prejudice and discrimination: Evolutionary, cultural, and developmental dynamics*. Boulder, CO: Westview Press.

Florian, V., & Mikulincer, M. (1998). Terror management in childhood: Does death conceptualization moderate the effects of mortality salience on acceptance of similar and different others? *Personality & Social Psychology Bulletin, 24*, 1104–1112.

Franco, F.M., & Maass, A. (1996). Implicit versus explicit strategies of out-group discrimination: The role of intentional control in biased language use and reward allocation. *Journal of Language & Social Psychology, 15*, 335–359.

Gagneux, P., Boesch, C., & Woodruff, D.S. (1999). Female reproduction strategies, paternity and community structure in wild West African chimpanzees. *Animal Behaviour, 57*, 19–32.

Gilbert, D.T. (1991). How mental systems believe. *American Psychologist, 46*, 107–119.

Glick, P., Fiske, S.T., Mladinic, A., Saiz, J.L. , Abrams, D., Masser, B., et al. (2000). Beyond prejudice as simple antipathy: Hostile and benevolent sexism across cultures. *Journal of Personality and Social Psychology, 79*, 763–775.

Goldstein, J. (2001). *War and gender: How gender shapes the war system and vice versa*. Cambridge: Cambridge University Press.

Goodall, J. (1986). Social rejection, exclusion, and shunning among the Gombe chimpanzees. *Ethology & Sociobiology, 7*, 227–236.

Goodall, J., Bandora, A., Bergmann, E., Busse, C., Metama, H., Mpongo, E., et al. (1979). Intercommunity interactions of the chimpanzee population of the Gombe National Park. In D.A. Hamburg & E.R. McCown (Eds.), *The great apes*. Menlo Park, CA: Benjamin/Cummings Publishing.

Gottlieb, G. (1991). Experimental canalization of behavioral development: Theory. *Developmental Psychology, 27*, 4–13.

Greenfield, P.M., & Childs, C.P. (1991). Developmental continuity in biocultural context. In R. Cohen and A.W. Siegel (Eds). *Context and development*. Hillsdale, NJ: Lawrence Erlbaum.

Grusec, J.E. (1971). Power and the internalization of self-denial. *Child Development 42*, 92–105.

Guarton, G.B. (1999). Beyond the dialectics of love and desire. *Contemporary Psychoanalysis, 35*, 491–505.

Guisinger, S., & Blatt, S.J. (1994). Individuality and relatedness: Evolution of a fundamental dialectic. *American Psychologist, 49*, 104–111.

Hallinan, M.T., Teixeira, R.A. (1987). Students' interracial friendships: Individual characteristics, structural effects, and racial differences. *American Journal of Education, 95*, 563–583.

Hamilton, W.D. (1964). The genetical evolution of social behavior. *Journal of Theoretical Biology 7*, 1–16, 17–52.

Hamilton, W.D. (1975). Innate social aptitudes in man: An approach from evolutionary genetics. In R. Fox (Ed.), *Biosocial anthropology*. London: Malaby Press.

Harker, K. (2001). Immigrant generation, assimilation and adolescent psychological well-being. *Social Forces, 79*, 969–1004.

Hasegawa, T. (1989). Sexual behavior of immigrant and resident female chimpanzees at Mahale. In P.G. Heltne & L.A. Marquardt (Eds.), *Understanding chimpanzees* (pp. 90–103). Cambridge, MA: Harvard University Press.

Hetherington, E.M. (1965). A developmental study of the effects of sex of the dominant parent on sex-role preference, identification, and imitation in children. *Journal of Personality and Social Psychology, 2*, 188–194.

Hinde, R.A. (Ed). (1983). *Primate social relationships*. London: Blackwell Scientific Publications.

Hoover, R., & Fishbein, H.D. (1999). The development of prejudice and sex role stereotyping in white adolescents and white young adults. *Journal of Applied Developmental Psychology, 20*, 431–448.

Hoxter, A.L., & Lester, D. (1994). Gender differences in prejudice. *Perceptual & Motor Skills, 79*, 1666.

Hrdy, S.B. (1999). *Mother nature*. New York: Pantheon Books.

Hummer, R.A., Rogers, R.G., Nam, C.B., & LeClere, F.B. (1999). Race/ethnicity, nativity, and U.S. adult mortality. *Social Science Quarterly, 80*, 136–153.

Irwin, C.J. (1987). A study in the evolution of ethnocentrism. In V. Reynolds, V. Falger, & I. Vine (Eds.), *The sociobiology of ethnocentrism*. Athens: University of Georgia Press.

Johnson, M.K., & Marini, M.M. (1998). Bridging the racial divide in the United States: The effect of gender. *Social Psychology Quarterly, 61*, 247–258.

Jolly, A. (1972). *The evolution of primate behavior*. New York: Macmillan.

Keefe, S.E., and Padilla, A.M. (1987). *Chicano ethnicity*. Albuquerque: University of New Mexico Press.

Kindlon, D., & Thompson, M. (2000). *Raising Cain: Protecting the emotional life of boys.* New York: Ballantine Books.

Lamb, B.C. (2000). *The applied genetics of plants, animals, humans and fungi.* London: Imperial College Press.

Lever, J. (1978). Sex differences in the complexity of children's play and games. *American Sociological Review, 43,* 471–483.

Lott, B., & Lott, A.J. (1986). Likability of strangers as a function of their sinner/loser status, gender, and race. *Journal of Social Psychology, 126,* 503–511.

Lumsden, C.J., & Wilson, E.O. (1981). *Genes, mind and culture.* Cambridge, MA: Harvard University Press.

Mayr, E. (1997) *This is biology: The science of the living world.* Cambridge, MA: Harvard University Press.

McKillip, J., DiMiceli, A.J., Luebke, J. (1977). Group salience and stereotyping. *Social Behavior & Personality, 5,* 81–85.

Mikulincer, M., & Florian, V. (2000). Exploring individual differences in reactions to mortality salience: Does attachment style regulate terror management mechanisms? *Journal of Personality and Social Psychology, 79,* 260–273.

Milburn, M.A., Conrad, S.D., Sala, F., & Carberry, S. (1995). Childhood punishment, denial, and political attitudes. *Political Psychology, 16,* 447–478.

Mills, J.K., McGrath, D., Sobkoviak, P., Stupec, S., & Welsh, S. (1995). Differences in expressed racial prejudice and acceptance of others. *Journal of Psychology, 129,* 357–359.

Montagu, A. (1995). Animadversions on the development of theory of touch. In T.M. Field (Ed.), *Touch in early development* (pp. 1–10). Hillsdale, NJ: Lawrence Erlbaum.

Nee, V., & Sanders, J. (2001). Trust in ethnic ties: Social capital and immigrants. In K.S. Cook (Ed.), *Trust in society* (pp. 374–392). New York: Russell Sage Foundation.Neuberg, S.L. (1992). Evolution and individuation: The adaptiveness of nonstereotypical thought. *Psychological Inquiry, 3,* 178–180.

Papademetriou, D. (1997–1998). Think again: Migration. Retrieved 10/6/2001 at http://www.ceip.org/files/Publications/Think_Again.as.

Pearson, P. (2002). Hard to imagine female bad guy? Think again. *USA Today,* January 29.

Pettigrew, T.F., & Tropp, L.R. (2000). Does intergroup contact reduce prejudice: Recent meta-analytic findings. In S. Oskamp (Ed.), *Reducing prejudice and discrimination* (pp. 93–114). Hillsdale, NJ: Lawrence Erlbaum.

Piaget, J. (1932/1948). *The moral judgement of the child.* New York: Free Press.

Quails, R.C., Cox, M.B., & Schehr, T.L. (1992). Racial attitudes on campus: Are there gender differences? *Journal of College Student Development, 33,* 524–530.

Reynolds, V. (1987). Sociobiology and race relations. In V. Reynolds, V. Falger, & I. Vine (Eds.), *The sociobiology of ethnocentrism.* Athens: University of Georgia Press.

Rossi, A.S. (1977). A biosocial perspective on parenting. In A.S. Rossi, J. Kagan, & T.K. Hareven (Eds.), *The family.* New York: W.W. Norton.

Rudman, L.A., Kilianski, S.E. (2000). Implicit and explicit attitudes toward female authority. *Personality & Social Psychology Bulletin, 26,* 1315–1328.

Schaffner, C.M., & French, J.A. (1997). Group size and aggression: "Recruitment incentives" in a cooperatively breeding primate. *Animal Behaviour, 54,* 171–180.

Seyfarth, R.M. (1983). Grooming and social competition in primates. In R.A. Hinde
    (Ed.), *Primate social relationships*. London: Blackwell Scientific Publications.
Shack, W.A., & Skinner, E.P. (Eds.). (1979). *Strangers in African societies*. Berkeley:
    University of California Press.
Sicotte, P. (2000). A case study of mother-son transfer in moutain gorillas. *Primates,
    41*, 93–101.
Sidanius, J., Levin, S., Liu, J., & Partto, F. (2000). Social dominance orientation, anti-
    egalitarianism and the political psychology of gender: An extension and cross-
    cultural replication. *European Journal of Social Psychology, 30*, 41–67.
Smetana, J.G. (1986). Preschool children's conceptions of sex-role transgressions. *Child
    Development, 57*, 862–871.
Solomon, S., Greenberg, J., & Pyszczynski, T. (2000). Pride and prejudice: Fear of death
    and social behavior. *Current Directions in Psychological Science, 9*, 200–204.
Stephan, W.G., Diaz-Loving, R., & Duran, A. (2000). Integrated threat theory and
    intercultural attitudes: Mexico and the United States. *Journal of Cross-Cultural
    Psychology, 31*, 240–249.
Strum, S.C. (1987). *Almost human*. New York: W.W. Norton.
Sugiyama, Y. (1999). Socioecological factors of male chimpanzee migration at Bossou,
    Guinea. *Primates, 40*, 61–68.
Thompson, D.B. (1999) Different spatial scales of natural selection and gene flow: The
    evolution of behavioral geographic variation and phenotypic plasticity. In S.A.
    Foster and J.A. Endler (Eds.), *Geographic variation in behavior: Perspectives on
    evolutionary mechanisms* (pp. 33–51). New York: Oxford University Press.
Thrall, P.H., Richards, C.M., McCauley, D.E., & Antonovics, J. (1998). Metapopulation
    collapse: The consequences of limited gene-flow in spatially structured popula-
    tions. In J. Bascompte and R.V. Sole (Eds.), *Modeling spatiotemporal dynamics
    in ecology* (pp. 83–104). Berlin, Germany: Springer-Verlag.
Tindale, N.B. (1974). *Aboriginal tribes of Australia*. Berkeley: University of California
    Press.
Tonnesmann, W. (1987). Group identification and political socialization. In V. Reynolds,
    V. Falger, & I. Vine (Eds.), *The sociobiology of ethnocentrism*. Athens, GA:
    University of Georgia Press.
Tooby, J., & DeVore, I. (1987). The reconstruction of hominid behavioral evolution
    through strategic modeling. In W.G. Kinzey (Ed.), *The evolution of human be-
    havior: Primate models*. Albany, NY: State University of New York Press.
Turiel, E. (1983). *The development of social knowledge*. New York: Cambridge Univer-
    sity Press.
Van den Berghe, P.L. (1981). *The ethnic phenomenon*. New York: Elsevier.
Waddington, C.H. (1957). *The strategy of genes*. London: Allen and Unwin.
Waddington, C.H. (1960). *The ethical animal*. London: George Allen & Unwin.
Walzer, M. (1997) *On toleration*. New Haven, CT: Yale University Press.
Wilson, D.S., & Sober, E. (1994), Re-introducing group selection to human behavioural
    sciences, *Behavioural and Brain Sciences 17*, 585–654.
Wilson, E.O. (1980). *Sociobiology: The abridged edition*. Cambridge, MA: Harvard Uni-
    versity Press.
Wrangham, R.W. (1987). African apes: The significance of African apes for reconstruct-
    ing human social evolution. In W.G. Kinzey (Ed.), *The evolution of human
    behavior: Primate models*. Albany: State University of New York Press.

# 8

# Global Conflict Resolution
## *An Anthropological Diagnosis of Problems with World Governance*[1]

*Christopher Boehm*

We live in a political world of dangerously disunited nations, states geared not only to economic, territorial, and ideological competition but to the violent settling of old scores and fighting out of national pride.[2] The policy concerns I write about are geared to a belief that normal diplomatic thinking needs to be stretched in new directions and that new theoretical perspectives may be of assistance in doing so. We are interested in the practical possibility of establishing a very different type of world order, one that makes it possible to readily and reliably police those who would wage war.

This would be a far cry from what we have today, for our problems with conflict and warfare are neither resolved nor even fully diagnosed. One way to approach such a diagnosis is to better understand the roots of these problems by looking into the political history of our species—a history that must be extended back into prehistory because human nature is involved. At a practical level, I believe we can use this theoretical advantage to better assess the amenability of armed conflict among nations to radical manipulation and suppression through global institution building.

Unfortunately, the habit of war among sovereign nations is deeply entrenched. Indeed, a remarkable species that sends people to investigate other celestial bodies has not yet managed to set up a really effective world government. To diagnose this problem, I look into some ultimate causes of conflict, but also into natural propensities that underlie our capacity for peacemaking. This large-picture approach will include a Darwinian analysis that takes into account today's human nature by examining an ancient human political career.

In important and fundamental ways, this career seems to have been amazingly consistent for tens of thousands of years. At base we have been, and are, a competitive and (under many conditions) pugnacious political animal. This will continue unless human nature changes, which is hardly likely—or unless our political environments and political practices are radically changed for the better, which might be within our power. Such changes certainly are conceivable, but as a practical matter the human nature I describe will tend to make this difficult.

The aim is to assess basic problems with world government in terms of contradictory basic tendencies in human nature, and to facilitate such a diagnosis I introduce two political models that are ethologically oriented. One I term the egalitarian band/tribal model. Essentially this is based on what might be called the primeval form of human political society: an egalitarian band of hunter-gatherers that deliberately excludes any alpha role and makes its decisions by consensus. Along with tribes, which are larger and more recent but politically similar, these bands are so deeply committed to egalitarianism that their leadership is never very strong, let alone coercive. Yet they govern themselves rather well in the absence of formal institutions.

Second we have the despotic chimpanzee model. This refers to patterns of hierarchical behavior that take place within territorial communities of wild chimpanzees and also in large captive groups. Chimpanzee politics are carried on through an alpha male system, and they provide a crude but useful model for certain of the more despotic types of political behavior in humans (Boehm, 1999; de Waal, 1982; Wrangham & Peterson, 1996). Politically the two models contrast sharply, but, because aspects of both egalitarian and despotic approaches emerge strongly in contemporary global political behavior, both will be useful diagnostically.

Using these two models in tandem will permit us to gain special insights into the possibilities for more effective world governance. The stakes are high, for we have moved from a world of nations in which destructive warfare is frequent to a world of nations that could accidentally or perhaps even deliberately destroy human life itself. Our troubled planet has a Security Council, but in fact it seems to have less security every year as major national nuclear arsenals remain potent enough to accidentally ruin the world environment, new nuclear arsenals are added, innovative methodologies for delivering weapons of mass destruction become more potent, and what was an unambiguous balance of thermonuclear terror in 1985 becomes increasingly blurred because of proliferation.

## AN AMBIVALENT HUMAN NATURE

"Human nature" has been around for a long time, as a concept people use when they wish to wax philosophical. Nonliterate people sometimes analyze motives of others in terms of human nature, and the ancient Greeks talked about it frequently in trying to define the human condition (see Arnhart, 1998). Over the past several decades, a deluge of books has appeared on the subject (e.g., Konner, 1982; Sober & Wilson, 1998; Wilson, 1978), but a frequent problem is that scholars too often treat one aspect of human nature at a time, on a laundry list basis, without considering the complex interactions of dispositions such as love or hate. As an extreme instance of oversimplification, scholars are prone to use human nature as a vehicle to characterize human behavior in terms of either-or propositions, as in, "Are human beings really warlike, or peaceful?" The eternal debate between Hobbesians and Rousseauians is a prime example.

Here, taking cues from Konrad Lorenz's ethological notion of a "parliament of instincts" (Lorenz, 1966; see also Eibl-Eibesfeldt, 1974; Lorenz, 1989; Masters, 1989), I adopt what I have called an "ambivalence" approach (Boehm, 1989, 1999) that assumes that human nature usually is not a matter of "either-or" but of "both-and." In broad philosophical terms, this means we are a mix of nasty and nice, rather than one or the other. Hobbes and Rousseau were both right.

In any human group, large or small, a fundamental problem is that of internal security. In assessing practical political problems that confront humanity, I suggest that there are dispositions that incline us to learn conflictive behavior quite readily, but also dispositions that foster the management and resolution of conflict. Both are important to the state of our political world, as are dispositions that respectively lead us to resent and appreciate superordinate control.

I suggest that with many of our more serious problems, the underlying causes are in part "Darwinian." Our flexible human nature is the product of a long history of natural selection, and individual humans are innately disposed to enter into conflict; indeed, competition and even fighting are behaviors readily learned under normal social stimuli. Unfortunately, this can apply also to coalitions or groups if serious environmental scarcities exist, and too often even if they don't. If one would prefer to believe that human nature does not contain such flexible dispositions, consider the facts. We know, anthropologically, that over time even the smallest and most peacefully inclined types of social units (hunting bands) will predictably experience homicides within the group, and that rather frequently there is killing between bands, as well.

The upside is that humans also seem to be innately averse to conflict within their social communities, for everywhere they try to manage and resolve their disputes. It is logical that propensities to fight and propensities to actively resolve conflicts would have evolved in tandem, for fighting provides certain competitive advantages to individuals (and sometimes to groups), while our evolved propensity to resolve and manage conflicts reduces the damaging side effects. Although these two traits are seen clearly in the oldest type of human society, the hunting band, they also hold for nations, which must either manage their internal conflicts or face civil war. At a grander level, an entire world of nations faces the same ancient dilemma. There is destructive conflict, and then there is conflict management as a means of actively trying to reduce its effects.

Until recently, the overall balance between tendencies to fight and tendencies to reduce the effects of fighting has at least been "tolerable"—in the ultimate and amoral evolutionary sense that the overall result has been survivable. We haven't yet done ourselves in as a species, even though warfare causes untold suffering. However, we now face a world rife with thermonuclear weapons and increasingly effective biological and chemical agents, weapons that can be delivered not only by nations but also by hard-to-target and sometimes suicidal nonnational political coalitions that may be disgruntled or vengeful, but that also may be ambitiously seeking world hegemony. An already very costly pattern of intergroup political competition is becoming increasingly complicated, and increasingly risky.

## THE "NATIONAL" APPROACH TO CONFLICT MANAGEMENT

An obvious and secure answer to this problem would be an impartially vigilant and highly invasive world government, one vested with power sufficient to intervene as needed for purposes of inspection and elimination of weapons that threaten all. What we have instead are two global political systems, neither of which provides the needed security. One is the United Nations, with its inability to coerce any of the great powers. Everyone knows what is wrong with the UN as a world policeman, but at the level of the global community of nations, there is little serious debate about how to reconstruct this entity so that it could be come truly effective. The hunter-gatherer model will provide a diagnosis that could be instructive.

The other global political system is an informal alpha-nation one, in which large nations committed to their national interests also have roles in being the world's policeman. Recently this superpower role has devolved on the United States, but there can be as many such "policemen" as there are alpha-nations with resources sufficient to play the role. The conflict of interest inherent in this "individualistic" policing role is a formula for disaster, and presently I enumerate a few examples of this. The chimpanzee model will clarify what is wrong with the present system, but also what aspects, if any, might be useful to a new world order.

At the level of diagnosis, why has our vaunted human rationality led us to be relentlessly unimaginative and ineffective in coping with a potentially ultimate problem that we have been well aware of for half a century?[3] Let us begin not with hunting bands and the great ape communities that preceded them in prehistory, but with single modern nations. Modern nations do quite a good job of preventing internal warfare within their frontiers, so let us consider a typical nation as a possible model for global governance.

Show me a nation, and I will show you—usually—a political success. The exceptions can be disastrous, as in the case of the former Yugoslavia, or merely unsuccessful as with the former Soviet Union aside from Chechnya. Other exceptions can combine short-term disaster with long-term success, as with the

U.S. Civil War. But by and large, nations all over the world are durable precisely because they do their job of preventing internal warfare.

When first created, nations presented a politically useful invention to the world. By this I mean that once nations started to appear, adjacent politically fragmented populations were obliged either to form nations of their own, or to become exploited by or absorbed into existing nations that were predatory. Inherent in this type of large organization is the political unification of population segments that originally were prone to factionalization and conflict. However, unlike warlike tribes, which only confederate ephemerally for specific purposes of defense or attack, nations are able to form permanent confederations out of their constituent elements because they are so good at keeping internal security. The problem with nations is that they keep the peace well at home—but are prone to fight with other nations.

The political theories that inform these standard political interpretations are as old as tribal politics itself. Nonliterate tribesmen understand basic political patterns much as political scientists, political anthropologists, and modern statesmen do, and one fundamental premise I just applied is that external threats stimulate internal unification. Others are that humans in groups are prone to conflict over scarce resources or territory, and that as groups we are prone to form coalitions, with allies, in order to balance power. Indeed, many of the anthropological principles that make sense of segmentary-tribal politics (e.g., Bohannan, 1954; Chagnon, 1983; Evans-Pritchard, 1940) work seamlessly for larger units like nations.

Internally, a nation unites a population in a way such that internal warfare is no longer a predictable outcome when serious internecine conflicts of interest arise. These may stem from competing economic interests or regional, religious, ethnic, class, or political-ideological bones of contention. A unifying national ideology helps, but ultimately, with large nations, it is coercive power at the political center that lies at the base of this successful arrangement. The alternative is to have a huge population that is prone to poorly regulated internecine conflict, and is likely to splinter asunder or become so weakened that it is vulnerable to conquest from the outside. It is difficult to find a major nation lacking either a large police force or a standing army.

A successfully stable nation has a centralized government that is committed to the preservation of an existing political union, and it must have the force available to follow through if other means of conflict resolution prove insufficient. After an incredibly bloody twentieth century, a question immediately comes to mind: Why haven't we simply patterned our world government on the many successful national governments we have before us as examples? In a sense we have: the UN looks quite a bit like a democratic national government writ large. But then we haven't, for the UN was absolutely powerless in the face of a perilous Cold War. For decades tensions between the two alpha-nations threatened all of humankind, and the global community stood by. The reason for this impotency is obvious enough, for sovereign nations refuse to submit to any higher authority. No political behavior is more predictable.

So why, at a lower level of political segmentation, do the constituent political units within nations submit to centralized control—when the nations of the world show no inclination to do this? This question is pregnant precisely because, in theory, at the world level a supernation or meta-nation should be able to end our ceaseless wars. It is tragic that humanity managed to get through just one year of the new millennium before its warfare pattern reasserted itself in a new and dangerous form.

## THE UNITED NATIONS AS IMPOTENT SUPERSTATE

At first blush, the UN with its General Assembly looks like a great big democratic nation. However, it cannot behave like a nation because its structure has been contrived to prevent this. The crucial job of conflict resolution is delegated to the Security Council, whose membership is heavily weighted in favor of militarily powerful nations, and in that council there is a veto with no recusal: any permanent member that objects can block any measure—including one directed at itself or one of its allies. Thus, the conflict-management function of this council is crippled in exactly the cases that are most likely to prove dangerous to the welfare of all.

Keep in mind that the UN army that engaged in resisting the North Korean and eventually Chinese invasion of South Korea did so when Mainland China was not a UN member and Taiwan held the Chinese seat. So when China became involved, it was not sitting on the Security Council. At the time, the Soviet Union was boycotting the UN because of the China issue, so it could not veto the UN police action against North Korea. Normally, UN police actions are directed at less powerful polities with neither a seat on the Council nor a veto-wielding Great Power to shield them from intervention.

In conjunction with the absence of an effectively centralized political structure for decision making, the UN lacks two other crucial political features of nations. One is the capacity to forcefully demand taxes. The other is a substantial standing army or police force that provides the coercive force needed for conflict management and other key governmental functions—including, of course, taxation. These liabilities are easily sufficient to cripple the UN whenever a serious conflict develops with either a superpower or its close ally in the mix.

The existence of such liabilities is not accidental. If an effective diagnosis of the world security problem is to be achieved, one must look into the motives that led certain constituent nations, the largest and most powerful ones, to emasculate their own peacemaking organization. It is to make a contribution in this direction that I now introduce our two evolutionary models, which involve principles derived from the disciplines of biocultural anthropology and primate ethology.

## THE BAND/TRIBAL POLITICAL MODEL

Ethnographers have documented the behavior of several hundred hunting bands worldwide, for extant foragers have been available for study on all continents—save for Europe and the Middle East. The great majority are nomadic, just as their prehistoric precursors surely were. With respect to politics, there is a rule of thumb that applies to every last group of these nomads: they are politically egalitarian.

The tribal people who followed and largely replaced these mobile foragers had domesticated animals and plants and they lived in larger settlements that very often were permanent, but they remained vehemently egalitarian in their political behavior. I refer separately to these tribesmen from time to time, because they do a few things politically that egalitarian foragers do not do in their smaller nomadic groups. One is to form confederations, and the other is to engage quite frequently in intensive warfare and raiding, in addition to killing for revenge.

It is impossible to understand the sociopolitical history of humans, and our political nature itself, without taking this phenomenon of deliberate political egalitarianism into account. I am by no means suggesting that humans are innately egalitarian as opposed to hierarchical and that the marked hierarchies that later appeared with chiefdoms, kingdoms, and nations were some kind of environmental or cultural accident. The relations between innate human hierarchical tendencies and this prehistoric preference for egalitarianism must be clarified before we can fully understand the political dynamics that presently hobble the UN, and see how deeply they are grounded in human nature.

There was a time when many anthropologists believed that people in hunting bands were just naturally equal, that is, that something akin to primitive anarchy reigned because human nature was devoid of dominance tendencies. By this view, the social and political hierarchies that came later were merely environmental effects, stimulated probably by modern population densities. This erroneous belief was facilitated by a Rousseauian perception of hunting societies as being naturally nonviolent and naturally nonhierarchical, and the result was some really serious confusion about human political nature. If some societies were despotically hierarchical and others egalitarian, at first blush it made sense to say that human nature must be a blank slate—that environments could impose any behavioral program they wished to.

That earlier implicit viewpoint can now be challenged definitively, and this is important in terms of building institutions for global governance: we are not likely to succeed unless we take our stronger natural propensities into account, realistically. Two cultural anthropologists, Bruce Knauft and Carol Ember, have demonstrated that in spite of being politically egalitarian, people in bands are far from being uniformly peaceful and nondominant. For one thing, hunting bands internally have substantial homicide rates, many being comparable statistically to violent urban scenes in our own country (Knauft, 1991). Homicide is perhaps the ultimate form of domination, and everywhere humans are prone to do it. For another, the majority of these bands engage in some type of intergroup conflict every year or so (Ember, 1978), often in the form of smallish revenge parties, and only a handful show anything like a total absence of conflict between bands. A few nomadic bands even go to war as entire groups, and in aboriginal Australia this pattern appears to be at least 1,000 years old (Tacon & Chippendale, 1994; see also Kelly, 2000).

In my role as a biocultural political anthropologist, I have tried to make sense of these ethnographic facts by suggesting that egalitarianism in bands is by no means due to a human nature that is so noncompetitive that we are just "naturally" egalitarian. Rather, egalitarianism involves a deep political tension between individuals who are motivated to dominate, and a rank and file that decides it simply will not be dominated (see Boehm, 1999). This can be demonstrated ethnographically, for people in bands have antiauthoritarian ideologies, and as moral communities their behaviors reflect this strongly. The rank and file astutely and effectively sanction (and thereby collectively dominate) stronger group members who deviate from a rule that can be stated as follows: no individual has the right to despoil, boss around, or otherwise dominate any other person in the group, and essentially every household head, male or female, must be at political parity (see Boehm, 1999).

This means that a clever species which is innately hierarchically inclined (see Masters, 1989; Wilson, 1975) and is well set up to be violently dominant (Daly & Wilson, 1988) is using domination by groups to avoid domination by individuals, and this tells us something quite different about human nature. It is the dominance and submission tendencies in that nature that make the formation of social hierarchies highly probable, and the twist is that sometimes, in small societies, the direction of domination can be reversed so definitely that the subordinates are firmly in charge—having first defined themselves as political equals.

These individuals know that if they were to stand alone they would be dominated, but that if they individually give up on their personal chances of becoming a dominator in order to ensure that they themselves will not be dominated, they can live in a "society of equals." That way the highest status they allow to anyone, no matter how talented or physically or psychically powerful, or how adept at leadership, is that of *primus inter pares* (Fried, 1967). Given a human nature that fosters status rivalry leading to individual dominance, a society of "firsts among equals" will not simply stay in place. Group members must work continuously at policing upstarts, if they wish to overcome the natural tendency of humans to form pyramid-shaped hierarchies based on individual dominance (Boehm, 1993; see also Erdal & Whiten, 1994, 1996; Lee, 1979).

That dominance tendencies can be rather strongly predisposed in individuals is shown by the fact that in spite of a shared egalitarian ideology, all bands at one time or another will have to sanction aggressive upstarts who ignore this social contract. Faced with a would-be dominator who wishes to make decisions for the entire group, or despoil other men of their women or goods, or haughtily treat others as unequals, or who even begins to kill people as a habit born of domination, a band has two choices. It can submit, or it can collectively cut down the dominator by forming a political coalition. I call such coalitions moral communities (Boehm, 2000).

Bands know exactly what they are doing in this respect. Criticism or ridicule may well do the job, for in a small group these are very effective weapons of social control. But if the upstart has a thick skin, and a few do, the band as a moral community has in reserve not only ostracism and expulsion from the group, but also execution as a final solution. Elsewhere (Boehm, 1993), I have identified instances of bands putting political upstarts to death on a number of continents, so we may assume that a potentially powerful tension between would-be dominators and their resentfully retaliatory groups is universal at the level of nomadic bands—which, I remind you, are always egalitarian. We may also assume that such tensions are ancient, and therefore associated with human nature itself.

An egalitarian lifestyle does not mean total equality in all things, as the term might suggest. There is room for individual achievement and ascendancy in certain areas that bring status. There are always superior hunters, whose efforts are praised. There may be shamans. There are always individuals whose advice is favorably weighted in the decision-making process because of their experience or sagacity. But these are not "offices," for in each category there is room for as many outstanding people as qualify (see Fried, 1967). And special statuses are not transferred to descendants on a dynastic basis, for that would affront the community with its egalitarian ethos. Any standing of merit must be earned, and having high social status does not deny it to another who might qualify. Nor does it entitle one to act as a political superior.

These egalitarian societies operate quite efficiently as groups, and manage to do so in spite of the fact that strong leadership is not allowed to emerge. Either the entire band meets to decide important issues that concern everyone, or frequently people may talk things over in sub-groups as they work their way toward a consensus. Either way, there is no voting, for consensus requires at least formal agreement on everybody's part. Otherwise, the group either remains undecided—or else it splits (see Boehm, 1996).

With universal commitment to this means of group decision making, in bands there obviously is no role for a dictatorial leader, or even one who tries to exert strong influence. If the band has a headman, his job is merely to help to facilitate the consensus—not to decide its content. What happens with dissenters? If a consensus cannot be achieved, then the band knows it cannot take collective action to cope with the problem in question. Usually, this is a decision about where to migrate next, and if a move is mandatory for ecological reasons, the band simply splinters, with each faction following its own subsistence strategy.

Fissioning is not good for a band's standard of living. In these small groups of 40 to 100 souls, individuals know one another very well. Aside from being highly sociable, they realize that they have good economic reason to stick together. This is because if a band falls below a certain number of hunters, the custom of equally sharing all of the large game meat that is acquired will not pay off very well because these major kills are made on a very sporadic basis. The name of the statistical game is variance reduction (see Kelly, 1995), and with a sizable band the result is a steady if moderate intake of high-quality protein and fat for every member of the group. This amounts to an informal social security system—one that surely is ancient.

A band of political peers who share their large game and otherwise may help those in need can be likened, in important ways, to a nation that has an effective system of social welfare. However, in many other ways this band-level political arrangement contrasts starkly with that of a nation-state. A hunter-gatherer band has no real specialists in governance, and very few other specialists aside from medical practitioners. Each family is an independent unit of production, basically, even though we have seen that hunters pool their large-game kills. The band has no coercive force at the political center; indeed, if a headman or one of its other more influential members tries to stop a fight by intervening physically, he is almost as likely to be injured or killed himself as he is to succeed in his mission of conflict resolution (e.g., Lee, 1979). Because of this lack of centralized authority, there seems to be a ceiling on band size that is political, as well as ecological. When a band grows large enough to develop serious factions, it tends to fission.

The same is true of egalitarian tribes, which similarly lack centralized power-figures to authoritatively damp conflicts. In fact, virtually everything I have said about band politics also applies to tribal politics. A tribe may be defined formally as a politically egalitarian sociopolitical unit which subsists on domesticated plants and animals instead of hunting and gathering as nomadic bands do, and tribes tend to be both larger and settled in one place. But in every tribe there exists an egalitarian ethos, and leaders are aware that they cannot speak or act with any real authority. Decisions are made by consensus, just as with bands (Boehm, 1996), and too much factionalization can result in fissioning because the conflict management process is so fragile.

Egalitarianism works satisfactorily in small groups that can fission in this way. This political approach has had a very strong run in human natural history, for hierarchical societies with centralization of political power arose only within the past 6,000 years or so, with the advent first of weak chiefdoms, then authoritative chiefdoms or primitive kingdoms, then early civilizations and empires, and finally modern nations. At the beginning of the eighteenth century, there were still major regions of the world where this transition from egalitarian tribes (or bands) to the hierarchical types that followed had not yet begun.

## THE EVOLUTION OF NATIONS

Now, let us consider the hierarchical, politically centralized end of this political spectrum. Strong chiefdoms, primitive kingdoms, early civilizations, and national states all have social hierarchies with people of high and low status, and generally such statuses are inherited in family lines. Ideologically, the strictly egalitarian ethos is a thing of the past: these larger populaces share an acceptance of authoritative leadership—as long as this serves general needs and is not gratuitously despotic. Coercive force at the political center is tolerated for purposes of conflict intervention, and also for social control. Societies that are centrally regulated in these ways can become very large, indeed, without becoming prey to serious factionalization, internecine armed conflict, and fissioning.

Consider well-centralized chiefdoms or large primitive kingdoms of the type that surely led to ancient states such as Mesopotamia, Egypt, Mexico, and Peru (see Service, 1975). With such nonliterate societies, we invariably find dynastic principles in operation. Certain socially superior clans or families are earmarked to retain wealth, position, and power, whereas and social hierarchy is incorporated into the political ethos in ways that give legitimacy to rulers as long as they are reasonably generous and not too cruel. At the political or religious center, we find that special individuals redistribute wealth that is originally donated by "commoners," and this enables those of high status to have a better standard of living—yet, at the same time, when commoners are facing subsistence problems, they can have their special needs addressed from a centralized storehouse. Thus, a dynastic system of economic and social privilege doubles as a social security system.

What about nations? A modern democratic state will set aside any strong dynastic principles of leadership, as may a totalitarian nation, but the economic redistribution function that we saw nascent in hunting bands will continue through taxation and welfare programs. Unlike bands and tribes, in nations there is a special standard of living for leading citizens and officers of the government, and attempts by socialist/communist regimes to create true socioeconomic leveling at a national scale have invariably failed. This is because those same regimes must develop centralized power, and such power, be it hereditary or achieved, always seems to lead to "perks."

If we further compare such politically and economically centralized societies with bands and tribes, the political differences are substantial not only in ideology but also in practice. The smaller societies are deeply suspicious of placing even moderate power in anyone's hands, and to avoid this they keep it diffused within the group. In the larger societies people either understand and accept the need for centralized control, or else rulers simply impose power they have available at the political center, with loyal standing armies to back them up.

Functionally a major advantage of well-centralized nations, over bands and tribes, is that these nations do not tolerate feuding. Feuding is a formalized, self-perpetuating, tribal invention that involves highly disruptive (yet rule-bound and partly restrained) armed conflict between clans or tribes (see Boehm, 1986). At a larger scale, such emotionalized internecine conflict readily leads to uncontrolled "civil war." That is why well-centralized polities quickly suppress feuding, using the abundant coercive power they have. A problem, with nations, is that the same coercive power that ensures internal order can become the tool of despots, and one answer to this problem is an effective system of checks and balances. But today fewer than half of the nations in the world have chosen this path, and many live with despotism.

## WHERE DOES THE UNITED NATIONS STAND?

With this anthropological background, let us consider the UN, which is the only formal system of governance the world possesses. First of all, like individual hunter-gatherers the constituent nations can, in a way, vote with their feet: They can resign their membership. (Functionally, this is perhaps similar to a family's leaving its band if it doesn't like the company—except that nations are not nomadic. They must stay in place physically after such a rupture.) In contrast, within individual nations the constituent units (such as states, republics, or provinces) cannot readily secede: usually they must fight for the right of secession, and normally they haven't sufficient power to attempt this.

A second similarity to egalitarians in small groups comes in the sphere of leadership. The secretary-general of the UN wears a title that smacks of powerlessness, and he behaves accordingly. He may come to exercise considerable influence, but this cannot be backed by force. This is very similar to headmen in bands and to tribal chiefs. All these leaders must keep a low profile until a consensus or majority opinion is reached, and essentially none has any formal authority to act independently. In this sense, the UN seems to wear some of the trappings of a nation, but it does so without permitting any real centralized authority to develop. As with bands and tribes, things are kept that way by design.

Essentially, all these organizations are politically acephalous. This "headlessness" means that no individual can independently make and implement important decisions for the group—even urgent decisions such as coping with internecine conflict. In a nation, by contrast, powerfully centralized governance is feasible because wealth is gathered through non-voluntary taxation and this makes possible a standing army or national police force. Thus, in nations governance from the center has definitively replaced the decentralized, populist approach to self-governance that is found in bands or tribes. In its political style, the UN is far closer to a tribe, or better a weakly centralized tribal confederation, than a nation.

The UN *seems* to have a politically centralized structure, for there is a General Assembly, a Security Council, and a secretary-general whose duties at least are suggestive of being presidential. But let us examine these organs critically.

The General Assembly is famous for coming up with resolutions that carry no clout beyond the force of world moral opinion—a force that can be highly influential but often is ignored by willful nations—even in the face of economic sanctions. The Security Council is dominated by an oligarchy chosen according to the historical military power of its members, and not for their sagacity in governance. But in spite of these problems can the Security Council, at least, be likened to an effective national government?

One major problem is the veto. In effect, the UN Security Council is able to intervene in quarrels between nations only if none of the five original nuclear superpowers—its permanent members—is involved. I emphasize that they will use their vetoes not only to avoid interference in their own affairs of state, but also to protect smaller allies from such interference. By contrast, within a typical nation there is a centralized decision process that need not be hamstrung by internal differences of opinion; indeed, if a serious conflict arises, a government must have the power to act quickly and decisively from above before such tensions explode.

This raises the issue of brute force. Aside from this often hamstrung centralized decision process, in the UN there is the absence of any permanent means of acting decisively in resolving political conflicts. The Security Council has no standing army, no budget for major military operations, and no real tax base. So, even if the Council does make a decision it must then seek to finance the intervention in question. In a nation, it is the freedom to make decisions in conjunction with the ready means to back them up that makes it possible to keep internal order on a decisive and preemptive basis.

If we consider the UN as an attempt to build a supernation with effective conflict resolution powers, its designers hobbled this organization in a way similar to what people face in egalitarian bands or tribes when family or clan factions come into conflict and a peacemaker is needed. Initially, pleading and persuasion sometimes do the job, but there is no certain basis for anyone to step in and to end a more serious conflict through a show of stern authority backed by possibility of forcefully dominant intervention. This situation of political impotency is exacerbated by the fact that whereas a dissident faction in a band or tribe may be able to remove itself spatially from the conflict, which does ameliorate it, the world's nations are permanently situated. One party cannot leave for another planet to avoid a conflict.

## EGALITARIANISM, NATIONAL SOVEREIGNTY, AND HUMAN NATURE

Why was the UN designed to be inadequately centralized? It certainly was not because the founders thought that effective peacemaking was not important to the world, for that was the organization's chief mission. The best brief answer would be "national sovereignty." Indeed, the type of egalitarian feelings that drive individual political behavior in a small band or tribe can be compared quite directly with feelings of sovereignty at the national level. The psychological and political dynamics are very similar, whether individuals or large groups are involved.

In both hunting bands composed of a hundred or so individuals and in our global band of scores of nations, there is a strong concern for the freedom of action of the subsidiary "political unit" involved, be it individual or national. If individual tribesmen or hunters are predictably vehement in their insistence upon personal autonomy, sovereign nations are perhaps still more vehement about holding on to their full freedom of action as players in international affairs. The issue, in both cases, is to be free from domination or control by some superordinate authority, and this interesting similarity between egalitarian individuals and sovereign nations can be fully understood only if human nature is taken into account.

Biocultural anthropology provides a sophisticated means of doing this if one is careful to differentiate sharply between so-called "hard-wired behaviors," which are so well programmed that they will predictably appear in much the same form wherever a species lives, and behavioral predispositions, which are quite flexible because they have evolved in conjunction with cultural traditions. It is these much more flexible dispositions that we will be speaking about. Whenever we find a general feature of human life that seems to be universal, such as this very flexible tendency to form *some* type of social hierarchy within every group, we may assume that human nature is making that type of behavior especially easy to learn.

With our species dominance tendencies express themselves ubiquitously. For instance, in all human societies adults control their offspring. And even in bands of hunters there are noteworthy inequalities of status (and, to some extent power) among adults, including within the family. Often our political hierarchies are like pyramids, with alpha individuals at the top, but in highly egalitarian bands or tribes, we have seen that there is a very different type of arrangement that nonetheless is hierarchical (Boehm, 1993).

There are ethological basics that underlie this wide range of hierarchical behaviors. Like other great ape species, humans are given to domination and submission. If you weren't aware of this, watch an elementary school playground at lunch hour. In spite of strictures to the contrary by teachers, students compete physically, exert the same earmarks of dominance and submission as other social mammals, and form political coalitions to enhance their dominance potential. Boys do more of this than girls (see Blurton-Jones, 1972), so we might even be talking partly about a male human nature (Wrangham & Peterson, 1996), but the general patterns apply to both sexes.

In adult life, humans everywhere seem to prefer domination—or at least personal autonomy—to submission, so it is clear that human nature is helping us to be attracted to freedom of action, as opposed to being controlled. In a basic form this resentment of domination can also be seen in our closest phylogenetic relatives—chimpanzees, bonobos, and gorillas (Boehm, 1999). But at the same time, our nature disposes us to accept dominant parental control, and we may also accept control voluntarily as adults—if the advantages seem to outweigh the detriments. This means that if a central authority is good to the people, and protective, they may accept its control willingly.

There are two other routes to political centralization (see Weber, 1947). One is based on the threat or use of force: dominant control is imposed from above on the basis of fear that trumps desires for individual autonomy. Another is that people become so taken with a charismatic leader that they voluntarily submit through identification with the power of another. So separately or in combination, fear, political identification, or simple self-interest and need for protection can overwhelm or modify the basic individual inclinations that favor personal autonomy.

When it comes to nations that are based on voluntary covenant, rather than on imposition of power or charismatic domination, our strong propensities to preserve freedom of action at the local level are traded off judiciously so that a minimum of personal freedom is sacrificed in order to have a centralized government that can protect its constituents from the ills that stem from impotency at the political center. The greatest of these ills is internecine armed conflict, which can tear any community apart—including a global community.

It seems extremely unlikely that an adequately centralized world authority will come into being through forceful imposition on the part of one nation, for there are too many major nuclear powers for this to be possible. A charismatic leader who could unite a troubled world and create some acceptable centralized authority is imaginable, but improbable. So basically any effectively centralized and stable world government will have to be the result of voluntary covenant. The question is, why wasn't a well-centralized—but democratic—national model followed in setting up the UN in the first place, and why hasn't such a model guided its further development? An ethologist's answer is that human nature favors autonomy at all levels. A political anthropologist's answer would be that this is particularly true at the national level. Therefore, national sovereignty is the stumbling block. A question I address later is, why can't we analyze the ways nations were formed—with their constituent political units giving up their sovereignty either because of perceived advantage, charismatic attraction, or fear—and then apply the insights to problems we face with the UN?

There is one other possibility, at least in the land of political fantasy. Groups having centripetal tendencies are likely to unite when they face a threat from without, and the world community of nations might suddenly become eager to create a strong central authority—if there were a serious extraterrestrial threat against our planet. A basic decision-making structure is already there, in the form of the Security Council. In a situation in which no one would want to use the veto, one readily imagines the creation of a decisive command and control over an integrated military force for the defense of all. If such a threat were durable, this centralized military force might become a permanent fixture, and useful also when nations collided here on earth.

With a standing army created and the Security Council veto eliminated, true political centralization would have taken place. At the level of nations, often it is in fact realistic external pressures, in the form of other nations, which have led them to centralize. The question is, are there actual earthly threats that could provide such an incentive for pan-national unification? I argue in the conclusion that there may be, and that one likely candidate appeared just a few months before I began to write this chapter.

## THE ALPHA MALE/ALPHA-NATION MODEL

If he is firmly established at the top of his wild community's political hierarchy, a chimpanzee alpha male can dominate any individual in the group on a one on one basis, and he also can face down any coalition of males that unites to oppose him (Goodall, 1986). This he accomplishes largely through spectacular intimidation displays, which reinforce his dominance on a generic basis. The methodology is direct: Daily he erects his long black hair and dashes around madly, daring any member of his group to stay on the ground where he is and ignore his mighty display. He knows all but instinctively that his fellows are naturally given to status rivalry, and he perceives that they are constantly working in coalitions to depose him. He also knows that if he doesn't keep these rivals cowed, he could be in for serious trouble.

In doing field work with wild chimpanzees, I have observed such displays hundreds of times, and normally every group member starts up a tree as soon as a displaying alpha even comes close. If deference is not shown in the form of flight accompanied by submissive pant-barks or frightened screams, the alpha will attack. The "attack" usually will not result in physical wounding, but this depends on how the alpha assesses the intentions of individuals not quick to get out of his way. If a known serious adversary seems to be pointedly ignoring his display, the attack can be vigorous, and the other chimpanzee can be seriously roughed up—or else the alpha can run into a fight.

From the standpoint of a motivated competitor who is ready to go head to head, the way to announce that one is going actively after the alpha's job—and his rank—is simply to stay in place and ignore his display. The alpha will predictably try to cow his opponent, but if the latter is a prime male who is really well motivated, or has effective backing from coalition partners, a dominance instability can result with no clear alpha. A persisting conflict scene can go on for months, and eventually the challenged alpha must decide whether to bluff strongly and, if necessary, fight with his rival in an attempt to hold on to his dominance, or to give in by submissively pant-grunting to him. Once he exhibits submissive signals—or his rival does—there will be no further problem. One will be dominant, and peace will return to the community. An analogous situation prevailed with United States and the Soviet Union, with a decades-long dominance instability that was eventually resolved in the United States's favor.

Why has natural selection kept a type of tendency that produces such status rivalry in place for 5 million years? The chimpanzee alpha male uses his power of intimidation to gain preferential access to estrous females, particularly during the small window of periovulation when fertilization chances are excellent, and he takes over better feeding patches when foraging in company: This is so routine that others often anticipate his interests and move aside (see Goodall, 1986). There can be little doubt that he increases his reproductive success by behaving dominantly, even though the energetic costs of frequent intimidation displays are high. Similar arguments would apply to the other *Pan* species, the bonobo (see Kano, 1992), and surely to the Paleolithic humans who put the finishing touches on our own political nature (Boehm, 1999). In all three species, individual status rivalry and competition for resources lead to the formation of social hierarchies.

It is worth emphasizing that in his elite role the chimpanzee alpha also invests energy in acts that do not increase his competitive genetic advantages within the group in any direct way. He may take on something like a leadership role occasionally, for instance when the males of his community go on patrol or when they mob a predator (Boehm, 1991). However, his most challenging, constant, energetically expensive, and socially useful contribution to group life involves a different application of alpha power. This involves his interventions in conflicts of others. This is done in the wild (Boehm, 1994; Goodall, 1986) and even more so in captivity (de Waal, 1982, 1989), where social proximity seems to increase conflict levels. I emphasize that he can even intervene in conflicts between other high-ranking adult males, acting as impartial peacemaker.

The effect is to simultaneously reinforce his social dominance and substantially assist others by keeping them from hurting one another. Superficially, the appearance is hardly one of altruism: When two individuals are beginning to quarrel by vocalizing hostilely or starting to engage physically, the alpha male will erect his hair and charge right at them. Their reaction is to disengage and avoid him, often climbing trees, and this enables their feelings of hostility to subside. They may be prone to resume the conflict, but the alpha knows this and he sits down on the ground somewhere between them, keeping an eye on things. This damps their tendency to resume the fray.

As with humans, this is definitely a "considered" as opposed to a stupidly "instinctive" reaction on the alpha's part. I say this because even though the intervener's strategies follow a single strategic direction in terms of his obvious motivation to stop fights, the tactics vary widely. For instance, at Gombe National Park in Tanzania I once saw alpha male Goblin stop a serious grappling-and-biting fight between two females up in the treetops by hurling the two downward so that they would have to disengage in order to break their falls, and then he quickly herded one of them back up to the treetop and then herded the other to the base of the tree and away from it to keep them separated while they calmed down. He used these inventive tactics because of logistics: in the canopy, he could not really display at or between them. In another case, I saw adult male Satan first try to stop a serious fight between two adolescent males by using the usual terrestrial tactic: he charged right at them. They were so engaged with grappling and biting each other that they remained oblivious of his presence, so his backup strategy was to reach in with his great arms and (with difficulty) pry them apart (Boehm, 1994). It is clear, then, that like humans chimpanzees dislike the effect of conflict on their social environment.

It will be the alpha male who performs in this role if he is present, but chimpanzee communities are subject to continuous fissioning and fusion and he is not necessarily present in a given subgroup. Goblin was away when Satan, as number two, intervened in the adolescent conflict described above; had Goblin been there it would have been his own prerogative, as alpha, to do the intervention. If a conflict is between infants or juveniles, usually Goblin will ignore the situation and let one of the mothers intervene to separate the fighters. However, if the mothers happen to be absent when juveniles fight, Goblin will intervene.

So a chimpanzee alpha male is a concerned bully. He is never shy about taking what he wants, and others both resent this and, in the case of more politically motivated males, covet and challenge his status. (They regularly form coalitions to diminish or usurp his power.) As an apparent altruist, he has a major role in keeping aggressions of others from becoming seriously maladaptive. He puts significant energy into the mission of preventing serious fighting, but, in doing so, in part he may be assisting his own reproductive success. By this I mean that he enhances his dominance status by exerting control as peacemaker, and it might even be said that his more aggressive interventions can substitute for general intimidation displays. At the same time, however, he is helping his genetic competitors within the group in a major way, by keeping them from hurting or killing one another.

## Comparison of Alpha Chimpanzee with Putative UN Counterpart

Let us compare alpha-chimpanzee Goblin with a typical UN secretary-general. The secretary-general of the UN is the formal leader of our world of nations, but he hasn't the power-role of a chimpanzee alpha male. What decision power there is, is invested in the Security Council, which of course is seriously impeded by the Great Power veto and lack of an independent military budget.

If we compare a chimpanzee alpha with the Security Council itself, this organization is unable to intervene with authority in disputes between major powers, whereas an alpha male chimpanzee can intervene forcefully even when high-ranking males begin to fight. Thus, the chimpanzee political model does not apply to the UN. Where it does apply, is to an individual nation. The average nation has centralized, powerful leadership, which is forceful enough, militarily, to intervene and make peace when internal factions are motivated to fight.

There is still another application for the chimpanzee model, an important one. In our global community of nations, it is diagnostic that we use the term "superpower." "Alpha-power" would do the same job semantically, for the world community of nations seems to feel about its superpowers much as individual chimpanzees do about their alpha male. The feelings are ambivalent, for dominant manipulation from above curtails freedom of action, and, in the case of nations it curtails national sovereignty—a word that is all but sacred in any political vocabulary. However, this is exactly the same bully to look to for help if there is a serious dispute to be resolved.

The peacekeeping roles of alpha-nations are perhaps less obvious than those of wildly charging chimpanzee alphas, but frequent references to the United States (often with NATO) as the "world's policeman" make the similarity of functions clear enough. If need be a dominant chimpanzee will apply force selfishly to gain either political or economic or mating advantage, and if need be he also will use force to impartially stop fights. But in fact most of his manipulations are based just upon the threat of force. He is a consummate bluffer who will use physical coercion only if he has to.

These same characterizations would seem to fit the former Soviet Union and United States in the last half of the twentieth century, if only within their two separate spheres of influence where these two powerful presences tended to stabilize the internal tensions among their clients and satellites. Today, the United States is widely referred to as the last remaining superpower, and again the chimpanzee shoe fits to the degree that a self-interested alpha-nation at least tries to pacify *certain* conflicts.

These are important parallels. Chimpanzees are ambivalent about their dominantly exploitative and manipulative alpha male—who also comes in handy for peacekeeping—and nations have similar reactions to superpowers, whose roles are similar. Furthermore, the Cold War period can be likened to a protracted dominance instability in a community of apes, the policing role being less effective at the global level because two would-be alphas were vying for ascendancy. The period since then has involved a single dominant alpha situation with the United States taking the lead and NATO partners providing backup, which is analogous to the backing a well-established chimpanzee alpha male receives from his coalition partner(s).

## Problems with the U.S. Alpha Role

It is time for some concrete examples which will show that alpha chimpanzees are perhaps more effective than their human national counterparts when it comes to conflict management. With respect to global conflict resolution, a forceful-intervention strategy succeeded in stabilizing but definitely not in resolving the conflicts in Bosnia, Kosovo, and Macedonia, whereas the Hutu-Tutsi massacres in Central Africa badly needed intervention that simply was not forthcoming. A problem that becomes immediately obvious is that the narrow national interests of the intervening superpower can affect the efficacy of peacekeeping efforts.

For instance, in the Bosnian conflict the United States eventually allied with Croatia, a nation that had and still has noteworthy fascist tendencies, to stop a rebellion by Serbs, who still considered themselves to be a U.S. World War II ally against the Nazis. Whatever the accuracy of this Serbian perspective, the United States did take sides moralistically in the conflict it was trying to mediate, favoring the seceding Moslems and later the Croatians. This was partly because it was in a hurry to expediently balance power so it would not have to engage its armies on the ground, and partly because from the beginning the Serbs were taken to be the villains. As a result, the "solution" was seriously flawed—for reasons I explain.

The chimpanzee approach to conflict management is quite different. The alpha male normally focuses on the conflict—and not on the parties and their relative culpability or on his ties to them (see Boehm, 1994; de Waal, 1982). This impartial approach holds also for humans in bands and tribes, for when communities intervene in disputes in order to "manage" them, usually they deliberately avoid sorting out the good guys from the bad (see Hoebel, 1964). The point is to find a morally neutral compromise that enables both parties to set aside their grievances, and this strategy is followed quite deliberately. When the eighteenth-century Serbs I studied ethnohistorically went to compose a feud between two willing clans in the same tribe, the mediators had a saying to the effect that "one party should not go home singing and the other lamenting" (Boehm, 1986). This widely applied principle is based on sound reasoning. If both parties to a dispute feel that they have achieved at least some of their goals and that the other side hasn't, they are much less likely to renew the conflict.

Let us consider more closely the facts in Bosnia. Initially, all three sides were committing gruesome atrocities, but eventually the Serbs moved far into the lead. The peacemakers decided to think in terms of good guys versus culprits, and they used their new allies the Croatians to balance power and thereby created a military stalemate that facilitated a cease-fire. This one-sided, moralistic policy approach did have an immediate effect, but it went against sound principles of conflict management, which look to the longer term. The Serbs, seeing themselves as victims of a hostile, unfair intervention based on political betrayal, are very likely to strike again.

I emphasize that this instance of dubious competence on the part of a superpower coalition was not misguided in its goals: the idea was to prevent atrocious ethnic slaughter in Europe and stabilize a region close to NATO. But for the long term, the methodology was seriously flawed because war criminality was not kept separate from conflict management. If the Versailles settlement after World War I provided a lesson, it is that even-handedness is of the essence.

The U.S. superpower coalition also sat on its hands during the Hutu-Tutsi slaughter—presumably because Europe and its stability were not involved. My point is that as the world's "policeman," individual alpha-nations or alpha-coalitions like NATO may sometimes be better than nothing, but inevitably they mix their national interests with the ideal role of impartial mediator. In part, this is because their political constituencies are not prepared to risk significant loss of life unless national self-interest is directly involved. A supra-national agency would not have this problem.

An even more striking example of faulty conflict mediation is the offices of the United States in the Palestinian conflict. Over time, the U.S. government has shown a pro-Israeli bias that is quite predictable in terms of U.S. ideals and voting patterns, but that seems far from fair in the minds of even moderate Palestinians, from whom substantial additional territory has been seized since the formation of the Israeli state. Under Israel's originally very beleaguered circumstances, strategic territorial expansion was quite understandable. Defensive military advantage was the issue. However, the same lands were then annexed by sending in permanent settlers, which basically amounts to territorial aggression no matter how it is rationalized. At Camp David, it is no surprise that the Palestinians felt they were being offered a raw deal at the same time that the United States, as supposed impartial arbitrators, called the return of merely a major portion of the economically useful lands a "good deal."

What we seem to have, in our global community of nations, is an alpha-nation that cannot separate its own interests and biases from the impartiality requirements of effective peacekeeping. This flaw has implications that go far beyond an inability to successfully stop and resolve specific, localized conflicts. The problem in what once was Palestine has helped to create a dangerously divided world, and also has nurtured a serious problem of global "terrorism." In this context, we need to take a serious look at what chimpanzee alpha males and band and tribal communities are doing right, when they consistently seek even-handed solutions to the conflicts in their midst.

It is clear that the United Nations does have a structural role that concentrates on intervention in conflicts, and its track record shows that sometimes, under its aegis, coalitions of nations may provide the means to do precisely that. But unlike an alpha male chimpanzee, the UN cannot intervene in conflicts among high-ranking nations because of the veto and the absence of a dominating military force. This creates a serious ongoing power vacuum with respect to policing functions, which is filled, if at all, by a Great Power whose essential mission is to advance national and not global interests.

## IMPROVING THE UNITED NATIONS

In the 1990s the alpha-nation approaches of the Bush-Baker and Clinton-Albright regimes did not make the most of the unique window of political opportunity that arose with the disintegration of the Soviet Union. Lamentably, this is an understatement. It has taken only a single decade for a new global divisiveness to appear, and with proliferation continuing dangerously the new tensions are not likely to be stabilized on an unambiguous basis by a mutually intimidating, "lose/lose" balance of nuclear terror as was the case during the Cold War.

This "mutually assured destruction" type of political stabilization involved both parties having very large nuclear arsenals, both parties having stable governments with the civilian component in control, and both parties having well-developed economic infrastructures at risk, as well as millions of people living in numerous, easily targeted large cities. At this writing there is at least one very poorly developed nation, Pakistan, which possesses nuclear weapons and is not necessarily stable in its government. There are several others, with only moderately developed infrastructures, that in their own minds have very good reason for seeking revenge against the world's alpha-nation and have already developed alternative methods of mass annihilation. They are trying to develop nuclear weapons, as well. In addition, there is the complex web of quasi-independent guerrilla cells that we refer to as "terrorists," some nationally created, some nationally sponsored, others more nebulous, many of which have "internationalized" the idea of wars of national liberation. (At least one of them has serious aspirations to world dominance.) Obviously, it would be impossible to employ a large nuclear arsenal against any of these organizations—either as a threat or in actuality.

Aside from problems of targeting, there is another feature of "international terrorism" that presents problems for global political stasis. Balance-of-terror theory requires that both parties have well-centralized leadership and—obviously—that neither party be so intent on wreaking destruction on the other that a suicidal approach becomes likely. The September 11 attack on New York City showed that people can be trained in large numbers in kamikaze techniques even if they are not defending a nation, and it remains to be seen whether holding host nations responsible for terrorist attacks is a viable response. For instance, a thermonuclear attack on a Western city might leave no local paper trail or other clues to dissuade host nations from providing such weapons.

To go with this dangerous new set of new circumstances, and to the everlasting discredit of the post–Cold War U.S. regimes, there has been no clear and enforced policy on nonproliferation of nuclear or other national weapons of mass destruction. Instead, in addition to a large community of individualistic sovereign nations, some of them arming to the teeth, we now have a loosely knit "shadow nation" of terrorists that seems to need relatively few weapons because of its ingenuity. There is a genuine possibility that militant components of this shadow organization might be given nuclear weapons by some vengeful nation that has the capability to make them. If so, then aside from specific strategies of revenge the targets are likely to be nations that are wealthy and politically manipulative, and ones that fail to be even-handed in their powerful roles as peacemakers. This describes the "sole remaining superpower" quite nicely—as much of the world sees it—but also its NATO allies. Add this all up, and it is easy to argue that our planet is in need, and soon probably in dire need, of firm but even-handed central governance.

The actual dangers faced by the world as a whole run a wide gamut. Even a thermonuclear attack by terrorists in the United States or Europe would not threaten human life in its entirety, but an exchange between India and Pakistan could create serious global problems, and an unlikely accidental exchange between the United States and either China or Russia could be globally disastrous at the level of radioactive pollution. There is no systematic or enforceable plan in place, or in process, to guarantee that large existing nuclear arsenals will be reduced to levels that preclude massive global damage, or that proliferation of other weapons of mass destruction will be curtailed, and the reason is clear. Everyone knows that national sovereignty would stand in the way of rigorous—that is, invasive—inspection.

For the past decade, what we have had, instead, is a powerful alpha-nation that perhaps was concerned about these issues—but was neither well focused in its foreign policy, nor prepared to call for riding roughshod over the sovereignties of other nations, because this would call its own freedom of action into question. To many, this alpha-nation has seemed self-serving, unfocused, unimaginative, and often quite inconsistent in its approaches, and as a matter of global public policy we need something far more effective. For one thing, we need a peacemaker that does not stir further conflict in that very role, as the United States has done in what was once Palestine.

National sovereignty will have to be heavily compromised if we are to make our global community of nations more like a well-regulated modern nation than an inopportune cross between an acephalous egalitarian band and a despotic chimpanzee community dominated by an alpha male. What we have, at present, is an informal world political community that in *realpolitik* terms is much like a community of chimpanzees: a pecking order of nations with bully-nations at the top but with rivalrous lesser nations industriously arming in order to raise their relative status. The scene is definitely reminiscent of a chimpanzee community. However, the apes benefit greatly from alpha dominance because they have consistent, even-handed, and effective peacemaking. With nations, the alpha-system seems to create almost as many problems as it solves.

Formally, as an alternative, we do have a "world government" of sorts. But I have demonstrated that it is set up to be more like an acephalous hunting band, or a tribe, than like a modern nation which can act decisively to stop internal conflicts. So both of our systems are seriously flawed. The policy question is, can either of these systems be made to work properly, or can they be more usefully combined?

If we are to consider an improved alpha-nation system as one potential path to better world governance, there is another feature, beyond consistency and impartiality, which presently is lacking. Generosity would seem to be crucial to the human alpha role, in the sense that if the world is to be run by alpha-nations, they need to be economically forthcoming not just because helping others is good, but because impartiality and generosity from the global center can help to unite the world around an alpha-nation. At issue is the kind of respect that UN peacekeeping forces once enjoyed, in an earlier era when they were never attacked.

The United States was in this position for a few years after 1945, until the Cold War began to dominate its original Marshall Plan approach. But even after U.S. foreign policy became more "manipulative" in response to Soviet and Chinese threats, the flow of foreign aid was significant—if increasingly less impartial and global. Today, the foreign-aid portion of America's enormous GNP is very much smaller; in fact, it is merely a small fraction of what Scandinavian nations are contributing. Furthermore, its distribution is extremely lopsided because Israel and Egypt are the main recipients. The perceived effect is not one of altruism, but of political manipulation. The world's alpha feels itself to be generous if one listens to its distinguished senators, but it is widely viewed as being otherwise. Its global image problems go far beyond poor "public relations."

To say the least, this international alpha system needs serious overhauling, and it may well be that it could never work very well in a divided world. This is because if the alpha-nation is to be universally generous economically, and if it is to resolve conflicts impartially, it will be obliged to assist its enemies and avoid being partial to allies. The alternative is to build a meta-nation at the global level, one that has the same centralized prerogatives of invasiveness and use of force as are found within a single nation. The structure is already present in the UN. What if the UN was given the right of taxation to support not only a permanent military force, one that could outgun any national force or combination thereof, but also generous, impartially disseminated foreign aid.

Crucially, the Security Council veto would have to be removed and representation on the council broadened. As things now stand, national sovereignty would be a major obstacle—as would the Great Power habit of wagging the entire dog. To address this problem, it might be possible to revamp the structure of the UN so as to create checks and balances that would assuage the fears that go with loss of sovereignty. But surely this task would be far trickier than that faced by single multiethnic nations that historically faced similar internal problems and have succeeded in coping with them.

One actual development that could help to transform national policies in this direction is the currently vivid "terrorist threat"—which looks as though it could have some real staying power. Initially, much of the world of nations rallied behind the United States as victim of imaginative urban guerrilla warfare—in part, because many other nations face similar threats. However, in treating "terrorists" as a unitary category, the problem has been vastly oversimplified. There are free-ranging anti-U.S./anti-Western terrorists, there are heavily state-sponsored terrorists of the same type, then there are much more narrowly focused "wars of national liberation" that happen to use "terrorist" methods, and there are various shades in between. There also are so-called "rogue nations," themselves prone to train urban guerrillas, which are arming themselves because they wish to rise in the world power hierarchy—just like young male chimpanzees whose aim is ultimately to challenge the alpha male. There are also nations like India and Pakistan whose intense rivalries are regional. If these various types are not clearly differentiated, clumsy attempts to neutralize the attendant dangers could further polarize the world into "haves" and "have-nots," Islamics versus Westerners, or other types of armed camps.

Perhaps it is optimistic to suggest that there are some potent seeds of world political centralization in all of this. But certain developments could further unite the global community precisely because all would feel threatened together. A terrorist organization's taking out Paris or New York with a thermonuclear device would be a likely strong stimulus—much stronger, obviously, than the September 11 attack on New York. But as a practical matter, how could a *trustworthy* international government be set up? For one thing, the potential major players are enmeshed in a wide range of conflicts with one another, and this means that there is no Great Power that could stand above the fray and incur the trust of all the principals as it took a leadership role in working toward a new world order. A charismatic leadership approach also seems unlikely.

What is needed is a centralized ruling entity whose impartiality will seldom be called into question because a rigorous system of checks and balances preemptively curbs partisan behavior. National leaders, when their rule is democratically based as opposed to imposed, are generally trusted in the ultimate sense that that the office they occupy is trusted. Obviously, this is not because democratic leaders are considered by nature or upbringing to be predictably trustworthy. Rather, it is because preemptive checks and balances are in place to make sure that the trust is not misplaced when the wrong personality or situation comes along.

This democratic approach is based on a not-so-sanguine assessment of human nature. It seems to assume that potentially there will be a major dose of "alpha male chimpanzee-type" selfishness in many leaders, and that this must be headed off at the pass. This distrust of leadership power is highly reminiscent of bands and tribes, and at the level of further developing the UN, there has been no serious effort to get past it in a practical and effective way. There are, in fact, checks and balances there, such as dividing functions between the General Assembly and the Security Council, and the veto. But the veto provides a check so strong that it is crippling for major decisions.

Creating a workable set of checks of balances that would allay the distrust of nations, many of which have waged destructive war with each other and many of which have bitter ideological and cultural bones to pick with others, seems far more daunting than doing the same thing within a nation. If the UN were slated to become militarily "alpha," the institution-building challenge would be enormous, for the checks and balances would have to foreclose the possibilities of capricious or partisan decisions—yet enable decisive decision making in difficult cases involving Great Powers. Because I promised a diagnosis rather than a total blueprint, I shall not try to spell out how this could be done. However, the will to arrive at such a solution definitely would be strengthened by a perceived and serious threat to the entire global community of nations or to most of them.

## THE LARGER PICTURE

National sovereignty is deeply imbedded in our political and cultural life, and this is no accident. It looks very much like the "individual sovereignty" of egalitarian tribesmen, or the sovereignty of individual tribes in a large region having many tribes. We can even see some rudiments of this in individuals of the two *Pan* species' dislike of being dominated, for both chimpanzees and bonobos form coalitions to lessen the power and control of those ranking above them (Boehm, 1999). With a pattern that holds at so many levels, we must assume that an anciently formed human nature could be partly responsible. The fact that in today's mobile hunting bands the issue of individual autonomy ("sovereignty") is so strongly and universally emphasized tells us something about human political nature in the Upper Paleolithic, and our nature remains similar today because natural selection acts basically as a conservative force. We all-too-readily identify with our nations, and rejoice in their sovereignty, because that is our recent history. But an ancient nature helps to shape that history.

We may assume that human political nature has been both hierarchically inclined and also quite culturally flexible for at least 40,000 years. With respect to this political flexibility, if you were to look at the world as of a mere 500 years ago, you would find one wholly egalitarian continent: Australia had nothing but nomadic hunting bands. Then there was Africa, with a few egalitarian hunters and many egalitarian tribesmen, but also with many chiefdoms and a few primitive kingdoms. There were several other continents that had earlier spawned the six early civilizations, but by 500 years ago they were largely or partly tribal with a number of chiefdoms, and sometimes kingdoms or empires. A few hundred years later, there were several continents with nations, democratic or otherwise, and nation-based empires. All known stages of human political evolution were represented by then—aside from a global supernation as the ultimate form of centralized government. Our first attempt at that was not until the League of Nations, which was more ineffective than the present UN.

For thousands of years, there has been a tendency for the size and density of local human populations to increase, and political centralization has increased proportionately. Over recent centuries, this has been accomplished in two ways: either through imposition by theocratic leaders, secular kings, or military dictators, or else by popularly setting up nations with checks and balances as in ancient Greece or the United States in the 1770s. Today, with no realistic possibility of an absolutely dominant superpower emerging, and with little possibility of national sovereignties being set aside in the interest of world peace, as I see it the penultimate stage of human political evolution seems to be in abeyance.

## A SPECIFIC DIAGNOSIS

The two anthropological models have shed some significant light on why it is so difficult to take the next logical step with respect to world government and what our alternatives may be. One reason we can't really centralize world governance is, obviously, national sovereignty. I have also raised the issue of trust. There is also the fact that in certain cases the UN and the informal alpha-nation system can (in fact) work effectively, each on its own, and this engenders hope or denial. All these factors reinforce the tendency to muddle along, rather than face the issue of giving up sovereignty. We also have seen instances, as with Operation Desert Storm, in which these two basically flawed systems can work together fairly effectively—for a time. The occasional successes make it clear that the present machinery is far from useless.

What can political anthropology tell us more specifically about obstacles and possibilities with respect to global centralization of power? We must ask how early tribal societies sometimes managed to set aside their egalitarian preoccupations as they began to accept the benefits of having strong chiefs who they supported voluntarily. We must ask, also, how people living in moderately centralized hierarchical chiefdoms came to form states having far more central authority. With respect to the origins of early states we are dependent on archaeological evidence and must speculate a great deal (see Service, 1975). However, archeological questions about how egalitarian tribes evolved into hierarchical chiefdoms (see Earle, 1991) are more readily enriched by means of recent ethnographic data.

For instance, the historical Montenegrin Serbs I studied in my capacity as cultural anthropologist (Boehm, 1983) began as an ephemeral confederation of fiercely independent tribes, which coalesced only when the Ottoman Empire threatened their autonomy. Otherwise, they feuded. Over several centuries of intermittent but sometimes extreme external pressure, they moved gradually into becoming a chiefdom, with theocratic leaders who worked as hard as they dared, sometimes even hiring assassins to take out their opponents, to increase their central authority, and thereby to control feuding. These military bishops succeeded only to a degree, but then, suddenly, by means of a forceful and atrocious secular coup, Montenegro was turned overnight into a despotic kingdom in 1850. Previously, the rank and file, with their individual tribal leaders representing them, had been recalcitrantly ambivalent as control from the political center was gradually increasing. They perceived the benefits, but still loved their autonomy. Finally, it had to be brute force that did the trick—with one clique of high-status tribes taking over central control and imposing universal taxation.

In terms of internal order, the tribesmen had been aware of the benefits of political centralization, for their noncoercive but high-ranking military bishops sometimes were persuasive enough to stop feuding among the tribes—feuding that not only disrupted civil life but also made the confederation much more vulnerable to outside attack by a powerful predatory empire. Once a bloody military coup brought in strong, coercive centralized leadership, the tribesmen accepted their nationhood with pride, but still with some ambivalence. With feuding ended, Montenegro suddenly became a well-ordered nation-state—ready, in 1911, to start the first Balkan War that led directly to the World War I.

Does this ethnohistorical sequence provide lessons for our world of nations? In terms of the final sequence described earlier, the answer is no because it is very difficult to see the UN being empowered by means of a military coup. I emphasize that there are over half a dozen major nuclear arsenals in the world, and that any of these nations could resist any global coup that threatened its precious sovereignty. However, the fact that the Serbian tribesmen were merely ambivalent during the period when their essentially powerless bishops were slowly increasing their power at the political center does supply some food for thought. As members of the tribal confederation saw the benefits of having somewhat stronger leaders, their concern about individual tribal sovereignty began to fade. It seems possible that they would have eventually centralized their government even without the coup, but instead this was done by force.

What this suggests is that using a "federal" model for world governance might be attempted on a gradualistic basis. This transition would have to be well strategized, in the sense that each nation would cede some power to the global political center while procuring perceptually obvious benefits to its national security.

Another example at the level of brute force is the now-defunct Zulu Empire in Africa (see Service, 1975). Rather than being a response to threats from an external state, as with the Montenegrin Serbs, the Zulu Empire arose through conquest opportunities; as it expanded, its advantage was in being well centralized politically, whereas its adversaries were merely acephalous tribes. As in Montenegro's final transition, this exemplifies sheer coercive force as a route to effective centralization. Because I have already ruled out the *imposition* of a global government today, the Zulu example is of little use heuristically.

A different route to centralization is through the entirely voluntary agglomeration of smaller units, and we can model this quite neatly by using the Iroquois Confederacy described by Louis Henry Morgan (1901). There, half a dozen large and independent tribes created a long-term but entirely voluntary confederation by using a system of checks and balances that may well have been emulated, in part, by the founders of the U.S. Constitution. They did so chiefly for purposes of self-defense and territorial expansion. The Iroquois confederation definitely was not a chiefdom, for a strict philosophy of political egalitarianism continued to prevail: The council of elders had no authoritative leader, the political center had no standing army, and any of the six tribal "nations" could secede at will. In making decisions it had to be a consensus— or nothing at all. In a sense, the UN is at a very similar stage of political development, and of course the Iroquois never really centralized. The question remains, How is such an organization transformed into a "state"?

What I see, as I write, is a dangerous world—a world of sovereign nations that in one sense is unifying temporarily against the common threat of global terrorism, but in another sense is polarizing into a new and bellicose divisiveness. These new divisions are not structured in a way that invites a reasonably unambiguous (and at least relatively safe) Soviet-U.S. style balance of terror. As nuclear weapons begin to fall into the hands of "rogue nations" that have both major political ambitions and major grievances against today's alphas, and as they become more likely to fall into the hands of sometimes suicidal dissident guerrillas who are extremely difficult to target and control, the "external threat" to well-established large nations could become ultimate. It was a similar type of stimulus—hostilities with neighboring tribes—that led the Iroquois to confederate. In doing so they created elaborate checks and balances that guarded against despotism and inspired trust. However, they were far from being fully federated, and after these once-united six Indian nations took different sides during our Revolutionary War, their powerful confederation fell apart after having flourished for centuries.

The Iroquois nations had the advantage of being contiguous in space, and of being fairly similar culturally, which made them predictable to one another. This made for considerable trust, even though such trust had to work hand in hand with ingeniously constructed checks and balances—which are always a sign of *mistrust*. At today's global level, the problem of trust is exacerbated because there are such extreme ethnic and religious differences among the nations of this world.

Fortunately, in our divisive and potentially violent community of nations there are at least a few recent cultural trends that might work in favor of global cultural unification. We are moving toward the world's having a dominant language, English. At the level of cultural values, the U.S. film industry is extremely influential, and the same is true of television and, more recently, the Internet. Whether one agrees with the particular values or not, world culture is continually being homogenized not only by "modernization," but also by the specific culture of its alpha-nation.

Perhaps equally important, in the very important economic sphere the often-reviled multinational corporations are creating serious and growing technological and economic interdependencies among nations that will greatly add to the calculated costs of warfare. More generally the movement toward free trade has had similar effects. Creation of new, Nuremburg-style international courts is another relevant advance. Any and all of these factors could help to mitigate the practical problem of mistrust among nations, and all acting together, in conjunction with a new kind of political threat, might have some unforeseen consequences.

## CONCLUSIONS

This chapter has been an experiment in bringing a deep, biocultural anthropological conceptual framework to the problem of formulating macropolicy in the area of global governance. In addition to the focus on past and present cultural patterns in various well-known types of political society, I also have taken account of the evolutionary prehistory of our species—a factor that in important ways constrains or helps to shape our possibilities today. I am speaking of a handful of ingrained political propensities that not only seem to affect human patterns of behavior in a wide spectrum of natural environments and societal types, but also may be found, in somewhat different forms, in apes we are closely related to phylogenetically.

Implicit in all the arguments I have made is the following premise: If we are to think realistically about reshaping our system of global governance—a reform that is seriously overdue—then basic political patterns, those which have a deep phylogenetic history in our species, must be given more respect in our practical calculations. This is by no means an argument that innovation is impossible because humans somehow are "genetically determined." It is an argument that we must not be naïve in trying to cope with the effects of a rather well-defined political nature that has been formed over millions of years.

In spite of our deeply felt dispositions to keep the peace, this nature is prone to cause conflict between both individuals and groups, and it makes for difficulties in accepting superordinate authority unless we can clearly see the benefits in doing so and can trust our governors not to turn legitimate control into despotism. It is no accident that the same problems arise in hunting bands and tribes, in tribal confederations, in modern democracies, and also, now, in our global community of nations.

I have focused on the issue of sovereignty, with its deep roots in a human political nature, which is both culturally flexible and reasonably predictable in some of its main out lines. I feel that we have been on solid ground in identifying tendencies to dominance and tendencies to resent being dominated, tendencies to fight, and tendencies to resolve conflicts caused by fighting. These innately structured ambivalences underlie, constrain, and even help to shape our actual political behavior as cultural animals.

Unfortunately, another area in which one can be confident in bringing in human political nature is with respect to ethnocentrism (see LeVine & Campbell, 1971). Humans everywhere tend to make invidious comparisons between themselves and others, and the political history of the twentieth century tells us that in conjunction with our capacity for warfare, xenophobia has contributed immensely to the destructiveness (and cruelty) we are capable of. This same capacity for ethnocentrism will present a major obstacle to any kind of world political integration because, in addition to a predictable moral condescension that makes it relatively easy to kill outsiders, ethnocentrism also breeds political mistrust. This is unfortunate, for trust appears to be the best and possibly the only route to better global security. Those who would experiment with global political centralization can ignore this issue only at the peril of all.

A viable world government would need to be eminently trustworthy, that is, effectively checked-and-balanced but not hobbled—a delicate adjustment given the strength of sovereign feelings and the increasingly strong need we have for a truly powerful arbitrator of disputes. It would have to be highly impartial in dealing coercively with stubborn conflicts. To pay administrative and military expenses, it would need to tax the nations of the world, and it would enhance its global standing as keeper of the peace if it could also redistribute substantial monies to nations that were in hardship.

At present, the UN looks far more like an egalitarian band or tribe than like either a despotic chimpanzee community, which has a powerful and reasonably even-handed peacemaking despot or like a well-centralized democratic national government, which has adequate coercive force to effectively prevent civil war but is kept on a strict leash by checks and balances. Insofar as the preferred model I have come up with is a democratic national government, rather than an autocratic national government, this is at least a major start in the right direction.

For a long time, World Federalists have been telling us that we would have a far more predictable and safer planet if this well-centralized national model, based on a democratic type of polity with strong checks and balances, could be invoked straightforwardly and completely at a level that was global. Their goals are eminently rational, but one sometimes gains the impression that they are not fully aware of what they are up against. For some reason, the dispositions for autonomy that emanate so predictably from human nature become particularly intense when associated with issues of sovereignty, be this tribal or national. This tenacious problem will be difficult to address in the absence of a discernible external threat, one dire enough to make substantial loss of sovereignty seem like a reasonable trade-off against gaining security and ensuring survival. Such a threat might well be on the horizon, but it will not come from outer space. It will come from urban retreats and caves, and from ambitious nations—ones that established alpha-nations deem to be "rogues"—that wish to increase their global influence.

Beyond the now very specific threats from international terrorism, or from nuclear exchanges by nations such as India and Pakistan, lie future threats—some surely not yet imagined. Even a layman can make generalized predictions about advances of technology, and particularly about the all too predictable advances in genetic engineering techniques. We cannot dismiss the possibility that a charismatic misanthrope might simply do away with humanity. Such a person (or organization) would need only to create an ever-changing AIDS-like virus that circulated through the air and entered the human body through the skin, and the game would be up for a talented but potentially very destructive species.

Some organization must be created to control not only the increasing risks of active warfare between states, but also weapons of mass or total destruction, including research and development in these fields. Global policy will have to be aggressively invasive, and it will have to impinge on national sovereignty pervasively. The problem is fear of the political unknown—in the form of world government.

As a political anthropologist, I have taken a biocultural perspective partly to identify obstacles by taking human nature into account, but partly to bring a sense of possibility to a task the world of nations seems to have given up on—with nothing more than Band-Aids in place. I have offered some general diagnostic guidelines as to why global power-centralization, though certainly a logical next step in human political evolution, will face special obstacles that are deeply rooted in human nature. There is no call for undue pessimism, for that same nature offers us possibilities in the form of our great inventiveness, a will to survive, and also, very importantly, a deeply ingrained propensity to reduce conflict.

Our inventiveness will definitely be stretched, as we try to devise ways of controlling conflicts without permitting an insidiously wider system of control from creeping in. Dealing with deeply felt commitments to national sovereignty will call for true inventiveness in institution building, but at least the UN is on the right path insofar as it is already set up as a democratic institution. I say this because the only way around the problem of national sovereignty will be through trust, and the checks-and-balances approach has worked adequately in creating a guarded type of trust within nations.

World political centralization has its obvious dangers. A potentially despotic, capricious, and willful UN organization, armed to the teeth, is a frightening specter. But a world without adequate political centralization may present even more peril. My prediction, as a political anthropologist, is that it will be only when the second type of danger becomes so obvious and imminent that it decisively outweighs the first, that we will begin to use our imaginations to construct a more viable supernation. However, one should never underestimate the innovative potential of a species whose very inventiveness could now destroy a planet.

## NOTES

1. This treatment of the modern political world and its problems was originally conceived as the final chapter of my recent book, *Hierarchy in the Forest.* One major precedent for such a treatment is Roger Masters's "World Politics as a Primitive Political System," published in the journal *World Politics* in 1964, but otherwise usually when nations are likened to tribes, the basis for the comparison is nontechnical. For support, I wish to thank the Templeton Foundation, which recently provided funds for research on hunter-gatherer conflict resolution, and the Simon J. Guggenheim Foundation for an ongoing fellowship to conduct research on conflict resolution, which made it possible to write this chapter. In addition the Harry Frank Guggenheim Foundation funded an ethnographic project on egalitarianism among bands and tribes, and also a two-year research project in Africa that investigated conflict interventions among wild chimpanzees. I also wish to thank Hayward Alker and Peter J. Richerson for useful comments.

2. In this chapter, I shall use the terms "nation" and "state" more or less interchangeably, but when I refer to the internal security structure of a country I will use the term "nation."

3. In using the term "unimaginative," I am referring not only to people in government who deal with foreign policy, but also to their constituencies. For a long time, there have been a handful of people of vision who have conceived of a world federalist system that would go far beyond what was attempted with the League of Nations and is being attempted with the UN. These people have formed organizations and formal platforms, and their proposals are eminently rational. However, they openly acknowledge that general support of their position is extremely weak. The present analysis focuses on factors that might help foreign policy officials and politicians to rethink their positions on the trade-offs between loss of national security and benefits of effective global governance.

## REFERENCES

Arnhart, L. (1998). *Darwinian natural right: The biological ethics of human nature.* Albany: State University of New York Press.

Blurton-Jones, N. G. (Ed.). (1972). *Ethological studies of child behavior.* Cambridge: Cambridge University Press.

Boehm, C. (1983). *Montenegrin social organization and values.* New York: AMS Press.

Boehm, C. (1986). *Blood revenge: The enactment and management of conflict in Montenegro and other tribal societies.* Philadelphia: University of Pennsylvania Press.

Boehm, C. (1989). Ambivalence and compromise in human nature. *United States Anthropologist, 91,* 921–939.

Boehm, C. (1991). Lower-level teleology in biological evolution: Decision behavior and reproductive success in two species. *Cultural Dynamics, 4,* 115–134.

Boehm, C. (1993). Egalitarian society and reverse dominance hierarchy. *Current Anthropology, 34,* 227–254.

Boehm, C. (1994). Pacifying interventions at Arnhem Zoo and Gombe. In R.W. Wrangham, W.C. McGrew, F.B.M. de Waal, & P.G. Heltne (Eds.), *Chimpanzee cultures*(pp. 211–226). Cambridge: Harvard University Press.

Boehm, C. (1996). Emergency decisions, cultural selection mechanics, and group selection. *Current Anthropology, 37,* 763–793.

Boehm, C. (1999). *Hierarchy in the forest: The evolution of egalitarian behavior.* Cambridge, MA: Harvard University Press.

Boehm, C. (2000). Conflict and the evolution of social control. *Journal of Consciousness Studies, 7,* 79–183.

Bohannan, P.J. (1954). The migration and expansion of the Tiv. *Africa, 24,* 2–16.

Chagnon, N. (1983). *Yanomamo: The fierce people.* New York: Holt, Rinehart and Winston.

Daly, M., & Wilson, M. (1988). *Homicide.* New York: Aldine de Gruyter.

de Waal, F.B.M. (1982). *Chimpanzee politics: Power and sex among apes.* New York: Harper and Row.

de Waal, F.B.M. (1989). *Peacemaking among primates.* Cambridge, MA: Harvard University Press.

Earle, T. (1991). *Chiefdoms: Power, economy, and ideology.* New York: Cambridge University Press.

ibl-Eibesfeldt, I. (1974). *Love and hate: The natural history of behavior patterns.* New York: Schocken.

Ember, C. (1978). Myths about hunter-gatherers. *Ethnology, 17,* 439–448.

Erdal, D., & Whiten, A. (1994). On human egalitarianism: An evolutionary product of Machiavellian status escalation? *Current Anthropology, 35,* 175–178.

Erdal, D., & Whiten, A. (1996). Egalitarianism and Machiavellian intelligence in human evolution. In *Modelling the early human mind.* Cambridge, UK: MacDonald Institute for Archeological Research.

Evans-Pritchard, E.E. (1940). *The Nuer: A description of the modes of livelihood and political institutions of a Nilotic people.* Clarendon: Oxford.

Fried, M.H. (1967). *The evolution of political society: An essay in political anthropology.* New York: Random House.

Goodall, J. (1986). *The chimpanzees of Gombe.* Cambridge, MA: Harvard University Press.

Hoebel, E.A. (1964). *The law of primitive man: A study in comparative legal dynamics.* Cambridge, MA: Harvard University Press.

Kano, T. (1992). *The last ape: Pygmy chimpanzee behavior and ecology.* Stanford, CA: Stanford University Press.

Kelly, R. (2000). *Warless societies and the origin of war.* Ann Arbor: University of Michigan Press.

Kelly, R.L. (1995). *The foraging spectrum: Diversity in hunter-gatherer lifeways.* Washington, DC: Smithsonian Insititution Press.

Knauft, B.M. (1991). Violence and sociality in human evolution. *Current Anthropology 32,* 391–428.

Konner, M. (1982). *The tangled wing: Biological constraints on the human spirit.* New York: Henry Holt.

Lee, R.B. (1979). *The !Kung San: Men, women, and work in a foraging society.* Cambridge: Cambridge University Press.

LeVine, R.A., & Campbell, D.T. (1971). *Ethnocentrism: Theories of conflict, ethnic attitudes, and group behavior.* New York: Wiley.

Lorenz, K. (1966). *On aggression.* New York: Harcourt Brace and World.

Lorenz, K. (1989). *The nature of politics.* New Haven, CT: Yale University Press.

Masters, R.D. (1989). *The nature of politics.* New Haven, CT: Yale University Press.

Morgan, L.H. (1901). *League of the Ho-De-No-Sau-Nee or Iroquois.* Vol. I. New York: Burt Franklin.

Service, E. (1975). *Origin of the state and civilization: The process of cultural evolution.* New York: Norton.

Sober, E., & Wilson, D.S. (1998). *Unto others: The evolution and psychology of unselfish behavior.* Cambridge, MA: Harvard University Press.

Tacon, P.S., & Chippendale, C. (1994). Australia's ancient warriors: Changing depictions of fighting in the rock art of Arnhem Land, NT. *Cambridge Archaeological Journal, 4,* 211–248.

Weber, M. (1947). *The theory of social and economic organization* (A. Parsons, Ed.). New York: Free Press.

Wilson, E.O. (1975). *Sociobiology: The new synthesis.* Cambridge, MA: Harvard University Press.

Wilson, E.O. (1978). *On human nature.* Cambridge, MA: Harvard University Press.

Wrangham, R., & Peterson, D. (1996). *Demonic males: Apes and the origins of human violence.* Boston: Houghton-Mifflin.

9

# Violence and Its Antidotes
## Promises and Pitfalls of Evolutionarily Aware Policy Development

*Nancy Dess*

Violence—genocide, war, hate crimes, rape, domestic abuse, bullying, tiffs, and spats—impacts most lives in the United States. Yet, as noted by Alfred Blumstein of the National Consortium on Violence Research, "it is hard to imagine a public-policy arena that has been more impervious to input from research" (Blumstein, 2000). It is to this imperviousness that this volume speaks. Illuminating some of the barriers to the formulation of effective violence-reduction policies may reveal paths through or around them. The light shone on the problem is thinking about the human species' trek through evolutionary time, on the assumption that doing so will enhance our understanding of contemporary violence and peacemaking. Because humans are social, political, cultural creatures, policy processes—from how policy is formulated to how it is received—are included among those processes assumed to be amenable to evolutionary analysis.

Enhanced understanding does not ensure positive change, of course. Indeed, like Tinbergen's classic piece "On War and Peace in Animals and Man" (1968), the chapters in this volume make clear the robustness of some of the impediments to change on a large scale. Few authors are sanguine about changes coming easily or soon. However, new understanding promises new initiatives, new justifications for existing initiatives, and new critiques of curiously failed policies.

In the last decade or so, modern evolutionary theory has fertilized a remarkable bloom of theoretical and empirical work in psychology and related fields—a neo-Darwinian revolution in the social/behavioral sciences. Amidst the enthusiasm, verbal firefights have flared, both within the ranks of evolutionarily minded scientists and between that cohort and its critics. The harshest exchanges have centered on hot button issues, such as sexuality, race, and aggression. The heat of these debates has obscured important conceptual distinctions, quickened old ghosts, raised defenses, closed ranks, hurt feelings, and polarized positions that may be reconcilable. Of those who jumped into the fray, some have made headway with complex issues whereas others have tossed gasoline on the bonfire, scuffled over high moral ground, or run for cover.

Scientists can be found in all groups. Many, though, have run for cover. Few scientists venture into policy waters. They hope that their research will matter some day. Yet, even in the best of circumstances—an important issue, interesting ideas and data, a receptive audience—they feel that they lack preparation, time, or incentives for thinking about policy. Most do. And, given the mottled history of the evolution/aggression debate, the topic of violence can seem more like a minefield than the best circumstance. Not surprisingly, then, finding contributors for this volume was not easy, despite strong consensus that:

- violence is an important issue
- the evolutionary perspective is relevant to it
- scientists should participate more in policymaking
- even less well informed people routinely weigh in on policy

In the end, a fine array of chapters representing diverse mixtures of scientific and policy expertise was assembled. In addition to offering recommendations to the policy community, the chapters provide models for exploring the policy implications of evolutionary scholarship and, hopefully, will encourage more scientists to do so.

Nobody, however, imagines that the work ahead for scientists and policymakers will be easy. Formidable challenges remain, some rooted in the history and politics of the evolution/aggression debate and others in unhelpful conceptual habits. Understanding and overcoming these challenges is prerequisite to fulfilling the promise of an evolutionary approach.

## HISTORY AND POLITICS OF THE EVOLUTION/ AGGRESSION DEBATE

### Ideology

Cultural ideology and the philosophies that distinguish political factions bear on reactions to evolutionary thinking about human behavior. A hallmark of American ideology is individualism—a view of the individual as the most meaningful unit of causal and moral agency. The hero, the scoundrel, the entrepreneur, and the rugged individualist are all American icons. Collectivism is of lesser value, if not anathema. This polarity has not diminished since the "Red Scare" of communism in the mid-twentieth century. If declining civic engagement (Putnam, 2000) and antipathy to collective solutions to child care, poverty, education, and health care crises are any indication, individualism has continued to rise.

Individualism is itself amenable to evolutionary analysis.[1] According to Guisinger and Blatt (1994), *individuality* and *relatedness* comprise an evolved dialectic that, in cultural context, can develop in a balanced or unbalanced way. An example of the latter is the nurturance of autonomy and relative neglect of interdependence in Western societies. One cognitive product of growing up in an individualistic society is the tendency to underestimate the role of circumstances in behavior, such that attributions to internal/dispositional motives prevail. Originally termed the *fundamental attribution error* due to its robustness in mostly white U.S. college samples, recent research shows that an extra-individual perspective—attention to situation, person/situation interactions, or group goals—is common among non-Westerners (Norenzayan & Nisbett, 2000) and in some U.S. subpopulations (Vandello & Cohen, 1999). Thus, the "fundamental" attribution error is not fundamental to being human but rather reflects disparate care-and-feeding of the psychological substrates of individuality and relatedness. In dominant American discourse, one is rose, the other weed.

Individualism, as ideology and folk theory of behavior, conflicts with the evolutionary concepts of ultimate causation and humans' inherent sociality. It resists the tenets of evolutionary analyses that locate important influences on behavior in the distant past and in social context (Bloom, this volume). In particular, attributing free will to individual agents implies a path-independence to behavior that appears to run straight up against the canalization and accommodation to rearing conditions central to evolutionary accounts of human development (Fishbein & Dess, this volume; Hrdy, 1999). Although the free will/determinism dichotomy is one of the oldest existing philosophical problems, the tension may be more apparent that real: An evolutionary approach to human cognition, behavior, and culture promises to resolve it by deconstructing its dichotomous nature (e.g., McCrone, 1999). In the meantime, harsh contrasts between the totally free individual and the highly constrained one will maintain certain ideological struggles.

Individualism also resists social-structural accounts of behavior, including perpetrating and being a victim of violence. In the United States as in many other countries, the poor, children, women, people of color, religious and sexual minorities, and immigrants suffer disproportionately from violence. These patterns seem to invite accounts in terms of political and economic structure, including those elaborated within an evolutionary framework (Fishbein & Dess, Masters, and Mealey, this volume). For one thing, those groups have little or no political power. Children and noncitizen immigrants cannot vote, institutional barriers to voting in poor and minority communities persist, and, at this writing, the U.S. Senate includes only thirteen women and no African

Americans or Latinos/as. Yet social-structural accounts are resisted by an ideology that insists upon the individual as autonomous agent; on this view, social structures and institutions themselves are not agentic but rather reflect the behavior and will of free individuals.

A better balance between individuality and relatedness would promote receptiveness to evolutionary and other situated approaches to policy, not to mention the health of the nation (Triandis, 2000; Wilkinson, 1997). A starting place is a shift in the balance of political power between individualist and collectivist sensibilities—ideally in electoral politics but also in the conceptual grounding of policymakers and the advocacy community more broadly in the biopsychosocial model offered by contemporary evolutionary thought. To promote these shifts, how policies derived from these approaches serve individual interests and shared superordinate goals can be articulated.

## Challenges from the Right

Obstacles to evolutionarily aware policy, in general and with respect to violence reduction, arise from ideology associated with the far right of the political spectrum. Individualism is embraced more firmly on the Right than on the Left (Emerson et al., 1999). A good illustration is 1996 presidential candidate Bob Dole's retort to Hillary Clinton's book, *It Takes a Village*, the thesis of which is collective social responsibility for raising children. In his convention speech, Dole proclaimed, "I am here to tell you: It does not take a village to raise a child. It takes a family . . . individual accountability must replace collective excuse." Although this indicates a willingness to make some exceptions to individual responsibility for children,[2] it also indicates that the line is drawn firmly around the nuclear family. Given that this political ideology opposes evolutionary reasoning, opposition from the Right can be anticipated.

The Religious Right—for practical purposes, conservative Protestant Republicans—has other problems with an evolutionary approach. The implications of evolution for God and religiosity have been the subject of fascinating debates, but for religious fundamentalists the matter is settled: Evolution contradicts God's Special Creation of Man (used advisedly), and evolutionists therefore are promoting atheism. Macroevolution opponents who advocate for "creation science" and its new incarnation, "intelligent design," continue to work to eliminate evolution from school curricula or, failing that, to add creationism to them. In 2001 alone, proposals to promote creationism in or eliminate evolution from curricula were introduced in nine state legislatures and four school boards.

At a general level, this religious agenda aims to rescue children from a meaningless, amoral life. According to one intelligent-design proponent, "When you look to the idea that you and I are basically random events and random happenings, that left me feeling void and empty as a human being. . . . That says there's no reason for laws, or for moral behavior" (J.L. Omdahl, quoted by

McMurtrie, 2001). To be sure, averting existential desperation and amorality is a noble cause, and organized religion is a paradigm in which much of the global population accomplishes it (see Solomon et al., this volume). However, most world religions have worked out a place for macroevolution in their cosmology, and most macroevolution adherents have done the same or otherwise found meaning, order, and beauty in the world. For creationists, however, no such accommodations are possible.

Antievolution fervor also has been linked specifically to violence. In 1999, House Majority Whip Tom DeLay (R–Texas) attributed the 1999 Columbine High School massacre to children being taught about evolution, to wit, "that they are nothing but glorified apes who are evolutionized out of some primordial soup of mud." Some fundamentalists even regard psychology on the whole as a satanic religion (see Solomon et al., this volume). Blaming violence on evolution by politicians partial to corporal punishment, the death penalty, and the flexing of military muscle may appear paradoxical but, as it happens, not from their point of view: despite a clear empirical relationship between right-wing authoritarianism (RWA) and aggressiveness, high-RWA individuals perceive themselves as "caring" (McHoskey, 1996).

Traditionalism regarding gender roles bears consideration in this context. "Traditionalism" is an orientation that is expressed in terms of, among other things, veneration of male authority and male control of female sexuality. This orientation is exemplified in the Promise Keepers, an all-male Christian organization devoted to reinvigorating American patriarchy—that is, male coalition building and social control. Rhetoric advocating sensitivity and caring is overshadowed by remarkably bald male aggressiveness. At an event called Passage, for example, young men are promised that they will "pick up the weapons necessary to take on the challenging pursuit of manhood . . . experience what it takes to become a skillful explorer and mighty warrior [and make] the transition from survivor to dangerous disciple" (Promise Keepers, 2002). Even though this may be an extreme case, the linkage of traditionalism to right-wing politics is reflected clearly in Republican Party platforms (e.g., against affirmative action and abortion rights) and the gender gap in political affiliation (more men among staunch Republicans and Independents; Norrander, 1997; Saad, 1999). It also is reflected in the differential (under)representation of women in the Republican Congressional contingent: Only three of the 13 women in the Senate and 18 of the 59 women in the House are Republican.

Neither men nor women hold a monopoly on any political slant or psychological attribute. Indeed, the very question of what "man" and "woman" mean and how a categorical construction of gender may foreclose human potential is receiving intense scrutiny (e.g., Butler, 1990; Fausto-Sterling, 2000). At a minimum, gender is multidimensional and interacts with many other variables in predicting ideology (e.g., Watkins et al., 1998). Yet, in the context of a binary view of gender, convergent evidence from cross-cultural studies and from our

nearest relatives indicates that male dominance perpetuates gendered differences and inequities and a propensity toward violence.[3] Although human cultures vary tremendously in how violent or peaceable they are, males
everywhere are on average more violent than their female counterparts (Goldstein, 2001). Male-dominant cultures currently are the norm, and they resist
female empowerment through mechanisms including brute force (e.g., the Taliban's public torture and execution of women, suttee or immolation of Indian
women), custom (e.g., property rights favoring males, denial of education to
girls), and socialization (e.g., internalized gender roles, identification with the
aggressor). Less the symbolic processes and formal institutions unique to humans, such systems resemble the male-dominant, largely despotic social organization of chimpanzees (Boehm, this volume; de Waal, 1989a).

Male dominance—and the aggression correlated with it—is not the only
mode for humans or our kin. Matrilineal female-dominant (e.g., the Mosuo of
China) and gender-egalitarian (e.g., the Minangkabau of Indonesia) cultures do
exist, and they are comparatively pacifistic. Globally, high female clout predicts
less intense state violence (Caprioli & Boyer, 2001). This pattern echoes bonobo
society, in which female coalitions rule and aggression within and between
groups is minimal (de Waal, 1995). Violence among bonobos is quelled through
high levels of intimate physical contact throughout life, which fosters close
attachments, reduces anxiety, and calms aggressive outbursts. If intimate contact is a quintessentially primate way of promoting affiliation and diffusing
anger (Field, 1999; Sheline et al., 1994; Silk, 1998)—and the enormous meaning accorded a handshake at top diplomatic levels hints that it is—proscriptions
against physical affection and female sexuality in male-dominated societies
permit the escalation of aggression.

Thus, research with many cultures and species indicates that the still small
voice of women on U.S. policy can effectively moderate violence and speak for
peace. This notion is no mere stereotype of femininity. Although a heterogeneous lot, American women *do* tend to be less social-dominance oriented and
more politically progressive, collectivistic, committed to social justice, and supportive of reproductive rights than men (Day & Hadley, 1997; Madson & Trafimow, 2001; Pratto et al., 1994). On the basis of these attributes and shared
goals, they have joined international coalitions such as Women Waging Peace
and Women's Peacepower Foundation. Activist female coalitions are more
likely to unsettle traditional social categories and to cultivate gender equity,
which may in turn facilitate the formulation and implementation of violence-
quelling, peace-promoting policies. Consideration of evolutionary views on
peacemaking also may increase, if differences with apparently competing perspectives can be negotiated (see Challenges from the Left and Science Wars,
below). Women's collective voice is, however, still very small, and given the
fundamentals of conservative ideology, it probably is unreasonable to expect
accommodation by the far Right to increase its volume.

## Challenges from the Left

The political Left is exquisitely sensitive to progressive thought, intellectualism, history, and the social context in which policy decisions are made. It also has been home to collectivist policies and female empowerment. In these respects, the Left is congenial to consideration of evolutionary reasoning. However, red flags are jerked aloft on the Left at the specter of oppression conducted under the banner of evolution. Being vigilant to oppression by the powerful is a good idea; indeed, we may be compelled to it (Boehm, this volume). It is true that Charles Darwin distinguished "civilized" from "savage" human societies, an idea that racists have exploited ever since. It also is true that principles of evolution have been co-opted to justify oppression in the form of inhumane economic practices (Herbert Spencer's Social Darwinism), eugenics (as did the Nazis), and political persecution (Lysenkoism).

A moment's reflection, however, reveals the illogical coalition implied by Social Darwinism (unbridled capitalism), Nazism (genetic determinism), and Lysenkoism (a Marxist version of nongenetic selection). These movements do not follow inevitably or uniquely from any core principle of evolutionary theory. The relationship has worked the other way around, that is, "People generally found in Darwin what they wanted to find" (Proctor, as cited by Conley, 2001). In this regard, there is nothing special about evolution. In human history, oppression has been pursued in the name of myriad constructs—religious obligation, philosophical mandate, historical warrant, scientific deduction, and so on. In many cases, as with evolution, the oppression was underdetermined by, if not logically disconnected from, the original concept.

Unfortunately, after more than a century of "spinning," the Left's objections to evolution are a muddle of legitimate concern, straw argument, knee-jerk reaction, and ignorance of modern evolutionary science. In many a liberal mind, evolution is guilty by association with colonialism, Hitler, *The Bell Curve* (Herrnstein & Murray, 1994), and other instruments of oppression. Ad hominem attacks in the popular press continue to reinforce earlier conditioning. For instance, writer Natalie Angier, perceiving antifeminism in research by some evolutionary psychologists, calls them "evo psychos"; though her complaint actually is not with evolutionary thinking in general, the aspersion paints a broad and nasty swath. So it goes that "evolution" elicits a negative visceral reaction and the specter of vast right-wing conspiracies. Once elicited, these covert responses need little further validation to control overt behavior—including omnibus condemnation of an evolutionary approach to policy.

In 1992, a scientist pushed the buttons of left-leaning politicians, and evolution took the hit along with the scientist. Frederick Goodwin, then head of the former Alcohol, Drug Abuse and Mental Health Administration, gave a speech about a federal initiative for violence research in which he compared the inner city to a jungle and young men living there to monkeys genetically prone to violence and hypersexuality. Goodwin's ideas suffered a host of conceptual problems, including a view of affluent society as superceding nature (with urban "jungles" a "return to what is more natural"), inference from population-based genetics to group differences, and failure to:

- Consider alternate paths to "antisocial" behavior (Kinner, this volume)
- Distinguish the psychosocial construct of aggression from the sociopolitical one of criminality (Kinner, this volume)
- Appreciate the role of racial and economic bias in the so-called criminal justice system

Politically and ethically, the speech was a disaster.[4] Had he meant to, Goodwin hardly could have done a better job of invoking negative stereotypes about African American men. He showed sensitivity to cost-effectiveness but none to social justice, despite a well-publicized legacy of racism in government-sponsored research (e.g., the Tuskegee syphilis study, psychosurgery and sterilization programs, exclusion from clinical trials). To the contrary, he capitulated to individualism, explaining that targeting inner-city youth for biomedical intervention would be palatable to a public averse to "social engineering of society."

Condemnation of Goodwin's plan was swift and sure. Groups from the Congressional Black Caucus to the Association of Black Psychologists, along with powerful congressmen such as Senator Edward Kennedy (D-Massachusetts) and Representative John Dingell (D-Michigan), killed the initiative and secured Goodwin's resignation. The initiative and Goodwin's job, however, were not the only casualties. For good measure, Kennedy and Dingell declared that knowledge about nonhuman primates "is a preposterous basis" for analyzing anything as complex as "the crime and violence that plagues our country today." This omnibus rejection of evolutionary analysis of human behavior far exceeds the scientific, political, and ethical dimensions of the Goodwin episode. As discussed further below (see Overcoming Anthropodenial), much of the passion generated by Goodwin's remarks stems not from partisanship or ideology but from the profound offense taken by many people—across party, color, and cultural lines—at being reminded that they are animals. Every person involved in the episode (and reading this volume) is a primate that shares more than 90% of its genome with monkeys and more than 98% with *Pan* species (chimpanzees and bonobos). Yet the sense that humans are not animals is so keen that references to one's (or one's group's) animal nature are fighting words.

An irony in the Goodwin episode is that all parties appeared to share the view that humans have slipped the surly bonds of animalhood. Goodwin's critics did not suggest that he erred by failing to compare everyone to monkeys. Rather, in the tradition of John the Elephant Man ("I am not an animal!") Merrick, they protested that they were "not animals" (e.g., Schiller Institute, 2001), that humanhood was being reserved for groups other than African American men. Indeed, by comparing the inner city to the jungle and inner city youth to monkeys, Goodwin did imply that a comparison to monkeys was less apt for, say, a white suburbanite who shoots his wife, beats his son's hockey coach to death, or wants to personally bomb Afghanistan and Iraq back to the Stone Age. If asked directly, Goodwin surely would plead good intentions and agree that all humans belong to the same species. But it is too late. Because African Americans, indigenous peoples, and other groups often have been denied status as human beings, the time to appreciate their and their allies' point of view and the true meaning of a comparative perspective on violence was before an ill-advised policy was formulated.

Contemporary evolutionary thinking about human behavior encompasses many ideas dear to the Left—reciprocity, social responsibility, coalition politics, nonviolent conflict resolution, gender equity, crucial roles for social learning and culture, and others. Unfortunately, many left-leaning people are scared away from this treasure trove by inaccurate, clumsy or naïve depictions of it, not to mention the racial-superiority campaigns by the likes of J. Philippe Rushton. The usefulness of an evolutionary approach to the Left's agenda will only be appreciated when their righteous concern about it is addressed.

## Right and Left Teamed Against Evolution: A Case Study

So often, the political Right and Left are at odds with each other about the way the world does or should work. Sometimes, however, they find themselves on the same side of an issue, pursuing a common objective for different reasons. A case in point is a resolution introduced in the Louisiana legislature in May of 2001 by Representative Sharon Weston Broome (HCR-74). It read in part:

Be it resolved that the Legislature of Louisiana does hereby deplore all instances and ideologies of racism, and does hereby reject the core concepts of Darwinist ideology that certain races and classes of humans are inherently superior to others.

Here, then, was a measure that equated evolution with Darwin, declared it an ideology rather than a scientific theory, linked it explicitly to a social evil and, on its face, was progressive. It was politically clever, daring opponents to vote against a condemnation of racism.

The House Education Committee passed the resolution, but not unanimously: All six Democrats voted "yeah" and were joined by three Republicans; the other five Republicans voted "nay." The measure fared less well in the full House, passing only in an amended form that condemned racism with no reference to evolution or Darwin. One interpretation of this measure's fate is crass party politics. This fits with the fact that 100% of the opposition in committee and the later amendment came from Republicans. However, the full House membership has a strong Democratic majority (70%) and still approved only the evolution-free amended bill. The House is overwhelmingly white (80%), so perhaps the bill was wrestled to the ground by politicians—Democrat and Republican—unmoved by racial oppression, civil rights, and the leadership of the African American woman who sponsored the resolution.

These analyses may have some merit, given the complexities of race, gender, party affiliation, and ideology in Southern politics. They ignore, however, the substantive themes in the debate. The first, obvious theme is the putative link between evolution and racism, which resonates particularly with the Left. Tracing modern racism back to Darwin may be a canard, but it is a scholarly sounding one that appeals to deep, authentic suspicion as well as to political opportunism (see also Science Wars, below). Its flaws were exposed in testimony from Joseph Graves, professor of evolutionary biology and African American studies at Arizona State University (see Foreword). An expert on evolution, philosophy of science, and the race/genetics debate (Graves, 2001), he explained how the Darwin-to-racism claim is "historically inaccurate and grossly misrepresents the history of racism in the Western world," how "in the historical balance, Charles Darwin was one of the good guys," and how, perversely, minorities already underrepresented in the sciences would suffer most from the resolution's likely impact on education (cited in Conley, 2001).

The second, less obvious theme is the Religious Right's crusade against evolution. Some facts suggest that the resolution was motivated by a hidden agenda—the teaching of creationism in the schools. The resolution did refer to the need to revise curricula, and Broome indicated, more specifically, that passage of the resolution would require disclaimers in science textbooks regarding evolution—a creationist strategy that has been implemented in several states and attempted in others. She had served on the state advisory board for the Christian Coalition and earned a graduate degree from a university founded by fundamentalist Pat Robertson. In addition, testimony supporting the resolution was offered by a representative from Concerned Women for America, an organization that promotes the teaching of creationism. Finally, the Darwin-to-racism claim figures prominently in the writings of creationists such as Henry Morris, founder of the Institute for Creation Research,[5] who, in *The Troubled Waters of Evolution* (1974), proclaimed that "evolutionary thinking is at the root of modern racism and racial conflicts" (as cited in Conley, 2001).

The religious motive for this resolution juxtaposes the agendas of the Left and Right in a peculiar way. Protestant Fundamentalism, especially in the South, has historical ties to the civil rights movement, coalition politics, and leaders from the African American community, such as the Reverend Martin Luther King Jr.. On the other hand, Protestant Fundamentalism also is central to the U.S. white supremacist movement. Would that the political pursuits of creationists were associated only with the noble alliance with progressives for civil rights, but apparently they are not. For example, after pinning racism on Darwin in one book, Henry Morris wrote in another:

Often the Hamites, especially the Negroes, have become actual personal servants or even slaves to the others. Possessed of a genetic character concerned mainly with mundane matters, they have eventually been displaced by the intellectual and philosophical acumen of the Japhethites and the religious zeal of the Semites. (in *The Beginning of the World*, 1991, as cited by Trott, undated)

Ironically, then, creationist cosmology has spawned both condemnation of evolution as racist and doctrine about God's design of genetically different human castes. Although the Bible arguably has been used more extensively than Darwin to justify racist policies, no ban on it is pending in Louisiana. Rather, it is being used as a platform from which to launch multiracial, multiparty attacks on evolution. (See Scott, undated, for a wry commentary on this double standard.)

The vigilance of African Americans and other disenfranchised groups to oppressive schemes, especially from government and science, is prudent. Their distrust has been earned. Sadly, though, that vigilance can be exploited in harmful ways. A tragic example is the popularity of conspiracy theories about AIDS. According to one version, AIDS was developed by the U.S. government in a genocidal plot to kill black and gay people. In a 1995 *Miami Herald* survey, two-thirds of the African Americans surveyed either believed in or were undecided about this theory. Other versions reject the idea that HIV causes AIDS or is sexually transmitted. Adherents including ACT UP-San Francisco and South African President Thabo Mbeki have stymied efforts to control and treat AIDS, such as safe-sex practices and AZT treatment for pregnant women. The case of the Louisiana evolution-and-racism resolution similarly is a brew of understandable suspicion, bad information, and murky political motives.

There is no doubt that upon reading the title of this volume, many on the far Right will assume a tome of godlessness, anarchy, and moral rot, while some on the far Left will assume an apologia for an oppressive status quo. Little can be done to prevent such prejudices and the out-of-hand rejection they ensure. However, healthy alliances of moderates on the Left and Right are possible. In the case of evolutionary perspectives on violence, their emergence will depend on identification of common goals, sound education about what evolution does and does not imply, and trust. Where the will for constructive alliance exists, this volume should be a useful tool.

## The Science Wars

The intrigues of academe are fascinating to academics but utterly uninteresting to most everyone else. Bearing this interest gap in mind, how evolution has fared in the academic arena is outlined here only briefly, to highlight those threads in the fabric of this story about history and politics. Lengthy analyses of the Science Wars can be found elsewhere (e.g., Gross & Levitt, 1997; Ross, 1996).

Evolution, as fact and theory, is the bedrock of contemporary biological science around the world. Due to the overwhelming evidence for macroevolution on Earth, its occurrence is granted in biology departments everywhere, excepting the odd American creationist holdout. Evolutionary theory has developed far beyond Darwin's germinal notion of natural selection or "survival of the fittest." It is a vibrant enterprise, with lively debates about the processes through which species and their attributes arise—individual versus group selection, gradual accretion versus punctuated equilibrium, environmentally sensitive mutation rates, reproductive isolation and genetic drift, and so on. Evolution provides a research framework that is rare in its unifying potential.

In academe generally, interdisciplinarity has blossomed in the last decade, with collaborations springing up between departments and divisions on campuses around the world. "Area studies" bridge sociology, anthropology, literature, and political science. Behavioral neuroscience bridges psychobiology, physics, and chemistry. Cognitive science bridges psychology, biology, philosophy, and math. Evolution is a key player in some of these emerging fields. For example, at the First International Conference on Social Cognitive Neuroscience in 2001, evolutionary biologists, political scientists, social and experimental psychologists, anthropologists, philosophers, and neuroscientists explored cells-to-society models of empathy, prejudice, intersubjectivity, and other topics. Scholars everywhere are reaching across disciplinary boundaries in exciting ways, enriching themselves, their students, and our understanding of the world.

Yet a deep rift between the humanities and the "traditional" sciences—biology, chemistry, physics[6]—has precluded integrative, consilient (Wilson, 1998) understandings of human behavior. The stage for the drama may have been set by the prehistorical roots of human yin and yang, Descartes's body/soul dualism (1600s), and the Age of Reason (1700s). By the mid-twentieth century, what C.P. Snow (1959) called "the two cultures" were entrenched:

Literary intellectuals at one pole—at the other the scientists. . . . Between the two a gulf of mutual incomprehension–sometimes (particularly among the young) hostility and dislike, but most of all a lack of understanding. (p. 4)

During the 1960s to 1970s in the United States, the Science Wars heated up as progressive-Left factions in sociology, anthropology, and history joined the humanities against the "traditional" sciences. The terms of the battle shifted in the 1980s to 1990s, when English translations of 1960s to 1970s European philosophy gave birth to American postmodernism. Postmodern attention to class, race, sexuality, and gender suggests a natural alliance with the Left; indeed, adherents have been called the "academic left." That label, however, is misleading: Postmodernists eschew the Left's progressive liberal agenda on grounds that it shares with traditional science untenable Enlightenment-era assumptions about the nature of truth and knowledge. From postmodernism emerged an antiscience, antiliberal sensibility within academe that in many institutions catalyzed tension into civil war.

Use of military metaphor here could be criticized, but it is used advisedly. As suggested by Snow's quote, the rift between the two academic cultures is not a collegial debate. Attempts at rapprochement are drowned out regularly by recrimination, disdain, and vicious attacks. At two major research universities (Stanford and Duke), the acrimony culminated in the cleaving of the anthropology department into two independent units, with biological anthropology home to the "traditional" science orientation (Naturalist Side) and cultural anthropology home to the postmodern orientation (Postmodern Side). A comparable rift has deepened divisions within many psychology departments.

How, then, to understand the contemporary conflict? Substantively, it can be distilled to tension between the Naturalist pursuit of general rules of the physical universe and the Postmodern pursuit of particular, culturally situated interpretations of life. Equipped primarily with quantitative tools, Naturalists aim to *discover* how the world works; Postmodernists, equipped primarily with qualitative tools, study how meaning is *created* in social contexts. Beyond this, characterization of the two sides would be fruitless. For one thing, it could not be neutral. For another, neither position is unitary: The Naturalist camp is home to everything from particle physics to experimental social psychology, and the Postmodern camp is home to social constructivism, critical and feminist theory, science studies, and other projects.

A more important reason for avoiding elaboration is that the details of the two substantive positions, as irreconcilable as some are, do not account for the acrimony. The communication gap Snow identified decades ago is a major culprit. Over time, barriers to constructive exchange have grown tall and thick. There is no common language (or "discourse") to serve as a medium for discussion. Many scientists, for instance, would be baffled by "conversation on the project of problematizing the privileged, patriarchal discourse of objectivism by interrogating the aporia of truth and binary opposition."

In addition, recruits to each camp now are exposed to secondhand (mis)representations of the other camp's tenets more than to the tenets themselves. The derivative nature of understanding on both sides has been aggravated by the crisis in K–12 education and specialization in higher education. Through a sort of intellectual reproductive isolation, new generations of Naturalists are taught little about philosophy whereas budding Postmodernists are taught little about science. Many *do* learn about how each side is perceived by the other, that is, that Postmodernists are incomprehensible naysayers who disguise sloppy thinking with winks and nods, whereas Naturalists are operatives of oppressive powers-that-be, smug money-grubbers wholly lacking in insight. Aspirants who would like to learn more are warned against taking the other side too seriously, lest they waste time or, worse, be tainted by it.

Although most academics are either disinterested in the conflict or manage equanimity, two relatively small groups of more vocal, more polarized, and polarizing individuals prosecute this internecine warfare. In the academic context, this manifests as fights over faculty positions, tenure, student loyalty, and control of resources. The conflict has all the hallmarks of classic intergroup bias, that is, in-group favoritism and out-group derogation (Fishbein & Dess, Solomon et al., this volume). At its worst, it is the academic equivalent of the Israeli-Palestinian conflict—vitriole, subterfuge, martyrdom, and protracted battle that renders the contested turf uninhabitable unless a sensible, fair resolution is achieved.

Evolutionary thinking has suffered in the Science Wars in two ways. First, by virtue of presumed location within the Naturalist camp, evolution has been critiqued by Postmodernists as a potentially inappropriate and immoral paradigm for addressing human behavior (for a primer, see Slife & Williams, 1995[7])—inappropriate, to the extent that applying the methods of "natural science" to humans wrongly assumes that they are "natural objects" (Slife & Williams, pp. 198–199), and immoral to the extent that evolutionary reasoning entails genetic determinism and biological reductionism, by which the "agency, meaning, and morality of human life are threatened" (p. 158). Determinism and reductionism also carry the historical baggage of Nazism and other eugenics programs (see Challenges from the Left, above), a red flag that Postmodernists hoist when evolution comes up, as did vanguards of the Left before them.[8]

These critiques impede full participation of evolutionarily minded scientists in policy work. Fortunately, defusing them is relatively easy. One can:

- Agree that everything one knows is, by definition, human knowledge and unavoidably influenced by culture
- Acknowledge that one assumes rather than knows that humans belong to the natural world
- Endorse a soft reductionism, that is, assume some coherence and stability in a physical universe at many levels of organization, while rejecting genetic determinism as straw argument.

These replies simply demonstrate a rudimentary understanding of the nature of science (see Rutherford & Ahlgren, 1991, Chapter 1) and modern evolutionary thought (see False Dichotomies, below). One can further stipulate that ethologist Konrad Lorenz was a Nazi, noting, in fairness, that this is not true of Dutch ethologist Niko Tinbergen, who survived Nazi persecution to accept the 1973 Nobel Prize with him—but *is* true of philosopher Martin Heidegger, a founding father of postmodernism. Identifying common ground, agreeing to disagree, and widening the lens of historical retrospectives can lower the temperature and narrow the gap between camps. An excellent example may be found in Wheeler Vega's (2001) incisive examination of the dispute between feminist and evolutionary scholars over Thornhill & Palmer's (2000) book, *A Natural History of Rape* (see also Mealey, this volume).

The second cost to evolutionary reasoning of the Science Wars is the lost potential for collaboration with differently trained people who are smart and thoughtful. Aside from those most committed to the Wars, plenty of academics are eager to engage substantive issues in a serious, productive way. Evolutionarily minded scientists can find within the postmodern universe colleagues with whom they can begin to communicate and from whom they can learn a great deal. Past the rancor and between naïve claims to scientific objectivity and postmodern nihilism, there is common ground. For instance, social constructivists assume that human knowledge is constructed in a cultural context and that humans (including scientists) can "know" things for which there is no referent in empirical reality; these assumptions about human meaning-making are entirely compatible with evolutionary theory and empirical evidence (Donald, 1991; Schumaker, 1995; Solomon et al., this volume). Together, evolutionarily minded scientists and postmodern-leaning colleagues also could usefully explore the possibility of *meaning* in the lives of animals without language or cultural institutions, compare views of diversity and "universality" from exclusively human versus comparative perspectives, and so on.

Passionate debate is healthy, but venom is not. The Science Wars—in the latter sense—have not been good for national policy. In a speech to academics in 1997, Representative Vern Ehlers (R-Michigan) noted that the emergence of an antiscience philosophy had driven Snow's "two cultures" further apart and charged the audience with responsibility for bridging them (Jones, 1997). Everyone—most of all, the world beyond academe—will benefit when proliferation of models for productive, civil exchange reduces the Science Wars to a skirmish and, finally, to a chapter in academic history.

## CONCEPTUAL HABITS IN NEED OF BREAKING

History and politics operate at a social and institutional level to influence evolution's standing in policy discussions. This section addresses five conceptual habits that operate at the individual level to influence discussions and collective decision making. Although interrelated, they are distinguished here to facilitate the development of habit-breaking strategies. These habits have outlived any usefulness they may once have had and/or are demonstrably wrong. In either case, it is time for renewed efforts at giving them up.

### Deconstructing False Dichotomies

Humans can think holistically as well as categorically. As it happens, people in Western cultures are prone to categorical thought (Nisbett et al., 2001). This propensity manifests in the persistence of false dichotomies in thinking about behavior. A prime example is the so-called "nature versus nature" debate, in which "nature" refers to genes and "nurture" refers to environmental events. The dichotomy pits genetic determinism against radical environmentalism. According to the former, behavior unfolds from genes in a predictable way, like a blueprint. According to the latter, environmental contingencies and contexts control behavior. The dichotomy gives rise to questions such as, "Is violence caused by genes or upbringing?"

Although this sort of question still appears in public discourse and some textbooks, in science the "nature-nurture" debate" is a red herring. Genetic endowment and environmental influences are inextricably intertwined. As David Lykken put it in *The Antisocial Personalities* (1995), "Without experience, a genotype is nothing more than a damp spot on the carpet" (p. 85). Recursive, reciprocal gene/environment interactions at individual (Plomin & Neiderhiser, 1992) and cultural (Deacon, 1998; Donald, 1991) levels figure prominently in contemporary theories. Ideas about development, learning, and natural selection turn on how the environment influences gene expression and, therefore, actually creates the phenotypes on which various selective pressures then act. Put simply, deterministic, either/or thinking about the role of genes and the environment in behavior is obsolete. Their relationship clearly is a probabilistic, transactional one (see Gottlieb, 2000, for a highly readable overview).

The interaction between genes and experience has been amply demonstrated with respect to aggression. In rhesus monkeys, impulsive aggressiveness varies considerably among individuals (Suomi, 1999). Inappropriate aggression often leads to social ostracism, which, for a highly social animal, is an enormous liability. In the wild, inappropriately aggressive young males are driven out of the troop, usually to an early death. Impulsive aggression has been linked to a low level of the neurotransmitter serotonin, which, in turn, has been linked to one form of a particular gene (LS allele for 5-HTT). It may seem, then, that this gene is a "risk factor" for bad social outcomes. It turns out, however, that monkeys with the gene are social losers only if they are peer reared; with maternal care, they grow up to be unusually socially competent. Gene/environment interactions also influence aggression in mice (Miczek, Maxson, Fish, & Faccidomo, 2001) and people (see Kinner, this volume, on individual differences and Masters, this volume, on omnibus effects).

Suomi's research demonstrates that the very same gene that puts an individual "at risk" of an undesirable outcome also may put the individual "at risk" of a desirable one. The behavioral expression of genes and its consequences for the animal depend critically on rearing and other circumstances. People intent on identifying and eliminating "bad" behavior genes would do well to heed this lesson. Although examples from behavioral genetics focus on understanding variation among individuals, the basic principle—that the biological potential for aggression does not ordain it—applies just as well at the group and species level.

Another false dichotomy concerns whether humans are by nature violent or peaceful. Is Nature the "state of war" asserted by Hobbes and "red in tooth and claw" as imagined by Tennyson or is it, as per Rousseau, a peaceable kingdom? A look around the globe at the tremendous variation in how violent or peaceable different cultures makes this seem like a sensible question: Which condition represents our true nature, and which represents our nature trumped by circumstances? As beguiling as this question may be, it makes more sense in terms of habits of mind—dichotomous thinking, determinism, literary archetypes, worst fears, or highest aspirations—than as a question worth answering. The study of human cultures over time and comparative research with diverse primate species clearly indicates that aggression and peacemaking are both integral parts of the human social/motivational repertoire; moreover, they interact in a complex fashion, sometimes appearing mutually inhibitory and other times appearing synergistic or dialectical. Numerous works from psychology, anthropology, primatology, and other fields support this emerging view of human nature and how individual and cultural experience influences its expression (e.g., Aureli & de Waal, 2000; de Waal, 1989a, b; Robarchek & Robarchek, 1997; Ury, 2002). Humans have a capacity for cruelty and killing unequalled by other species. We also have the ability to proactively prevent aggression by building prosocial affiliations, deescalate aggression by literally or figuratively turning the other cheek, and reconcile after fights to restore or strengthen relationships—even to make friends with former mortal enemies. Although conflict may be inevitable, violence is not. It is within humans' nature to avert it and foster peaceableness.

Policy decisions grounded in either pole of the nature/nurture or violent/peaceful dichotomies will err in terms of the populations they target or the over- or underestimation of potential impact of interventions. For example, a belief that males are "innately" aggressive is consistent with school policies and economic institutions that encourage ritualized violence and tacitly condone "penalty" violence in the context of contact sports (Conroy et al., 2001; Silva, 1983). More generally, a belief in a violent human nature—allowing for, perhaps, a modest amount of early childhood malleability—can lead to underestimation of the ability of individuals and entire groups to abandon seemingly entrenched violent norms for a more peaceful existence (Robarchek & Robarchek, 1997). Despite being at odds with empirical evidence and counterproductive, these dichotomies have been kept alive by the powerful emotional, political, and ideological forces addressed above (History and Politics), and by the proclivity of the Western mind for dualisms. They might lose some of its appeal if these coercive influences are exposed and the research providing persuasive alternative models is more widely disseminated.

## Overcoming Anthropodenial

In *The Ape and the Sushi Master*, Frans de Waal (2001) observes, "I often get the impression of being surrounded by two distinct categories of people: those who do and those who don't mind being compared with animals" (p. 10). Although people do seem to vary in this way, the former attitude is more deeply rooted in Western culture than is the latter. In the united States, pointing out that someone is an animal generally is not considered a compliment. Indeed, a snarled "They are animals!" is often aimed at whole groups of people behaving in ways culturally associated with "base instincts" and impaired human faculties such as intellect and moral reasoning. It is ironic that the behavior earning the epithet often is massively destructive or sadistic behavior for which there is no parallel in other species.

De Waal coined the term "anthropodenial" to refer to the rejection of humans' animalness. Although it may vary across individuals and cultural groups, there is evidence that it is deeply rooted in human evolution. Specifically, humans' cognitive capabilities compel awareness of our corporeal nature and mortality. Thoughts about "creatureliness," then, elicit a primal terror against which we vigorously defend through intergroup bias, the quashing of in-group dissent, and belief in an afterlife (Goldenberg et al., 2001). Thus, the tendency to resist thinking about human behavior in the context of continuity with other species is culturally endorsed and proximately reinforced by anxiety reduction.

Anthropodenial stands in the way of evolutionary reasoning because humans' continuity with other species is an inescapable implication of evolution. Fortunately, it is a habit of mind that can be managed. First, evolutionary reasoning also implies human uniqueness, and people who wish or need to focus on ways in which humans are different from other animals can be edified by that differentness. Second, the power of animalness reminders to elicit anxiety is probably can be defused by high self-esteem and strong, secure attachments early in life (Florian & Mikulincer, 1998; Mikulincer & Florian, 2000). Therefore, its power can be attenuated with policies promoting psychological wellness and high quality child care. Overcoming anthopodenial in these ways would increase receptiveness to evolutionary reasoning, as well as emotionally satisfying appreciation for the creaturely world of which we are a part.

## Challenging Aggression Myths

Cultural mythology about the nature of aggression can be antithetical to effective problem solving. An example is the construction of extreme or collective violence as inexplicable. In the aftermath of the Columbine school massacre, for instance, a commentary in the *Los Angeles Times* was entitled, "Seeking to Make Sense Where There Is None" (Hewitt, 1999). Another example is the construction of violence as madness—something of which "normal," "rational" people are incapable. To be sure, there are instances of violence that are, at first, difficult to comprehend and for which a role for bona fide mental illness is plausible—such as the man with a brain tumor who climbed a campus tower in 1966 and shot 46 people, killing 15, and the Houston mother reportedly suffering from severe postpartum depression who drowned her five children in 2001. Yet even these are not simple cases. The first—of Charles Whitman—included a history of domestic violence and combat training, the second—of Andrea Yates—social isolation, the overwhelming demands of a large family, and a religious fundamentalist belief system in which her despair was readily understood as the Devil's doing. Similarly, attributing violence on a large scale, such as genocide, to chaos or the mind of a madman is belied by the degree of organization and number of individuals necessary to prosecute the campaign.

From media sensations to the commonplace, then, violence is amenable to systematic analysis in terms of distal (evolutionary, developmental) and proximate (e.g., neurochemical, social context) factors that fuel or moderate (e.g., impulse control; Masters, this volume) aggressive behavior. One can indeed "make sense" of the Columbine tragedy. As represented in the media in recent years, a recurrent theme in school shootings is that of revenge by boys harassed by peers and lacking high-quality adult supervision (see quotes in Solomon et al., this volume). Consistent with this depiction, aggression is elevated among children who are "bully-victims" (both bully and are bullied) and who were physically abused by caregivers (Salmivalli & Nieminen, 2002; Shields & Cicchetti, 2001); moreover, aggressiveness is more "power based" among boys than among girls (Roland & Idsoe, 2001). Related observations have been made in other species. For example, young male hamsters exposed to aggressive adults during puberty are more likely to later attack smaller hamsters than are nonsubjugated controls (Delville et al., 1998), and young orphaned male elephants lacking supervision by adult bulls can become violent gangs, even engaging in the highly unusual practice of killing rhinoceroses (Slotow et al., 2000). Add cultural support for male aggressiveness (e.g., violent mass media, sports, video games) and human weaponry that renders physical prowess moot (high-powered rifles, semiautomatic handguns), and the mysteriousness of episodes like Columbine yields to understanding.

Construals of violence as incomprehensible or mad are themselves understandable. Several factors likely contribute to them. First, they may (accurately) reflect our inability to predict precisely the who/what/when/where of many violent outbursts. Despite all the factors that have been identified as important to aggression, "point predictions" remain probabilistic, and especially elusive with respect to rare, devastating cases. Being unable to confidently predict the next outburst creates a sense of randomness that can be interpreted as fundamental inexplicability. Second, these construals may serve the psychically protective function of scapegoating individuals or out-groups, the resulting distancing of which decreases the sense of personal vulnerability to becoming a perpetrator or victim (e.g., Link et al., 1999).

Finally there is the matter of reducing our sense of responsibility for solving problems, either personally or collectively through policy. Cultural constructions of cosmic order or disorder and of normalcy versus deviance are socialized deeply and experienced noetically—viscerally, as unequivocally true. Not all violence is perceived as morally reprehensible; killing (as in war or the death penalty) or brutality (as in boxing) can be positively socially sanctioned. But violence that is perceived as reprehensible appears to call first for blame—finding the evildoers and giving them their just desserts—and only later, if at all, for dispassionate understanding. That is, people are prone to conflating causal analysis of a problem with moral judgment, to analyzing a problem in terms of assigning responsibility, that is, determining who should act (or should have acted) rather than identifying variables contributing to the events' oc-currence (Brickman et al., 1982). The tendency in Western cultures in particular is to eschew assignment of shared responsibility or attributions to society rather than to individuals, be they perpetrators or victims (see Ideology, above). So it is that proclaiming that one can *understand* why Ted Bundy, the serial killer, murdered dozens of women often is *heard* as exoneration of him, when the latter are is not implied at all.

This conflation of understanding and blame is apparent in the courtroom (Bloom, this volume). A startlingly clear example occurred in Maryland in 1994. Kenneth Peacock had come home unexpectedly and found his wife, San-dra, in bed with another man; several hours later, he shot her in the head with a hunting rifle (see Buss, this volume). Although Peacock could have received 25 years in prison, Judge Robert E. Cahill sentenced him to just 18 months— and that, reluctantly, with a recommendation for work release—saying, "I se-riously wonder how many men married five, four years would have the strength to walk away without inflicting some corporal punishment. I am forced to impose a sentence . . . only because I think I must do it to make the system honest" (*Los Angeles Times*, 1994). Clearly, the judge's view of mate homicide as understandable under the circumstances was conflated with the moral and legal judgment he rendered, to an extent exceeding the conflation generally codified in law.

The tendency to conflate causal analysis with moral judgment of individuals can stimulate policy processes directed more at assignment of blame, retribu-tion, sympathy, and deservingness than at analysis and problem solving (e.g., Appelbaum, 2001). The American public's enthusiasm for harsh criminal pen-alties, the boom in the prison industry, and the political virtue of being "tough on crime"—all despite overwhelming evidence from many species that pun-ishment is an impractical, ineffective way of managing behavior—can be un-derstood in these terms.

In terms of public policy, these myths about violence afford shortsighted, inadequate perspectives. Violence occurs for a reason. An affirmative, ambitious agenda of understanding the complex underpinnings of violence and combining that knowledge with prudential judgment (Arnhart, 1998) will, in the long run, more effectively reduce its likelihood overall and in high-risk situations and populations. In terms of utilizing an evolutionary perspective, this agenda must include replacing simplistic "naturalistic fallacies" (i.e., what is "natural" is good and right) with more sophisticated views of humans' behavioral, cog-nitive, cultural, and moral nature.

## Avoiding Oversimplification

Simplicity is appealing. People often respond well to a simple explanation. Policymakers, advertisers, and others exploit this fact when they sweep away gray areas and complexities, declaring them mumbo jumbo and asserting instead an unadorned, "plainspoken" truth. Scientists also admire simplicity, in the form of parsimony: Given two explanations that are equally valid accounts of a phenomenon, they prefer the simpler one. But as Albert Einstein warned, "Things should be made as simple as possible—but no simpler." The third challenge to developing evolutionary sound policy resides in the unique complexity of human social life.

Violence and its antidotes occur at intrapersonal, interpersonal, intergroup, and international levels of organization. Aggression research tends to focus on one or another level. Choice of focus may reflect closely held theoretical or metatheoretical positions (Bloom, this volume), but also may reflect personal interests or aptitudes and pragmatic issues, such as time constraints on how many interesting ideas one can pursue. Whatever the reasons, separate endeavors on different levels leave open the question of how mechanisms critical at one level relate to mechanisms at other levels. Take the example of silicofluorides (SiFs) and impulsive aggression (Masters, this volume). Assuming the validity of the key arguments—that impulse control has been critical to moderation of violence in human evolution, that SiFs interact with heavy metals to compromise its brain mechanisms, and that this makes violence more likely where SiFs are high—important questions also must be addressed at the social structural level. For instance, what sociopolitical forces lead to the unequal distribution of SiFs, and to what extent do those forces also shape *violent crime statistics* as opposed to violence itself? Research on environmental racism (e.g., Allen, 2001) and on the inequitable treatment of minorities and the poor at many points in the so-called criminal justice system (e.g., Poe-Yamagata & Jones, 2000) provides some pieces to this puzzle. Moving from one level of analysis to another, however, does not require leaving an evolutionary framework. The macrolevel politics of any primate are as amenable to evolutionary analysis as is brain function (e.g., Boehm, this volume; de Waal, 1989a; Masters, 1989). But human politics—of, for instance, race and class—are complicated, and those undertaking such an analysis will benefit from collaboration with differently minded people.

Another example in the same vein is discrimination between in- and outgroups, a process central to intergroup conflict in many species (Fishbein & Dess, Solomon et al., this volume): Does the same apply to interpersonal conflict, such as domestic partner abuse (Buss, this volume), with gender mediating "in-group" and "out-group" identities? Perhaps so (Reitz, 1999); this should be the case if a dialectical relationship between self and others undergirds all social relationships (Guisinger & Blatt, 1994). But perhaps not (Jennings & Murphy, 2000). Or perhaps violence in intergroup and interpersonal contexts are the same in some ways but differ in others (Romero, 1985).

A final example comes from research on prosocial physical touch. Touch is an essential factor from the earliest moments of any mammal's life, playing a critical role in physical, behavioral, emotional, and social development (Field,

2001). Touch is a key component of affiliation, including conflict resolution, among social mammals (see Challenges from the Right, above). According to Robin Dunbar in *Grooming, Gossip, and the Evolution of Language* (1998), some social functions of touch were assumed by language as the size of stable human groups grew, with concomitant evolution of brain structures. How fully does symbolic communication "substitute" for physical touch in terms of affiliation? Are the same brain and hormonal systems activated by a kind word as by a hug and, if so, at what age do they converge? Does a nod of assent seal a deal as firmly as does a handshake? Can mass symbolic communication foster peacemaking as effectively as direct intimate contact? Conceptualizing how reconciliation and peacemaking are the same and how they differ on scales from dyad to globe will be crucial to designing policies that will succeed on those scales.

Avoiding oversimplification and, instead, cutting across the different levels at which complex social phenomena such as violence and peacemaking are organized is a thorny but important challenge: To the extent that mechanisms of intergroup and interpersonal violence are shared, interventions aimed at early, common antecedents will be effective and efficient. To the extent that the mechanisms are more idiosyncratic to contexts, interventions will have to be tailored to those contexts. As a first step toward accurately assessing continuities and discontinuities across levels of analysis, researchers and policymakers should develop a shared conceptual framework for thinking about those levels—a framework as simple as it can be, but no simpler.

### Bridling Wishful Thinking

The final challenge consists of wishful thinking about constraints on human violence. Many a candidate for what distinguishes humans from all other species has been advanced: toolmaking, tool use, an outsized neocortex, a self-concept, facility with numbers, language, political savvy, culture. As psychologists, anthropologists, and biologists have learned more about other species, these candidates have, one by one, lost some or all of their luster. One candidate yet to stumble is wishful thinking—the ability to conjure up a past, present, or future far rosier than reality may warrant. As far as we know, only humans have the cognitive ability to construct from whole cloth psychological and cultural realities with emotional, behavioral, social, and moral force (Schumaker, 1995). Wishful thinking has many rewards. Individuals who overestimate the degree of control they have over events, underestimate their foibles, and generally expect good things to happen are at lower risk of anxiety, depression, and associated health outcomes (Taylor, 1991); the collective benefits of cultural worldviews were described by Solomon et al. (this volume).

Surely, though, the benefits of "positive illusions" are not limitless. Relevant in the present context are instances of wishful thinking with particularly faulty premises, which, if used in the formulation of policy, can be expected to impede effective problem solving. One example derives from the idea discussed above (False Dichotomies) that humans are innately peaceable. A corollary is that violence is "unnatural" and thus psychologically aversive for the perpetrator—that is, motivated by unpleasant emotions such as anger or fear and, at best, a necessary evil or impulse for all but the true psychopath (Kinner, this volume). There can be no doubt that committing violence against others can psychologically wound the perpetrator. In *An Intimate History of Killing: Face to Face Killing in 20th Century Warfare,* for example, Bourke (1999) presents heart-wrenching accounts of shame, fear, and guilt associated with warfare and describes the intensive measures often needed to train men to kill. Juxtaposed against this sorrowful tableau, though, she documents how killing is experienced by many combatants as thrilling, a "joyful slaughter" (p. 18). An illustrative case in a chapter titled "The Pleasures of War" reads:

I secured a direct hit on an enemy encampment, saw bodies or parts of bodies go up in the air, and heard the desperate yelling of the wounded or the runaways. I had to confess to myself that it was one of the happiest moments of my life. (Henry de Man, quoted on p. 19)

Bourke summarizes, "Fear, anxiety, pain; these are only too familiar in combat. But excitement, joy, and satisfaction were equally fundamental emotions, inspired by imagining that they had scored a good, clean 'kill'" (p. 31).

Although Bourke focuses on face-to-face combat, her psychological analysis of violence in that context likely generalizes to violence in other contexts. In the early 1990s, it was hard to miss the excitement in the cockpit-taped voices of American pilots successfully targeting Iraqi ground forces during Desert Storm. The accoutrements of killing in war—glee or steely coldness, unprovoked attack, atrocities, trophies, stalking, planning and intentionality, and so on—are recognizable in reports of violence in humans and other species of many kinds (e.g., predatory and/or affective aggression; Vitielo & Stoff, 1997; also Fishbein & Dess and Buss, this volume). Preventing violence and promoting peaceableness are worthy policy goals for many reasons, including minimizing the psychological harm to violence perpetrators. However, interventions to reduce violence should not be designed on the premise that anticipating, engaging in, or remembering violence is, fundamentally, either emotionally aversive *or* positive. The temporal dynamics and context dependency of subjective experience of aggression are far more complicated than that.

Another bit of wishful thinking is an idyllic view of how peace can be achieved. In this halcyon vision, happiness and contentment beget peace: The young live stress-free lives, surrounded by doting, peaceable adult models and, thus, only peaceableness and its concomitants can fill their growing behavioral and psychological quiver. Children *do* learn a great deal from observing others and the consequences of their behavior, as famously demonstrated by Albert Bandura in the "Bobo doll" studies of the social learning of aggression. Clearly,

availability of models of nonviolent conflict resolution and other prosocial behaviors have a key role to play in the development of peaceableness, as do
physical affection and other aspects of high-quality child rearing (see Fishbein
& Dess, Kinner, Solomon et al., this volume; Hrdy, 1999).

It is tempting, then, to lay plans for promoting peaceableness by eliminating
"obvious" threats to it, from models of and rewards for aggression to unmet
needs, frustrations, anxiety, and negative emotions of other sorts. The problem
is that an agenda for peace that excludes all traces of aggression, distress, or
privation is not only of questionable feasibility but also, quite probably, will
be ineffective. Evidence concerning the coevolution of fear, love, and anger
strongly suggests that the optimal level of anxiety and aggression in human
societies—that is, the level at which peaceableness is maximized—may not be
zero. Among nonhuman primates, intimate contact (hugging, grooming, etc.)
in the face of fear or stress and in the aftermath of hostility is a crucial context
in which affiliative bonds are formed and strengthened from an early age (de
Waal, 1989b, especially Chapter 1; Harlow & Mears, 1983; Silk, 1998). Just as
young cats hone their predatory skills on easy prey provided by adults, young
monkeys and apes learn about coping with stress and reconciliation when they
encounter pint-sized morsels of fear and aggression in a supportive social context.

The same is very likely true for humans. Consider the means by which
unusually peaceful societies keep the peace (Bonta, 1997). Some of these practices are, from an idyllic point of view, shocking. An example is the creation
of double-bind anxiety in children. An Inuit parent may, for instance, teasingly
tell an older child to kill his baby brother, or allow children to cuddle and protect
a small animal then encourage them to kill it. Bonta argues that contradictory
messages—of love and meanness, of trust and mistrust—teach children not to
take for granted others' peaceful intent, rather to be vigilant to and proactive
about threats to peace. He also notes that adults in peaceful societies care ten-
derly for infants but teach them as youngsters that they are nothing special.
For instance, Semai children in Malaysia "quickly learn that they are helpless
to control events around them and are totally dependent on the good will and
support of the group" (p. 302). These strategies, according to Bonta, favor the
development of peaceful social relations over aggressive ones.

Shall we assume, then, that policies that foster childhood anxiety, helplessness and low self-esteem will reduce violence? Hardly. A great deal of psychological research suggests that this would generate undesirable outcomes
including aggressiveness, poor peer relations, depression, even death (Deci &
Ryan, 1995; McLaren & Brown, 1989; Seligman, 1975). So rapid institution-
alization of Inuit or Semai rearing practices in the United States is ill-advised,
models of peaceableness though their societies may be.

The contrast between this literature and the socialization practices gleaned
in Bonta's review seems to comprise a paradox akin to the roller-coaster of

news about whether eating oat bran is healthy. Fortunately, the paradox can be resolved. The cultural context of a particular socialization practice is critical to its effects on child welfare and adult functioning, including aggressiveness. The sort of teasing and "rejection" that Inuit children experience occurs in the context of a community in which:

- They can indeed count on others to meet their needs.
- They learn that they are valuable as group members.
- Peacefulness is culturally valued above aggression.
- Few adult models of violence exist.
- Instances of aggression that do occur are not rewarded.

In such a context, these strategies promote equanimity, albeit not great happiness at all times. Given a cultural worldview that, in contrast, prescribes autonomy, self-sufficiency, and a readiness to fight in response to infractions—U.S. society, for instance—the same strategies may yield instead the psychological and social risks well documented in the predominantly American research literature.

Available evidence, then, does not support an idyllic view of achieving peace by eliminating all insecurities and preventing aggression in all of its forms. Although this may be bad news for dedicated wishful thinkers, it need not kill hope. Cornel West, University Professor at Harvard, has said, "Hope for me has nothing to do with optimism. I am not optimistic. There is not enough evidence out there to convince me that things are going to get better." Hope, he posits, motivates striving despite uncertainty about eventual success, indeed in the face of reason to doubt it. Reducing violence and fostering peace will require simultaneous reforms as grand as a shift in worldviews, as concrete as new daycare policies, and as difficult as embracing all of what it means to be human, not just what we wish to believe about it ourselves. It will require hope.

## CONCLUSION

Scientists, policymakers, and public policy advocates have good reason to be hopeful about improving the human condition by reducing violence and fostering peace. Cross-cultural differences in levels of violence provide prima facie evidence that as a species, we are capable of far more benevolent, just, and healthful living than exists in many places. Grounding policies in the clear-eyed view of the kind of animal that we are—even when the answers belie simple dichotomies and belie precious myths or illusions—offers the greatest chance of achieving these worthy goals.

## NOTES

1. Left aside here is the untenable claim that individualist ideology follows from the "selfish gene" concept. This claim suffers many fatal flaws, chief among them the problem of crossing levels of analysis (gene, individual, group). Extensive critiques are available elsewhere.

2. This is true only to a limited degree. In the last decade, conservatives have led a national campaign to lower the age at which children can be tried as adults, serve hard time, and receive the death penalty.

3. The relationship among gender, politics, violence, and peace has been examined extensively from many theoretical perspectives. The present treatment is limited to a few points relevant to evolutionary thinking.

4. Writer Tom Wolfe (1996) observed of Goodwin's reference to the "jungle": "That may have been the stupidest single word uttered by an American public official in the year 1992."

5. In connection with discussion above of gender and ideology, it is interesting that none of the 29 board members, officers, or representatives governing the Institute for Creation Research is a woman.

6. Common administrative terms for science are problematic. For example, "natural sciences" implies a contrast with unnatural ones, "physical" with metaphysical, "social" with asocial. None is apt, so they are avoided here.

7. These authors of the postmodern persuasion provide an example of a wildly inaccurate view of evolution (pp. 139–140). Note also their effort at distinguishing *identification* of assumptions and *rejection* of them; the interested reader can decide whether they succeed.

8. De Waal (2001), who is Dutch, relates a meeting at the rim of the rift: "An older social psychology once shocked me by reacting to my declaration that I was a European ethologist with 'So, you must be a Nazi!'"

## REFERENCES

Allen, D.W. (2001). Social class, race, and toxic releases in American counties, 1995. *Social Science Journal, 38,* 13–25.

Appelbaum, L. (2001). The influence of perceived deservingness on policy decisions regarding aid to the poor. *Political Psychology, 22,* 419–442.

Arnhart, L. (1998). *Darwinian natural right: The biological ethics of human nature.* Albany: State University of New York Press.

Aureli, F., & de Waal, F.B.M. (2000). *Natural conflict resolution.* Berkeley: University of California Press.

Blumstein, A. (2000). Violence: A new frontier for scientific research. *Science, 289,* 545.

Bonta, B.D. (1997). Cooperation and competition in peaceful societies. *Psychological Bulletin, 121,* 299–320.

Bourke, J. (1999). *An intimate history of killing: Face to face killing in 20th century warfare.* New York: Basic Books.

Brickman, P., Carulli Rabinowitz, V., Karuza Jr., J., Coates, D., Cohn, E., & Kidder, L. (1982). Models of helping and coping. *American Psychologist, 37,* 368–384.

Butler, J.P. (1990). *Gender trouble: Feminism and the subversion of identity.* New York: Routledge.

Caprioli, M., & Boyer, M.A. (2001). Gender, violence, and international crisis. *Journal of Conflict Resolution, 45,* 503–518.

Conley, J. (2001). Is Darwinism racist? Creationists and the Louisiana Darwin-racism controversy. Retrieved at http://www.princeton.edu/~jconley/DarwinRacism, on January 11, 2002.

Conroy, D.E., Silva, J.M., Newcomer, R.R., Walker, B.W., & Johnson, M.S. (2001). Personal and participatory socializers of the perceived legitimacy of aggressive behavior in sport. *Aggressive Behavior, 27,* 405–418.

Day, C.L., & Hadley, C.D. (1997). The importance of attitudes toward women's equality: Policy preferences among Southern party elites. *Social Science Quarterly, 78,* 672–687.

Deacon, T.W. (1998). *The symbolic species: The co-evolution of language and the brain.* New York: W.W. Norton.

Deci, E.L., & Ryan, R.M. (1995). Human autonomy: The basis for true self-esteem. In M.H. Kernis (Ed.), *Efficacy, agency, and self-esteem* (pp. 31–40). New York: Plenum Press.

Delville, Y., Melloni, R.H. Jr., & Ferris, C.F. (1998). Behavioral and neurobiological consequences of social subjugation during puberty in golden hamsters. *Journal of Neuroscience, 18,* 2667–2672.

de Waal, F.B.M. (1989a). *Chimpanzee politics: Power and sex among the apes.* Baltimore, MD: Johns Hopkins University Press.

de Waal, F.B.M. (1989b). *Peacemaking among primates.* Cambridge, MA: Harvard University Press.

de Waal, F.B.M. (1995). Bonobo sex and society. *Scientific American, 272,* 82–88.

de Waal, F.B.M. (2001). *The ape and the sushi master: Cultural reflections of a primatologist.* New York: Basic Books.

Donald, M. (1991). *Origins of the modern mind: Three stages in the evolution of culture and cognition.* Cambridge, MA: Harvard University Press.

Dunbar, R. (1996). *Grooming, gossip, and the evolution of language.* Cambridge, MA: Harvard University Press.

Emerson, M.O., Smith, C., & Sikkink, D. (1999). Equal in Christ, but not in the world: White conservative protestants and explanations of Black-White inequality. *Social Problems, 46,* 398–417.

Fausto-Sterling, A. (2000). *Sexing the body: Gender politics and the construction of sexuality.* New York: Basic Books.

Field, T. (1999). American adolescents touch each other less and are more aggressive toward their peers as compared with French adolescents. *Adolescence, 34,* 753–758.

Field, T. (2001). *Touch.* Cambridge, MA: MIT Press.

Florian, V., & Mikulincer, M. (1998). Terror management in childhood: Does death conceptualization moderate the effects of mortality salience on acceptance of similar and different others? *Personality & Social Psychology Bulletin, 24,* 1104–1112.

Goldenberg, J.L., Pyszczynski, T., Solomon, S., Kluck, B., & Cornwell, R. (2001). I am not an animal: Mortality salience, disgust, and the denial of human creatureliness. *Journal of Experimental Psychology: General, 130,* 427–435

Goldstein, J.S. (2001). *War and gender.* Cambridge: Cambridge University Press.

Gottlieb, G. (2000). Environmental and behavioral influences on gene activity. *Current Directions in Psychological Science, 9,* 93–97.

Graves, J.L., Jr. (2001). *The emperor's new clothes: Biological theories of race at the millennium.* New Brunswick, NJ: Rutgers University Press.

Gross, P.R., & Levitt, N. (1997). *Higher superstition: The Academic Left and its quarrels with science.* Baltimore, MD: Johns Hopkins University Press.

Guisinger, S., & Blatt, S.J. (1994). Individuality and relatedness: Evolution of a fundamental dialectic. *American Psychologist, 49,* 104–111.

Harlow, H.F., & Mears, C.E. (1983). Emotional sequences and consequences. In R. Plutchik & H. Kellerman (Eds.), *Emotion: Theory, research and experience.* Vol. 2. *Emotions in early development* (pp. 171–197). New York: Academic Press.

Herrnstein, R.J., & Murray, C. (1994). *The bell curve: Intelligence and class structure in American life.* New York: Free Press.

Hewitt, J.P. (1999, April 23) Seeking to make sense where there is none. Los Angeles, CA: *Los Angeles Times.*

Hrdy, S.B. (1999). *Mother nature: A history of mothers, infants, and natural selection.* New York: Pantheon Books.

Jennings, J.L., & Murphy, C.M. (2000). Male-male dimensions of male-female battering: A new look at domestic violence. *Psychology of Men & Masculinity, 1,* 21–29.

Jones, R.M. (November 1997). Congressman Ehlers on science policy. Retrieved at http://www.aip.org/enews/fyi/1997/fyi97.140.htm, on January 18, 2002.

Link, B.G., Phelan, J.C., & Bresnahan, M. (1999). Public conceptions of mental illness: Labels, causes, dangerousness, and social distance. *American Journal of Public Health, 89,* 1328–1333.

*Los Angeles Times* (1994, October 19). 18-month sentence for wife-killer sparks outcry. Associated Press.

Lykken, D.T. (1995). *The antisocial personalities.* Hillsdale, NJ: Lawrence Erlbaum.

Madson, L., & Trafimow, D. (2001). Gender comparisons in the private, collective, and allocentric selves. *Journal of Social Psychology, 141,* 551–559.

Masters, R.D. (1989). *The nature of politics.* New Haven, CT: Yale University Press.

McLaren, J., & Brown, R.E. (1989). Childhood problems associated with abuse and neglect. *Canada's Mental Health, 37,* 1989, 1–6.

McCrone, J. (1999). A bifold model of freewill. *Journal of Consciousness Studies, 6,* 241–259.

McHoskey, J.W. (1996). Authoritarianism and ethical ideology. *Journal of Social Psychology, 136,* 709–717.

McMurtrie, B. (2001, December 21). Darwinism under attack. *Chronicle of Higher Education,* p. A8.

Miczek, K.A., Maxson, S.C., Fish, E.W., & Faccidomo, S. (2001). Aggressive behavioral phenotypes in mice. *Behavioural Brain Research, 125,* 167–181.

Mikulincer, M., & Florian, V. (2000). Exploring individual differences in reactions to mortality salience: Does attachment style regulate terror management mechanisms? *Journal of Personality & Social Psychology, 79,* 260–273.

Nisbett, R.E., Peng, K., Choi, I., & Norenzayan, A. (2001). Culture and systems of thought: Holistic versus analytic cognition. *Psychological Review, 108,* 291–310.

Norenzayan, A., & Nisbett, R.E. (2000). Culture and causal cognition. *Current Directions in Psychological Science, 9,* 132–135.

Norrander, B. (1997). The independence gap and the gender gap. *Public Opinion Quarterly, 61,* 464–76.

Plomin, R., & Neiderhiser, J.M. (1992). Genetics and experience. *Current Directions in Psychological Science, 1,* 160–163.

Poe-Yamagata, E., & Jones, M.A. (2000). And justice for some: Differential treatment of minority youth in the justice system. Available online at http://www.buildingblocksforyouth.org/justiceforsome/jfs.html.

Pratto, F., Sidanius, J., Stallworth, L.M., & Malle, B.F. (1994). Social dominance orientation: A personality variable predicting social and political attitudes. *Journal of Personality & Social Psychology, 67,* 741–763.

Promise Keepers (2002). Retrieved at http://www.promisekeepers.org, January 14, 2002.

Putnam, R.D. (2000). *Bowling alone: The collapse and revival of American community.* New York: Simon & Schuster.

Reitz, R.R. (1999). Batterers' experiences of being violent: A phenomenological study. *Psychology of Women Quarterly, 23,* 143–165.

Robarchek, C.A., & Robarchek, C.J. (1997). *Waorani: The contexts of violence and war.* Belmont, CA: Wadsworth.

Roland, E., & Idsoe, T. (2001). Aggression and bullying. *Aggressive Behavior, 27,* 446–462.

Romero, M. (1985). A comparison between strategies used on prisoners of war and battered wives. *Sex Roles, 13,* 537–547.

Ross, A. (1996). *Science wars.* Durham, NC: Duke University Press.

Rutherford, F.J., & Ahlgren, A. (1991). *Science for All Americans* (pp. 15–22). Washington, DC: American Association for the Advancement of Science.

Saad, L. (1999). Independents rank as largest U.S. political group. Gallup Poll News Service. Retrieved at http://www.gallup.com/poll/releases/pr990409c.asp, on January 15, 2002.

Salmivalli, C., & Nieminen, E. (2002). Proactive and reactive aggression among school bullies, victims, and bully-victims. *Aggressive Behavior, 28,* 30–44.

Schiller Institute Web site. Retrieved at http://www.schillerinstitute.org/programs/prog_6-23_camd-leaf.html, January 12, 2002.

Schumaker, J.F. (1995). *The corruption of reality: A unified theory of religion, hypnosis, and psychopathology.* Amherst, NY: Prometheus Books.

Scott, B. (undated). Open letter to Rep. Sharon Weston Broome (Louisiana). Retrieved at http://secularsouth.org/show.php?column = bible_belt&story_id = 10, on January 17, 2002.

Seligman, M.E.P. (1975). *Helplessness: On depression, development, and death.* New York: W. H. Freeman.

Sheline, J.L., Skipper, B.J, & Broadhead, W.E. (1994). Risk factors for violent behavior in elementary school boys: Have you hugged your child today? *American Journal of Public Health, 84,* 661–663.

Shields, A., & Cicchetti, D. (2001). Parental maltreatment and emotion dysregulation as risk factors for bullying and victimization in middle childhood. *Journal of Clinical Child Psychology, 30,* 349–363.

Silk, J.B. (1998). Making amends: Adaptive perspectives on conflict remediation in monkeys, apes, and humans. *Human Nature, 9,* 341–368.

Silva, J.M. (1983). The perceived legitimacy of rule violating behavior in sport. *Journal of Sport Psychology, 5,* 438–448.

Slife, B.D., & Williams, R.N. (1995). *What's behind the research? Discovering hidden assumptions in the behavioral sciences.* Thousand Oaks, CA: Sage Publications.

Slotow, R., van Dyk, G., Poole, J., Page, B., & Klocke, A. (2000). Older bull elephants control young males. *Nature, 408,* 425–426.

Suomi, S.J. (1999). Behavioral inhibition and impulsive aggressiveness: Insights from studies with rhesus monkeys. In L. Balter & C.S. Tamis-LeMonda (Eds.), *Child psychology: A handbook of contemporary issues* (pp. 510–525). Philadelphia, PA: Psychology Press/Taylor & Francis.

Taylor, S.E. (1991). *Positive illusions: Creative self-deception and the healthy mind.* New York: Basic Books.

Thornhill, R., & Palmer, C.T. (2000). *A natural history of rape: Biological bases of sexual coercion.* Cambridge, MA: MIT Press.

Tinbergen, N. (1968). On war and peace in animals and man. *Science, 160,* 1411–1418.

Triandis, H.C. (2000). Cultural syndromes and subjective well-being. In E. Diener & E.M. Suh (Eds.), *Culture and subjective well-being* (pp. 13–36). Cambridge, MA: MIT Press.

Trott, R. (undated). Is the ICR's Henry Morris racist? The Talk.Origins Archive. Retrieved at http://www.talkorigins.org/faqs/racism.htm, on January 16, 2002.

Ury, W.L. (2002). *Must we fight?* San Francisco, CA: Jossey-Bass.

Vandello, J.A., & Cohen, D. (1999). Patterns of individualism and collectivism across the United States. *Journal of Personality & Social Psychology, 77,* 279–292.

Vitielo, B., & Stoff, D.M. (1997). Subtypes of aggression and their relevance to child psychiatry. *Journal of the American Academy of Child & Adolescent Psychiatry, 36,* 307–315.

Watkins, D., Akande, A., Fleming, J., Ismail, M., Lefner, K., Regmi, M., et al. (1998). Cultural dimensions, gender, and the nature of self-concept: A fourteen-country study. *International Journal of Psychology, 33,* 17–31.

Wheeler Vega, J.A. (2001). Naturalism and feminism: Conflicting explanations of rape in a wider context. *Psychology, Evolution & Gender, 3.1,* 47–85.

Wilkinson, R. (1997). *Unhealthy societies: The afflictions of inequality.* London, UK: Routledge.

Wilson, E.O. (1998). *Consilience: The unity of knowledge.* New York: Alfred A. Knopf.

Wolfe, T. (1996). Sorry, but your soul just died. Retrieved at http://www.brainmachines.com/body_wolf.html, on January 16, 2002.

# Index

# About the Editors and Contributors

**Richard W. Bloom,** Ph.D., is Dean, College of Arts and Sciences; Professor of Political and Clinical Psychology; and Director, Terrorism, Intelligence, and Security Studies, at Embry-Riddle Aeronautical University, Prescott, Arizona. He is a past-president of the Military Psychology Division of the American Psychological Association; Fellow of the Society of Personality Assessment; and diplomate of the American Board of Professional Psychology (clinical). He carries out policy analysis, reviews applied research, and consults with both government and industry on aviation security threat assessment; terrorism; covert action, counterintelligence, and personnel security; and information warfare.

**Christopher Boehm,** Ph.D., is Professor of Anthropology and Director, the Jane Goodall Research Center, University of Southern California. He has done field work with both humans and African great apes. His research interests with humans (including Montenegrin Serbs) include moral communities and social control, tribal systems, feuding and warfare, and the evolution of sociality. His primatological research interests (with wild chimpanzees) are in conflict resolution behavior and vocal communication. His most recent book is *Hierarchy in the Forest* (Harvard Press), which deals with the evolution of egalitarianism. He is currently working on a book on the evolution of conflict resolution under a J.S. Guggenheim Fellowship.

**David M. Buss,** Ph.D., is Professor of Psychology at the University of Texas at Austin. He received the American Psychological Association (APA) Distinguished Scientific Award for Early Career Contribution to Psychology in 1988, the APA G. Stanley Hall Award in 1990, and the APA Distinguished Scientist Lecturer Award in 2001. His books include *The Evolution of Desire: Strategies of Human Mating* (Basic Books, 1994); *Evolutionary Psychology: The New Science of the Mind* (Allyn & Bacon, 1999), which won the Robert W. Hamilton Book Award in 2000; and *The Dangerous Passion: Why Jealousy Is as*

*Necessary as Love and Sex* (Free Press, 2000). He has extensive cross-cultural research collaborations on the topics of homicide, stalking, conflict between the sexes, status and reputation, and the strategies of human mating.

**Nancy Dess,** Ph.D., is Professor of Psychology at Occidental College. She is a Fellow of the American Psychological Association and, from 1999 to 2001, served as its Senior Scientist. Her primary research concerns the relationship between eating and emotion in humans and other animals; a particular interest is in why individual differences in the perception of tastes predicts emotionality, stress vulnerability, and the organization of food-rewarded behavior. In other professional activities, she advocates for a fuller understanding of nonhuman animals and human nature, for science education, and for utilization of empirical research in the formulation of effective and humane public policy.

**Joshua D. Duntley** is a doctoral student in the Individual Differences and Evolutionary Psychology program at the University of Texas at Austin. He received his undergraduate degree in Psychology from The State University of New York at Plattsburgh. He is currently conducting research examining the psychology of homicide, suicide, stalking, and family relationships.

**Harold D. Fishbein,** Ph.D., is Professor of Psychology at the University of Cincinnati. He has taken sabbatical leaves at Harvard University, The Philadelphia Child Guidance Clinic, University of California at San Diego, University of Pittsburgh, University of Chicago, and SNDT Women's University in Bombay, India, where he was a Fulbright Lecturer. He has been writing in the area of the genetic/evolutionary bases of human development since the publication of his first book in 1976. His second book appeared in 1984, and his third, *Peer Prejudice and Discrimination,* in 1996. That book was the first winner of the Eleanor Maccoby Book Award from the American Psychological Association. The revision of this book will appear in July 2002.

**Joseph Graves, Jr.,** Ph.D., is Professor of Evolutionary Biology at Arizona State University–West. In 1994, he was elected a Fellow of the Council of the American Association for the Advancement of Science. Professional distinctions include serving as Secretary for the Division on Integrative and Comparative Issues in the Society of Integrative and Comparative Biologists and as a member of the external advisory panel for the National Human Genome Center at Howard University. His research concerns the evolutionary genetics of postponed aging and biological concepts of race in humans, with numerous publications and appearances in documentary films on these topics. *The Emperor's New Clothes: Biological Theories of Race at the Millennium,* his book on the biology of race, was published by Rutgers University Press in 2001. He also has been a leader in addressing the underrepresentation of minorities in science and efforts to improve the teaching of science, particularly evolutionary biology in Arizona public schools.

**Jeff Greenberg,** Ph.D., is Professor of Psychology at the University of Arizona. His research is focused on the determinants and consequences of the need for self-esteem, and the psychological functions of culture and prejudice. Specific topics include Terror Management Theory, Cognitive Dissonance Theory, stereotyping, psychodynamic perspectives on motivation, depression and self-awareness, and self-concept.

**Stuart Kinner** is in the final year of a research Ph.D. in the School of Psychology, University of Queensland, Australia. Born in Belfast and with a background including criminal intelligence analysis and public health (illicit drug trends) research, he draws from a wide range of applied experience. He is an associate member of the Australian and New Zealand Association of Psychiatry, Psychology and Law (ANZAPPL), and serves on the committee for the Australian Psychological Society (APS) College of Forensic Psychologists. His dissertation focuses on emotional and cognitive typologies underlying antisocial behavior; however, his current research interests extend to empathy and theory of mind, developmental crime prevention, and social policy relating to antisocial behavior.

**Roger D. Masters,** Ph.D., is Nelson A. Rockefeller Professor of Government Emeritus at Dartmouth College. After studies at Harvard and Chicago, he specialized in human nature and political thought. He is currently President of the Foundation for Neuroscience and Society and is on the Council of the Association for Politics and the Life Sciences. Recently, he has worked in evolutionary psychology, with special emphasis on the behavioral implications of neurotoxicology. Having published in other fields—books including *Fortune Is a River: Leonardo Da Vinci and Niccolo Machiavelli's Magnificent Dream to Change the Course of Florentine History* (Free Press) and *The Nature of Politics* (Yale)—in recent years he has focused on scientific studies of toxins that modify health and behavior.

**Linda Mealey,** Ph.D., is Professor of Psychology at the College of St. Benedict in St. Joseph, Minnesota, and adjunct Associate Professor at the School of Psychology at the University of Queensland in Brisbane, Australia. Her research combines her interests in sexuality, evolution, animal behavior, individual differences, and law. Most recently, she has been looking at evolutionary models of psychopathology, including psychopathic personality (*Behavioral and Brain Sciences* 18:523–599) and anorexia nervosa (*Human Nature* 11:105–116). She also has been working in the area of rape and rape prevention strategies (*Jurimetrics* 39:217–226) and has developed an evolutionary taxonomy of ethics. In 2000, she published *Sex Differences: Developmental and Evolutionary Strategies* (Academic Press).

**Tom Pyszczynski,** Ph.D., is Professor of Psychology at the University of Colorado at Colorado Springs. He is interested in the human need for self-esteem and meaning, unconscious processes, self-deception, and how defensive needs interfere with human growth and development. Over the last fifteen years, most of his work has been centered on exploring issues related to terror management theory, which he developed with his colleagues Jeff Greenberg and Sheldon Solomon. They recently completed a book, *In the Wake of 9/11: The Psychology of Terror,* published by the American Psychological Association in the summer of 2002, in which they apply their theoretical perspective to the problem of global terrorism.

**Sheldon Solomon,** Ph.D., is Professor of Psychology at Skidmore College. He is an experimental social psychologist who is generally interested in motivational underpinnings of human behavior and specifically in the effects of uniquely human awareness of death on human affairs.